Discourse and Communication

# Research in Text Theory
# Untersuchungen zur Texttheorie

Editor
János S. Petöfi, *Bielefeld*

Advisory Board
Irena Bellert, *Montreal*
Maria-Elisabeth Conte, *Pavia*
Teun A. van Dijk, *Amsterdam*
Wolfgang U. Dressler, *Wien*
Peter Hartmann †, *Konstanz*
Robert E. Longacre, *Dallas*
Roland Posner, *Berlin*
Hannes Rieser, *Bielefeld*

Volume 10

Walter de Gruyter · Berlin · New York
1985

# Discourse and Communication

New Approaches to the Analysis of Mass Media Discourse and Communication

Edited by
Teun A. van Dijk

Walter de Gruyter · Berlin · New York
1985

*Library of Congress Cataloging-in-Publication Data*

Main entry under title:
Discourse and communication.
 (Research in text theory = Untersuchungen zur Texttheorie ;
 v. 10)
 Includes indexes.
 1. Mass Media and language--Addresses, essays, lectures. 2.
Discourse analysis--Addresses, essays, lectures. I. Dijk, Teun
Adrianus van, 1943– .
 II. Series: Research in text theory ; v. 10.
 P96.L34D57  1985       001.51        85-16071
 ISBN 0-89925-105-6 (New York)
 ISBN 3-11-010319-2 (Berlin)

*CIP-Kurztitelaufnahme der Deutschen Bibliothek*

**Discourse and communication** : new approaches to the analysis
of mass media discourse and communication / ed. by Teun A. van
Dijk. — Berlin ; New York : de Gruyter, 1985.
 (Research in text theory ; Vol. 10)
 ISBN 3-11-010319-2 (Berlin)
 ISBN 0-89925-105-6 (New York)
NE: Dijk, Teun A. van [Hrsg.]; GT

Printed on acid free paper (pH 7, neutral)

© Copyright 1985 by Walter de Gruyter & Co., Berlin 30.
Printed in Germany
Alle Rechte des Nachdrucks, der photomechanischen Wiedergabe,
der Herstellung von Photokopien — auch auszugsweise — vorbehalten.
Satz und Druck: Arthur Collignon GmbH, Berlin 30.
Bindearbeiten: Lüderitz & Bauer, Berlin

# Preface

There are two vast fields of research that, despite their common interest for text, talk and communication, seem to virtually ignore each other: the study of mass communication on the one hand and discourse analysis on the other hand. There is a small link between the two disciplines in the form of a method of description, viz. content analysis, but linguistics and especially current developments in discourse analysis have as yet had little influence as an explicit basis for such a method of research. In fact, one central element in mass communication processes, viz. the 'message' itself, has received little autonomous attention in mass communication research. And conversely, linguists or discourse analysts have shown little interest in mass media discourses and their socio-cultural and cognitive contexts. The studies collected in this book have been written to help bridge this gap of happy single-mindedness in the two disciplines. Although both fields of research have been remarkably interdisciplinary in their development, a discourse analytical approach to mass media texts and communication seems to be an important lack on both sides. Such a lack is detrimental for their further development. We hope that the chapters in this book will provide first suggestions of how on the one hand media messages can be analyzed in more systematic and explicit terms, and how on the other hand results in mass communication research about the production, the uses and socio-cultural functions of media discourses may shed light on the analysis of such dimensions for other types of text and talk in society.

This book is divided in two parts. The first part contains articles that have been written with a 'didactic' goal in mind. They provide introductions, surveys and theory for various domains of communication and information research, mainly about mass media messages. Here we find both introductions to various directions of media discourse analysis, and brief characterizations of different genres of media discourse, such as news, advertising, and communication campaigns. To stress the broad and interdisciplinary scope of communication studies, this part also features articles about automatic information retrieval, persuasion and manipulation, and international communication. The second part of this volume features articles that have a more applied nature. They provide theoretical extensions, case studies, and critical approaches to mass media discourse. Apart from dealing again with specific media genres, such as news, advertising, film, or TV-programs, these papers also address specific topics, such as the portrayal of foreigners, ethnic groups or terrorist violence in the media.

Since the analysis of information and communication, even within the mass media alone, pertains to a multitude of different discourse and context types, and deals with numerous special issues, the selection of articles collected here must, to a certain extent, be relatively arbitrary. Yet, the variety of approaches in this volume also shows how and where discourse analysis can or should be applied and further developed. And also from a theoretical and methodological point of view, it is obvious that the intersecting fields of discourse analysis and (mass) communication research have a common ground where our analysis is still in its infancy. The formal and systematic approach of linguistic discourse analysis, indeed, cannot simply be extended to the study of media messages and complex communication issues, if only because of the often vast data bases that require description in mass communication research. The contributions to this volume nevertheless contain many suggestions how new theory formation and analysis, or the account of specific and relevant media — and hence social — problems could take shape. It may be hoped, therefore, that this volume will stimulate further research in the discourse analysis of media and communication.

T. A. v. D.
*Summer, 1984*

Contents

Preface . . . . . . . . . . . . . . . . . . . . . . . . . . . . . . . . . . . . . . . . . . . . . . . V

Teun A. van Dijk
Introduction: Discourse Analysis in (Mass) Communication Research    1

Part I. Introductions, Surveys, Theories

George Gerbner
Mass Media Discourse: Message System Analysis as a Component of
Cultural Indicators . . . . . . . . . . . . . . . . . . . . . . . . . . . . . . . . . . . .   13

Ian Connell and Adam Miles
Text, Discourse and Mass Communication . . . . . . . . . . . . . . . . .   26

Howard H. Davis
Discourse and Media Influence . . . . . . . . . . . . . . . . . . . . . . . . .   44

Douglas S. Solomon and Barbara A. Cardillo
The Elements and Process of Communication Campaigns . . . . . . . .   60

Teun A. van Dijk
Structures of News in the Press . . . . . . . . . . . . . . . . . . . . . . . .   69

Kim B. Rotzoll
Advertisements . . . . . . . . . . . . . . . . . . . . . . . . . . . . . . . . . . . .   94

W. John Hutchins
Information Retrieval and Text Analysis . . . . . . . . . . . . . . . . . . 106

Rom Harré
Persuasion and Manipulation . . . . . . . . . . . . . . . . . . . . . . . . . . 126

Cees J. Hamelink
International Communication . . . . . . . . . . . . . . . . . . . . . . . . . 143

Part II. Applications, Extensions, Critical Approaches

Günter Bentele
Audio-Visual Analysis and a Grammar of Presentation Forms in News
Programs: Some Mediasemiotic Considerations . . . . . . . . . . . . . . 159

Claire Lindegren Lerman
Media Analysis of a Presidential Speech: Impersonal Identity Forms in
Discourse . . . . . . . . . . . . . . . . . . . . . . . . . . . . . . . . . . 185

Theo van Leeuwen
Rhythmic Structure of the Film Text . . . . . . . . . . . . . . . . . . . 216

John Hartley and Martin Montgomery
Representations and Relations: Ideology and Power in Press and TV
News . . . . . . . . . . . . . . . . . . . . . . . . . . . . . . . . . . . . 233

Charles Husband and Jagdish M. Chouhan
Local Radio in the Communication Environment of Ethnic Minorities
in Britain . . . . . . . . . . . . . . . . . . . . . . . . . . . . . . . . . . 270

John D. H. Downing
'Coillons ... Shryned in an Hogges Toord': British News Media Discourse on 'Race' . . . . . . . . . . . . . . . . . . . . . . . . . . . . . . 295

Philip Schlesinger and Bob Lumley
Two Debates on Political Violence and the Mass media: The Organisation of Intellectual Fields in Britain and Italy . . . . . . . . . . . . . . 324

Biographical Notes . . . . . . . . . . . . . . . . . . . . . . . . . . . . . 351

Name Index . . . . . . . . . . . . . . . . . . . . . . . . . . . . . . . . 357

Subject Index . . . . . . . . . . . . . . . . . . . . . . . . . . . . . . . 363

TEUN A. VAN DIJK

# Introduction: Discourse Analysis in (Mass) Communication Research

*1. From Content Analysis to Discourse Analysis of Media Messages*

For outsiders it is surprising to conclude from the vast amount of mass communication research since World War II that comparatively little attention has been paid to the systematic analysis of what mass communication seems to be primarily about, viz. *texts* (messages, discourse, etc.). Indeed, most work deals with various sociological or socio-psychological theories of mass media institutions, of audiences or effects, or the relations between media on the one hand and society and culture on the other hand. The study of the mass mediated messages themselves is usually relegated to a predominantly methodological approach, viz. that of so-called 'content analysis'. Thus, to take just one example, McQuail's recent introduction to mass communication theory (McQuail, 1983), contains one, 25-page, chapter on media content, of which again large part deals with more general properties of news. Systematic discourse analysis of media messages hardly goes beyond modest applications of 'structuralist' or 'semiological' approaches inspired by the work of French theorists of more than 15 years ago (cf. e.g. Bentele, ed., 1981; Merten, 1983). Current results from linguistic discourse analysis are as yet ignored in mass communication research (see de Beaugrande & Dressler, 1981; and van Dijk, ed., 1985, for many references to that work).

There are several reasons for this notable lack of both classical and modern mass media research. First, linguistics itself simply had little to offer to those interested in the analysis of media discourse. Until the beginning of the 1970s, linguistic grammars were limited to rather abstract descriptions of isolated sentences and did not account for the various levels or dimensions of whole 'texts'. Interest for media discourse, then, was limited to sister-disciplines such as stylistics, rhetorics or semiotics. Unified models for the description of 'text' or 'discourse' only became to be elaborated during the 1970s. But most discourse analysts hardly paid any attention to the texts which, apart from everyday conversation, they are confronted with most frequently, viz. those of the media. Second, mass media research has primarily emerged within the social sciences, such as political science and sociology, and therefore rather focussed on macro-phenomena such as institutions, the audience or public, large-scale processes of effects, or overall functions of media in society. Indeed, the influence of the media — and its vatious modalities (high or low impact) — was reconstructed at a rather high level of abstraction and seldom at the level of the actual texts that would have such influence or the actual recipients and their internal cognitive processing of such texts. Third, the nature of the questions asked in mass communication research was conducive to the analysis of large amounts of message data, for which only rather superficial and mostly quantitative methods were available. A subtle stylistic analysis of, say, many thousands of texts (the output of only a month of news of one average newspaper) is simply not a feasible undertaking.

Although there are certainly other (historical, practical, methodological or theoretical) reasons for the lack of systematic discourse analysis in media research, it should be emphasized at the same time that message analysis was not altogether absent either. Ignoring for a moment the more distant roots of media analysis in and before our century, we witness increasing interest during the 1960s for what is still commonly called 'content analysis'. After Berelson's classical book (1952) and the collection of conference papers edited by Pool (1959), the Annenberg School Conference of 1966 resulted in the highly influential book of papers edited by Gerbner et al. (1969), a book that appeared in the same year as Holsti's (1969) introduction to content analysis in the social sciences and the humanities. Indeed, both the Gerbner et al. book and the Holsti introduction showed that content analysis was not just a theoretical approach of mass communication research, but an interdisciplinary method 'for the objective, replicable and quantitative' description of texts. Besides the media, also poetry, dreams or psychiatric discourse could be analyzed with such a method. And first linguistic, stylistic and even logical foundations were provided for the definition of the crucial 'units' of analysis that must precede quantitative treatment of data. Finally, the important help of computers, both for limited automatic analysis and for statistical treatment of results, was called in, as was exemplified for instance in the General Inquirer project published several years before (Stone, et al., 1966). We had to wait more than 10 years, before the uses of computers in Artificial Intelligence research, e.g. at Yale, on text processing significantly changed these early attempts, and we now witness the first steps in the automatic understanding an summarization of news stories (Cullingford, 1978).

Content analysis as it was elaborated in the 1960 continued in the 1970s, although that decade hardly seemed to provide new orientations or new paradigms. A decade later, Krippendorff's (1980) introduction was a welcome replacement for Holsti's, but its bibliography hardly contained substantial new contributions from the seventies. In other words, the major interests, both theoretically and methodologically, seemed to lie elsewhere in mass communication research, and inspection of a current introduction to the field, such as the one already mentioned by McQuail (1983) can illustrate that point. Or else, content analysis is used as part of necessarily large scale projects involving fundamental questions of the media, such as the 'cultural indicators' research directed by George Gerbner, as it is also summarized in this book. Indeed, cultural changes cannot simply be detected only by meticulous micro-analyses of a few media messages. Selected signaling devices, or indicators, are to be described in many (kinds of) media discourse in order to assess such important social phenomena through media analysis. Similarly, other kinds of content analysis will of course provide at least partial insight into properties of media discourse, such as the prevalent themes of the news, the kind of actors in news, advertisements, TV-programs or film, or style in the headlines. That is, content analysis *is* interested in principles of description when it tries to account for the basis of unitization, and in this way also structural properties of media discourse can be attended to, at least from a quantitative point of view.

Yet, the second half of the 1970s also brought suggestions for a more explicit and systematic account of media discourse. Some of this work clearly rejects the principles of 'classical' content analysis and the aims of media research in which it is embedded (often associated with the 'American' approach in mass communication). Much of this new look in media research is based in Britain. Thus, the well-known Glasgow University Media Group published in 1976 its first 'bad news' study about TV-news, followed in 1980 by a book on 'more bad news', in which systematic analysis of both text and film yielded the conclusion that industrial news is biased in favor of the 'dominant' position of government or factory directors. In a somewhat different vein, this critical analysis of the media has also been the characteristic of media research by the Centre for Contemporary Cultural Studies at Birmingham, under its earlier direction by Stuart Hall (Hall, et al., eds. 1980). In his review of the media research of the Centre, Hall (1980) formulates the break with the classical (quantitative, American, stimulus-response) approaches as follows: "(our) approach defined the media as a major cultural and ideological force, standing in a dominant position with respect to the way in which social relations and political problems were defined and the production and transformation of popular ideologies in the audience addressed" (p. 118). This concern for the (re-)production of ideologies in and through the media is also manifest in the special interest for discourse analysis in the work of the Centre. Current French thinkers (such as Barthes, Lacan, Foucault, Althusser, Laclau, etc.) have been a major inspiration for such approaches. Both this work, and the work of the Glasgow University Media Group are represented in this volume, viz. by the chapters of Connell & Mills, and by Davis, respectively. Details about the theoretical backgrounds and the methodological principles of analysis of these two directions of research can be found in those chapters.

Although this work is becoming more influential only by the end of the 1970s and in the 1980s, it also has its predecessors in earlier research. For instance, Cohen's (1972) book about the Mods and the Rockers extensively pays attention to the way these youth groups are transformed into 'folk devils' by the media. This analysis is an example of what Hall calls the 'production of popular ideologies'. In fact, Hall and his collaborators (1978) had shown themselves how this process works in crime reporting, such as the media coverage (or rather: construction) of 'mugging' as a pervasive social 'problem'. Although these studies do not (yet) apply systematic discourse analysis, there is explicit attention for the ideological analysis of media messages. Instead of the more manifest units of quantitative content analysis, we thus approach an account of underlying meanings or processes of 'signification'. That classical methods of content analysis can be usefully combined with such a critical, ideological analysis, was already shown by Halloran and his associates (1970) in their study of the media coverage of a Vietnam demonstration in London. In other words, there is no strict distinction between content analysis on the one hand and explicit discourse analysis on the other hand, e. g. along the quantitative-qualitative dimension or according to whether observable or latent categories are studied. Another good example of this integration of methods and critical analysis is the Hartmann & Husband (1974) study about racism in the media.

Whereas most of the work mentioned above has been done by social scientists, some British (and Australian) linguists have recently started to pay attention to the relations between language and ideology in the media (Fowler et al., 1979). They start, so to speak, at the other end, viz. with a close analysis of the grammatical structures of media messages about an event (e. g. the West-Indian carnival) in different newspapers. They are able to show that a syntactic analysis of sentences alone may already reveal biases in the description of facts, e. g. through the deletion of agents/subjects in sentences if these are the agents of negative acts (e. g. 'The mugger was killed' instead of 'The police killed the mugger'). It is obvious that a complete discourse analysis can trace further properties of media messages that go beyond those of syntactic structure of single sentences. It is however important to stress that ideological positions, interests or power, can also be 'signalled' through such apparently 'context-free' language characteristics as sentential syntax (see also Kress & Hodge, 1979).

Several of the papers in part II of this volume can be located in this tradition of critical or ideological analysis of mass media discourse, as it has been developed especially in Britain. The contributions of Schlesinger & Lumley, Downing, Husband & Chouhan, and Hartley & Montgomery, provide such special 'readings' of media messages. Despite their differences, they all deal with the representation or the accounts of 'others' (minority groups, foreigners, or 'terrorists') in the media.

*2. From discourse analysis to the analysis of complex communicative events*

We have observed above that various directions of media research in the 1970s have laid the foundations for a discourse analytical approach to mass mediated messages. Discourse is no longer just an 'intervening variable' between media institutions or journalists on the one hand, and an audience on the other hand, but also studied in its own right, and as a central and manifest cultural and social product in and through which meanings and ideologies are expressed or (re-)produced. In other words, we here find the beginnings of a sound theory of media discourses, even if many social scientists will of course take (media) discourse primarily as the basis for an 'inferential framework', that is, as 'expression', 'indicator', 'signal' or as 'stimulus' for other, 'underlying', phenomena in culture and society, such as ideologies, power, dominance, discrimination, racism and sexism, media access of elites, or the uses and effects of the media with the audience. These relations between 'text' and 'context' are of course crucial, and no full-fledged theory of the media is adequate without such explicit inferences. This does not mean, however, that our insight into the structures of media discourse is more than fragmentary at the moment. On the contrary, most extant work focuses on rather specific features of media discourse, viz. those features which intuitively are found relevant for inferences about important social or cultural factors.

It goes without saying that an adequate analysis of the relations between media texts an contexts requires a more systematic approach to media discourse. All levels and dimensions of analysis need to be attended to, from 'surface' properties of presentation, lay-out, graphical display in printed discourse, or intonation, paraverbal and nonverbal features in spoken media discourse, on the one hand, through an analysis of syntactic structures, lexical style or rhetorical devices, to the 'underlying' meanings, connotations or associations, or the pragmatics of speech acts performed. And such systematic analyses should be made for a large variety of discourse types in the media, not only of news, but also of advertising, film, TV-programs (talk shows, etc.), and so on. Comparison between different media genres may then yield specific properties for different genres but also commonalities, e. g. of style, rhetorical devices, event or actor descriptions, implicit meanings or modes of coherence. Despite the encouraging studies mentioned above, this programmatic enumeration also suggests that most of the work is still ahead of us.

Some of the papers contributed to this book address these various structural features of media discourse. Lindegren-Lerman, for instance, examines the subtle devices journalists may use in the representation of controversial or 'problematic' propositions in Nixon's public declarations about the Watergate affair. On the other hand, van Leeuwen in his contribution deals with a complex 'surface' phenomenon in film and film text, viz. rhythm and intonation. And also Bentele, in his chapter on TV-news programs, shows what linguistic or 'grammatical' approaches can contribute to media discourse analysis. My own contribution tries to specify some properties of news discourse in the press. Besides the usual distinctions between several levels of analysis, such as the distinction between overall, semantic macrostructures, and local relationships of coherence, this chapter proposes that news has a conventional 'news schema', or superstructure, consisting of a hierarchical organization of news item categories. Similar 'schemata' may be made explicit also for other media discourses, whether written/printed, or spoken, and including non-verbal acts and film (for details about such news structures, see also van Dijk, 1984b, 1986).

*The cognitive and social context*

Besides this urgent need for more textual analyses of media discourse, also the well-known features of the context, such as processes of production and reception, as well as the social and cultural situations need of course further attention. We have suggested that most work in mass media research in fact is about these social dimensions of the communicative process. Yet, in accordance with the prevalence of macro-level approaches in sociology, there is also a lack of more detailed, micro-studies of media processes, both in production and in reception. For the production of news, a few recent studies (Tuchman, 1978, Fishman, 1980) have begun to pay attention to the more detailed production and interpretation processes in the everyday activities of journalists. Daily interactions between journalists, or between journalists and other newspersons such as newsactors, sources, witnesses, or representatives of organizations, need to be further analyzed for their strategies, routine acts, commonsense categories, or other principles of understanding. Detailed observation and analysis is necessary of decision making processes in e. g. editorial meetings, also to make explicit the understanding and the uses of the well-known newsvalue criteria in the selection or the (re-)construction of news events as news items. From our discourse analytical point of view, for instance, it is imperative that we come to know how final news items in the press or on TV are the ultimate results of a complex *sequence of text processing stages*. It has not sufficiently been realized that most news items are not directly based upon personal observations or experiences of journalists, but rather the result of a series of textual transformations of various forms of antecedent discourses, such as telex messages, reports, interviews, press conferences, documents, police records, eyewitness testimony, and so on. In other words, most news production is a form of text processing. We should investigate which linguistic, cognitive and social factors impinge on this process. Cognitive models of discourse comprehension, for instance, will be necessary to account for the strategies used by journalists in these respective processing stages (see van Dijk & Kintsch, 1983, for detail). At this point, a cognitive theory of news values can be built into the cognitive (re-)production model to account for the special, socio-cultural and institutional constraints upon news reporting.

Similar remarks hold for the reception process. Theories of media effects abound, but there is no theory that models in detail the processes of media discourse understanding, the formation of knowledge and beliefs, the interaction of personal or social opinions or attitudes on that process of acquisition, and hence upon the 'effects' consisting in the transformation of knowledge, beliefs or attitudes. The 'stages' of media effects as they were proposed by e. g. McGuire (1973) a decade ago are merely rough designations of the various steps of such a process. Detailed memory models, both in experimental psychological terms, and in terms of computer simulations in Artificial Intelligence, will be needed to fill in the required applications in media research. Using a newsreport in an international weekly as our example, we have demonstrated how complex such processing of news discourse in readers (or hearers) may be (van Dijk & Kintsch, 1983). It goes without saying, however, that earlier insights in the field of persuasion analysis, whether from a socio-political or philosophical and sociological point of view (as is the case in the chapter by Harré), need to be integrated into such highly complex models (Roloff & Miller, eds., 1980).

Next, communicative events such as the production and the consumption of media discourse have their goals and functions. In the light of the previous paragraph, we may therefore expect that again a micro-analysis of the 'uses' of media messages may shed further light on problems that have been studied in more global terms before (Blumler & Katz, eds., 1974). Thus, in our own current research about ethnic attitudes in everyday conversations (e. g. van Dijk, 1984a), we have found how people use media information in the construction of ethnic opinions and attitudes, and how they take media as 'evidence' in conversational strategies of self-presentation and persuasion. Detailed conversational analysis, thus, yields more insights into the actual uses of media discourses in realistic social situations and other communicative events. Both from a cognitive and from a linguistic and social point of view, such insights also allow us to specify what exactly the 'agenda setting' function of the media amounts to. A socio-cognitive model of discourse production indeed may account for the role of such 'topic structures' in the production of new texts and in the participation in talk about media-induced topics and their degree of social relevance.

And finally, a decade of research in sociolinguistics and the ethnography of communication (Gumperz & Hymes, 1972; Bauman & Sherzer, 1974, Saville-Troike, 1982) has shown how practically all features of discourse, as well as those of discourse production and understanding, are systematically related to the many features of the socio-cultural context. This means that we also need detailed ethnographic observations about the production and uses (participation) of communicative events in the media, both for communicative events (e. g. talkshows) 'in' the media, as well as those 'by' the media, i. e. with media users als participants. Such analyses may shed light upon such issues as the shared cultural basis of common understanding (and hence of cultural presuppositions), the uses of different formal styles in the media, conditions of code switching (e. g. between a dominant media language and a dialect or a minority language), the socio-cultural functions of various media discourses, the ritual nature of specific media discourses or programs, and so on.

At this latter point we also find a link with the important study of international and cross-cultural forms of media discourse, production and uses (see Hamelink's chapter in this volume). Economic and cultural dominance in communication is not only a macro-phenomenon, but also is actualized in the details of media texts and their uses. Explicit comparison of media products across nations and cultures allows us to specify which thematic, stylistic, rhetorical, schematic, or other features of media discourse are imposed (or not) by dominant communication monopolies. In this way not only ideologies may be transmitted (see e. g. Dorfman & Mattelart, 1971; Dorfman, 1980, UNESCO, 1980; Smith, 1980; Richstad & Anderson, eds., 1981, and many other sources), but also the very ways of production, writing, and reading/viewing. In other words, the hypotheses of cultural domination (of the third world by the first world) at the macro-level need to be further strengthened and tested at the micro-level of detailed discourse and communication analysis along the lines briefly sketched above (for details, see van Dijk, 1984b).

These final paragraphs may sound convincing but are of course highly programmatic. Yet, both theoretically and descriptively, we at the moment have the instruments to perform such a task. Linguistic, cognitive and social discourse and communication analysis only needs to be applied in and extended towards the systematic account of media discourse. And conversely, the study of mass communication should only realize that besides their own models of communication, media structures and uses, a micro-level approach, such as the one proposed in discourse analysis, may be fruitful. Fruitful also for a thorough study of typical 'macro-problems', such as cultural and communicative dominance patterns in (the media of) our world. Recent work in both interpersonal and mass communication studies has shown that such new developments in linguistics, discourse analysis, cognitive psychology and micro-sociology are being picked up in the detailed, and explicit account of what communication, whether in production, reception or interaction, will always basically involve: discourse.

*Bibliography*

Bauman, Richard, & Sherzer, Joel (eds.). (1974). *Explorations in the Ethnography of Speaking*. London: Cambridge University Press.

de Beaugrande, Robert, & Dressler, Wolfgang (1981). *Introduction to Text Linguistics*. London: Longman.
Bentele, Günter (ed.). (1981). *Semiotik und Massenmedien*. Munich: Ölschläger.
Berelson, Bernard (1952). *Content Analysis in Communication Research*. Glencoe, Ill.: Free Press.
Blumler, Jay G. & Katz, Elihu, eds. (1974). *The Uses of Mass Communications*. Beverly Hills: London: Sage.
Cohen, Stanley (1972). *Folk Devils and Moral Panics*. London: MacGibbon & Kee (new edition, published by Robertson, Oxford, 1980).
Cullingford, Robert (1978). *Script Application: Computer Understanding of Newspaper Stories*. Ph. D. thesis, Yale University.
van Dijk, Teun A. (1984a). *Prejudice in Discourse*. Amsterdam: Benjamins.
van Dijk, Teun A. (1984b). Structures of International News. A Case Study of the World's Press. University of Amsterdam: Dept. of General Literary Studies, Section of Discourse Studies. Unpublished Report for UNESCO.
van Dijk, Teun A. (1986). *News as Discourse*. New York: Longman.
van Dijk, Teun, A. (ed.). (1985). *Handbook of Discourse Analysis*. 4 vols. London: Academic Press.
van Dijk, Teun A., & Kintsch, Walter (1983). *Strategies of Discourse Comprehension*. New York: Academic Press.
Dorfman, Ariel (1980). *Reader's nuestro que estás en la tierra. Ensayos sobre el imperialismo cultural*. Mexico: Nueva Imagen.
Dorfman, Ariel, & Mattelart, Armand (1971). *Para leer El Pato Donald*. Valparaiso: Ediciones Universidad.
Fishman, Mark (1980). *Manufacturing the News*. Austin, Tx.: University of Texas Press.
Fowler, Roger et al. (1979). *Language and Control*. London: Routledge & Kegan Paul.
Gerbner, George, et al. (eds.). (1969). *The Analysis of Communication Content*. New York: Wiley.
Gumperz, John, & Hymes, Dell, eds. (1972). *Directions in Sociolinguistics: The Ethnography of Communication*. New York: Holt, Rinehart & Winston.
Glasgow University Media Group (1976). *Bad News*. London: Routlegde & Kegan Paul.
Glasgow University Media Group (1980). *More Bad News*. London: Routledge & Kegan Paul.
Hall, Stuart (1980). "Introduction to Media Studies at the Centre". In: Hall, et al. eds. 117—121.
Hall, Stuart, et al. (eds.). (1980). *Culture, Media, Language*. London: Hutchinson.
Hall, Stuart, et al. (1978). *Policing the Crisis*. London: Methuen.
Halloran, James D. et al. (1970). *Communications and Demonstrations*. Harmondsworth: Penguin Books.
Hartmann, Paul, & Husband, Charles (1974). *Racism and the Mass Media*. London: Davis Poynter.
Holsti, Ole (1969). *Content Analysis for the Social Sciences and the Humanities*. Reading, Mass.: Addison-Wesley.
Kress, Gunther, & Hodge, Robert (1979). *Language as Ideology*. London: Routledge & Kegan Paul.
Krippendorff, Klaus (1980). *Content Analysis*. Beverly Hills & London: Sage.
McGuire, William J. (1973). "Persuasion, Resistance and Attitude Change". In: I. de Sola Pool et al., eds. *Handbook of Communication*. Chicago: Rand McNally, 216—252.
McQuail, Denis (1983). *Mass Communication Theory*. Beverly Hills & London: Sage.
Merten, Klaus (1983). *Inhaltsanalyse*. Opladen: Westdeutscher Verlag.
Pool, Ithiel de Sola (ed.) (1959). *Trends in Content Analysis*. Urbana: University of Illinois Press.
Richstad, Jim, & Anderson, Michael H., eds. (1981). *Crisis in International News*. New York: Columbia University Press.
Roloff, Michael E., & Miller, Gerald R. eds. (1980). *Persuasion*. Beverly Hills/London: Sage.
Saville-Troike, Muriel (1982). *The Ethnography of Communication*. Oxford: Blackwell.
Smith, Anthony (1980). *The Geopolitics of Information*. New York: Oxford University Press.
Stone, Philip J. et al. (1966). *The General Inquirer. A Computer Approach to Content Analysis*. Cambridge, Mass.: MIT Press.
Tuchman, Gaye (1978). *Making News*. New York: Free Press.
UNESCO. (1980). *Many Voices, One World*. Paris: Unesco.

Part I. Introductions Surveys Theories

GEORGE GERBNER

# Mass Media Discourse: Message System Analysis as a Component of Cultural Indicators

Personal tastes and selective habits of cultural participation limit each of us to risky and usually faulty extrapolation about the media experiences of large and diverse populations. The very qualities that draw our attention to exciting plots and to information relevant to our own interests detract from our ability to make representative observations about the composition and structure of large message systems such as mass media discourse.

Mass media discourse reflects policies of media institutions and enters into the cultivation of conceptions in ways that can be investigated. Therefore, informed policy-making and the valid interpretation of social concept formation and response require the development of some indicators of the prevailing winds of the common symbolic environment in which and to which most people respond.

Such indicators are representative abstractions from the collectively experienced total texture of messages. They are the results of analysis applicable to the investigation of the broadest terms of collective cultivation of concepts about life and society. Philosophers, historians, linguists, anthropologists, and others have, of course, addressed such problems before. But the rise of the industrialized and centrally managed discharge of massive symbol-systems into the mainstream of common consciousness has given the inquiry a new urgency and social policy significance. Becoming aware of mass-produced sources of consciousness can also be a liberating experience.

Before we discuss the terms and measures of the analysis, we need to consider the special characteristics of mass media discourse. That consideration will touch upon the nature and distinctive features of public communication in a cultural context whose messages are largely mass-produced and/or distributed by complex industrial structures. The description and definition of the concepts of cultivation and publication, and of their relationships to mass publics created and maintained by mass communication, will complete the background necessary for the development of an approach to message system analysis of mass media discourse.

*Public Communication*

Distinctive characteristics of large groups of people are acquired in the process of growing up, learning, and living in one culture rather than another. Individuals may make their own selections through which to cultivate personal images, tastes, views, and preferences. But they cannot cultivate what is not available, and will rarely select what is rarely available, seldom emphasized, or infrequently presented.

A culture cultivates patterns of conformity as well as of alienation or rebellion after its own image. In fact, I define culture as a system of messages that regulates social relationships.

The communications of a culture not only inform but form common images; they not only entertain but create publics; they not only reflect but shape attitudes, tastes, preferences. They provide the boundary conditions and overall patterns within which the processes of personal and group-mediated selection, interpretation, and interaction go on.

Communication is interaction through messages. Messages are formally coded symbolic or representational events of some shared significance in a culture, produced for the purpose of evoking significance. Social interaction through such messages is the "humanizing" process of Homo Sapiens. The terms of this interaction define for members of the species the realities and potentials of the human condition. These terms provide functional perspectives of existence, priority, value, and relationships; they cultivate public notions of what is, what is important, what is right, and what is related to what.

A word of *cultivation*. The term is used to indicate that our primary concern is not with bits of information, education, persuasion, etc., or with any kind of direct communication "effects". It is with the common context into which we are born and in response to which different individual and group selections and interpretations of messages takes place. Instead of measuring change causally attributed to communications injected into an otherwise stable system of messages, our analysis is concerned with assessing the system itself. That assessment is a first step toward investigating the role of message systems in establishing and maintaining stable conceptions of reality. These are conceptions that persuasive and informational efforts are usually "up against."

*Public* is another word of special significance. It means both a quality of information and an amorphous social aggregate whose members share a community of interest. As a quality of information, the awareness that a certain item of knowledge is publicly held (i. e. not only known to many, but *commonly known that it is known to many*) makes collective thought and action possible. Such knowledge gives individuals their awareness of collective strength (or weakness), and a feeling of social identification or alienation. As an amorphous social aggregate, a public is a basic unit of an requirement for self-government among diverse and scattered groups. The creation of both the awareness and the social structure called public is the result of the "public-making" activity appropriately named *publication*. ("Public opinion" is actually the outcome of eliciting private views and publishing them, as in the publication of polls.)

Publication as a general social process is the creation and cultivation of knowingly shared ways of selecting and viewing events and aspects of life. Mass production and distribution of message systems transforms selected private perspectives into broad public perspectives, and brings mass publics into existence. These publics are maintained through continued publication. They are supplied with selections of information and entertainment, fact and fiction, news and fantasy or "escape" materials which are considered important or interesting or entertaining, and profitable, (or all of these) in terms of the perspectives to be cultivated.

Publication is thus the instrument of community consciousness and of governance among large groups of people too numerous or too dispersed to interact face to face or in any other personally mediated fashion. The truly revolutionary significance of modern mass communication is its broad "public-making" ability. That is the ability to form historically new bases for collective thought and action quickly, continously, and pervasively across previous boundaries of time, space, and culture.

The terms of broadest social interaction are those available in the most widely shared messages of a culture. Increasingly these are mass-produced message systems. Whether one is widely conversant with or unaware of large portions of them, supportive or critical of them, or even alienated from or rebellious of them, these common terms of the culture shape the course of the response.

The institutions producing the most pervasive systems of messages are central to public acculturation, socialization, and the conduct of public affairs. Every society takes special steps to assure that authorative decision-making in the field of public-making is reserved to the key establishments of the power structure, be that religious, secular, public, private, or some mixture of these. The provisions conferring authoritative control to key establishments may be in the form of state monopoly, public subsidy, tax privileges, protection from public interference with private corporate control (as under the First Amendment to the U.S. Constitution), or some combination of these.

The oldest form of institutionalized public acculturation is what we today call religion, the cultural organization that once encompassed both statecraft and the public philosophy of a community. Two more recent branches are the offspring of the industrial revolution. One of these is public education or formal schooling for all, born of the struggle for equality of opportunity, and sustained by the demand for minimum literacy, competence, and obeisance in increasingly mobile, de-tribalized, de-traditionalized, and non-deferential societies. The other major branch of institutionalized public acculturation is mass communication.

*Mass Communication*

Mass communication is mass-produced communication. It is the extension of institutionalized public-making and acculturation beyond the limits of handicraft or other personally mediated interactions. It is the continuous mass production and distribution of systems of messages to groups so large, heterogeneous, and widely dispersed that they could never interact face-to-face or through any other but mass-produced and technologically mediated message systems. This becomes possible only when technological means are available and social organizations emerge for the mass production and distribution of messages.

The key to the historic significance of mass communication does not rest, therefore, in the concept of "masses" as such. There were "masses" (i. e. large groups of people) reached by other forms of public communication long before the advent of modern mass communication. The key to the cultural transformation long before the advent of modern mass communication. The key to the cultural transformation which mass communication signifies is the *mass production* of messages forming message systems characteristic of their technological and industrial bases.

The media of mass communications — print, film, radio, television — are ways of selecting, composing, recording, and sharing stories, symbols, and images. They are also social organizations acting as "governments" (i. e. authoritative decision-makers) in the special domain of institutionalized public acculturation. As such, they are products of technology, corporate (or other collective) organization, mass production, and mass markets. They are the cultural arms of the industrial order from which they spring.

Mass media policies reflect and cultivate not only the general structure of social relations but also specific types of institutional and industrial organization and control. Corporate or collective organization, private or public control, and the priorities given to artistic, political, economic or other policy considerations govern their overall operations, affect their relationships to other institutions and shape their public functions. The general context of public consciousness today may have more to do with industrial power, structure and control than with anything else.

*Mass Media Message Systems*

Mass-produced and/or distributed media discourse is thus both a record and an instrument of industrial behaviour in the cultural field. Its analysis can shed light on its actual controls and functions, independently from policy intentions, rationalizations, and pretentions or from assumptions and claims about its effects. Such analysis is not a substitute for the study of policies and effects. Rather it is a source both of hypotheses for those investigations and of independent results that can help illuminate, support or counter them. But it can also yield strategic intelligence and results that cannot be obtained in any other way, such as explaining why certain issues, problems, courses of action, etc. become salient to large numbers of people at certain times. Message system analysis of mass media discourse is one leg of the three-legged stool of comprehensive cultural indicators, including three types of investigations; institutional policy analysis, message system analysis, and cultivation analysis. (See Gerbner, et al., 1973a)

*The Analysis*

Message system analysis is thus designed to investigate the aggregate and collective premises presented in mass media discourse. It deals with the "facts of life" and dynamic qualities represented in the systems. Its purpose is to describe the symbolic "world," sense its climate, trace its currents, and identify its functions.

The results make no reference to single communications. They do not interpret selected units of symbolic material or draw conclusions about artistic style or merit. That is the task of essaying works of personal and selective relevance, not necessarily representative of a system of image and message mass-production. Message system analysis seeks to examine what large and heterogeneous communities absorb but not necessarily what any individual selects.

The analysis extracts from the discourse its basic presentation of elements of existence, importance, value, and relationship, and then re-aggregates these elements into larger patterns along lines of investigate purpose. The analysis pivots on the reliable determination of these elements and is limited to clearly preceived and reliably coded items. That limitation does not mean that message system analysis pays attention only to surface structure cues (words, etc.) of discourses. Nor does it leave out the semantic, pragmatic, and other systematically assessible dimensions of messages. It only means that, unlike artistic and literary criticism of a traditional kind, useful for purpose of revealing personal interpretation and unique insight, message system analysis deals with the common elements of discourse such as thematic distribution, propositional context, characterization and action structure, social typing, fate (success, failure) of character types, and other reliably identifiable representations and configurations. If one were to use the perceptions and impressions of casual observers, no matter how sophisticated, the value of the investigation could be reduced, and its purpose confounded. Only an aggregation of unambiguous message elements and their separation from personal impressions left by unidentified clues will provide a valid and reliable standard for comparison with the intentions and claims of policy makers and the perceptions or conceptions of audiences.

What distinguishes the analysis of public, mass-mediated message systems as a social scientific enterprise from other types of observation, commentary, or criticism is the attempt to deal comprehensively, systematically, and generally rather than specifically and selectively or *ad hoc* with patterns of collective cultural life. This approach makes no prior assumptions about such conventionally demarcated functions as "information" and "entertainment," or "high culture" and "low culture." Style of expression, quality of representation, artistic excellence, or the nature of individual experience associated with selective exposure to and participation in mass-cultural activity are not relevant for this purpose. What is informative, entertaining (or both), good, bad, or indifferent by any standard are selective judgments applied to messages in a way that may be quite independent from the functions they actually perform in the context of message systems touching the collective life of a large and diverse populations. Conventional and formal judgments applied to selected communications may be irrelevant to general questions about the presentation of what is, what is important, what is right, and what is related to what in mass-produced message systems.

It should be stressed again that the characteristics of a message system are not necessarily the characteristics of individual units composing the system. The purpose of the study of a system *as system* is to reveal features, processes, and relationships expressed in the whole, not in its parts. Unlike most literary or dramatic criticism, or, in fact, most personal cultural participation and judgment, message system analysis focuses on the record of industrial behavior in the cultural field and its symbolic functions.

*Symbolic functions*

Symbolic functions are implicit in the way basic elements of a system are presented, weighted, loaded with attributes, and related to each other. Such elements are time, space, characterizations (people) and their fate (success, failure; domination, submission, etc.). Dynamic symbol systems are not maps of some other "real" territory. They are our mythology, our organs of social meaning. They make visible some conceptions of the invisible forces of life and society. We select and shape them to bend otherwise elusive facts to our (not always conscious) purposes. Whether we know it or intend it or not, these purposes are implicit in the way things actually work out in the symbolic world.

On the whole, and in the long run, institutional interests and pressures shape the way things work out in most collective myths, celebrations, and rituals. Mass-produced message systems (as all standardized and assembly-line products) are even more power-ridden and policy-directed. Various power roles enter into the decision-making process that prescribes, selects and shapes the final product. In the creation of news, facts impose some constraints upon invention; the burden of serving institutional purposes is placed upon selection, treatment and display. Fiction and drama carry no presumption of facticity and thus do not inhibit the candid expression of social values. On the contrary, they give free reign to adjusting facts to institutional purpose. Fiction can thus perform social symbolic functions more directly than can other forms of discourse.

Symbolic functions differ from those of nonsymbolic events in the ways in which causal relationships must be traced in the two realms. Physical causation exists outside and independently of consciousness. Trees do not grow and chemicals do not react "on purpose," although human purposes may intervene or cause them to function. When a sequence of physical events is set in motion, we have only partial awareness and little control over the entire chain of its consequences.

The symbolic world, however, is totally invented. The reasons why things exist in the symbolic world, and the ways in which things are related to one another and to their symbolic consequences, are completely artificial. The laws of the symbolic world are entirely socially and culturally determined. Whatever exists in the symbolic world is there because someone put it there. The reason may be a marketing or programming decision or a feeling that it will "improve the story." Having been put there, things not only stand for other things as all symbols do, but also *do* something in their symbolic context. The introduction (or elimination) of a character, a scene, an event, has functional consequences. It changes other things in the story. It makes the whole work "work" differently.

A structure may accomodate to pressure in a way that preserves, or even enhances, the symbolic functions of an act. For example, the first response of television program producers to agitation about violence on television was to eliminate violent women characters, thereby reducing violent acts but also making women involved in violence totally victimized. In other words, we found that when the proportion of violent characterizations was selectively (and temporarily) reduced, the imbalance in the risks of victimization between groups of unequal social power increased, thereby strengthening the symbolic function of violence as a demonstration of relative social powers (Gerbner, 1972).

In another study (Nunally, 1960), the opinions of experts on 10 information questions concerning the mentally ill were compared with mass media (most fictional and dramatic) representations of mentally ill characters. The mass media image was found to diverge widely from the expert image. The "public image," as determined by a attitude survey along the same dimensions, fell between the expert and the media profiles. Thus, instead of "mediating" expert views, the media tended to cultivate conceptions far different from and in many ways opposed to those of the experts. What may be seen in isolation as "ineffective" communication was, on the contrary, powerful media cultivation "pulling" popular notions away from expert views. The symbolic functions of mental illness in popular drama and news may well be to indicate unpredictability, danger, or morally and dramatically appropriate punishment for certain sins — all very different from its diagnostic and therapeutic conceptions.

The study of specific message structures and symbolic functions reveals how these communications help define, characterize, and decide the course of life, the fate of people, and the nature of society in a symbolic world. The "facts" of that world are often different from those of the "real" world, but their functions are those of the real social order. For example, in U.S. television drama, male characters outnumber female characters more than three to one. They dominate the symbolic world, and present more than their share of activities and opportunities. Fiction, drama, and news depict situations and present actions in those realistic, fantastic, tragic, or comic ways that provide the most appropriate symbolic context for the emergence of some institutional and social significance that could not be presented or would not be accepted (let alone enjoyed) in other ways.

*Terms of Analysis*

Message system analysis thus investigates industrial behaviour in message mass-production for large and heterogeneous populations. The analysis suggests collective and common features and functions of public image formation. The schema and methods of analysis are designed to inquire into those dimensions of mass media discourse that identify elements of *existence*, *importance*, *values*, and *relationships*. Figure 1 summarizes the questions, terms, and measures of analysis relevant to each dimension.

The dimension of existence deals with the question "What is?", that is, what is available (can be attended to) in public message systems, how

| Dimensions | Existence | Priorities | Values | Relationships |
|---|---|---|---|---|
| *Assumptions about*: | WHAT IS? | WHAT IS IMPORTANT? | WHAT IS RIGHT OR WRONG, GOOD OR BAD, ETC.? | WHAT IS RELATED TO WHAT, AND HOW? |
| *Questions*: | What is available for public attention? How much and how frequently? | In what context or order of importance? | In what light, from what point of view, with what associated judgments? | In what over-all proximal, logical, or causal structure? |
| *Terms and measures of analysis*: | ATTENTION Prevalence, rate, complexity, variations | EMPHASIS Ordering, ranking, scaling for prominence, centrality or intensity | TENDENCY Measures of critical and differential tendency; qualities traits | STRUCTURE Correlations, clustering; structure of action |

Fig. 1. Dimensions, Questions, Terms and Measures of Message System Analysis

frequently, and in what proportions. The availability of shared messages defines the scope of public attention. The measure of attention, therefore, indicates the presence, frequency, rate, complexity, and varying distributions of items, topics, themes, etc., presented in message systems.

The dimension of *importance* addresses the question, "What is important?" We use measures of *emphasis* to study the context of relative prominence and order or degrees of intensity, centrality, importance. Measures of attention and emphasis may be combined to indicate not only the allocation but also the focusing of attention in a system.

The dimension of *values* inquires into the point of view from which things are presented. It notes certain evaluative and other qualitative characteristics, traits, or connotations attached to themes, events, items, actions, persons, groups, and so on. Measures of *tendency* are used to assess the direction of value judgments observed in units of attention.

The dimension of *relationships* focuses on the associations within and among measures of attention, emphasis, and tendency. When we deal with patterns instead of only simple distributions, or when we relate the clustering of measures to one another, we illuminate the underlying *structure* of assumptions about existence, importance, and values represented in message systems.

The four dimensions, then, yield measures of attention, emphasis, tendency, and structure. *Attention* is the typology or classification of units of discourse into categories of existence (subjects, themes, demographic characteristics, etc.); *emphasis* is the relative importance attributed to each unit attended to within the context of the discourse; *tendency* is the evaluative and other qualities attributed to each unit of attention; and *structure* is the ways in which categories of attention (existence) are related to emphasis (importance) and tendency (values) in the system. For a full and comprehensive analysis, all four dimensions should be included.

Message system analysis begins with the determination of appropriate samples and units of analysis, and the development of an instrument of analysis (coding and recording scheme). The sample should be large enough to permit the development of stable patterns and the assessment of the significance of differences in the distribution of characteristics. The units of analysis should correspond to the units of production as much as possible (newspapers, pages, films, programs, books for context units; stories, scenes, characters, themes, etc., for units of enumeration). The instrument of analysis should be as explicit as possible to facilitate reliable coding and the recording of observations.

*The Measures*

Let us now discuss each measure in greater detail and illustrate them with examples.

1. Attention indicates the presence (or absence) and frequency of selected elements of existence that a system of messages makes available for public attention. These can be a subject classification, list of themes, typology of characters, or any other category scheme relevant to the purpose of the investigation. The principal issue here is to determine "what is" in the system to which people can attend, and how frequently does each element appear in the system.

Most content analyses use the measure of attention to determine the occurrence of relevant items, themes, and other characteristics in press coverage, dramatic and fictional analyses, thematic study of magazine stories, ads, films, etc. For example, we have studied trends in media attention to mental illness (Gerbner, 1959); the relative amounts of attention that the press systems of different countries devoted to the outside world (Gerbner and Marvanyi, 1977); the representation of teachers, schools, and students in the mass media of 10 countries (Gerbner, et al, 1973b); the image of the "film hero" in one year's feature film production of six countries (Gerbner, 1969); and the demography of the dramatic character population of U.S. television drama (Gerbner and Signorielli, 1982). A typical attention item has a subject title or question, (i. e. "Foreign News," "Occupation," "Character's Success or Failure," "Character's Age,") and several answers, including "cannot code," "uncertain, mixed," and "other-write in," as well as the most relevant substantive categories.

2. Emphasis is a measure of the relative importance of a unit of attention in the sample. Emphasis directs attention to some units at the expense of attending to other units. The headline or title of a story, its size and placement, the intensity of the mode of communication, the order of presentation, loudness, tone, prominence by other means such as duration, focus, detail, etc. and certain design characteristics are marks of emphasis. Emphasis is always a relative measure and an element of context. Therefore ranks, scales, and other measures of relative value are suitable for indicating emphasis. Frequency (a measure of attention) may also denote emphasis, but there ale elements of discourse that are prominent for their relative rarity, while others may receive emphasis by repetition. Therefore, a measure of emphasis that is separate from frequency is sometimes desirable.

The emphasis code (rank order, scale number, etc.) is generally attributed to the unit of attention. It answers the question: Now that we have established that something exists in the system and thus may be attended to (attention), let us note how prominent or important it is.

Message system analysis may feature the units of attention that receive the highest emphasis, such as a study of headlines in a comparative investigation of national press perspectives (Gerbner, 1961) or an investigation of leading characters in television drama (Gerbner and Signorielli, 1982). Usually, however, separate and independent measures of attention and of emphasis can illuminate different facets of the system. For example, we have found that one general feature of the representation of women and minorities on American television is that even when their numbers exceeds their proportion of the real population (which is rare), they are more likely to play minor or secondary than major or leading parts (Gerbner and Signorielli, 1979).

3. Tendency is a measure of the evaluative or other qualitative characteristics attributes to a unit of attention. It is often a scale defined by such adjectives as good—bad, right—wrong, positive—negative, active—passive, strong—weak, smart—stupid, successful—unsuccessful, or whatever is germane to the purpose of the investigation. A group of such scales may stem from and define a factorial structure of dimension of meaning or personality types such as semantic differential scales. The measure of tendency attempts to answer the question: Now that we have established the distribution of attention and emphasis in the system, in what evaluative, qualitative, judgmental light is each unit presented?

Measuring tendency is clearly separate from coding attention and emphasis; whether something is good or bad does not depend on its frequency or prominence. However, the ultimate combination (an element of structure) may determine its meaning. The frequency and prominence of good things certainly impresses us differently from the frequency and prominence of bad things.

Although tendency is thus usually an element of the structure of a message system, presented in conjunction with the other measures, it can also be the principal feature of the investigation. For example, a study of ideological tendencies in the French press showed that different political organs reported a criminal case in different light, even when shifts of attention and emphasis were considered equal (Gerbner, 1964).

4. Structure is that aspect of the context of a message system that reveals underlying relationships among the other dimensions. These relationships are "underlying" in that they are not necessarily given in single units but are characteristics of the system as a whole. A story may present a violent criminal as an "ex mental patient," a doctor as wise and authoritative, and a politician as opportunistic. If the *majority* of stories in a message system present mental patients as violent, doctors as omniscient, and politicians as venal, we are dealing with structural characteristics of the system ("stereotypes") whose meaning for the policies that produce it and the assumption it may cultivate are very different from that of isolated portrayals.

Most of the studies cited in the bibliography and virtually all full-fledged message system analyses investigate the underlaying structure of message systems. Some also relate that structure to theories of the cultural functions of institutions and to theories of cultivation and media effects. Examples of such research can be found in the development of our theory of "mainstreaming" (Gerbner, Gross, Morgan, and Signorielli, 1980) and its application to political orientations (Gerbner, Gross, Morgan, and Signorielli, 1982).

The analysis of mass media message systems can thus provide a framework in which comprehensive, coherent, cumulative, and comparative mass-cultural information can be systematically assembled and periodically reported. Indicators relevant to specific problems or policies can then be seen in the context of the entire structure of assumptions cultivated at a particular time and place.

These indicators will not tell us what individuals think or do. But they will tell us what most people think or do something *about* and suggest reasons why. They will tell us about industrial policy and process in the cultural field mass-producing shared representations of life and the assumptions and functions embedded in them. They will help understand, judge, and shape the symbolic environment that affects much of what we think and do in common.

*Bibliography*

Gerbner, G. (Fall 1959). "Mental Illness on Television: A Study of Censorship." *Journal of Broadcasting* 3, 292–303.

Gerbner, G. (Summer 1961). "Press Perspectives in World Communications: A Pilot Study." *Journalism Quarterly* 38, 313–322.

Gerbner, G. (Autumn 1964). "Ideological Perspectives and Political Tendencies in News Reporting." *Journalism Quarterly* 41, 495–509.

Gerbner, G. (Summer 1966). "Images Across Cultures: Teachers in Mass Media Fiction and Drama." *The School Review* 74, 212–229.

Gerbner, G. (1969). "The Film Hero: A Cross-Cultural Study." *Journalism Monograph* 13, 1–54.

Gerbner, G. (1972). "Violence in Television Drama: Trends and Symbolic Functions." In G. A. Comstock and E. A. Rubinstein (eds.) *Television and Social Behavior* 1. *Content and Control*. U.S. Government Printing Office, Washington, D.C. 29–93.

Gerbner, G., Gross, L., and Melody, W. (eds.) (1973a). "Cultural Indicators: The Third Voice." In *Communications Technology and Social Policy*. John Wiley & Sons, New York, 555–573.

Gerbner, G., Gross, L., and Melody, W. (eds.) (1973b). "Teacher Image and the 'Hidden Curriculum.'" In *Communications Technology and Social Policy*. John Wiley & Sons, New York, 555–92.

Gerbner, G. and Gross, L. (Spring 1976). "Living with Television: The Violence Profile." *Journal of Communication*, 173–199.

Gerbner, G. and Marvanyi, G. (Winter 1977). "The Many Worlds of the World's Press." *Journal of Communication*, 52–66.

Gerbner, G. and Signorielli, N. (1979). "Women and Minorities in Television Drama, 1969–1978." The Annenberg School of Communications, University of Pennsylvania, Philadelphia, Pa.

Gerbner, G., Gross, L., Morgan, M., and Signorielli, N. (Summer 1980). "The 'Mainstreaming' of America: Violence Profile No. 11." *Journal of Communication*, 100–127.

Gerbner, G., Morgan, M., and Signorielli, N. (1982). "Programming Health Portrayals: What Viewers See, Say and Do." *Television and Behavior: Ten Years of Scientific Progress and Implications for the 80's*. (The National Institute of Mental Health update of the original report of the Surgeon General's Scientific Advisory Committee on Television and Social Behavior). Washington, D.C., 291–307.

Gerbner, G., Gross, L., Morgan, M., and Signorielli, N. (Spring 1982). "Charting the Mainstream: Television's Contributions to Political Orientations." *Journal of Communication*, 100–126.

Gerbner, G. and Signorielli, N. (October 1982). "The World According to Television." *American Demographics*, 15—17.

Nunnaly, Jum C. Jr. (1960). *Popular Conceptions of Mental Health; Their Development and Change*. Holt, Rinehart and Winston, New York.

IAN CONNELL AND ADAM MILLS

# Text, Discourse and Mass Communication

*Sociology and Mass Communication: Revision or Reformation?*

To speak of the 'mass media' at once invokes a now well-established body of critical opinion and assumption concerning not only the character of certain types of public signification, but also how they relate to and affect other social processes. For instance, it has long been assumed that the 'mass media' — radio, cinema and now television — are the instruments of the destruction of (genuine) popular culture and the vehicles for a homogeneous and standardised 'mass culture'. Moreover, it has long been assumed that the social effects or costs of the (apparent) imposition of this 'mass' culture are clear: — the creation of a homogenous audience lacking in discrimination and incapable of differentiated response and the constitution of a network of social relations constantly monitored and mediated by the institutions of public signification. Because of such assumptions the so-called content of the 'mass' media has long been the source of concern and the focus of considerable interest.

We pick up the story of this concern and interest at a moment of reformation, a moment in which some of the more monolithic assumptions were opened up to questioning. Drawing upon the resources of the 'interpretive' critique of normative and positivist sociologies, the reformers began to question whether the media were capable of producing unilateral effects, and whether it was useful to consider that the media were the sole sources of "definitions of the world", whether there might not be other sources which permitted of alternative definitions.

The notion that the media made available definitions of the world and stereotypical social characters led to some empirical work on how they were socially constructed or "manufactured" (cf. Cohen and Young, 1976), but in a rather restricted way. For the most part the processes of manufacture were quite narrowly interpreted by analysts as those institutionalised ways and means for gathering the "raw material" (though little was done to demonstrate how they had become 'institutionalised'), and not to the (semiotic) ways and means of its transformation into journalistic stories of one sort or another. As to the products manufactured, then, little was done except to assert that they *expressed* certained pre-determined meanings. It was argued that the relation beween medium and audience was more fittingly conceived of as an interaction or exchange (cf. Halloran, 1970). But this did not draw on or initiate any particulary novel empirical work, nor did really disturb the notion of the products as "vehicles for meanings", which have been established elsewhere, in other social sites.

So, although some well-worn analytic and conceptual cliches concerning the various media and their social impact were shaken up and others were more or less shaken out (that "emphasis upon the viewer as *tabula rasa*, as wide open just waiting to soak up all that is becamed at him", denounced by Halloran for example), the concerns and questions which followed the reformation were not such as to lead to the wholesale abandonment of what had by then become the mainstream interests. This reformation was no potential revolution — by no means an "epistemological break". While some critical distance was put between the established and emerging concerns, a fundamental continuity in conception and methodological procedure was also maintained. One, major consequence of this continuity was that, in the main the analysis of media discourses remained as, at best, a variation, and sometimes a sohistication of, *content analysis*. Moreover it was to become a fairly low priority.

The quite peripheral status of the analysis of discourses in the context of this reformed sociological perspective also had to do with the perception of other problems requiring immediate attention. One such was the seemingly perennial one ot the 'impact' or 'effect' of the media of so-called 'mass' communication as such, or, on a somewhat less grand scale, of particular 'messages'. (Again, this conception of the product as a 'message' with all the attendant connotations of consistency and coherence had an easy, untroubled passage through the reformation).

This 'effects-research' hat taken one of two main courses. Either it had drifted towards market research. Confident that the basics of 'mass' communication had been fully understood, some saw the work in future as an "engineering rather than a theoretical" task (cf. Bauers, 1960). It was now down to manipulating the known variables to a client's advantage, whether the client was selling soap, a political party or politician. This was, and still is, the bread-and-butter business of media research. In other cases, it drifted to more 'honourable' concerns with the media's impact upon democratic procedures, social issues or social policies. Often the effort was to determine by what means their deleterious effects (the promotion of a moral laxity in matters sexual, the sensationalisation of 'serious' political matters, or the encouragement of violence and aggression) could be contained, modified or, even better, countered.

Underpinning each there was a seemingly unshakeable conviction that the media were for good or, more often, ill effective. This, though in various ways qualified, was one of the field of study's axioms. The reformatory studies stuck to this conviction, expressing it in terms of television's power to define. This supposed definitional power was not the issue so much as how it was exercised, with what effects on particular social groups. The virtual absence of any interest in audience research can be regarded as a symptom of the extent to which television and other media were regarded as powerful, as capable of setting the agenda of public interest.

*Constraints and Determinations*

James Halloran, Director of the Mass Communications Research Centre (still the major English research institution in this field), and his colleagues were foremost among those to question notions of 'influence' that had informed previous effects research. They argued that "there is much more to the influence of television than can possibly be assessed through direct changes in attitude and opinion, as these have normally been measured (1970b, p. 67). As they saw it, "the concentration on attitude change as a primary criterion of influence has meant that other important areas have been neglected" (p. 67). That is to say, 'influence' was a process not exhausted by that one, particular case of 'attitude change'; television could still, or also, be influential in setting and maintaining attitudes which were already present. Thus, in their view, "television can help set standards, confer status, define norms, provide stereotypes, convey a sense of what is approved and what is not approved, structure our fields of discourse and frameworks of expectation and generally provide us with our pictures of the world" (p. 67).

In a more recent statement Peter Golding and Graham Murdock have put the point this way: "given the insistent pressure to maximise audiences and revenues, there is not surprisingly a consistent tendency for the commercial media to avoid the unpopular and tendentious and to draw instead on the values and assumptions which are most widely legitimated, which almost inevitably means those which flow authoritatively downwards through the social structure" (1977, p. 37—8). The provisional character of the earlier statement given in its use of 'can' had, by the time of Golding and Murdock's, been dispensed with. The certainty of their statement is by no means exceptional. But, given this view, it is difficult to see how it can also be assumed that consumers of these commercial media can have any measure of autonomy, an autonomy suggested by that 'interactionist' perspective recommended by Halloran earlier. Moreover, even were we to accept this view, it leaves us none the wiser as to the (discursive and other) processes by which the 'flow downwards' is accomplished.

This attempted reformulation — a reformulation which has come virtually full-circle to the presupposition of televisual potency that was initially to be qualified — was, however, only one among a number of other concerns. In *Demonstrations and Communications* (1970), the study which did more than any other to establish the reformed order of interests and approaches, Halloran, Elliott and Murdock suggested that there had been an over concentration upon supposed effects which had excluded empirical work being done on other equally important questions. They cited, among other things, the production processes by which 'messages' were put together and transmitted: economic planning and policy making, and the study of the 'professionalisation' of the 'mass' communicator. These were some of the 'main attractions' in the years following the publication of *Demonstrations and Communications*. (Its lead has now been followed by a number of studies including Elliott, 1972; Schlesinger, 1978; Chibnall, 1977; and Alvarado and Buscombe, 1976).

The overall orientation of this work has been, then, to fill out knowledge of the working environment and routines of television journalism especially, and of the determinations (or 'constraints' which has been the usual way in which determinations have been conceived of in this work) operating on them. Given this orientation, what, if anything, has been accomplished in respect of identifying and analysing specific media discourses? The short answer is, very little!

The most recent and most controversial instance of this kind of research is the work of the Glasgow Media Group. The basic task which this group set itself in both *Bad News* and *More Bad News* was to demonstrate once-and-for-all that the news provided by both the BBC and ITN constantly fails to meet the editorial criteria of impartiality and balance. What distinguishes their treatment of this familiar accusation is the contention that the failure is routine and not merely an occasional lapse. This is demonstrated, to their satisfaction at any rate, when during the first four month of 1975 there were only 17 occasions when someone was shown to speak against the government's incomes policy as compared with the 287 occasions when it was argued for. (Actually all this demonstrates is the acknowledgement of all that has been constitutionally required of broadcasters, namely *due* accuracy and *due* impartiality. For a fuller discussion of this point, cf. Connell, 1980). So, they conclude that "viewers were given a misleading portrayal of industrial disputes in the UK when measured against the independent reality of events" and that "the news was organised and produced substantially around the views of the dominant political group in our society". What they refer to as "the bland assertion of objectivity and impartiality" serves, they assert, "to obfuscate what is in fact the reproduction of the dominant assumptions about our society".

This work once again demonstrates the limitations of the sociological reformation. Once again many of the themes from the 'mass thesis' are reproduced here — the notion that the media are controlled by the peculiar interests of a powerful elite and the further notion that of course the media are successful in generalising those interests by nothing more complex than deception.

In a recent estimation of another tradition of media research, one which has, in part, drawn upon the same critical resources and is represented by instances of Hall's work (1975, 1976 for instance) and Williams's (1974, 1976 for instance), Graham Murdock and Peter Golding have made it clear that for this reformed sociology the principal object of attention was not so much the definitions of situations or frameworks of assumption as such which the media employed, but rather more their sources. They have said, on what they perceived as a "tendency to over-privilege texts as objects of analysis" that "one recurrent theme in recent analysis of news is the detection of frameworks of understanding within which news is constructed. These are discovered in the analysis of texts by a circumspect reading of the assumptions and nuances of routine journalism. This work is often brilliant and insightfull. It does not, however, tell us anything of the social derivation of such frameworks" (1979, p. 212). So this sociological analysis of cultural production has been more concerned with the "analysis of social relations and social structure", that is, with who shares the frameworks identified and with how they have come to be part of the rhetoric and character of news.

So, although particular studies have been concerned to establish the definitions and the inferential structure of news reports about the anti-Vietnam war demonstration (Halloran *et. al.*, 1970), the definitions of prejudice (Elliott, 1972), to establish "the way race-related material ... handled in the media contributes towards the definition of the situation" (Hartmann and Husband, 1972), or to denounce news stories of industrial affairs (G. U. M. G., 1976, 1980), these have not been their only nor their main concern. Fundamentally such analyses have viewed studies of discourses as "a variety of content analysis and as such they suffer from the familiar but intractable problem of inference" (Murdock and Golding, 1979, p. 206). The point of such analysis is perceived to be to gain insight into *something other* than the immediate object of attention — the text or 'message vehicle'; to gain insight into the "sets of relations and of determinations they exert upon the production process." (1979, p. 207) — relations and determinations which texts are seen to *express*, but often in a disguised way. In other words, analysing messages for this sociology, is a kind of surrogate, a sometimes unavoidable expedient, for the real thing, namely, the *direct* analysis of the web of social relations of production.

*The More or Less Missing Text*

It is with some justification that Murdock and Golding have complained of a lack of attention to what we may think of as the social relations of communication. But there are a number of problems with the alternative they propose. In some mysterious way the object of analyses becomes *a-social*. In their view, and it is a view common to this sociology, any analysis properly concerned with the social would look elsewhere than texts to discover social relations and structures. Texts may be socially constructed and may express socially shared meanings, but they are not themselves social! For this sociology the text ist simply an 'artefact', a given stability which is fixed once and for all.

Given this view, there is hardly even respect for the texts as a certain structure or order of signs, a received combination of discourses which are, nevertheless, open to reconstruction or recombination as they are appropriated and consumed. The content analyses that have been mounted, deconstructed texts willy-nilly, with scant regard for their immanent structures and the meanings these were capable of sustaining. What structure there was, was that imposed by the act of analysing the content. There was little to suggest that this was recognised as an effect of one, special kind of appropriation, that others were possible, or that texts were structured independently of their consumption. Moreover whether the manifest aim of the content analysis was to determine the definitions of a particular situation, or how already delimited social groupings were 'labelled' or 'stigmatised' (Young, 1971; Cohen, 1972, Cohen and Young, 1973; Hall, *et al.*, 1978), texts were deemed capable of expressing or representing and amplifying only one definite meaning, that established in the course of the analysis — what the texts *really* meant.

The determination of 'the meaning' seemed a relatively easy and straightforward business. Underpinning the seeming easiness of it all was the notion that media discourses were semantically transparent: a meaning or set of meanings is formed up (usually) by ruling groups and this is then carried to other, subordinate groups more or less clearly via the media. The signs ('message vehicles') of which the text are composed were conceived merely as instruments for conveying the meaning which had already been established.

It is somewhat surprising that such notions survived the reformation, given some of the critical resources which were drawn upon. Symbolic interactionism or ethnomethodology (cf. Meltzer *et al.*, 1975) or as Dreitzel has termed it, "the phenomenological analysis of consciousness" (1970) has clearly informed the reformation, yet its potential for questioning the supposed 'transparency' of meaning was virtually overlooked. For Cicourel, for example, social interaction consisted in "mutual typifications" which were always "tentative and being tested over the course of the interaction" (p. 25). These 'stimuli' had to be interpreted as meaningful or relevant, which in turn pre-supposed mechanisms or "basic rules that permit him to identify settings that could lead to appropriate invocation of norms" (p. 25). The 'basic rules' provided "a sense of social order that is fundamental for normative order (consensus or shared agreement) to exist or be negotiated and constructed" (p. 30).

Such propositions could have led to the identification of 'basic rules' for the production and consumption of say television news stories. But it did not, at least as far as the reformed sociological perspective were concerned. It did not for a numer of reasons. Much of this perspectives rhetoric was devoted to denying the existence of a consensus or of 'consensual meaning'. It might have been better were it to have attempted to determine the conditions under which such meaning could be produced. Murdock observed that such work confused social structure with actors' sense of social structure: social structures did not exist precariously, but did not exist independently of actors' accounting practices (Murdock, 1974). In other words 'objective' structures were denied. And, furthermore, as Dreitzel in his assessment argued "communicative behaviour rests on work and power relations as well as on language; and, if we comprehend the typification schemes of language as the most fundamental basic rules of everyday life, we also have to notice that even language is subject to distortions caused by the condition of our life" (1970, p. XVII). The perception of these shortcomings proved too much, and the potential remained unexploited. The problematisation of notions of 'communicative transparency' did not really occur until the advent, albeit in fits and starts, of work informed by for instance structuralism and marxism reviewed through structuralism.

*The Structuralist Projection*

While the dominant sociological tradition of mass-communications research was being revised from within its principal theoretical supports were being increasingly contested and eroded by the growing importance of what Jameson has called the 'structuralist projection' (Jameson, 1972 cf. pp. 101–102). Though it is clear that in no sense can structuralism be thought of as a single coherent theoretical enterprise, and that instead there are only structuralisms, what is equally clear is that these structuralisms were responsible for the successive 'break' in the field of media analysis which provided, or prepared the ground for the series of theoretical initiatives which have come to be collectively termed 'discourse analysis'. However, there is no clear, single line of development leading from structuralism to something called discourse analysis which now exists as a distinct, self-contained and unified theory; because it has been theorised in a number of different fields and has drawn on a number of different traditions it would be more accurate to say that it delineates an approach, or a way of thinking about media analysis. In this sense it is the concept of discourse analysis, or discourse theory which has opened a space in the field of media studies and the way that 'space' is used and developed depends, essentially, on the way the term itself has come to be characterized.

In its most general sense, structuralism is no more than a convenient term by which to designate a loose methodology developed in areas of knowledge as diverse as anthropology, psychoanalysis, Marxist theory, literary criticism and linguistics. Emerging primarily in France during the fifties, (though not achieving prominence and a certain notoriety until the seventies) what gave these areas of knowledge a certain general cohesiveness was their distinctive theoretical emphasis on a methodology based on linguistics. By the end of the sixties, and with the 'effects' paradigm of media research proving to be clearly inadequate, structuralism seemed to offer a way of transcending the static and inert models of mass communications proposed by the various media sociologies. In whatever areas the structuralist approach was applied, whether the 'object' under scrutiny was society, literature, myth, or whatever, the 'object' was considered a 'whole', or more correctly a totality of mutually dependent elements which, while comprising the whole, were subordinate to and, in the final analysis, dependent on and determined by the whole of which they were a part. From this point of view, language was the paradigm, *par excellence*, on which to base this approach. Firstly, because it was conceived as a self-contained system of mutually interdependent terms linked together by certain specific rules; and secondly, because language was seen to be concerned above all else with meaning and the production of meaning, not in an individual sense, but in the sense that language was both social and objective. Meaning in communication was understood to be possible not through the activity of an individual but by virtue of the objective rules and possibilities which were determined by the language system itself.

Probably the single most important exponent of this trend has been Lévi-Strauss who has consistently argued, not only for the synthesis of linguistics and the study of culture, but more radically for an approach which treats social systems as if they were, in fact, organised like languages. (Lévi-Strauss, 1972, p. 83) This approach, founded generally in the structural linguistics of Saussure, was expanded and developed over the fifties, primarily by Lévi-Strauss, but also in the work of Roland Barthes, to provide a general theory of the way culture was produced and organised. The paradigms advanced by these two figures proved to be of major theoretical importance for the structuralist initiative in mass-communications theory, constituting the basis for the early semiotic analysis of message systems. Ironically, however, the methodology derived from Saussurean structural linguistics and which gave semiotics its basic conceptual apparatus has subsequently been rejected (Jakobson, 1973: Williams, 1977: Pêcheux, 1982), and in retrospect it now seems that many of the developments within media analysis have been attempts to accomodate and overcome the limitations inherent in the methods and concepts borrowed from, what was essentially a Saussurean linguistics and applied to the media. Nevertheless, the advances made in these early paradigms have not simply been supplanted and totally superseded, but have continued to inform the newer, more developed theoretical positions in which media analysis has been thought.

*The Semiological Paradigm*

Despite the fact that Lévi-Strauss's Intervention was seminal for socio-cultural theory, setting the terms of both the structuralist problematic and the principles for a theory of discourse in the analysis of the social production of meaning, the work of Barthes and his development of semiotics provided the main point of departure for the structuralist approach to the mass media. In the ten years between the publication of *Mythologies* (Barthes, 1973) in 1957 and the emergence of semiotics on the periphery of communications theory, however, the principles of structuralism had been extended to a number of different fields, most notably by Althusser and his colleagues (Althusser, 1975, 1977) which were to have important repercussions on the analysis of the media. In general, the initial application of structuralist methods to the media were more concerned with discovering the rules and conventions governing signifying systems and in elaborating the principles of semiotics than in the rigorous analysis of specific message systems. Thus in the first phase of development, the horizon of structural analysis was limited to what Burgelin proposed as 'immanent analysis' (Burgelin, 1972), the aim of which was to uncover the internal organisation of the elements comprising a message in order to reveal the code by which they were articulated to form a structured whole. Though this approach was indebted to Barthes, the formalism of its method derived mainly from Lévi-Strauss's analysis of myth (Lévi-Strauss, 1972) and while this was a tentative start, it almost immediately revealed certain shortcomings in the paradigm on which it was based. Though Lévi-Strauss had argued that social meaning was produced through the organisation of language by the 'mythic discourse', which, as a structured system, was organised according to its own international logic (Lévi-Strauss, 1970 cf. pp. 11–12)), the formalism of his method proved to be an obstacle. Because the code and the rules were conceived in terms of their 'abstract' properties, independent of, and irreducible to, the 'contents' which they organised, the analysis elided the social relationship between source and receiver, production and reception, intention and effect. Consequently, applied to mass communications, this proved to be inadequate for a more developed analysis of the relations between institutions, messages and the social formation and the different 'moments' in the production and circulation of meanings and the field in which they produced their effects. Moreover, as Gerbner had prophetically observed in 1967, many areas of social conflict were being increasingly absorbed and mediated by 'the newer spheres of control, contest and attention in mass produced communications'. (Gerbner, 1972, p. 38)

Barthes, on the other hand, though principally concerned with extending a theory of signs — semiotics — to embrace all signifying systems (Barthes, 1967) had insisted on retaining the concept of ideology (Barthes, 1973). By integrating the study of semiotics and the production of meaning with a theory of ideology he attempted to demonstrate the processes by which certain signifying practices and certain meanings were elavated and generalised so that they organised the field of culture as a whole. However, the hesitation and ambiguity in his seminal discussion of the relation between signification and ideology revealed the central weakness of the structuralist methods drawn from Saussurean linguistics for the analysis of mass communications. Where the real force of his argument lay in its emphasis on signification as an active process for the production of meanings within specific systems or domains, his definition of ideology as a 'type of speech' suggested, on the contrary, that ideology comprised a single, unilateral system of meanings. In effect, his work implied that at the level of meaning, at least, the concept of 'langue' was impossible and instead, that the ideological work of the media consisted of constructing, organising and mapping together the disparate areas of social meanings. But though these insights could throw some light on the operation and multi-leveled coding of message systems by which meanings were inflected (Heck, 1973, cf. pp. 67) it could not answer questions concerning the political and institutional forces which determined the role of the media within society.

While the most important contribution of structuralist theory was its insistence on the specificity and irreducibility of signifying systems in general, its tendency to treat them abstractly and independently of social relations meant that a more located concept such as discourse was little more than a marginal term on the edge of the theoretical field. However, once the focus of analysis narrowed, the main direction of theoretical research turned to the study of the relations between 'messages' and the social structures within which they were produced and 'consumed', and this demanded certain revisions in the existing paradigms in order to account for, and include, the position of social agents, as sources and receivers within the circuit of communications. Thus in semiotic theory, for example, Eco (Eco, 1972) broke fundamentally with the Saussurean tradition by drawing substantially on Jakobson's work in his analysis of sign systems within television messages. Basically introducing the functions of addressor and addressee into the analytic framework, he suggested that because the transmitted message, as the sign-vehicle for a system of meanings, was produced and interpreted according to a number of codes whose meanings were determined the context of communication, he pointed to the fact that there was no necessary correspondence between the en-coding of the message and the moment of its de-coding. But the most significant advances in this area were made by the Centre for Contemporary Cultural Studies as part of a much broader attempt to situate the analysis of culture and cultural forms within the problematic of determination and the re-working of Marx's 'base-superstructure' metaphor (Hall, 1980). Generally, the work produced under the auspices of C.C.C.S (passim WPCS) was initially responsible for implementing and developing the insights offered by structuralism though they were modified and informed by the twin theoretical imperatives of maintaining the specificity of the concepts of culture and ideology.

Broadly, this body of work (hereinafter Cultural Studies) challenged and re-defined media theory at a number of different levels. It broke with the assumption that the media message, or text, was simply a transparent, neutral medium for the dissemination of ideas and values, and instead emphasised the critical importance of the structuring effects of signifying systems and the codes through which they were organised, but stressing equally, the disjunction between 'en-coding' and 'de-coding' (Hall, 1973a). At a more general level, Cultural Studies 're-located' media analysis and linked it with a much wider series of questions concerning the overall ideological, cultural and political significance of media institutions in relations to the social formation as a whole. Here the emphasis focussed on the centrality, authority and dominance of the media within culture and the specific role played by the media as, above all, active agencies producing, circulating and securing the reproduction of dominant political and cultural definitons of social life (Hall, 1973(a), 1973(b); Media Group, 1976). In this respect the media were seen to have both a transforming and mediating relationship with political institutions and their ideologies, and to work on and across the terrain of common-sense understandings by articulating and dis-articulating popular ideologies (Hall & Jefferson, 1975). Finally, media analysis was directed to a more complex understanding of language and representation in general. The idea that the meanings of language, or representation, simply reflected reality, or corresponded to the intentions of a mind or consciousness was rejected and replaced by a more sophisticated account which saw meaning as the product of specific, socially determined practices of signification (Hall, 1977 cf. pp. 27–29).

The central contribution of these developments lay principally in their systematic attempt to integrate the analysis of the mass media with the question and theorisation of ideology by using the major insights offered by the various structuralisms, not merely at the level of signification, but more generally at the level of social theory. But equally important, Cultural Studies opened a space in media analysis, for a number of other approaches, drawing variously on ethnomethodology, Hallidayan linguistics and the English 'culturalist' tradition with its emphasis on class, experience and cultural struggle.

*Structuralism and Ideology*

Following a different line of development, the two journals sponsored by the Society for Education in Film and Television, *Screen* and *Screen Education* provided the base from which a far more systematic attempt was made to mobilize and synthesise the various strands of structuralism. Though loosely concerned with film theory, specifically the practices and ideology of realism, this was used as the point of departure from which to elaborate a series of proposals concerning the relations between ideology, language and the social construction of 'the subject', or subjectivity through the process of signification and representation. The hypotheses advanced in *Screen* (Ellis, 1977: Eaton & Neale, 1981) drew far more centrally on the series of debates within structuralism and semiotics in the fields of film theory, 'structuralist marxism' and the psychoanalytic work of Lacan. While the theories expanded and advanced in *Screen* were less centrally placed with respect to mass communications as such they did overlap with the work of Cultural Studies and the 'dialogue' which occurred between these two lines of development intercepted the Anglo-American strand of empirical research posing of it a series of quite fundamental questions (For an account of the issues around which the major differences occurred see Coward, 1977, representing the *Screen* position, and for the reply see Chambers et al., 1977/'78 representing the C. C. C. S. position.)

The first results of this general convergence between media analysis and theories of signification and representation were to problematise the relation of the text to the practices which produced it and secondly to problematise the relation of the institution to the social formation. What immediately became clear was that it was impossible to theorise and analyse the institutional practices of the media without recognizing the effects of those practices on the messages, or 'texts' they produced. According to Hall (1973), for example, the different levels at which meanings were produced in the newsphotograph was a product of the transformational work of institutionalised practices and professional ideologies which actively articulated the pre-given meanings of social events into larger ideological domains. While this had been accepted in a weak form by sociologies of the mass media, for example McQuail had suggested that the media could not adequately be theorised as "merely neutral 'message-carrying' network" (1977, p. 77)., this insight had not been realised in terms of message analysis. But secondly, this pointed to another problem because the social and institutional practices which produced the text were themselves not free of meaning and were intimately bound up with forms of understanding regulated by institutional ideologies and professional commonsence. Since these too were considered to be 'representations', in the general sense, it was implied that these systems of understanding were, like the texts they produced, also organised according to an 'internal', or unconscious 'logic', operating independently and semi-autonomously, of which media professionals were simply the bearers. In the sphere of news and current affairs, for example, the Birmingham Media Group (1976) attempted to show the ways in which the recursive features of textural organisation were articulated with, and produced by the routine practices and 'spontaneous' wisdom of television journalism. But the most significant feature of this account was its proposal that television messages 'never deliver *one* meaning; they are, rather, the site of a plurality of meanings, in which one is preferred... as the most appropriate.' (1976, p. 53) In this respect the principal site of ideological labour was seen to consist, not merely in the process by which the meanings of social events were made to signify within the larger ideological system, but in the process whereby certain of those meanings were embedded within the map of dominant and 'preferred' meanings.

In general, the single most important aspect of this work lay in its reconceptualization of the role of the media in the social production of meanings. By advancing the semiotic paradigm in the study of mass communications it was shown that the media were, in a very real sense, engaged in cultural production, actively transforming its cultural 'raw-material' into texts which then, in turn, through the process of circulation and distribution constituted the 'raw-material' from which social classes produced themselves in the field of culture. The text was seen, not as the expression or reflection of a given segment of reality, but as a 'moment' in a more general circuit of meaning production: as Stuart Hall put it, texts are 'the products in some sense of a signifying practice, a practice which constructs and produces meaning'. (Hall, 1978, p. 26). These innovations, in many ways, took as their point of theoretical departure Vološinov's proposition that the sign, or in this case the text, 'does not simpy exist as part of reality — it reflects and refracts another reality.'(Vološinov, 1973, p. 10). Above all, this provide the basis from which to begin 'thinking' the text, not only as an object in reality, but as an active and constitutive element in the production of that reality. Furthermore, this principle finally and fundamentally called into question the 'traditional' polarity enshrined in some earlier theories of language, including Saussure's, between on the one hand words and ideas, and on the other objective, material reality. In effect, the emphasis in these arguments had been to recover the idea that meanings were the products of social practices and dependent on social relations which had been lost in the development of Saussurean structural linguistics as a general paradigm for the analysis of signifying systems. Thus, basing himself in Vološinov, Williams has suggested that 'the social creation of meaning through the use of formal signs, is then a practical material activity; it is indeed, literally, a means of production.' (Williams, 1977, p. 38) In the context of media analysis, then, the return of 'meanings' to social practices showed that media texts were objects of struggle in which the production of meaning coincided with social classes. But this also pointed to the fact that these meanings could neither be reduced simply to the text, nor to an abstract system of 'values and beliefs' as some media sociologies had postulated.

*From Semiology to Discourse Theory*

On the whole, this constitutes the ground which discourse theory and discourse analysis has yet to develop. Recent work has returned to the text in order to examine the specific properties of its discursive organisation, drawing widely on the insights of film and narrative theory. In these new developments the text has been theorised as a 'site' in which different and contradictory ideological discourses are articulated so that the text, as a coherent, expressive unity, is a 'fiction' whose coherence is produced by and is a condition of its ideological effectivity. This has been Macherey's argument (1977), for example, which has been used in the analysis of films to show that the text comprises a complex balance of ideological elements whose 'unity' is produced through the operation of specific narrative devices (Gledhill, 1978, pp. 9—10). Elsewhere this has led to an analysis of the text in terms of, what has been called its 'mode of address' (Neale, 1977, pp. 18—20) as an attempt to understand the representational strategies deployed within the text by means of which an 'implied reader' (Chatman, 1978, cf. chpt. 4) is constructed and through which the audience is 'positioned', or in Althusser's terms interpellated. There have also been some preliminary explorations of television news from the point of view of examining the conventions, immanent at the level of the textual discourse, to which the text must conform if it is to have the status and value of an objective news-report. (Connell, 1980, cf pp. 144—145 & p. 147). Similarly, narrative theory has been tentatively used in the analysis of news-stories which has attempted to show how the media produce the intelligibility of social events by organising their reports into forms determined by narrative structures (Bazalgette & Paterson, 1980/1 p. 55). In the area of audience research discourse theory has been used to analyse the social production of a text's meanings as the inter-action between the text and the social discourses which it encounters at the moment of decoding (Morley, 1980 pp. 9—11).

The direction of this more recent work in media studies has been informed, to a large extent, by substantial revisions, not only in the way in which the media as a whole has been understood, but also, and perhaps more importantly in the way the field of culture has been 're-thought' in the light of discourse theory. In rejecting certain marxist accounts and also sociological theories which have presumed an all powerful media, the general tendency, on a number of fronts, has been to emphasise the concept of struggle in conceptualizing the place of the media within society. Debray (1981) has argued, for example, that the 'field' of media production is not simply an aggregate of different sectors, but rather, is structured in dominance according to the pre-eminence of television. This point towards a more dynamic account of media production with the different sectors in conflict over cultural position and cultural authority. This also implies, therefore, that the text itself is, in some sense, a signifier, so that the cultural values and meanings carried by the text are determined both by the specificity of its production and by the position within the field from which it is produced and cannot simply be reduced to the internal or inherent properties of the text as such. Pêcheux (1982) has argued similarly, and more radically that social institutions, such as the media, are not merely the sites of competing discursive practices, but are, in fact, agencies for the production of realities and subjects for those realities. Correspondingly, the concept of discourse, or discursive practice, has been used to cut across the 'conventional' distinctions between thought and action, representation and reality, fiction and every-day life. Thus it has now been taken to specify a relatively discrete, socially constructed domain of significations, both producing and produced by a structured and structuring configuration of social relations which creates a specific field, or region, of reality inseparable from the system of meanings, knowledge and power of which the social individual is an effect and element in its articulation. (cf. Foucault, 1979, 1980; Gledhill, 1978; Heath, 1977/8) Here, the recent attempts to extend a more fully linguistic approach to an understanding of the relationship between language and ideology have provided an important complement to these theoretical departures (Fowler et al., 1979). Drawing on the functional linguistics of M. A. K. Halliday (cf. Halliday, 1979) Fowler and his colleagues have applied his theories to the media in order to explore the ways in which 'theories of reality' and relations of power are encoded in the discursive syntax of newspaper headlines and news reports.

Following a parallel line of inquiry Stuart Hall has drawn together the work of a number of figures, such as Williams (1977) and Laclau (1977), to suggest a way in which it might be possible to relate the text to practices and the text to the social formation (Hall, 1978). He has argued that these relationships could be thought of as the outcome of the class struggle in the field of culture through which, and by which, the social relations structuring the field reinforce and maintain the hegemony of the ruling alliance of class fractions. Thus as he puts it 'the cultural analysis of a particular text is always concerned with relating the internal contradictions of the discourse of one text with the contradictory form of the cultural-ideological field in which it is situated ' (1978, pp. 47–48) The pertinence of this, for Hall, is that it re-introduces the dimension of struggle into the analysis because the 'balance'of elements, the fragments of contradictory and antagonistic discourses, articulated within the text in relations of subordination and domination are the product of a continuous process of negotiation. The specific process is always , therefore, concerned with 'neutralizing' contradictions within the text and securing correspondences between the text and other class practices given elsewhere through the articulation of discourses across the cultural field. But this also suggests that the text is not simply the combination of pre-existing elements but is the result of their tranformation, through the process of articulation, into specific discourses by the media. In this sense, the text is a 'mosaic' of citations to other discourses — integrated and re-worked by the practices of signification deployed by the media in conjunction with practices of signification at other levels (the economic, the political) — re-presenting and producing a new system of meaning. This also implies, then, that the text can no longer be considered an inert artefact, but must instead be understood as a specific and constitutive social production of meaning with its own specific autonomy — a particular 'moment' crystallizing and expressing the social relations which it both pre-supposes and of which it is an active part in sustaining the balance of forces in an dynamic equilibrium.

While the approaches outlined here 'privilege' the text, they do not do so simply in order to analyse the immanent structures of the text, nor do they examine the text merely as a 'vehicle of meaning'; instead they emphasise that the text is an active element within social relations and is a constitutive process in the objective production of social meanings, that the text is, in other words, an element in the currency of hegemony. Clearly, however, much work, both theoretical and empirical, remains to be done, but if nothing else, at least the vitality of these different theoretical initiatives in 'mass' communications research have provided the basis and the possibilities for a more sophisticated understanding of the complex processes involved in the mass production and distribution of social knowledge. But, despite their obvious advances in a number of different areas, however, their presence within the mainstream of mass communications research is, in the end, conspicuous only by its overwhelming marginality!

*Bibliography*

Althusser, L. (1975, first published 1968). *Reading Capital*, New Left Books
Althusser, L. (1977). *Lenin and Philosophy and Other Essays*, New Left Books
Alvarado, M. and Buscombe, E. (1978). *Hazell, the Making of a TV Series*, BFI/Latimer
Bauer, A. and R. A. (1960). "America, Mass Society and Mass Media" in *Journal of Social Issues*, 16 (3)
Barthes, R. (1973,first published 1957). *Mythologies*, Paladin
Barthes, R. (1967). *Elements of Semiology*, Jonathan Cape
Bazalgette, C., and Paterson, R. (1981). "Real Entertainment: The Iranian Embassy Siege" in *Screen Education*, 37
Burgelin, O. (1972). "Structural Analysis and Mass Communications" in McQuail, D., (ed) *Sociology of Mass Communications*, Penguin, Harmondsworth
Chambers, I; Clarke, J; Connell, I; Curti, L; Hall, S; Jefferson, T. (Winter 1977/78). "Marxism and Culture" in *Screen* Volume 18, number 4.
Chatman, S. (1978). *Story and Discourse*, Cornell University Press, Ithaca, N.Y.
Chibnall, S. (1977). *Law-and-order News*, Tavistock Publications
Cicourel, A. V. (1970). "Interpretive Procedures and Normative Rules in the Negotiation of Status and Role" in Dreitzel, H., (ed) *Recent Sociology No. 2*, Collier—Macmillan
Cohen, S. (1972). *Folk Devils and Moral Panics*, McGibbon and Kee
Cohen, S., and Young, J. (1973). *The Manufacture of News*, Constable
Connell, I. (1980a). "Television and the Social Contract" in Hall, S., et al., (eds) *Culture, Media Language*, Hutchinson
Connell, I. (1980b). "Review of More Bad News" in *Marxism Today*, August
Debray, R. (1981). *Teachers, Writers, Celebrities, The Intellectuals of Modern France*, Verso
Dreitzel, H. (1970). "Introduction", Dreitzel, H., *Recent Sociology No. 2*, Collier—Macmillan
Eaton, M., and Neale, S. (1981). "Introduction", *Screen Reader 2: Cinema and Semiotics*, SEFT
Eco, U. (1972). "Towards a semiotic inquiry into the television message", in *WPCS 3*
Elliott, P. (1972). *The Making of a Television Series: a Case Study in the Sociology of Culture*, Constable
Ellis, J. (1977). "Introduction", *Screen Reader 1: Cinema/Ideology/Politics*, SEFT
Foucault, M. (1979). *The History of Sexuality, Vol. 1: An Introduction*, Allen Lane "Two Lectures" in Gordon, C., (ed.) *Power/Knowledge*, Pantheon Books, New York
Fowler, R.; Hodge, B.; Kress,G.; Trew, T. (1979). *Language and Control*, Routledge and Kegan Paul

Gerbner, G. (1972)."Mass Media and Human Communications Theory" in McQuail, D. (ed)
Glasgow University Media Group (1976). *Bad News*, Routledge and Kegan Paul
Glasgow University Media Group (1980). *More Bad News*, Routledge and Kegan Paul
Gledhill, C. (1978). "A contemporary film noir and feminist criticism" in Kaplan, A., (ed) *Women in Film Noir*, BFI
Hall, S. (1973a). "Encoding and Decoding in the television Discourse", CCCS Stencilled Paper
Hall, S. (1973b). "The Structured Communication of Events", CCCS Stencilled Paper
Hall, S. (1976). "Broadcasting, politics and the state: the independent-impartially couplet", Paper, Tenth biennial conference of the International Association for Mass Communications Research, University of Leicester
Hall, S. (1977). "The Hinterland of Science; Ideology and the Sociology of Knowledge" in *On Ideology*, WPCS 10
Hall, S. (1978). "Some Paradigms in Cultural Studies", Paper, Estratto da Annali, Istituto Orientale di Napoli
Hall, S. (1980). 'Cultural Studies and the Centre: some problematics and problems" in Hall, S., et al. (eds) *Culture, Media, Language*, Hutchinson
Hall, S., et al. (eds). (1980). *Culture, Media, Language*, Hutchinson
Hall, S., Clarke, J., et al. (1978). *Policing the Crisis*, Macmillan
Hall, S. and Jefferson, T. (eds). (1975). *Resistance Through Rituals*, WPCS 8
Halliday, M. A. K. (1979). *Language as Social Semiotic*, Edward Arnold
Halloran, J. (1970). *The Effects of Television*, Panther
Halloran, J., Murdock, G., and Elliott, P. (1970b). *Demonstrations and Communications*, Penguin, Harmondsworth
Halloran, J., Brown, R. L., and Chaney, D. (1970c). *Television and Delinquent Behaviour*, Leicester University Press
Hartmann, P., and Husband, C. (1972). "The Mass Media and Racial Conflict", in McQuail, D., (ed)
Heath, S. (1977/78). "Notes on Suture" in *Screen*, 18, 4
Heck, M. (1973). "The Ideological Dimension of Media Messages", CCCS Stencilled Paper 10
Henry, P. (1971). "On Processing of Message Referents in Contexts", in Carswell, E. A., & Rommetveit, R., (eds), *The Social Context of Messages*, Academic Press
Jakobson, R. (1973). *Main Trends in the Science of Language*, George Allen and Unwin
Jameson, F. (1972). *The Prison House of Language*, Princeton University Press, Princeton, N. J.
Kaplan, A. (ed) (1978). *Women in Film Noir*, BFI
Laclau, E. (1977). *Politics and Ideology in Marxist Theory*, New Left Books
Lévi-Strauss, C. (1972, first published 1958). *Structural Anthropology*, Penguin, Harmondsworth
Lévi-Strauss, C. (1970, first published 1964). *Mythologiques Vol. 1*, Jonathan Cape
Macherey, P. (1977). "Interview", in *Red Letters*, no. 5
McQuail, D. (ed). (1972). *Sociology of Mass Communication*, Penguin, Harmondsworth
McQuail, D. (1977). "The Influence and Effects of Mass Media" in Curran, J., et al., (eds) *Mass Communications and Society*, Edward Arnold
Media Group. (1976). "The 'Unity' of Current Affairs Television" in *Culture and Domination*, WPCS 9
Meltzer, B. N., et al. (1975). *Symbolic Interactionism, Genesis, varieties and criticism*, Routledge & Kegan Paul
Morley, D. (1980). *The Nationwide Audience*, BFI
Murdock, G. (1974). "Mass Communication and the Construction of Meaning", in Armistead, N., (ed) *Reconstructing Social Psychology*, Penguin
Murdock, G., and Golding, P. (1977). "Capitalism, communication and Class Relations", in Curran, J., et al., (eds) *Mass Communication and Society*, Edward Arnold
Murdock, G. and Golding, P. (1979). "Ideology and the Mass Media: the Question of Determination", in Barret, M., et al., (eds) *Ideology and Cultural Production*, Croom Helm
Neale, S. (1977). "Propaganda", in *Screen*, 18, 3
Pêcheux, M. (1982). *Language, Semantics and Ideology*, Macmillan

Schlesinger, P. (1978). *Putting 'Reality' Together*, Constable
Vološinov, V. N. (1973). *Marxism and the Philosophy of Language*, Seminar Press
Williams, R. (1974). *Television: technology and cultural form*, Fontana
Williams, R. (1976). "Communications as cultural science", in Bigsby, C. W. E., (ed), *Approaches to Popular Culture*, Edward Arnold
Williams, R. (1977). *Marxism and Literature*, Oxford University Press
Young, J. (1971). *The Drugtakers; the Social Meaning of Drug Use*, Paladin

HOWARD H. DAVIS

# Discourse and Media Influence

This paper describes and illustrates some of the results and implications of research which attempts to discover how the special properties of news media discourse are related to the structure and ideologies of mass communication systems. In recent years, this type of critical analysis has received an impetus from several closely related technical and theoretical developments.[1] This is especially true of the broadcast media, which have long been an object of critical research.

The first of the developments is a technical one, namely the relative ease of recording the largely ephemeral verbal and visual output of the electronic media. This is a prerequisite for detailed analytical work. It is less costly and technically more simple than ever before to capture televisual messages and isolate their component elements for analysis. Until the means of cheap and reliable recording became available, analysis of the characteristics of broadcast discourse was a cumbersome business and one which was highly dependent on ideas, methods and techniques borrowed from the print media and, to a lesser extent, film. The possibility now exists for an independently-derived set of analytical practices which do not impose prejudicial concepts and categories on the subject matter.

The theoretical developments are related to the increasing technical sophistication and cultural pervasiveness of the electronic media. Broadcasting has developed its own patterns and structures of discourse so that it is no longer appropriate to treat broadcasting as an analog of the printed word, 'with pictures'. Therefore, one cannot simply translate categories of content, units of measurement, criteria of relevance, etc. from one medium to another. In broadcasting, the relations of programme production, the media of transmission and the receptivity of audiences have evolved in quite novel ways which create special problems of analysis. Critical research has confronted

---

[1] 'Critical analysis' is used here to refer to media research which sets out to identify and explain the system of rules, conventions and codes which channel and restrict the flow of information through the mass media. It is not criticism of professional journalism as such although journalistic practices are important data. The present discussion is based on recent empirical contributions from the UK, especially the work of the Glasgow University Media Group (1976, 1980), but also work from the forthcoming Centre for Contemporary Cultural Studies, Birmingham (e. g. S. Hall *et al* 1978), Paul Hartmann (1975/6), David Morley (1976), Graham Murdock and Philip Schlesinger (1978).

these problems in part at least and has accordingly developed along the following lines.

It has sought to construct analytical categories in the first instance from the *practices* of cultural producers and to respect 'commonsense' criteria in its initial descriptions. This approach rests on the assumption that broadcasting output is a manufactured artifact and that the routine practices of journalists, writers, performers, etc. are circumscribed by and embedded in the conditions and institutional relationships of cultural organisations. These organisations are characteristically large in scale, bureaucratic and monopolistic, whether they operate 'commercially' or as state organisations in the 'public service'.

This sensitivity to the real world of media producers explains why much critical research has so far been *pre-theoretical*, in the sense that it has not specified detailed hypotheses nor has it provided all the necessary means for rigorously testing them. The first aim has been to accurately document and describe production processes; to disclose what is hidden and artificial behind the 'natural' appearances of talk, images and media personalities. Only then, through an empirically based description of professional norms, language behaviour and production codes can general explanations of media influence be generated.

Building on this essential foundation, critical research has sought to originate or adapt concepts and methodologies used in the analysis of other media and apply them to the electronic media. In a pragmatic and eclectic manner, the subdisciplines of content analysis, sociolinguistics, stylistics, pragmatics, semiotics and cultural criticism have all been pressed into service. What they have in common — and this is why they are useful for media analysis — is that they approach language as a means of establishing, maintaining and mediating social relationships. In seeking to develop new categories, critical analysis combines two 'problematics'. First, there are the questions of ideology, distorted communication and cultural hegemony which hitherto have been the province of social and political theories.[2] Secondly, there are problems of message encoding and construction which have led to a search for models of linguistic 'performance' that include the social assumptions, conventions or 'codes' which govern the production and reception of messages.[3] Where these interests converge, the broadcast message is not conceived as a statement or expression which is reducible to the intentions of writers, producers, editors and others but as a transformation of complex institutional processes.

---

[2] See, for example, Stuart Hall's discussion (1980) of the interaction in British 'cultural studies' between a 'culturalist' paradigm and a 'structuralist' paradigm articulated around the concept of ideology derived from Marx.

[3] Some of these problems are tackled from the point of view of semiology (cf. Eco, 1976) while others use a more narrowly defined sociolinguistic frame of reference (Bernstein, 1971).

The following presentation gives one example of the convergence between these problematics. It is based on the research of the Glasgow University Media Group into British television news and subsequent work by the present author on news language in the USA and Germany as well as Britain.[4] In this particular instance, the convergence is between the analysis of manifest and latent content on the one hand and the recurrent patterns of linguistic behaviour on the other. Both are an essential part of the object of the critical analysis of news discourse. Content analysis has traditionally made much use of word counts and categories based on names, keywords, descriptions, definitions, etc., where manifest content is the main focus of attention. The approach in terms of discourse analysis takes the same 'data' but construes them somewhat differently. For instance, a traditional content analysis of news media might involve frequency counts of keywords ('democracy', 'China', political slogans, etc.) across different media or through time. These keywords or expressions are then taken to be more or less directly indicative of other phenomena (change in political values, foreign policy, etc.) In critical discourse analysis it is acknowledged that what are essentially linguistic data require a treatment which is less mechanical, less concerned with manifest content and more aware of the power of language, and the varieties and contexts of language use. It is true that frequency counts are still necessary but generally only as a prelude to a study of use within the wider institutional and social context (where frequency may not be the best indicator of importance). The significance of media discourse is located in the often implicit explanatory frameworks and ground-rules of interpretation which must be 'read out' rather than simply 'read from' the discourse.

There are three sets of questions which may be asked in an analysis of both the superficial and deeper aspects of media discourse. They are

— who is speaking (especially when the 'speaker' is a newsreader, official spokesperson, teacher, or anyone speaking as an agent for an institution)?
— what are they saying (i.e. what does the speech manifestly denote and connote)?
— what do they mean (or what must we assume for their talk to be intelligible in its context)?

These questions will be used to situate the discussion of recent developments in the analysis of broadcast media discourse.

---

[4] See especially Glasgow University Media Group 1976, 1980; Davis and Walton, 1983a and 1983b. The author gratefully acknowledges the support of the Social Science Research Council for this research.

*Who is speaking?*

All statements imply an author. However, speakers or narrators in news broadcasting are not always or even usually, authors. Typically, the talk is either in a written-spoken mode authored by journalists and editors or a version of monologue or dialogue which is edited by someone other than the speakers. In this section, I consider the attempts which have been made to characterise the forms of speech in the mass media, particularly insofar as they use the idea of 'mediation'. As yet there is only incomplete agreement on the minimal constituent elements of the forms of broadcast talk but typologies tend to rely heavily on the commonplace distinction between 'direct' and 'indirect' speech. The problem is that categories like 'quotation' or 'report' need to be further differentiated as the forms or televisual presentation have become more technically versatile and elaborated. The problem here is not simply to list 'who gets on', who has the 'right to speak' or who may speak in an unmediated or partly mediated fashion. We also need to identify speech variations which are present by virtue of the media's attempt to maximise influence or otherwise incorporate its audiences. Some forms of broadcast discourse can be seen as more or less deliberate strategies of media influence, ways of 'getting the message across'. The problem is to determine whether these mediations transform in similar directions.

By definition, all broadcast news talk 'mediates'. The question at issue is how the mediation occurs and how speakers are differentially affected. In the first place, speakers are subject to an institutional selection process which amounts to a 'hierarchy of access'. Media personnel naturally occupy a special place but for the most part, the hierarchy resembles the hierarchies of power and privilege in society at large. This is amply demonstrated in the Glasgow Media Group's extended study of British television news, and industrial news in particular (Glasgow Media Group 1976; 1980). From this and other studies it is possible to formulate three rules concerning the relation between the hierarchy of access and the mediation of speech:

— the higher the status of speaker, the greater the relative amount of media attention
— the higher the status of a speaker, the more direct the presentation
— the higher the status of a speaker, the greater the tendency for media personnel to endorse the speaker's assumption.

The first rule on its own could be taken as evidence that the news media are simply reflecting an external world of facts, events and characters. However, the second and third rules show that more is involved. In four months of British television network news coverage of the economic crisis and the 'social contract' between the Labour government and the trade unions in 1975, the Glasgow Media Group found that both BBC and ITN made a very similar choice of interviewees and that interviewees were drawn from a narrow range in the leadership of government, industry and the trade unions. The measure of concentration is indicated by the fact that 14 of the 23 people who appeared in interviews were seen more than one occasion. (Glasgow Media Group 1980, 98–104).

The restricted pattern of access extends to the elements of reported speech and names mentioned in the bulletins, so that for example more than one third of reported statements on the 'social contract' came from the members of the interviewed group. While it may seem 'natural' for journalists to concentrate on the central actors in the social contract debate, even the members of this select group do not speak with equal emphasis. In the analysis of policies or solutions to economic crisis identified on television news it emerged that the overwhelming majority of all interview responses, reported statements and references were for supporting the policies of the 'social contract' (ibid., 440). Thus, where trade union officials were questioned about a pay claim, they were typically required to justify their members' action against an established background of an analysis that blamed inflation and the crisis in general almost exclusively on wage increases.

In addition to the hierarchy of access to the medium, which is replicated in most other mass media of information, speech is mediated in ways which are specific to broadcast news. These are partly but not entirely to do with 'technical' criteria like film and video editing, the audibility of radio circuits

*Fig. 1: Two reports of a speech*

*ITN News 17.10 17 May 1975*

*Newcaster:* Mr. Jack Jones, the leader of the Transport Workers Union, called today for what he called a 'positive response' from the trade unions to help the government fight the present economic crisis. Mr. Jones said that wages were not the main cause of inflation but the present trend for wages to increase faster than prices spelled economic disaster. Mr. Jones said the government could improve the situation by imposing a price freeze and bringing in certain import controls.

*ITN News 22.30 17 May 1975*

*Newscaster:* Mr. Healey found support from the leader of the Transport Workers Union, Mr. Jack Jones, who called for a positive response from trade unions to help the government fight the present economic crisis. Speaking at Poole in Dorset Mr. Jones said that wages were by no means the main cause of inflation, although he said the present trend for wages to increase faster than prices spelt economic disaster. Mr. Jones said that wage rises should be linked to the cost of living and the increase in the average earnings. He also said that the government could improve the situaton by imposing a price freeze and import controls.

and the mobility of outside broadcast units. For instance, it has often been observed that the visual contrast between managers seated behind desks and picketers at a factory gate is almost certain to enhance the relative authority of what the managers say. In other cases, the mediation is through editorial decisions which are often justified by professionals in terms of 'pressure of time'. There is an example of this in the reporting of a speech by a trade union leader at the time of the social contract. Compare the wording of the two reports in Figure 1 (totalling 78 and 107 words respectively) and in particular the information which is omitted from the shorter, evening report. The expanded version contains an opening phrase linking it with an earlier report ('Mr. Healey found support from . . .'), it gives geographical information ('Speaking at Poole in Dorset . . .') and contains a new sentence giving Mr. Jones' prescription for the index-linking of wage rises. There is a change from the slightly inelegant repetition in

> [Mr. Jones] called today for what he called a positive response from the trade unions . . .

to

> [Mr. Jones] who called for a positive response from trade unions . . .

And the sentence

> Mr. Jones said that wages were not the main cause of inflation but the present trend for wages to increase faster than prices spelled economic disaster

is expanded to

> Mr. Jones said that wages were *by no means* the main cause of inflation, *although he said* the present trend for wages to increase faster than prices spelled economic disaster.

From these two reports it seems that there are at least three types of information which can be 'dispensed with' in the interests of brevity and style. First, contextualising information 'Mr. Healey found support . . .', 'Speaking at Poole in Dorset . . .'), secondly, items of content (Mr. Jones' suggestion that wages should be index-linked) and thirdly, information about the internal organisation of the report itself (omission of the verb of saying). It can be argued that the overall effect of these changes is to blur the distinction between the 'voice' of the news and the 'voice' of the person being reported. However, this tendency enhances rather than undermines the artificial consensus on the meaning of inflation and wage rises because the hierarchy of access has already denied a voice to the majority of those who would challenge the consensus.

This description of the convergence between media and reported speech leaves one problem unresolved. In the process of shaping news sources to bring them into line with the assumptions and explanations of the broadcasting institutions, we observed not only that higher status sources are subject to less mediation but also that attributed statements (direct and indirect) from management and government sources are more frequent than attributed statements from labour and the trade unions (Glasgow Media Group 1980, 162). This means that lower status sources are more frequently referred to in indirect, unattributed ways which make it difficult, if not impossible to tell exactly whose words are being spoken. The impression created is quite unlike the merging of 'voices' described above. From a report of a mass meeting of car workers we have:

> The strikers were told that Chrysler should get out of Britain if they can't pay a living wage. The workers were being used as cheap labour and have become the poor relations of the car industry.
>
> (BBC, 21.00, 15 May 1975)

In the bulletin, this statement is followed by actuality shots of speakers at a mass meeting but they are speaking on a different subject, the vote. The argument about 'cheap labour' is mediated and 'distanced' from the speakers, whoever they are, in two ways: by the absence of any attribution and by the grammatical rendering (passives, past tense). 'Distancing' is a discourse characteristic which differentiates relatively direct, transparent speech from speech which is indirect, obscure, or even unintelligible. It has been argued that a great deal of both private and public discourse is elliptical and avoids direct or explicit statement (Lerman, 1983). But news at least *claims* to be direct and transparent in its reporting of facts, events and characters. In this example, however, the statement is distanced from any identifiable speaker and the 'living wage' topic is transformed by this indirect form of speech into an expression of another topic — the workers' intransigence. The 'living wage' does not become an object of discussion in the rest of the item; the distanced form renders it 'undiscussable'.

In the scale of mediation there is one further category: the implied statements or point of view of groups and individuals who only 'appear' when mentioned by others, non-media personnel. As a rule, they are neither interviewed nor quoted and their views are not sought directly. In the sample analysed by the Glasgow Media Group they included many from low-status occupational groups, pensioners, working class families as well as some ('top civil servants', 'the wealthy') from high status groups which tend to shun publicity. British Leyland employees can hardly be said to have been ignored by the news services, but the following item illustrates the priorities which are set by the established framework of interpretation.

> The engineering workers' President, Mr. Hugh Scanlon, has told Leyland workers that if they want to keep their jobs, constant and recurring disruption will have to stop. He told delegates at the union conference that Leylands 'deep-down malaise' couldn't go on. He said workers should stop criticising the government and management before taking a long look at themselves.
>
> (BBC *Newsday*, 8 May 1978)

In this item, the mention of Leyland workers does not guarantee that their point of view is expressed. We can infer that they are critical of Government and management but that is all. Without further information, the only possible reading of this item is that it is Leyland workers who have the power to prevent 'disruption' and cure Leyland's 'malaise'. While information from other sources would clearly show that the malaise had a variety of causes, this news item conforms to a general pattern which is premised on the assumption that the car industry's failure is to be explained by the failure of its workforce (Glasgow Media Group 1976, 256–268). This ideological assumption can remain unspoken because the alternatives find no expression within the prevailing hierarchy of access and routines of mediation.

So far I have concentrated on the characteristics of discourse which stem from the *referential* function of news and the selection and mediation of the talk. The pattern of transformations from direct speech to the varieties of reported speech and indirect reference is not a system of neutral channels but a system of mediation which articulates ideological bias without normally undermining news' credibility. It has been pointed out that this attention to reference neglects the other functions of language, especially the interpersonal or expressive functions (Leitner 1980, Kress 1983) and that style and presentation devices have a bias which is independent of referential bias.

A full analysis of this problem would involve a study of questions which are beyond the scope of the research reported here: do journalists aim to create certain effects? How are these expressed in forms of talk? What do audiences respond to?, etc. However, there are two points to be made in defence of an analysis of news discourse which gives primary importance to speakers' expression of content or to the relation between language and reality. The first is simply that broadcast news talk relates to its external environment according to strict rules and public conventions which define its referential or 'ideational' functions as paramount. 'Due accuracy and impartiality' (IBA Act, 1973) is a prescription for a particular language-reality relationship in broadcast news. Following Halliday's functional terminology (Halliday 1970, 143) we would expect the 'interpersonal' and 'textual' functions to serve this prescribed goal and therefore to share similar biases to the 'referential' function. Secondly, there is the evidence of news talk itself. In the system of 'news vaules' which can be inferred from the output, we find that persons, events, facts and processes which are 'new', 'important' and 'relevant' take precedence over those which are merely novel, entertaining, or visually exciting, i. e. those which might be said to function purely for the maximising of audiences or other 'interpersonal' reasons.

News texts are a form of public, institutional discourse constructed according to unusually strict and conventionalised procedures. The 'rules' govern every aspect of opening, closing, narrative structure, flow, informaton content, character selection, editorialising and other features. To this extent, news language can be said to be a system which, relative to private conversation, is highly formal and independent of both context and content. It is true that many newscasters are public personalities who have an image of sociability, closeness and informality. However, for the duration of the news itself, this 'persona' is deliberately suspended except in human interest stories and at the close of bulletins. The 'I' of the news is not the newscaster but the authoritative, institutional 'I' of a large-scale and inflexible 'cultural bureaucracy' (Burns 1977).

*What are they saying?*

In attempting to answer this question, critical analysis comes closest to the traditional aims and practices of content analysis. Its purpose is to analyse news texts to relate their manifest content to a variety of external factors. It may proceed at the macro-level through a study of 'topics', to determine presences and absences in relation to other frameworks of reference and other sources of information. Or it may take elements at the micro-level (vocabulary, descriptions, etc.) and consider their relationship to external objects of reference. Where critical analysis differs most from content analysis is in its deliberate attempt to view texts in their context, as the product of institutional processes of selection and codification which render apparently obvious meanings problematic and constrain the flow of information. It hardly needs to be stressed that the most important limits to what is said are set by the news 'agenda'.

Two brief examples will illustrate the approach at the macro level. In the Glasgow study of industrial relations reporting, a comparison was made between the contours of television's coverage of industrial life in Britain and the alternative picture offered by independently derived and publicly available official statistics. The findings show a significant amount of divergence. For instance, there is no consistent relationship between officially-recorded industrial stoppages and those reported by television news and when disputes are reported, there is no direct relationship between the amount of coverage they receive and their severity. In some sectors where the Department of Employment recorded industrial stoppages there were no news stories. In other sectors, news coverage was far greater than one would expect if news simply reflected the number of stoppages, working days lost and 'knock-on' effects. For example, in the first five months of 1975, the engineering industry recorded 25 per cent of the total days lost in all industries and received just over 5 per cent of total dispute reporting. On the other hand, the 2 per cent of Britain's employed population who make cars and other vehicles received nearly 25 per cent of television news' industrial coverage. Moreover, all three channels of British television made a similar selection of industrial stories and reported them at similar length. News discourse, then, is pre-structured by a process which accords significance in special ways. The topics or manifest themes of what is being said are conditioned by the news selection process or 'agenda-setting' as it is commonly called.

In the area of industrial coverage, the Glasgow study concluded that the 'heaviest' reporting (in terms of the statistical indices) was of the car industry, transport and communications, and public administration and services. News sense or commonsense identifies these industries as important in the following ways: they epitomise the problems of private and public manufacturing business at a time of stiff international competition, inflation and stagnation; and they express a concern for consumers (i.e. the news audience) who encounter disruption in the normal flow of goods and services. However, this provides an important clue to the relationship between what is being said and what is meant. In this example, the surface topics of wage bargaining, dispute procedures and industrial action regularly become expressions of an underlying topic, 'the state of the economy'.

The journalistic criteria of selection do not lead to a haphazard picture of industrial life. On the contrary, the picture is quite coherent and deviations from it are rare. A second example from another, related context illustrates the frame of reference which determines what is said in news discourse. A large proportion of the coverage of industrial and economic affairs in Britain in the early months of 1975 made direct or indirect reference to the 'social contract' between the trade unions (TUC) and the Labour government. This agreement was part of an attempt to ameliorate the economic crisis, especially the high rate of inflation, by holding down wage increases. It was a political policy based on the economic views of a large section of the Labour party. As a policy, it was at variance with the economic views of the Labour party left, the Conservative right and the majority of economists influenced by Keynsian economic models. However, it corresponded closely with the ideas of the Treasury. The television coverage of this period is notable not for reporting the 'social contract', but for using the same model for its own viewpoint and interpretations. Overwhelmingly, the social contract was given credibility on the news by a massive emphasis on the effect of wage-claims as the cause of the economic crisis. In the first four months of 1975 there were 17 occasions on national network news when someone appeared and argued against the government policy of no increase in real wages as a solution to the problem of inflation. There were 287 occasions when someone argued for these policies. By comparison other causes, such as structural imbalances or the lack of investment in British industry, received nothing like the same amount of attention.

Analysis of interviews often provides good illustrations of the pre-set agenda which delimits what is said. For example, in the coverage of the car industry in 1975 there was an interview with the convenor of shop stewards at the British Leyland Cowley plant. It was a rare statement of the well supported view that production losses were as much to do with management failings as with the actions of the labour force. However, the interviewer returned persistently to the theme of workers' disruption, making no concessions to the convenor's shift in topic.

54   H. H. Davis

> Convenor: ... Since April of last year, we have worked consistently, all of us, to try and avoid any disputes whatsoever. In fact most of the production that has been lost, has been lost through either breakdowns or shortage of materials and we do recognise that British Leyland is, has got a problem, a cash-flow problem, and we have worked very, very hard, both union and members, to try and eradicate this position.
> Interviewer: How does the prospect of no government cash for British Leyland strike you if the strike record doesn't improve?
> (Glasgow Media Group 1976, 224—5 and 264—5)

This should not be misinterpreted as an instance of the 'adversary' technique in which an interviewer deliberately challenges the interviewee's position in order to probe and provoke a lively debate. The interviewer's agenda simply takes no account of the interviewee's replies. Since the conduct and editing of interviews is always within the control of journalists and editors, their agenda will be the one which is privileged in any normal reading of the output. Whatever the interviewee may say does not alter the fact that 'what they are talking about' is worker-induced industrial trouble.

*What do they mean?*

With this question, we come to the most difficult yet the most important aspect of critical analysis. For it is here that the link must be made between content or linguistic analysis and sociological claims about media influence. The question turns on the degree to which the 'reading' given in terms of speakers, content categories, the distribution of lexical items, etc. can be said to be 'preferred'. Content analysis, or even functional analysis of language, must aim for maximum reliability and validity and a statement such as 'news focused predominantly on a particular view of wages as a prime cause of inflation' is based on procedures which can be reproduced and checked for accuracy and consistency. However, as critics point ot 'Texts can be read, and TV sets viewed, in different ways ... does anyone else read them and view them in the same way as media scholars do?' (Anderson and Sharrock 1979, 374). Setting aside the obvious differences between scholarly and other readings, there remains the serious question of the possibility of alternative accounts.

Assuming some degree of openness or variability in either a text, its reception or both, there are a number of logical possibilities. If the text is unitary and is a vehicle for a single account, this may be read either in a singular, congruent way or there may also be other (presumably 'discordant') readings. If the text contains multiple possibilities, there may be a multiplicity of readings or there may be only one. We can postulate a range of intermediate categories and variations on these themes. Although we need to know about the conditions and receptiveness of audiences, texts themselves contain internal clues which point to some rather than other possibilities. The evidence strongly suggests that news is generally a vehicle for a single account and that in ideologically sensitive areas attempts are made to close off possible ambiguities. Audience research has shown that receptivity can vary according to knowledge and social circumstances but there is no conclusive evidence that 'deviant' decodings are regularly made by any major audience category.

Much recent work on media content has stressed the consistency of the frameworks of interpretation used across a wide range of informational programming. Other studies have analysed the pattern of 'flow' in programme schedules as a whole and have arrived at similar conclusions. A few examples from British sources should suffice for the present argument. At least the following major categories of content have been studied in some depth:

— political (Parliamentary, non-Parliamentary, demonstrations, etc.);
— economic and industrial affairs (including industrial relations);
— foreign;
— crime and deviance;
— health and social welfare.[5]

These categories alone normally account for 80 per cent of the content of television news bulletins and there are additional 'thematic' studies (e. g. of race, women) which include some of the remainder. It is all the more significant, then, to find a whole range of studies based on a variety of working assumptions speaking with the same voice. Whether the terminology is that of systematic bias or distortion, agenda-setting, frameworks of interpretation, encoding, or vocabularies of motive, the conclusions are the same. Informational content is neither unmediated re-presentation of facts and events nor is it a complex expression of the diversity and contradictoriness of the social democratic society it purports to describe. Instead, it is the predictably structured artifact of routine professional practices which resolve the variety and contradictions of the world into simple binary distinctions (violent non-violent; extreme/reasonable; law-abiding/criminal; normal/abnormal; good/bad. etc.) based on an assumed identity of interest and perspective with the audience. One can impute motives, a world-view, a consistency of orientation, to the totality of bulletins, not just to each one individually. This 'ego', according to the kinds of research mentioned above is predominantly masculine, white, middle-aged, middle-class, metropolitan and liberal pluralist in orientation, with only slight variation between channels.

The sometimes repetitive and laborious process of accumulation which content analytic studies represent has been indispensable. It means that the face-value of broadcasting output can no longer be taken as a starting-point

---

[5] Representative studies include Halloran *et al* (1970), Pateman (1975) and Tracey (1978) on politics; the Glasgow University Media Group (1976, 1980), Hartmann (1975/6) and Morley (1977) on industrial news; Davis and Walton (1983a and b) on foreign news; Chibnall (1977) on crime and deviance; Golding and Middleton (1979) on health and social welfare.

or datum for other kinds of media analysis, whether they be concerned with audiences or with the production process. Any questions about 'effects', 'media influence', 'ideological impact', and so on have to adopt assumptions which recognise these detailed findings about the structuring of the output.

The case of industrial news will serve to illustrate the problem. The internal evidence of news item content and the external evidence of broadcaster's pronouncements confirm that industrial relations are seen as part of a legitimate institutional framework which ensures free collective bargaining and allows trade unionists the right to organise and withdraw their labour. The basis of economic life is a system of free exchange between individuals and there is sufficient convergence between the interests of employers and employees in the exchange of labour and wages for workable compromises to be reached. This view may be more or less 'unitary' or 'pluralist' in its recognition of legitimate competing interests but the moral necessity for compromise is invariably assumed.[6] Routine editorial decisions about 'balance' are derived from these assumptions which come in turn from the more explicit and elaborated framework 'parliamentary democracy'.

The Glasgow Media Group's study of vocabulary shows that the problem of meaning lies in the discrepancy between the framework of these assumptions (two sides of industry, market-place, bargaining, compromise) and the conceptual organisation of terms within the framework (Glasgow University Media Group, 1980, 171–189). In practice, the terms are not the fully interchangeable set that one might expect from their semantic possibilities. They are selected in ways which betray an alternative framework in which labour makes unreasonable or unrealistic claims on a rational industrial order.[7] For example, terms which are specific to action by employees (strike, work to contract) are used in identical ways to terms which embrace both parties (dispute, disruption). Thus the labels 'engine tuner's strike' and 'engine tuner's dispute' are interchangeable. This ignores or obscures the identity of the employer, makes labour the active party in disputes and, by implication, makes workers responsible. Significantly, the frequently used term 'trouble' ('And there was more trouble today . . .') is rarely specified as trouble for anyone in particular. We must assume it is trouble in general, for industry, for the economy, for us even. This in conjunction with the dispute label makes it likely that many viewers will come to see the workers involved in any industrial dispute as the 'trouble-makers' and as a threat to harmonious and orderly social relations.

The same study shows that the pattern of use of nouns and verbs in industrial reports limits even a 'pluralistic' interpretation of industrial relations.

---

[6] See Chapter 6 of Hyman and Brough (1975) for an examination of the 'unitary' and 'pluralist' interpretations of industrial relations.

[7] Note that the framework as such is not generally accessible through observation of particular instances. It can only be identified by a structural analysis of sets of terms and their relations. Relevant terms may not co-occur with great frequency, so an extensive sample is essential.

There are two significant absences: a vocabulary of motive for collective action by employees; and a vocabulary to describe employer's strategies. While both strategies certainly contribute to a 'bias against understanding' by underplaying causes, the constant preferring of certain key terms constitutes an ideological bias against labour in any normal reading of the output.

If this is part of the hidden meaning of industrial news what evidence is there for convergent or divergent readings? From viewing and listening research in the UK we know that there is a high propensity to consume news among a large majority of the population. We also know that a majority of all social classes consider broadcast news to be 'accurate' and 'trustworthy', whether or not they use other sources of news. This in itself, taken with the finding that people indulge in television viewing as a pastime and not necessarily because they intend to watch any particular programme, strongly suggests that highly divergent readings are likely to be uncommon. Blumler and Ewbank's (1970) and Hartmann's (1979) studies have direct relevance to the question of how industrial news is perceived. Blumler and Ewbank showed that trade unionists were generally disposed to receive information from the media and that with the exception of full-time 'officials' they were highly dependent on the broadcast media for their information about industrial affairs. Their results are at least consistent with the view that divergent readings are improbable among groups whose experience limits their access to alternative sources of information.

In a more recent survey, Hartmann (1979, 255–270) attempts to empirically establish a connection between news content and audience reception. The findings of a content analysis of industrial relations news were broadly consistent with those of the Glasgow Media Group and uphold the view that the news perspective is unitary and consistent in its interpretation of industrial conflict. Instead of simply inferring how this may lead to the shaping of audience perceptions and values, Hartmann explores the differences in perspectives on industrial relations between working and middle class groups and relates these to the content analysis. There is only moderate support in the findings for the idea of selective interpretation. Views of industrial relations were not polarized along class lines and there was a considerable degree of convergence between media perspectives and social perspectives on many issues. The similarities were found to be greatest among middle class respondents. Working class respondents were slightly more inclined to explain strikes in terms of economic causes but the differences between samples were small. One possible indicator of the direction of media influence was the finding that working class people who held views of a 'middle class' kind (e.g. giving 'bad communication' as a cause of strikes) were more reliant on media information than other working class people.

It is surprising how researchers have neglected the most obvious and compelling result of these and other studies (cf. Morley 1980) which look at the psychological and social equipment which people bring to the listening and viewing experience. The selectivity of responses occurs only within a limited range and what variation there is does not appear to be a direct function of social class. There is virtually no positive evidence that those audiences which are assimilated to the cultural framework generate divergent readings. Those groups which can be said to be excluded or partly excluded from this framework by reason of language, ethnicity or other criteria do not generate alternative readings either, they simply find no point of identification with the media discourse (Morley 1980, 142–143).

With this we come full circle to the original set of questions. Media discourse, and especially the discourse of broadcast news, is based on an image of the audience which owes more to tradition and professional mythology than to actual audience research. The capacity of the news to efface real social differences is measured by the fact that it is universally audible and intelligible in its preferred ways. Its credibility as neutral news is generally maintained. The connection between the broadcaster's image of the audience and the cultural and social assumptions of the discourse needs to be explored in future research. However, both work powerfully at a high level of generality to achieve orderly and integrated interpretations. What discourse analysis is able to show is that network news output owes its remarkable homogeneity and consistency of perspective in matters of social controversy not so much to the selective recruitment or political bias of journalists as to the institutional mechanisms which process facts, events and personalities through the filter of highly contentious assumptions about such matters as democracy, the causes of inflation, the status of speaker's opinions or the audience's capacity to understand. Critical analysis will continue to expose these assumptions and their damaging consequences for as long as there is a significant discrepancy between the claims and the reality of news discourse.

*Bibliography*

Anderson, D. and Sharrock, W. (1979). Biasing the news: technical issues in media studies. *Sociology* 13, 3.
Bernstein, B. (1971) *Class, Codes and Control*. Vol. I, Routledge & Kegan Paul, London.
Blumler, J. and Ewbank, A. (1970). Trade unionists, the mass media and unofficial strikes. *British Journal of Industrial Relations* 8, 32–54.
Burns, T. (1977). The BBC: *Public Institution and Private World*. Macmillan, London.
Chibnall, S. (1977). *Law-and-Order News*. Tavistock, London.
Davis, H. and Walton, P. (1983a). Sources of variation in news vocabulary: a comparative analysis. *Int. J. of the Sociology of Language* 40, 59–75.
Davis, H. and Walton, P. eds. (1983b) *Language, Image, Media*. Blackwell, Oxford.
Eco, U. (1976). *A Theory of Semiotics*. Indiana University Press, Indiana.
Golding, P. and Middleton, S. (1979). Making claims: news media and the welfare state. *Media, Culture and Society* 1, 1, 5–21.
Glasgow University Media Group (1976). *Bad News*. Routledge & Kegan Paul, London.
Glasgow University Media Group (1980). *More Bad News*. Routledge & Kegan Paul, London.

Hall, S. (1980). Cultural studies: two paradigms. *Media Culture and Society* 2, 1, 57–72.
Hall, S., Critcher, C., Jefferson, T., Clarke, J. and Roberts, B. (1978). *Policing the crisis: mugging, the state, and law and order.* Macmillan, London.
Halliday, M. (1970). Language structure and language function. In J. Lyons (ed.) *New Horizons in Linguistics*, Penguin, Harmondsworth.
Halloran, J., Elliott, P. and Murdock, G. (1970). *Demonstrations and Communication.* Penguin, Harmondsworth.
Hartmann, P. (1975/6). Industrial relations in the news media. *Industrial Relations Journal* 6, 4, 4–18.
Hartmann, P. (1979). News and public perceptions of industrial relations. *Media, Culture and Society* 1, 3, 255–270.
Hyman, R. and Brough, I. (1975). *Social Values and Industrial Relations.* Blackwell, Oxford.
Kress, G. (1983). Linguistic processes and the mediation of 'reality': the politics of newspaper language. *Int. J. of the Sociology of Language* 40, 43–57.
Leitner, G. (1980). BBC English and Deutsche Rundfunksprache. A comparative and historical analysis of the language on the radio. *Int. J. of the Sociology of Language* 26.
Lerman, C. (1983). Dominant discourse: the institutional voice and control of topic. In H. Davis and P. Walton (eds.) *Language, Image, Media* Blackwell, Oxford.
Morley, D. (1976). Industrial conflict and the mass media. *Sociological Review* 24, 245–268.
Morley, D. (1980). *The 'Nationwide' audience: structure and decoding.* British Film Institute, London.
Murdock, G. (forthcoming). *Beyond Youth Culture.* Constable, London.
Pateman, T. (1975). *Television and the February 1974 General Election.* British Film Institute, London.
Schlesinger, P. (1978). *Putting 'Reality' Together: BBC News.* Constable, London.
Tracey, M. (1977). *The production of political televisions.* Routledge & Kegan Paul, London.

DOUGLAS S. SOLOMON AND BARBARA A. CARDILLO

# The Elements and Process of Communication Campaigns

*Campaign Definition*

A campaign can be defined, generically, as "any systematic course of aggressive activities for some special purpose" (Stein, 1970; p. 214). From a more specific communication point of view, a campaign is defined as "a pre-planned set of communication activities designed by change agents to achieve certain changes in receiver behavior in a specified time period" (Rogers 1973 p. 277). An important distinction between these two definitions is that communication campaigns are defined as *a process within a limited time period*. Both definitions though indicate that a campaign has a definite purpose, something to be changed or achieved. Campaigns are often categorized based upon this purpose, with the three most common classifications being political campaigns, marketing/advertising campaigns, and public communication campaigns. The first, political campaigns, is usually attempting to encourage people to support a particular candidate or issue; marketing campaigns are usually aimed at getting people to buy a product; and public communication campaigns are usually designed to achieve some sort of social change. The differences in the structure, process, and elements of each type of campaign would provide an interesting analysis, however, this chapter will primarily focus on the elements and processes of public communication campaigns.

Historically, public communication campaigns have emerged as proactive rather than reactive (Paisley, 1981). That is, they have the power to affect decisions before problems occur as compared to two centuries ago when they were reactive strategies "against social problems that the political, legal, and economic systems were delinquent in solving" (p. 39).

In a recent historical overview, Paisley (1981) identified reform as the unifying principle of public communication campaigns. He defined reform in a generic sense as "any action that makes society better or makes the lives of individuals better" (p. 24). Reform, or life betterment, has been attempted within various classes of behavior. For example, health campaigns have tried to reduce the risk of cardiovascular disease (Maccoby and Farquhar, 1975; Farquhar and Maccoby, 1977; Maccoby and Solomon, 1981), to increase knowledge and use of family planning (Udry, 1974; Taplin, 1981), and to motivate and teach people how to quit smoking (McAlister, 1981). Other campaigns have attempted changes such as increased use of seat belts (Robertson, 1974), conservation of energy (Farhar-Pilgrim and Shoemaker, 1981), and prevention of wildfires (McNamara, et al, 1981).

*Essential Elements of a Campaign*

Since Hyman and Sheatsley's 1947 article on why information campaigns fail, communication rsearchers have been periodically analyzing campaign results and identifying both content and programmatic factors which contribute to the success of communication campaigns. Some of these research efforts will be briefly reviewed.

In 1979 Atkin reviewed the research evidence on mass mediated health communication campaigns and determined that one of the key issues is "how to define success." Mendelsohn (1972) found that informations campaigns have relatively high success if middle range goals are set as specific objectives. Other research efforts have supported these conclusions that successful campaigns are associated with realistic and explicit objectives, defined in the planning stage, which clearly specify the necessary conditions for a campaign to be considered successful (Novelli, 1977; Robertson and Wortzel, 1978); Maccoby and Alexander, 1980; Solomon, 1982).

Observers have also found that most campaigns are relatively short run, one time efforts, while the behaviors they are attempting to change must continue for a long time. In a study of consumer behavior and health care change, it was found that it is the cumulative effect of a campaign that creates behavior change and that this is achieved through repetition and reinforcement of messages (Robertson and Wortzel, 1978). In a review of four successful health campaigns Solomon (1982) found that the use of multiple channels reinforced each other and produced a synergistic effect. In the Stanford Three Community Study, Maccoby and Alexander (1980) cited the use of creative scheduling of messages as an important factor in the success of the campaign.

Campaign researchers have achieved consensus that along with realistic goals and long term strategies, evaluation is a third important element in success of public communication campaigns. Mendelsohn (1972) states:

> Published research on the effects of mass mediated information campaigns suffers from a serious flaw. Customarily, it reflects a consistent division of labor between the creators of messages and those who evaluate them. Most frequently, it reflects the post hoc efforts of researchers to evaluate information campaigns which were designed and implemented independently by anonymous communications practitioners without the active participation of the evaluators in the so called creative process (p. 51)

The evaluation problem is two-fold. As Mendelsohn points out, post hoc designs are often not evaluated within the context of the original goals of the campaign and researchers often cannot assess whether or not the campaign was a success. Another problem is that there is a lack of process analysis to determine the reasons *why* a campaign succeeded or failed (Solomon, 1982). In the Stanford study, Maccoby and Alexander (1980) found that regular feedback through process evaluation enabled them to identify the effectiveness of specific components ot the campaign.

This brief review has identified three of the elements that have consistently been found to be associated with successful campaigns. Now we discuss how these elements, along with others, help to structure a campaign as a process within a specific time period.

*Framework and Process of Campaigns*

This framework consists of three aspects which are basic to all communication campaigns: planning, implementation, and evaluation. For each aspect, we will focus on the most crucial elements by describing the importance and function of each.

*Planning*

The first element of a campaign, the planning, has many levels. However, we will present two essential steps: problem analysis and specification of objectives.

All campaigns, by their nature, must be designed to ameliorate or change some kind of pre-defined problem situation. It is crucial, therefore, that the problem be accurately assessed. This can be accomplished through careful problem definition, audience analysis, and selection of an appropriate change model.

Problem definition consists of determining the specific attributes of the problem situation. At this point it is often important to understand the problem from a communication point of view to determine whether or not it is an appropriate one to be dealt with by a communication campaign. For example, in reference to improving nutritional behavior, a campaign may only have a marginal impact on consumers because the problem is often defined more appropriately as a lack of resources. When individuals do not have a great deal of control over their financial resources, high knowledge or motivation to change may still not result in nutritional behavior change. Simply telling poor people of the joys of eating steak might motivate them but still not lead to change. Therefore, it is important to understand the attributes of a problem and whether or not it is communication-related or structural.

It is also essential to study the audience and know their demographic attributes as well as their psychographics. In understanding the audience, it is necessary to hypothesize a process by which messages distributed by the media can have an impact on the problem. For example, if one wishes to have adults purchase breakfast cereals, one approach would be to aim messages directly at adults. A second approach would be to direct messages through children's television and rely on kid's persuasive and often annoying powers to influence their parents to purchase the product. Therefore, a model is usually designed at this stage to determine the flow of messages and planned impact on various sub-audiences of the total population. In understanding target audiences, it is necessary to know their pre-existing levels of knowledge, attitudes, motivation to change, and behavior relevant to the problem. It is also important to understand their mass media use and interpersonal communication behavior in order to direct messages through the most appropriate, and potentially most effective, channels.

In addition to problem definition and audience analysis, another area of problem analysis is understanding the nature of the change hierarchy which applies to a particular situation. Ray (1973) has shown that depending upon the problem, different kinds of hierarchies of change can have differential effects on desired outcomes. For example, most campaigns assume that people should first be educated which therefore leads to knowledge gain, leading in turn to attitude change, and finally, to behavior change. While this may be the case in many problem areas, there have been a large number of problems where the audience already has acquired knowledge and developed favorable attitudes, and something else is blocking the path to behavior change. Smoking cessation is an example of this situation. Many people know that smoking is bad for them, want to quit, and yet are unable to do so. They simply lack the skills required to become and remain a non-smoker such as resisting peer pressure to smoke. In some situations, it may be more appropriate to try to change behavior first which often will lead to knowledge gain (i. e., information seeking behavior), and ulitmately to favorable attitudes. It is clear that understanding the intended change and where the audience currently is on a hierarchy of change will help the campaign planner to determine which hierarchy model to apply.

The second step in planning is to define the objectives of the campaign. Having completed the problem analysis step, the planner now has adequately defined the problem, has determined who the audience target groups will be, and understands how to achieve the desired change. Now both general and specific objectives must be defined which will indicate the kinds of outcomes that are desired. These objectives should include the number and types of people to be reached by messages, and indicate the expected percentage who will change as a result of these messages. For example, a campaign which is both employing mass media and interpersonal communication strategies should define objectives and target groups for each aspect of the campaign by determining the number of people to be reached, then calculating the percentage to change their attitudes, the percentage expected to change their behavior, and the percentage expected to sustain that behavior. If alternative behaviors are possible, objectives should be specified for each. Having created specific objectives, it is possible to estimate the potential success of a campaign, define alternative approaches, and redefine strategies when necessary. For example, if the probability of reaching an individual is 50%, and the probability of change is 50% and the probability of maintaining the change is 50% then one can readily see that out of 100 people, chances are that 12.5% (.5x .5x .5) will change. This analysis, which includes very optimistic probabilities, by the way, will sober up a planner who wants to change 90% of the audience.

The second major phase of the campaign process is implementation. In mass communication campaigns implementation consists basically of two components: message design and media planning. Message design is a sub-process of the overall campaign in which messages relating to the overall goals of the campaign are developed, tested through formative research, revised, and prepared for final implementation. In high quality campaigns, message design follows quite logically from the previous planning process. Message design itself has four sub-elements: defining the core message, determining the message source, selecting a theme, and creating treatments.

The first step is the creation of the core message itself. This is the generic message which the campaign designers, through their objective defining process and through their formative research, have defined as essential for achieving the campaign's overall objectives. These generic messages can be quite simple such as: "mother's milk is best" or can be quite complex such as those in a political campaign. Once a core message has been defined, it is the campaign designer's role to tailor this message into what is known as message treatments.

A treatment of a message is the format that the message will actually take when it is presented to the public. This could be a dramatic format, a testimonial format, a cinéma verité format, or many other kinds of potential message treatments. It should be noted that a great deal of research exists on many elements of the message design process (cf., McGuire, 1969; Schramm, 1972; Zimbardo, et. al. 1977).

Once the core generic message has been defined, it is important to determine appropiate sources to present the message. Many research studies have shown that the source of the message can greatly influence its perception by the audience as well as its effects on them. It is important that the source chosen be sufficiently credible with the proper kind of credibility (Rogers with Shoemaker, 1971). It is also stylistically important for the source to fit in with the content of the message. In the United States, a large number of dog food commercials include Western stars as their spokesperson which would not be suitable (although they are credible), for a perfume commercial, or vice versa.

A final aspect of message design which adds coherency to a campaign is to have themes, graphic logos, and other verbal and visual images that are consistent across various media products. By having similar visual and verbal imagery it is possible to increase the overall awareness of the campaign in the target audience, since presumably each exposure reinforces and is related cognitively to previous exposures. If all of the messages stylistically are quite different, their impact will probably be greatly diluted.

The second element of implementation is creating a media plan, and media planning has two sub-components: selecting channels and a media mix; and deciding reach, frequency and timing. The first step is choosing a particular medium or media to use. There are many reasons for using one medium over another. Certain media, such as broadcast media, are highly appropriate for short, relatively low information-density, repetitive messages. Print media on the other hand do not have the powerful reach into the audience's homes that broadcast media do, but rather are capable of handling a much higher information-density which can be controlled at the reader's own pace. Therefore, print and broadcast media can be used to supplement one another. Sometimes, certain media are more appropriate than others because of the message content. For example, to train individuals to wire a radio set, one might want to use film or videotape rather than printed material, particularly if movement and the color of the components is essential to learning. It is therefore important for media planners to consider the fit of the content with the medium chosen, as well as the relevance of the message to the medium.

Usually, communication campaigns use what is called a media mix. A media mix is a combination of media used to augment one another. It is hypothesized that utilizing a variety of media such as television, radio, booklets, newspaper columns, posters, billboards, etc., creates overall synergistic effect and provides a much greater impact than the individual media elements taken alone.

In actually using media, the planner must decide three key elements: reach, frequency, and timing. Reach is the number of individuals in a particular audience category who will be exposed at least once to the message. Frequency is the number of times the average individual has been exposed. And timing, which is really an element of reach and frequency, consists of the time of the day that a message, particularly broadcast messages, are shown. Obviously, different times of day have different kinds of people in the audience and have different size audiences.

*Evaluation*

The final phase in the campaign process is evaluation. All campaigns have some evaluation, which ranges from, "Gee my friends thought that campaign was great," to "we got six requests for our catalog," to highly complex psychological impact studies through field research on the outcomes of the campaign. The purpose of evaluation is to provide some kind of feedback on the impact of the campaign for future planning purposes. There are really two kinds of evaluations of campaigns. Summative evaluation, which looks at whether or not the campaign has met the objectives that were defined previously in the planning element of campaign process; and formative evaluation, which looks at the planning and implementation aspects of the campaign.

Formative research is particularly important in the campaign process because it helps in creating, testing, and revising messages. Formative research can be defined as research oriented toward the planning, implementation, and design process of campaigns. It is basically all the research conducted with the exception of the summative outcome research that measures the overall impact of the campaign. Formative research helps understand whether or not an audience is really being reached by the messages, and the kinds of people that constitute the audience. It is also able to study the short-term impact of each piece of media, such as the impact of a particular newspaper column or of a booklet.

There are many evaluation strategies which are typically used in campaigns. Some of them include surveys, such as telephone surveys or shopping center intercept surveys, that attempt to understand whether or not the campaign is achieving awareness in the audience. A. C. Nielson and other commercial ratings services provide a great deal of information on the television and radio audiences for any given time period. In this way, it is possible for a campaign planner to know the exact number of people in each audience category that was exposed to a message on a particular day and time. Other evaluations might include counting coupons sent in by people reading campaign materials in magazines, or counting requests for information. The point is that there are many kinds of evaluation strategies and all campaigns as a genre contain some kind of formal or informal evaluation.

*Conclusion*

Our goal for this chapter has been to clarify the structure and process of communication campaign. In doing so, we have pointed out the variations in purpose, level of effort and potential target groups for campaigns, as well as presenting the essential elements in the planning, implementation, and evaluation process.

While an understanding of all of these components and elements is crucial to effective campaigns, there must be equal emphasis placed upon how they are put together and processed within the specified time period of a campaign. This use of time has been mentioned in our discussion of individual elements, yet it must again be stressed that the elements of planning, implementation, and evaluation are not mutually exclusive steps in time. They are interdependent parts of the campaign process and may occur at several times, often in conjunction with one another. For example, planning involves getting to know the intended target groups. This is accomplished through the use of formative research techniques. Implementation involves message design which uses formative research for pretesting and refining messages, as well as planning for redesigning the objectives when necessary.

It is important to explicitly plan the campaign process and to periodically review and revise it. This means that the elements of the process must be sequences within a time framework. For example, a campaign planner must determine a time schedule for initial problem analysis and definition of objectives. These goals should then be presented on experts and potential target groups, then redefined. The process of interplay between planning, implementation, and evaluation should also continue throughout the campaign.

Perhaps through an understanding of the elements and processes of the campaign genre, some of the problems found in previous communication campaigns can be more easily overcome.

## Bibliography

Atkin, C. K. (1979). "Research Evidence on Mass Mediated Health Communication Campaigns." *Communication Yearbook 3*. New Brundwick, New Jersey: Transaction Press.

Farhar-Pilgrim, B. and Shoemaker, F. (1981) "Campaigns to Affect Energy Behavior." In R. Rice and W. Paisley (Eds.) *Public Communication Campaigns*. Beverly Hills, Ca: Sage Publications.

Farquhar, J., Maccoby, N. (Summer 1975). "Communication for Health: Unselling Heart Disease." *Journal of Communication* Volume 25:3.

Mendelsohn, H. (1973). "Some Reasons Why Information Campaigns Can Succeed," *Public Opinion Quarterly*, 37:1 (Spring), pp. 50—60.

Maccoby, N. and Alexander, J. (1980). "Field Experimentation in Community Intervention." In Munoz, R., Snowden, L., & Kelly, J. (Eds.), *Research in Social Contexts: Bring About Change*, Jossey-Bass.

Maccoby, N. and Farquhar, J. (Winter 1977). "Reducing the Risk of Cardiovascular Disease: Effects of a Community-Based Campaign on Knowledge and Behavior." *Journal of Community Health*, Vol. 3, No. 2.

Maccoby, N. and Solomon, D. S. (1981). "The Stanford Community Studies in Heart Disease Prevention." In R. Rice and W. Paisley (Eds.) *Public Communication Campaigns*. Beverly Hills, Ca: Sage Publications.

McAlister, A. (1981) "Antismoking Campaigns: Progress in Developing Effective Communications." In R. Rice and W. Paisley (Eds.) *Public Communication Campaigns*. Beverly Hills, Ca: Sage Publications.

McGuire, W. J. (1969). "The Nature of Attitudes and Attitude Change." In G. Lindzey and E. Aronson (Eds.) *The Handbook of Social Psychology*. 2nd. ed., Vol. 3. Menlo Park, Ca: Addison-Wesley Publishing Co.

McNamara, E. et al. (1981). "Communication Efforts to Prevent Wildfires." In R. Rice and W. Paisley (Eds.) *Public Communication Campaigns*. Beverly Hills, Ca: Sage Publications.

Novelli, W. (1977). "Improving Messages and Materials through Pretesting." In Proceedings of the Fourth National Cancer Communications Conference, DHEW Publication No. 78—1463; June.

Paisley, W. (1981). "Public Communication Campaigns: The American Experience." In R. Rice and W. Paisley (Eds.) *Public Communication Campaigns*. Beverly Hills, Ca: Sage Publications.

Ray, M. (1973). "Marketing Communication and the Hierarchy of Effects." In Clarke, P. (Ed.) *New Models for Mass Communication Research*. Beverly Hills, Ca: Sage Publications.

Robertson, L. S. (1974). Kelley, A., O'Neill, B., Wixom, C., Eiswirth, R., and Haddon, Jr., W. (1974). "A Controlled Study of the Effect of Television Messages on Safety Belt Use." *American Journal of Public Health*, vol. 64, no. 11.

Robertson, T. S. and Wortzel, L. H. (1978). "Consumer Behavior and Health Care Change: The Role of Mass Media." In C. Lovelock and C. Weinberg (Eds.) *Readings in Public and Non Profit Marketing*. The Scientific Press.

Rogers, E. (1973). *Communication Strategies for Family Planning*. New York: Free Press.

Rogers, E. with Shoemaker, F. (1971). *Communication of Innovations: A Cross-Cultural Approach*. New York: Free Press.

Schramm, W. (1972). "Nature of Communication Between Humans." In Schramm & Roberts (Eds.) *The Process and Effects of Mass Communication* (rev. ed.) Chicago: University of Illinois Press.

Solomon, D. S. (1982). "Health Campaigns on Television." In D. Pearl, L. Bouthilet, & J. Lazar (Eds.) *Television and Behavior: Ten Years of Scientific Progress and Implications for the Eighties*. Vol. 2: Technical Reviews, National Institute of Mental Health; U.S. Department of Health and Human Services.

Stein, J. (1970). *The Random House Dictionary of the English Language*. Random House, New York.

Taplin, S. (1981). "Family Plannning Communication Campaigns." In R. Rice and W. Paisley (Eds.) *Public Communication Campaigns*. Beverly Hills, Ca: Sage Publications.

Udry, J. R. in collaboration with Bauman, K. E. et al., with the assistance of Noyes, R. W. et al. (1974). *The Media and Family Planing*. Cambridge, Mass: Ballinger Publishing Co.

Zimbardo, R. et al. (1974) *Influencing Attitudes and Changing Behavior*. Menlo Park, Ca; Addison-Wesley.

TEUN A. VAN DIJK

# Structures of News in the Press

*1. Introduction*

The aim of this chapter is to propose an analytical framework for the structures of news discourse in the press. Given the complexities of textual structures, and hence also of news discourse, we restrict our focus to what we call the *global* organization of news. Intuitively, this means that we are dealing only with news structures beyond the sentence level, such as thematic and schematic structurel, and must ignore syntactic, semantic, stylistic or rhetorical features of sentences and sentential connections. Similarly, we also neglect issues of graphical organization, such as lay-out, and nonverbal properties of news, such as photographs. In other words, we are concerned with macro phenomena, rather than with the micro-organization of news discourse. Finally, we limit our discussion to news in the daily press, and do not analyze TV- and radionews.

By the 'thematic structure' of a discourse, we understand the overall organization of global 'topics' a news item is about. Such a thematic analysis takes place against the background of a theory of semantic macrostructures. These are the formal representation of the global *content* of a text or dialogue, and therefore characterize part of the meaning of a text. Schemata, on the other hand, are used to describe the overall *form* of a discourse. We use the theoretical term *superstructure* to describe such schemata. Schemata have a fixed, conventional (and therefore culturally variable) nature for each type of text. We assume that also news discourse has such a conventional schema, a 'news schema', in which the overall topics or global content may be inserted. In other words, schematic superstructures organize thematic macrostructures, much in the same way as the syntax of a sentence organizes the meaning of a sentence. Indeed, in both cases, we deal with a number of formal categories, which determine the possible orderings and the hierarchical organization of sentential and textual units, respectively. To wit, the category of Headline in a news discourse, has a fixed form and position in news items in the press. At the same time, this Headline has a very specific thematic function: it usually expresses the most important topic of the news item. We see that themes and schemes, macrostructures and superstructures are closely related.

With these theoretical instruments, we are also able to analyze another notion of discourse analysis, which is of particular importance in the characterization of news, namely, *relevance*. It will be shown, indeed, that news has what we may call a 'relevance structure', which indicates to the reader which information in the text is most important or prominent. Obviously, again, Headlines have a special role in such a relevance structure, because we just assumed that headlines express the most 'important' topic of the news.

Although the approach proposed above may contribute to an explicit structural account of news discourse, it tells us little about the (mass or media) *communication* dimension of news discourse. *Why*, for instance, have news items the kind of thematic or schematic structures we want to study? What is their role, function or effect in the *processes* of news production and reception? Obviously, there are social, cultural and cognitive constraints on such organizational properties of media messages. In other words, we assume that there is a systematic relationship between news text and context. Thus, it seems plausible that the structural forms and the overall meanings of a news text are not arbitrary, but a result of social and professional routines of journalists in institutional settings, on the one hand, and an important condition for the effective cognitive processing of news text by both journalists and readers, on the other hand. Therefore, we pay brief attention also to the *cognitive* dimension of thematic and schematic structures, but must neglect the social and institutional context of news production and use, which we can only refer to in a review section (Section 2).

Although this chapter is mainly theoretical, our examples are drawn from a large scale, empirical case study of the international press coverage of the assassination of president-elect Bechir Gemayel of Lebanon in september 1982 (van Dijk, 1984a and van Dijk, 1986). For this study 250 newspapers from 100 countries were collected, from which more than 700 articles were subjected to both quantitative and (especially) qualitative analysis. Hence, our observations about the thematic and schematic structures of news are made against the background of a rather extensive data base, even if we can give only a few examples here.

## 2. Backgrounds. The Study of News

Obviously, our approach to news structures from a discourse analytic point of view is not independent of insights obtained in other work on news or news discourse. Before we start our analysis, therefore, a few remarks are in order about the research done from different and similar perspectives. Indeed, the late 1970s have witnessed a rapidly increasing interest for the production, contents and organization of news in the media. Let us highlight only a few milestones of this development (see also the editorial introduction to this book and van Dijk, 1986, as well as the previous chapters).

Common to most studies of the news, is a sociological perspective, whatever the differences in actual frameworks of analysis. This may be a macrosociological perspective, interested in the institutional, professional and cultural context of news production. Or it may be a microsociological analysis of journalistic routines, taken for granted practical rules, and news values or ideologies which govern the daily activities of journalists in gathering and writing the news. And when attention is paid to the content, form or style of news items, such an analysis is primarily geared towards the assessment of social or cultural dimensions of mass media and communication, such as the political views, the institutional embeddedness or the ideological orientation of journalists or newspapers. Specific properties of news are seen as the probable or even necessary results of these social and cultural constraints. In other words, news discourse is hardly ever analyzed for its own sake, either as a specific type of (media) discourse, or as a specific socio-cultural accomplishment.

There are a few purely structural approaches to news discourse, e. g. by linguists, discourse analysts or by people working in domains such as semiotics, stylistics, or rhetoric. However, such structural studies are seldom comprehensive. They usually take news as an example or illustration of a structural analysis of specific discourse features, e. g. of lexical choice as a component of style.

We are convinced that both approaches are important and necessary, but also we think that they should be integrated. A 'pure' structural analysis is a rather irrelevant theoretical exercise as long as we cannot relate textual structures with those of the cognitive and socio-cultural contexts of news production and reception. The development of linguistics and discourse analysis in the 1970s has shown, indeed, that a 'context-free' approach to language, for instance in the construction of formal grammars, is one-sided at best and certainly empirically inadequate. Of course, the same holds for the analysis of news discourse. It is impossible to really account for the many *specific* constraints on news structures, without specifying their social (institutional, professional) conditions or their socio-cognitive functions in mass mediated communication. Why, indeed, would news have headlines, and why would these be big, bold and 'on top' of the news article? And conversely, a sound psychological, sociological or even economical analysis of news production and consumption can be incomplete at best, without a detailed characterization of the nature of the 'product' involved in these processes. Both the production processes and the cognitive understanding and memory of news, depend on the 'format' of this product.

Macrosociological approaches to the news are basically restricted to the institutional and professional dimensions of news production by journalists working for news agencies or newspapers (Tunstall, 1971; Boyd-Barret, 1980), or are concerned with the economic and ideological controls of news production and newspapers (e. g. Curran, ed. 1978; Gurevitch, et al. eds., 1982). Although these studies are certainly important in an account of the social and especially the ideological contraints upon journalists during news production, they seldom show *how* exactly such constraints work in the actual production process and in the final result: the news. Indeed, this is why we may call them macro-studies: they do not pay attention to micro-phenomena. There are exceptions though, mostly in the area of ideological analyses of the news, such as in the work of the Centre for Conteporary Cultural Studies in Birmingham (e.g. Hall, et al., eds. 1981). See also Cohen & Young, eds. (1981).

There is also an 'intermediate' level of analysis, viz. of the concrete organization of news production within news institutions (Roshco, 1975; Gans, 1979, Schlesinger, 1978, Golding & Elliott (1979). Such studies pay attention to the everyday routines, the division of labor, the hierarchical relationships, institutional constraints both from the management and the readers/sales, or the values and the culture that define the journalists' activities. Although such studies also seldom pay attention to concrete news analysis, they at least provide us rather direct insight into the professional constraints of news production, such as deadlines, beats, the editorial system, competition, and the everyday organization of news gathering and selection.

Although strict distinctions between macro- and microsociological approaches cannot (and should not, cf. Knorr-Cetina & Cicourel, eds., 1982) be made, the observation of everyday routines of news production may also take place in an even 'closer' perspective, e.g. in terms of ethnomethodology (Tuchman, 1978; Fishman, 1980). Various dimensions can be seen to 'work' at this micro-level of analysis. Not only professionalism, or ideology and news values, and not only the routine organization of news gathering practices can be observed in a detailed account of everyday practices of participants as institutional and social members. These frameworks or networks (webs) provide a device to routinely produce news as a form of 'reality construction'. They define how journalists 'see' the social world, and hence news events, and also their special tasks in the reproduction of such events through news articles in the press. Large parts of the news appear to be pre-formulated already by influential news sources, such as the police or other state or corporate institutions. Their accounts, in documents or press releases, of their own actions, already provide the journalist with a dominant definition of the situation. Through such approaches, which also have an interesting cognitive slant (they deal with the rules, the categories, the interpretation procedures journalists bring to bear in the reconstruction of news reality), we are able to link the macro-context of news with the actual meanings and forms of news discourse. But again, concrete text analysis, even in this perspective, is still scarce.

Finally, there are a series of studies, both by social scientists and linguists, that explicitly deal with news analysis per se. The work of the CCCS (Hall, et al. eds., 1981) has already been mentioned above. It derives part of its inspiration from French work in discourse and ideological analysis, and integrates a marxian analysis of media production with notions developed by structuralists such as Barthes, Pêcheux, and Althusser (see Connell & Mills, this volume).

Of a different perspective, but also aiming at a 'social' reading of news, is the work of the Glasgow University Media Group (1976, 1980, 1982). Their influential 'bad news' studies of TV-news programs, are systematic content analyses, also of interviews and visual dimensions of news, especially focusing on strike coverage in the news. They showed, among other things, that the assumption, if not the prescription of 'impartiality' of news representations (of public broadcasting companies like the BBC) is challenged by the biased account of strikes in favor of those in power, a bias that could be detected especially in small and subtle details of news reporting (style, turns in interviews, camara shots, etc.) (see Davis, this volume, for details). Although this news analysis is certainly systematic and more or less explicit, it does not yet account for news structures in a discourse analytical or linguistic perspective. Such a grammatical approach we find in e.g. Fowler, et al. (1979). They were able to show that news bias can even be expressed in syntactic structures of sentences, such as the use of active or passive constructions, which allow the journalist to express or suppress the agent of news acts from subject positions. Such an approach shows that even with the limited instruments of a grammatical analysis, we can find linguistic correlates of ideological positions (see also Kress & Hodge, 1979) of newspapers and journalists. Hartley (1982) also focuses on (TV-)news structures, but does so from a broader, semiotic discourse analysis point of view, which also allows the systematic account of news films, stills and pictures (see also Davis & Walton, eds. 1983).

Much of this work is done in Britain, which we may consider the most advanced and theoretically most diverse location of actual research on the news. Despite the substantial differences between the various approaches mentioned here, this work embodies an interesting integration of empirical and structural analysis with a more critical ideological dimension (see also Downing, 1980). Most American studies about news have a much more anecdotical nature (many are written by journalists). When they have a critical perspective, they focus on issues of distortion, civil rights or the organizational and corporate control structure of news production (Epstein, 1973; Diamond, 1978; Bagdikian, 1971; Altheide, 1974; Barrett, 1978; Abel, ed. 1981). Often such studies will be about concrete 'cases' of portrayal: how did the media cover the presidential elections, Watergate, the 'race riots' and similar social events? They may cogently 'describe' what is and what is not being covered, but will seldom actually analyze news items systematically. Nor will such studies probe into the deeper ideological frameworks that underly American news production.

Finally, and without even trying to be complete, we should mention the important work on news being done in Germany, e.g. by Strassner and associates (Strassner, ed. 1975; Strassner, 1982). Although this work has a linguistic bias, it also pays attention to the production and reception dimension of news. Other studies, such as Kniffka (1980) and Lüger (1983) focus on details of language and style of the news.

Concluding this brief survey of recent studies about news and news discourse, we find that most work focuses on the 'context' of news, such as practical, socio-cultural or ideological constraints on news production. Little work has been done on the details of news texts themselves, and still less about the exact relationships between text and context of the news. If news is analyzed, it is mostly its 'content', which is of course important, but only half of the story, literally. A few linguistic studies have revealed much about the local syntax and style of news language. What remains to be done in the years ahead is a thorough, systematic and theoretically founded, discourse analysis of news, on the one hand, and an integration of such an approach with the prevailing sociological approaches. Unfortunately, this chapter can only provide one small element to the first goal (for detail, see van Dijk, 1986).

*3. Thematic structures*

Language users, and therefore also newspaper readers, have the important capacity to tell what a text or conversation 'was about'. They are able, though with subjective and social variation, to say what the 'topic' of a discourse is. Thus, they can formulate the theme or themes of a news text, by statements like 'I read in the newspaper that the president will not negotiate with the Russians' or 'did you read who won the European soccer championship?'. In other words, language users can summarize fairly complex units of information with one or a few sentences, and these sentences are assumed to express the gist, the theme, or the topic of the information. In intuitive terms, such themes or topics organize what is most important in a text. They, indeed, define the 'upshot' of what is said or written (see Jones, 1977).

The various notions introduced in the previous paragraph can be theoretically reformulated in terms of semantic macrostructures (van Dijk, 1980). The ability of language users to derive such macrostructures from a text, is based on a number of linguistic and cognitive rules and strategies (van Dijk & Kintsch, 1983). These macrostructures are called 'semantic' because when we are talking about notions such as 'topic', 'theme' or 'gist' of a text, we are dealing with meaning and reference, and not, for example, with syntactic form, style or rhetorical devices. Also, we are not even talking about the (local) meaning of isolated words or sentences, but about the meaning of larger fragments of text or about whole texts. We do not assign a theme or topic to one sentence, but to larger stretches of talk or text. Hence, themes, topics and the semantic macrostructures we use to make these notions explicit, pertain to *global* structures of discourse. Take for instance the following brief news text:

> (1) WEINBERGER Vs. THE PRESS
>
> Defense Secretary Caspar Weinberger is so upset over media coverage of his controversial Mideast trip that he is considering barring reporters from accompanying him on his forthcoming visit to the Far East. Weinberger's main complaint: he thinks the press twisted the meaning of his remarks so that U.S
> 5 willingness to sell sophisticated weapons to Jordan came out as a final decision which brought an immediate protest from Israel. Says a Weinberger aide: "Do we really need these headaches when we're dealing with foreign governments?" The sensitive topic of arms sales probably won't come up to Weinberger's Far East trip, since neither China or Taiwan will be on his itinerary.
> 10 (From *Newsweek*, March 1, 1982, p. 7).

Although this short news text from a weekly, which itself may be a summary of more extensive news discourses, is not ideal to demonstrate the role of topics or macrostructures in the structure (or understanding) of discourse, it may be argued that it also has a few central topics. One aspect of this overall topic is signalled by the headline 'Weinberger vs. the press'. This is certainly a high level abstraction from the information in the text, since it is implied by the statement that Weinberger criticizes the press for having twisted his words in earlier arms talks. Yet, it is *also* a somewhat subjective, biased formulation of this level topic implied by the text, because it may suggest that Weinberger is opposed to the press in *general*, whereas the text only suggests that Weinberger is considering to bar the press from delicate foreign missions. Indeed, this last sentence expresses in somewhat more detail a more neutral overall topic of this text, which may be summarized e. g. as follows:

> (2) The U.S defense secretary, Weinberger, is considering to bar reporters from his next trip to the Far East, because he thinks that they might disturb delicate talks with foreign governments, as they had done during his arms talks in the Middle East.

And even this text may be further summarized, e. g. as follows:

> (3) Weinberger is considering not to take the press with him on his trip to the Far East, because earlier reporting had had negative results on relations with foreign governments.

and finally this summary allows even further abstraction into:

> (4) Weinberger is considering not to take the press on his trip.

From this example, we may conclude several things. First, there is not just one topic or possible summary of a text, but several. Summarization may take place on a continuum, from leaving out a few less essential details on the one end, until leaving out all information except the most relevant or essential, on the other end. Second, the topics we assign to a text, or the summary we make of it, are possibly subjective. We may infer from a text what is relevant or important for *us*. Indeed, *Newsweek* perceives Weinberger's consideration or decision as an act *against* the press, and summarizes the text in a headline that is consistent with that macro-topic. Third, part of the topics we have inferred from (or assigned to) this text, are formulated in the text itself: indeed, the first sentence of the original news text is virtually identical with our summaries (2) and (3). Fourth, topics are typically obtained by 'leaving out details' from a text. Such details may be dimensions of a situation described, such as normal reasons, components and consequences for action. But, summarization is not just a form of deletion. It may also involve generalization, e. g. 'Weinberger is upset about the press' could be a generalization of several different situations in which Weinberger did not like the actions of the press, e. g. when reporters distorted his earlier statements. Finally, abstraction may also take place by replacing a sequence of the text, e. g. describing a sequence of actions, by a single concept (proposition), which need not be expressed in the text at all. Indeed, a sequence of acts by Weinberger and his aides may in that case simply be summarized by the sentence 'Weinberger bars the press from his trip'.

In this first, intuitive analysis of an example we have found some important properties of macrostructures, and the principles that may be used to infer or derive macro-information (topics) from a text, e. g. by deletion, generalization and (re-)construction. These three summarizing principles are called *macrorules*. They reduce the complex, detailed meaning structure of a text into a simpler, more general and abstract (higher level) meaning of a text. And it is this higher level, overall meaning which we call the macrostructure of a text, and which we have also identified as the level at which we describe the topics or themes of a text. Macrorules, formally speaking, are *recursive*. They may apply again at each level of abstraction to produce even shorter abstracts. The result is a hierarchical macrostructure, consisting of several levels, each level consisting of a sequence of (macro-)propositions that 'summarize' a sequence of lower level (macro-)propositions. To avoid too many theoretical terms, we shall simply use the terms *thematic structure, theme* or *topic*. It is however understood that a theme in this case is not simply a word or a single concept, but a (macro-)proposition. Hence, 'Weinberger' or 'the press' or even 'censorship' is not, in our terms, a topic or theme of our sample text, but the sentence *Weinberger bars press from trip* does express a proposition and can therefore be a topic or theme of that text.

We have seen that topics may be subjective. This means that we should not simply say that a text 'has' a macrostructure, but that such a structure is assigned to the text by a writer or reader. In this sense, then, like meanings in general, themes or topics are *cognitive* units. They represent how the text is understood, what is found important, and how relevancies are stored in memory. This means that knowledge, beliefs, attitudes and ideologies may operate in the cognitive construction and representation of macrostructures. In order to summarize and globally understand the text about Weinberger, we must have a vast amount of political knowledge, knowledge that is not spelled out in the text, but presupposed by it: e. g. that it is possible or even customary that reporters accompany important government officials, that the press may distort the words of such officials, that biased reports may be a reason for political tensions, and so on. Thus, we may need complex social and political knowledge schemata, or *scripts* to understand what this text is about (Schank & Abelson, 1977; Schank, 1982).

Finally, the cognitive nature of macro-interpretation also requires a more process-oriented approach to the assignment of topics to a text. Whereas abstract macrorules derive topics from a *given* text, or rather from its underlying sequence of propositions, this is not what a reader actually does. During reading, the language user starting with the beginning of a text only has one or a few sentences and their meanings at his/her disposal. And with this limited information, but with the help of vast knowledge structures about the context or the type of text, the reader will try to derive a provisional topic as soon as possible, without waiting until the whole text has been read. In other words, readers use expedient *macrostrategies* for the derivation of topics from a text. For news discourse, these strategies have important textual devices to help build the thematic structure, viz. headlines and the lead. We have seen in our earlier example that the headline and the first sentence indeed seem so express at least part of the assumed macrostructure of the news item. Headlines and lead may therefore be used as expedient signals to make effective guesses about the most important information of the text. Note however that they express the macrostructure of the writer, rather than that of the reader: the reader may infer a different thematic structure, depending on his/her own beliefs and attitudes. And when a headline or lead is not an adequate summarizaton of the full overall meaning of a text, we may, either formally or subjectively, say that they are biased.

*4. Thematic structures in news discourse*

The theoretical approach outlined in the previous section still has a rather general nature. It holds for discourse in general, and is not specific for news discourse. The only rather specific observation we have made pertains to the special macrostructural role of headlines and leads in news discourse: they are used to express or to infer the theme or topic. There are however other specific features of thematic organization in news discourse, both from a structural and from a more dynamic, cognitive point of view.

Consider for example the news article, taken from the *Bangkok Post*, about the invasion of West-Beirut by the Israeli army (next page). Disregarding for a moment the schematic category names added in the margins, to which we return below, we first observe that the headline expresses only one topic from the thematic structure, viz. the invasion of West-Beirut by the Israeli army. Another important topic, mentioned in the lead, and opening the first sentence after the lead, viz. the assassination of Gemayel, is not mentioned in the headline. It follows that the headline is not so much incorrect as rather incomplete. If two important events are covered by a news item, a single headline can usually only express one of them, which is either the most recent event and/or the most important. Yet, in that case we often find a smaller headline above or below the main headline, as is also the case in the *Bangkok Post* article. Such secondary headlines usually express important causes or consequences.

The first sentence of the article then specifies some of the details of the second main topic: actors, instrument (bomb) and characteristics of the instrument, further participants (victims), and finally the consequences of the assassination. The second paragraph, also a complex sentence, similarly specifies some details of the other main topic, namely the reasons of the Israeli army for the invasion. So far, we obtain the following picture of the *realization* of the thematic structure in a news text: the highest or most important topic is expressed in the headline, the top of the complete macrostructure of the text is formulated in the lead, and the initial sentences or paragraphs of the text express a still lower level of macrostructure, featuring important details about time, location, participants, causes/reasons or consequences of the main events. This means that the linear, i. e. both left to right and high to low in terms of article lay-out, and linear in the sense of the reading process, organization of a news text is a *top-to-bottom* mapping of the underlying semantic macrostructure. In other words: the highest levels of the thematic structure are formulated first, and the lower levels follow.

The third paragraph of the text comes back to the assassination topic, and specifies personal and political characteristics of the main protagonist, Gemayel, as well as speculations about the political and military consequences of the assassination. And most of the rest of the text also provides particulars about the assassination, its backgrounds and consequences. This means that, when both story details and length are considered, the article nearly completely 'is about' the assassination of Gemayel, and only tangentially about the Israeli invasion of West-Beirut. Yet, the headline suggests that the latter topic is more important, even when it merely covers one small paragraph of the text. Here, we find an instance of what may be called 'skewed' headlining: one topic from this text, organizing only part of the information in the text, is promoted to the main topic. And the topic which structurally speaking dominates most of the story is merely expressed by an inserted heading across part of the article. The reason for this 'bias' in signalling topics by headlines need not be ideological or political, but seems to be determined by an implicit journalistic rule of news organization: last main events are more important. This rule is based on the actuality principle of the press. What we see in the *Bangkok Post* also happens in other newspapers that cary both the story of Gemayel's assassination and the invasion of West-Beirut. The invasion is the 'latest development', and therefore may get more prominence, 'over-

HEADLINE — **Israeli troops re-enter west Beirut**

*From: BANGKOK POST, September 16, 1982, p.1*

LEAD — BEIRUT — Israeli forces moved into west Beirut yesterday to "insure quiet" after the assassination of Lebanese president-elect Bashir Gemayel, the Israeli military command in Jerusalem said.

## After Gemayel's assassination

MAIN EVENT — Unidentified assassins killed Gemayel Tuesday with a 204-kg (450 lb) bomb that took more than 26 lives, wounded 60 other people and returned Lebanon to relentless sectarian violence.

CONSEQUENT ACTION 1 — "As a result of the assassination of Bashir Gemayel, Israel Defence Forces entered west Beirut in order to prevent possible severe occurrences and in order to insure quiet," a statement by the Israeli military command said.

EXPECTATIONS — The death of the Maronite Christian, only nine days before he was to be inaugurated as Lebanon's president, raised fears of a new round of fighting between Gemayel's troops and Muslim forces in the deeply divided country.

MAIN EVENT (cont.) — The Government, shocked at the first assassination in Lebanese history of a person elected president, delayed confirming the death of the 34-year-old right-wing leader for nine hours.

CONSEQUENT EVENTS — All crossings between east and west Beirut were closed and panicky residents jammed gas stations and bakeries stocking up in fear a continued closure would lead to shortages of essential items.

An Israeli Army spokesman said the border between Israel and Lebanon was sealed off yesterday for all but military personnel, barring journalists and other civilians from crossing the frontier.

VERBAL REACTION — "With great pain I face this shocking news with the strongest denunciation for this criminal act," Prime Minister Chefik Wazzan said late Tuesday in an official statement about Gemayel's death.

President Elias Sarkis ordered seven days of official mourning and a state funeral yesterday in Gemayel's hometown of Bikfaya.

MAIN EVENT (cont.) — Six hours after the blast, Gemayel's mangled body was pulled from the rubble. Government sources said it could only be identified by his ring.

### PLOT

DIRECT ANTECEDENTS — Despite the charges of a plot, no one claimed responsibility for the blast.

Gemayel was elected over the protests of most Muslims, who remembered his role as the Phalangist military commander during the bitter 1975-76 civil war. — HISTORY

Twice before — in March 1979 and February 1980 — enemies tried to kill Gemayel with car bombs. The second blast killed his 18-month-old daughter.

"The news of the cowardly assassination ... is a shock to the American people and to civilised men and women everywhere," President Reagan said in a statement issued from the White House. — VERBAL REACTION 1

### CRIMINAL

VERBAL REACTION 2 — In Jerusalem, Israeli Prime Minister Menachem Begin cabled his condolences to Gemayel's father, Pierre, saying he was "shocked to the depths of my soul at the criminal assassination."

CONTEXT — US Mideast envoy Morris Draper yesterday met with Begin in Jerusalem and vowed to negotiate an Israeli and Syrian withdrawal from Lebanon despite complications caused by Gemayel's death.

Begin's Press spokesman, Uri Porath, said Begin and Draper agreed to work out a timetable for the withdrawal of all foreign forces from Lebanon.

VERBAL REACTION 3 — Meanwhile in Rome, PLO chairman Yasser Arafat yesterday urged Israel to "return to its senses" and negotiate for a peaceful settlement of the Middle East conflict.

In a 19-minute speech at the Inter-Parliamentary Union, boycotted by Israeli delegates, Arafat blamed Israel for the murder of Gemayel and called on the parliamentarians to set up a special panel to investigate Israel's "war crimes" in Lebanon. He accused Israel of trying to turn Lebanon into a "protectorate." — UPI, AP

shadowing' earlier events. These then may become mere causes, conditions or reasons for the later events. The constraint on this rule is of course that the latter event must also be of high news value, as is the case for the Israeli action. What we witness here is an aspect of the so-called *relevance structure* of the news text. The thematic structure represents a formal or subjective collection of topics, which each organize part of the meanings of the text. Yet, the news item may by various devices express or assign different relevance values to the topics of this hierarchy, e. g. by the headline, lead or linear order of the text. If we represent the thematic structure of the news item in the *Bangkok Post* in a schematic diagram (see Figure 1), we observe that the text need not follow the thematic structure form left to right, or even from top to bottom: the consequence of the assassination, viz. the invasion, is mentioned first and in the most prominent position (on top, in bold type). Thus, relevance may supersede thematic hierarchy. Yet, we have also observed that of a given topic, we *first* may expect the highest level information, as is also the case for the assassination.

Let us try to identify the other, lower level topics of the story, in their order of realization in the text, starting with the third paragraph, and taking each paragraph as a thematic unit:

(5) (a) Death of F. may lead to new fighting in Lebanon
 (b) The shocked government delayed the news
 (c) Residents panicked
 (d) The Israeli-Lebanese border was closed
 (e) Wazzan strongly denounced the murder
 (f) Sarkis announced official mourning and burial
 (g) Body of G. found hours later
 (h) No one took responsibility for the assassination
 (i) Moslems opposed Gemayel's election
 (j) There were earlier attacks against Gemayel
 (k) Reagan says the news is a shock for the American people
 (l) Begin cabled condolences to the father of Gemayel
 (m) Draper continued negotiations in Israel
 (n) Begin and Draper will work out time table for withdrawal
 (o) Arafat, in Rome, urged Israel to settle peacefully
 (p) Arafat accused Israel of the murder and of war crimes.

We see that the order of presentation of the themes is not only determined by thematic importance, but also by the principle of *recency* we have met above. We first find themes that are about immediate or delayed consequences of the assassination (themes a. through e): declarations of officials, reactions of the citizens. Only then we get more information about the main event itself: when and how the body was found, who could have done it, and only with topic (i) we arrive at the conditions and possible reasons or backgrounds of the assassination: controversial election and earlier attacks. All this information is still highly general. The story in the *Bangkok Post* is, as it were, itself a summary of the stories as they were provided by the news agencies (here UPI and AP). This article, for instance, merely specifies that

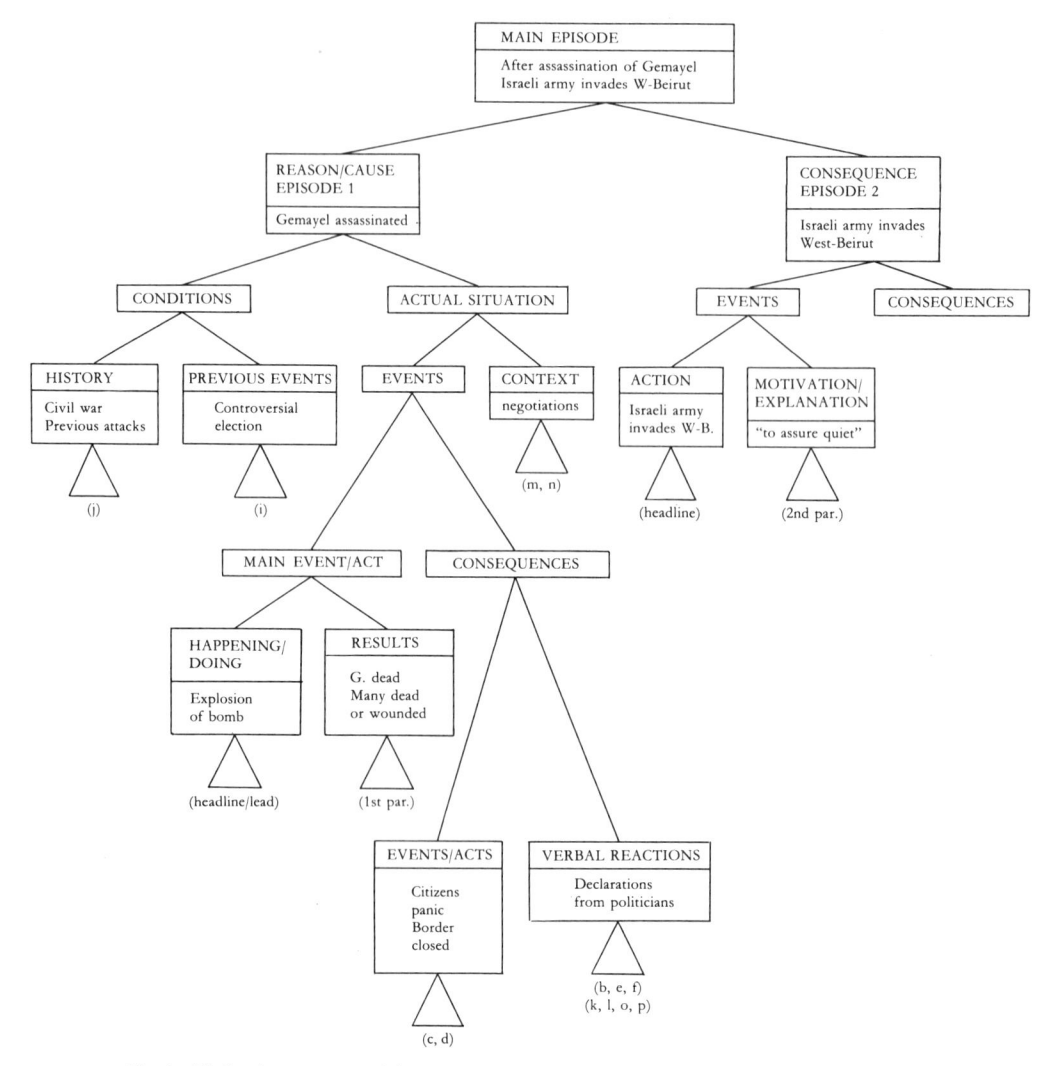

```
                          ┌─────────────────────────────┐
                          │        MAIN EPISODE         │
                          │ After assassination of Gemayel│
                          │ Israeli army invades W-Beirut│
                          └─────────────────────────────┘
                                ╱              ╲
                ┌──────────────┐              ┌──────────────┐
                │REASON/CAUSE  │              │CONSEQUENCE   │
                │EPISODE 1     │              │EPISODE 2     │
                │Gemayel assassinated│        │Israeli army invades│
                │              │              │West-Beirut   │
                └──────────────┘              └──────────────┘
```

Fig. 1: Thematic structure of the news item in the Bangkok Post. Topics in lower case, semantic categories in upper case. Letters refer to the topics listed in (5) on p. 20. Triangles indicate macrostructural organization of topics.

the Moslems "remembered his role as the Phalangist military commander during the bitter 1975–76 war", but does not specify what Gemayel actually did during the civil war, as many other newspapers do in their coverage of the assassination. Nor does the newspaper detail the political reasons for the opposition against Gemayel. The reader does not get such details, but can obviously reconstruct such details through specific knowledge about the situation in Lebanon obtained from previous press reports, that is, from a so-called *model of the situation* in memory. This model is the memory representation of accumulated experiences and information about a given situation as they were interpreted by an individual (van Dijk & Kintsch, 1983; van Dijk, 1984b). This model provides specifics, and the elements in the text may 'remind' (Schank, 1982) of information elements from the model. At the same time, the reader will of course activate more general knowledge and attitudes about civil wars, about Moslems or Christians, and about the possible atrocities committed during a civil war. This general, socially shared, script information is combined with actual, personal ('remembered') model information, and with the new information in the news text, to form a new model, namely about the actual events of the assassination and the invasion. At the same time, this new model may be used to *update* the previously existing, more general, model of the situation in Lebanon. Cognitively speaking, thus, the aim of reading a newspaper article is to construct a particular model of the situation or event the text is about, and through such a particular 'picture' of the actual situation, to update more general models. These, finally, may be used to form or change more abstract scripts or frames, e. g. about civil wars, international politics or specific actors, such as Israel or the USA in our example.

The themes of a news text are not only relevant in the construction of a general meaning structure of the text itself, its so-called 'text base' (Petöfi, 1971), but they also have an important role in the activation, the retrieval and the (trans-)formation of situation models in memory. In general, then, high level topics of a text, may also become high level 'topics' (macropropositions) in the representation of a model. And conversely, what we have represented as the high level 'definition of a situation' may be used to construct topics for a text. In our example, for instance, specific models about the Lebanese actions of the Israeli army, or attitudes about the Mid-East policy of the Israel government, may lead to a high level representation of the assassination not simply as a condition or reason for the Israeli action, but as a 'pretext' for control over West-Beirut. This is at least the overall evaluation of many newspapers and commentators.

When we inspect the other themes in the list given in (5) above, we see that as from theme (k), the focus again rests on the consequences of the assassination: declarations by important news actors (Begin, Reagan, Arafat), and further information about the actual political context of the whole event, viz. the negotiations about the withdrawal of foreign (Syrian, Israeli) troops from Lebanon.

If we compare this linear realization of the respective topics ot this text with the hierarchical structure given in Figure 1, we notice that the overall *strategy of news discourse production* proceeds according to the following moves or steps:

(i) Activate the *model of the actual situation*, as it has been formed by interpretation of other press reports, agency dispatches, and other knowledge and beliefs about the situation in Lebanon and the Middle East.
(ii) Derive an overall *thematic structure* from this situation model with the goal of expressing these themes through a news text (in a communicative context, for which the journalist also has a model, which we however ignore here).
(iii) Decide which of the main themes of the thematic structure are most *relevant* or important, given a system of news values, or other journalistic norms, routines or ideologies, such as recency, negativeness, elite persons, elite nations, etc.
(iv) Start actual production by expressing the relevant main theme as a headline, and the rest of the top structure of themes as the lead of the news item.
(v) Main themes about main events are, at a next lower level of macrostructure, formulated as the first sentences/paragraphs of the text.
(v) Each next paragraph deals with a next lower topic, according to the following production principles (writing strategies):
    a. Important consequences come first.
    b. Details of an event or actor come after overall mentioning of the event or person
    c. Causes or conditions of events are mentioned after the event and its consequences.
    d. Context and background information comes last.

Of course, the steps in this complex strategy are hypothetical and approximate only. They explain in cognitive terms what a journalist (must) do during the writing of a news text, and how this process results in the characteristic structures of a news item in the press. We find several central monitoring devices in this production process, viz. general *scriptal knowledge* and general *attitudes* or idelologies (including news values), general *models* of the situation, the *thematic structure* of the text to be produced about this situation, and finally a system of practical *production moves* that operate in the actual realization, linearization and expression of the themes. These controlling instances together define the *relevance structure* of the actual news item, for the journalist as well as for the reader. Since the thematic structure tells us what topics are more general, and which ones are more detailed, it also provides a ready-made organizational strategy for production: take high level themes first, and work from top to bottom, observing the relevance criteria. This means that in actual news texts we get, as it were, a cyclical delivery 'in installments' of each topic: first the top levels of each triangle (see Figure 1), and next the respective lower levels of each triangle, and apparently (at least for this example), going from right to left (consequences before events, events before conditions).

Note that these cognitive production strategies are rather different from the production of other than news stories. There, in principle, each topic is finished, starting with details (or an occasional initial summary, especially in everyday conversational stories (see Ehlich, ed. 1980; Quasthoff, 1980), and from left to right, that is from causes, conditions, circumstances or a setting to the actions or events themselves, with the results or consequences last (we ignore specific literary transormations here). As soon as news stories imitate this narrative pattern, in which linearity of thematic realization matches the linearity of the events, it is no longer the relevance criterion that plays a major role, but an esthetic, persuasive, or other principle, such as the creation of dramatic 'tension'. Some news reports about the assassination of Gemayel, for instance in popular mass newspapers (e. g. German *Bild Zeitung*), indeed have such a partially narrative organization (to which we come back in the next section).

We now have some insight into the formal and cognitive nature of themes or topics in (news) discourse, and into their hierarchical organization and their linear realization in a news item. We have found that several controlling principles are at work in the realization of a thematic structure in the text. Apparently, the realization depends on specific *semantic categories* for the organization of actions, events or situations, such as 'conditions', 'consequences', 'details', 'reasons', or 'participants'. This is indeed the case. The organizational concepts of the thematic structure appear to be useful in the production (and understanding) of news if we assume that 'consequences' come before 'conditions' according to a general recency principle. The same holds for the *specification* relations that relate macrostructures with microstructures, and hence with the actual words and sentences of the text. Whereas macrorules and macrostrategies derive topics from the local microstructures, specification operations work in the other direction. Given a topic, they 'elaborate' it. Again, this is not an arbitrary process, and especially in news articles, it appears to follow rather special constraints. Details of an action, for instance, are not necessarily given in their (chrono)logical order. In our example, we saw that the first paragraph first specifies the agent participants, then the time or date, then the instrument and its characteristics, then other participants (victims), and then an overall (assumed) consequence. The third paragraph gives further identification of the main participant, Gemayel, as a Maronite Christian, and further details about the 'sectarian violence' mentioned in the first paragraph: fighting between Gemayel's (Christian) troops and Moslem forces. This continues in the following paragraphs, each adding one detail to the representation we have about the main event, about Gemayel, about the political situation, about the consequences of the assassination and about the international reactions. In other words, the specification relations for a news theme follow a specific categorial 'track', in such a way that each category is cyclically treated in more or less detail (depending on the length of the article or the size of coverage): Main act, main participants, other participants, properties of main participants, properties of the event (time, place, circumstances), consequences, conditions, context, history, and again details of all these categories, in decreasing order of relevance. Further empirical research will be necessary to specify the exact rules or strategies involved in these 'inverse macro-operations' of specification and linear ordering of thematic realization in a news text.

The principles we have described for the strategic production of news discourse also hold for its strategic reading, comprehension and memorization by the reader. Headlines and leads are read and interpreted first and their formal or semantic information initiate a complex process of understanding (see van Dijk & Kintsch, 1983):

> (i) They are first recognized as newspaper headlines and leads, and thereby establish or confirm the communicative context model 'I am reading the newspaper', involving specific interests, goals and beliefs.
> (ii) They activate knowledge and beliefs about headlines and lead, e. g. as formal indicators of importance, and this importance may be 'taken over' (or not).
> (iii) Their underlying propositions activate and instantiate relevants scripts and models from memory. After activation, and given the parameters of the communicative context (time, occasion, interests, goals), such scripts, attitudes and models provide the basis for the decision 'I am (not) interested in having information about this topic or issue'.
> (iv) They indicate or express relevant macrotopics, which may be strategically used to build the highest levels of the text base and particular situation model for this article. This provisional high level topic(s) may be used as top down monitoring device for the comprehension and organization of the rest of the text (see Kozminsky, 1977).
> (v) First paragraphs are used to build full macropropositions, to confirm (or reject) the initial macro-assumptions of the reader, and to further extend the macrostructure and the model of the text. The same happens for the further paragraphs, which provide lower level details of the global meaning.
> (vi) The discontinuous delivery of topics in the news text can be strategically brought under control by the monitoring function of the central topics, the hierarchical structure of the themes, and the semantic categories (e. g. 'cause' or 'consequence') of sub-topics. That is, a 'scrambled' topic structure can be 'unscrambled' again by the thematic structure.

Although these theoretical assumptions are based on empirical work about other types of text, we still have to find out experimentally whether indeed they also hold for news discourse comprehension (see Thorndyke, 1979).

## 5. *News schemata*

Having discussed the macrosemantics of news discourse, we now turn to the macrosyntax. That is, we assume that news items also have a conventional *form*, a schema that organizes the overall content. To distinguish such a global form of organization from (semantic) macrostructures, we use the theoretical term *superstructures*, but for ease of reference we also simply use the more general term 'schema'.

The notion of 'schema' has a long tradition in psychology, where it was used by Bartlett (1932) to denote organization of knowledge in memory. This notion was picked up again in the 1970s to denote knowledge clusters that above were called 'scripts' or which Minsky (1975) called 'frames' (Norman & Rumelhart, eds. 1975). Such knowledge structures also extend to what people know about the organization of action or specific discourse types, such as stories (Rumelhart, 1975). Following suggestions from structural poetics, semiotics, and linguistics, it was proposed that such story schemata can be described by some kind of 'grammar', viz. a *story grammar* (Mandler, 1978). Much like a linguistic grammar specifying syntactic structures, such a story grammar consists of (i) a set of characteristic categories, and (ii) a set of formation rules, which specify the linear and hierarchical ordering of the categories in a 'well-formed' narrative structure. Since the end of the 1970s, a rather fierce debate has been developing about the formal and empirical adequacy of such story grammars (Black & Wilensky, 1979; van Dijk, ed. 1980; Wilensky, 1983 and commentaries). The idea of a story grammar was especially critized by researchers in Artificial Intelligence. They argued that, apart from formal problems, story grammars were superfluous: story structures could simply be accounted for in terms of action structures, that is, with terms such as 'plan' or 'goal'.

This is not the place to discuss the details of this debate. In fact, both approaches have much in common, e.g. because also the story grammars feature action theoretical terms. And both directions of research lack important theoretical distinctions. Thus, we should carefully distinguish between the structure of action and the structure of *action discourse*. Since stories are a special type of action discourse (and not each action discourse is a story), it should be borne in mind that people's description of human actions is not necessarily organized in the way actions are organized. To wit, natural stories in conversation often feature a kind of summary, which is of course not a property we find in action sequences such a story is about. Next, both in AI approaches and in story grammars, no systematic distinction is made between the global, overall description of a story, and its local description in terms of sentences or propositions.

Therefore, we assume that superstructures or schemata of stories can be explicitly described in terms of conventional categories and rules (or strategies). Yet, such categories and rules do not operate on a local, but on a global level. The categories, thus, pertain to global meaning units, that is, to macropropositions or themes, and must have a conventional nature. They must parse a natural story into units that are typical for stories in our culture. If stories always begin with a summary, for instance, it makes sense to introduce the conventional category of Summary as part of the narrative structure. In several branches of discourse analysis, such categories for global formal units have been often proposed. Thus, Labov & Waletzky (1967), already suggested that natural stories feature such categories as Orientation, Complication, Resolution, Evaluation and Coda (see also Labov, 1972).

This is exactly what we want to do for news discourse. Whatever the contents, and therefore independent of local and global meanings of news discourse, we assume that there is a fixed, conventional schema, consisting of categories that are typical (at least in part) for news discourse. Each category must correspond to a specific sequence of propositions or sentences of the text. The order of categories, as it is specified by the rules, therefore also determines the overall ordering of the respective sequences or episodes (van Dijk, 1982).

News schemata, due to their conventional nature, are at least implicitly known by their users in an given culture, that is by journalists and readers. Obvious categories for such a news schema are for instance *Headline* and *Lead* (initial capitals are used to signal the use of superstructure categories). Since in our culture practically all news discourses are headed by a Headline, we may take Headline as the first, opening category of the schema. Many newspapers, however, do not have a separate Lead, marked by bold type, so that that category is optional. In Figure 2 we have tried to represent these and the other categories to be discussed here.

Much like syntactic structures of sentences, also schemata of texts may have specific *semantic constraints*. That is, we may not simply insert *any* (macro-)proposition into each category. This is also the case for Headline and Lead, as we have seen before. They both directly express the highest level macropropositions of the news discourse. Together, then, they function as a

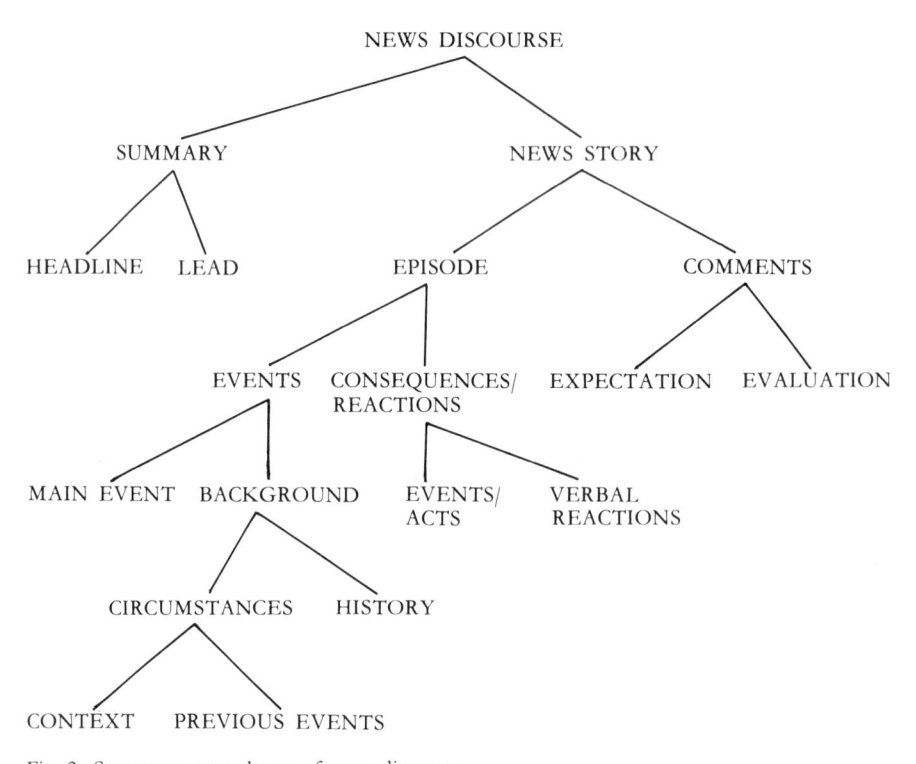

```
                          NEWS DISCOURSE
                         /              \
                   SUMMARY              NEWS STORY
                   /     \              /         \
            HEADLINE   LEAD      EPISODE         COMMENTS
                                  /    \          /      \
                              EVENTS  CONSEQUENCES/  EXPECTATION  EVALUATION
                              /   \    REACTIONS
                             /     \      /    \
                      MAIN EVENT  BACKGROUND  EVENTS/  VERBAL
                                    /    \    ACTS   REACTIONS
                                   /      \
                            CIRCUMSTANCES  HISTORY
                              /      \
                             /        \
                       CONTEXT    PREVIOUS EVENTS
```

Fig. 2: Superstructure schema of news discourse

summary for the news discourse, and we therefore group them together under the higher level category of *Summary*. We have noticed above that such Summaries can also be found in everyday, conversational stories (Quasthoff, 1980). Similarly, syntactic categories may be related to specific phonological constraints, such as stress and intonation. The same holds for Headline and Lead, but then in relation to graphical lay-out: they are printed 'on top', 'first', in large, bold type and if there are more columns, across several columns. These 'expression' rules, of course, may be somewhat different for each culture or newspaper.

Other well-known news categories are for instance *Background* and quotations, which we will call *Verbal Reactions*. Background must dominate those portions of the text in which information is given which is not as such part of the actual news events, but provides general, historical, political or social context or conditions of these events. Then, we should of course not forget to introduce a category that dominates the description of these very news events, which we may call *Main Event*. And, to remind readers of what 'happened before' (and hence to activate their relevant situation model), we often find a category of *Previous Events*. In our analysis of the news item from the *Bangkok Post*, next, we found that due to a recency principle, news has special attention for results or consequences of events. Therefore, we introduce the general category of *Consequences*, which may organize all those events that are described as being caused by the Main Event. The same article showed that sometimes there is not just one main event, but several. In formal terms, this means that the category of Main Event is *recursive*: it may be repeated (at least theoretically) $n$ times, much in the same way as the syntactic category of Adjective is recursive ('A big, high, beautiful ... tree'). A slightly different way of ordering Main Events, is to consider them, not as an arbitrary series, but as one coherent unit, e.g. as an *Episode*, for which for instance certain semantic constraints hold. The first Main Event of an Episode in that case might require to be filled with a theme which is a cause or condition of the theme to be filled by the second Main Event of an Episode. (Notice that formal categories of schema do not themselves have such meaning relations as 'cause' or 'consequence' among each other. This is only the case for the themes or macropropositions that are inserted into the slots of the schema).

At the end of a news article, we often find a *Comment* section, containing conclusions, expectations, speculations, and other information — often from the journalist — about the events. Like several other categories of the schema, this category is of course optional: we also have a well-formed news article without such Comments.

Finally, there is a complex *Background* category to attend to. We may leave it unanalyzed, and insert here all macropropositions that summarize portions (episodes) of the text that are not about the main news event(s) or their consequences. Yet, there are various types of background, and we assume provisionally that they can be routinely dinstinguished — at least by professionals. Thus, we have *History* as the category that organizes all news information of a general historical nature: events in the past that are indirectly related with the present situation or events. In our example of the assassination of Gemayel, information about the civil war in Lebanon is a good example. Such information provides a historical perspective to the *whole* of the actual situation, and hence only indirectly to a specific event in the actual situation, viz. the assassination. History is different from Previous Events, because the latter category is about a specific event, which rather directly precedes the actual main events, and which may be taken as a cause or direct condition of the actual events. And finally, we may use the category of *Context* to organize information about this actual situation we just mentioned, and in which the actual main event is a significant element. Thus, the negotations of Draper about Lebanon form the actual political context of the assassination of Gemayel.

Although it is possible to provide rather strict theoretical specifications for these various background categories, their application to concrete texts may sometimes be less easy, especially if there is only little and highly integrated background information. In that case, history, previous events and context might merge. In our example, for instance, the information about the election of Gemayel might be taken as Previous Events, viz. as those events that are recent and that probably are a direct condition or even cause of the actual assassination. Yet, the election (and therefore also the new election after Gemayel's death) might also be taken as Context, viz. as 'controversy about the presidency of Lebanon'. Similarly, the previous attacks against Gemayels life could be seen als Previous Events, and in that case the actual assassination is represented simply as the third attack in a row. But, since they occurred much earlier, and as part of the aftermath of the civil war, they might also be seen as History. These difficulties of categorial assigment, and hence of pratical analysis, are not serious however. They just show that also schematic superstructures may have some ambiguity, and depend on the formal or personal interpretation of the information in the text. It is however important that we *in principle* can make such distinctions, because they may be relevant for some type of news text, even when in other news texts some of the categories are absent, may merge or allow 'ambiguous' assignments.

*Rules and strategies*

Now we have informally introduced the tentative categories of a news schema, we should of course also know how they are *ordered*. After all, the ordering of the categories must also determine the ordering of information in the text, such as the sequential realization of topics as we discussed it in the previous section. Some of the ordering principles are straightforward and have been discussed above. Thus, Summary (Headline and Lead) always come first, and Comments mostly last. Then, it may be assumed that most news texts start with Main Event after the Summary. Analysis of empirical data form many newspapers from many countries shows that this is indeed the case (van Dijk, 1984a, 1986). The information about the bomb attack against Gemayel (time, location, instrument, circumstances) usually opens the 'body' of the text. Next, various background categories may appear in the text, such as History or Context. For theoretical reasons, we assume that Previous Events and Context are 'closer' to the Main Events and therefore should preferably follow the Main Event category, and this is indeed often the case. Yet, the rules are much less strict in this case. We may also have History first and Context later. Ordering, thus, is optional in this case. Verbal reactions are usually ordered toward the end of the article, before Comments, as we also find in the *Bangkok Post* article (which has no comment section at the end).

From these few indications about ordering rules, we may conclude that some rules are fairly strict and general, whereas others have a much more optional nature, being no more than 'preferences', which may differ from culture to culture, newspaper to newspaper, journalist to journalist. In that case, the formal rules are no longer algorithmic, but become variable (as many sociolinguistic rules are, see Sankoff, 1980), or even expedient strategies (van Dijk & Kintsch, 1983). We touch upon well-known problems of linguistic theory here, such as the distinction between formal rule systems and the actual and variable *uses* of such systems. From our cognitivistic point of view, there is no real problem, however. Both rules and strategies have a cognitive nature, and language users may use both fixed rules as they are shared in a community, more variable rules, and context bound, goal-directed strategies in the production and understanding of discourse. We already discussed the possibility that relevance principles may affect the final structure of a news item. This means that categories that usually come toward the end of a news item, such as Verbal Reactions, Comments or Consequences, may be placed in an earlier position if the information in such categories is sufficiently relevant. In formal terms, such permutations or deplacements can be described as *transformations* of a (canonical) schema. Thus, in general, relevance transformations involve fronting of categories.

A much more interesting and difficult problem problem, however, is the characteristic *discontinuous* ordering of news discourse. In the previous sections, it was already observed that themes in the news may be delivered 'in installments'. Details about the Main Event of the assassination of Gemayel may be given throughout the text, in decreasing degrees of relevance or specification. Since themes are the contents of news category slots, this implies that also the categories themselves are realized discontinuously in the text. Indeed, Main Event will open the body of the news story, but the category will 'come back' in the rest of the story. Similarly, early in the article we may already find some fragments of Comments or Verbal Reactions (see also the *Bangkok Post* article). This problem is serious because the schema not only should tell us what categorial functions themes in the news may have, but also in what conventional or canonical order they appear. The theoretical intricacies of this problem cannot be discussed in detail here. We assume that both the thematic and the schematic structure of a news discourse have an abstract nature. That is, independent of the actual *realization* of these structures, they represent the themes and their interrelations, and the typical news functions (categories) these themes may have in the text. In actual production, other constraints begin to operate, such as relevance, recency, and maybe others. This means that the news schema becomes the input (one input among other knowledge and principles) to *production strategies*. These strategies tell the writer which themes, and which categories should come first, and *how much* information from each theme or category. If we now use the news schema in Figure 2 as part of a production strategy, we should not merely realize the text from left to right, but also from top to bottom *within* each category. That is, first the highest level information of Main Event, then maybe the highest information in Consequences, then high level information of History or Context, and so on, and then reverting back to lower level information of Main Event, and similarly for the next categories. Such a strategy can operate easily because the terminal contents of each category have a macrostructural organization: we need only 'read off' the top levels from each topic to know which information is most 'general' and therefore which information should come first. This is also the strategy followed by *readers* in their recall of texts: high level macro-propositions are recalled first and best (van Dijk & Kintsch, 1983).

Our last few remarks suggest that a purely formal, structuralistic approach to news schemata has its limitations. It allows us to specify fixed, canonical structures of news, but hardly the many variations and the context-dependent strategies. It does not account for the interaction of several constraints that work 'at the same time', such as themes, (partial) schemes, relevance and recency principles. These have a cognitive nature, and the actual structure of news discourse should therefore be characterized in terms of all the information that goes into the strategies of production. Relevance decisions have some general, shared conditions (such as the news values of journalists), but also more specific constraints which derive from the knowledge of the actual situation, and hence from our models. The assassination of Gemayel is not only important, and the theme not only relevant in news discourse about such an event, because it is a violent (negative) event, a crime and directed against an elite person, as the news values would specifiy for selection or attention. It is also the special political situation in Lebanon, and the role of the president in restoring order in that country, which makes *this* assassination so prominent. Moreover, it fits a pre-established pattern that organizes the model of journalists about the situation in Lebanon and the Middle East (violence, factional strife, international conflict, etc.). And because the assassination fits this known pattern, it is also easier to 'see' and 'interpret' as a news event, and therefore can be assigned more importance and higher relevance. Only a cognitive model can account for all these complex constraints. Not only text production 'as such' is involved, but also the uses of scripts and models, the socio-political interpretation of news events, and the institutional constraints and routines of newspapers in the transformation of news events into news discourses. A cognitive approach can embody and integrate these various constraints and information types, both for the journalist and for the reader. It explains production processes, and also the results of such processes in actual new structures. The same holds for processes of understanding, which we discussed for themes in section 4 (see Findahl & Höijer, 1981; Höijer & Findahl, 1984; van Dijk & Kintsch, 1983; van Dijk, 1986). In line with the findings in the cognitive psychology of stories, for instance, we assume that text schemata facilitate comprehension, storage and retrieval from memory. And despite the negative results in some experimental work (e.g. Thorndyke, 1979, who didn't use proper news schemata), we assume that both the thematic structure and the schema of news help the reader to organize information in memory, which is a primary condition for (better) recall and use of that information.

If news schemata are professionally known and shared they also will facilitate production of news. They organize the sometimes bewildering complexity of news themes, and allow the journalist to strategically search his/her memory, or 'outside' information bases, such as documentation services. Indeed, journalists may routinely look or ask for (more) 'background' about a news event, and thereby show that such a category is canonically expected to occur in the news item. The same may hold for other social news production routines and their relation with the cognitive processes of news writing.

*6. Conclusions*

In this chapter we have made proposals for the systematic analysis of news structures in the press, focusing especially on global structures such as topics or themes, and superstructural schemata. From a brief survey of some studies about news in the last decade, we concluded that few work is specifically concerned with the structures of news discourse per se. Most research has a sociological bias, and deals with professional routines, institutional control, or with news ideologies. Some microsociological approaches and a few recent linguistic studies, however, come closer to an account of the meanings and forms of news. A discourse analytical orientation may integrate such different directions of research.

The global analysis of news discourse deals with higher level structures, which extend beyond the study of individual words or sentences. In this chapter, we distinguished between global meanings or topics, accounted for in terms of semantic macrostructures, on the one hand, and formal schemata, accounted for in terms of superstructures, on the other. It was shown how themes and schemata are related in news discourse. One typical property of both is for instance that they are realized discontinuously throughout the news text. News schemata are defined with the help of conventional news categories, such as Summary, Main Event and Background, and their respective sub-categories. It was finally shown that to account for the actual structures of news, in which principles of relevance and recency also play an important role, a cognitive and strategic orientation should be given to the formulation of theme and schema uses in news discourse. This cognitive approach also provides the link with the social constraints of news production (routines, news values, and ideologies).

*Bibliography*

Abel, Elie (ed.). (1981). *What's news. The media in American society*. San Francisco: Institute for Contemporary Studies.
Altheide, David L. (1974). *Creating reality. How TV news distorts reality*. Beverly Hills, Ca: Sage.
Bagdikian, Ben H. (1971). *The information machines*. New York: Harper and Row.
Barrett, Marvin. (1978). *Rich news, poor news*. New York: Crowell.
Bartlett, F. C. (1932). *Remembering*. London: Cambridge U.P.
Black, John B. & Wilensky, Robert (1979). An evaluation of story grammars. *Cognitive Science* 3, 213–229.
Blumler, Jay G. & Katz, Elihu, eds. (1974). *The uses of mass communications*. Beverly Hills, Ca: Sage.
Boyd-Barret, Oliver (1980). *The international press agencies*. London: Sage/Constable.
Cohen, Stanley & Young, Jock, eds. (1981). *The manufacture of news. Deviance, social problems and the mass media*. London: Sage/Constable.
Curran, James (ed.). (1978). *The British Press: A Manifesto*. London: Methuen.
Davis, Howard & Walton, Paul, eds. (1983). *Language. Image. Media*. Oxford: Blackwell.
Diamond, Edwin (1978). *Good news, bad news*. Cambridge, Mass.: MIT Press.
Downing, John (1980). *The media machine*. London: Pluto Press.
van Dijk, Teun A. (1980). *Macrostructures*. Hillsdale, NJ: Erlbaum.
van Dijk, Teun A. (1982). Episodes as units of discourse analysis. In: D. Tannen, ed. *Analyzing discourse: Text and talk*. Washington, DC: Georgetown UP., 177–195.
van Dijk, Teun A. (1984a). *Structures of international news. A case study of the world's press*. Report for Unesco. University of Amsterdam. Dept. of General literary studies. Section of Discourse Studies.
van Dijk, Teun A. (1984b). Episodic models in discourse processing. In: R. Horowitz & S. J. Samuels, (eds.) *Comprehending oral and written language*. New York: Academic Press.
van Dijk, Teun A. (1986). *News as discourse*. New York: Longman.
van Dijk, Teun A. (ed.). (1980). *Story comprehension. Poetics* 8, nrs. 1–3 (special issue).
van Dijk, Teun A. & Kintsch, Walter (1983). *Strategies of discourse comprehension*. New York: Academic Press.
Ehlich, Konrad (ed.). (1980). *Erzählen im Alltag*. Frankfurt: Suhrkamp.
Epstein, Jay (1973). *News from nowhere*. New York: Random House.
Findahl, Olle & Höijer, Birgitta (1981). Studies of news from the point of view of human comprehension. In G. Cleveland Wilhoit & Harold de Bock, eds. *Mass Communication Review Yearbook*. Vol. 2. Beverly Hills, Ca.: Sage, 393–403.
Fishman, Mark (1980). *Manufacturing the news*. Austin, Tx: University of Texas Press.

Fowler, Roger, Hodge, Bob, Kress, Gunther, Trew, Tony. 1979. *Language and control*. London: Routledge & Kegan Paul.
Gans, Herbert J. (1979). *Deciding what's news*. New York: Pantheon Books.
Glasgow University Media Group. (1976). *Bad News*. London: Routledge & Kegan Paul.
Glasgow University Media Group (1980). *More bad news*. London: Routledge & Kegan Paul.
Glasgow University Media Group (1982). *Really bad news*. London: Writers and readers.
Golding, Peter & Elliott, Philip (1979). *Making the news*. London: Longman.
Gurevitch, M., Bennett, T., Curran, J. & Woollacott, J. (eds.). (1982). *Culture, Society and the Media*. London: Methuen.
Hall, Stuart, et al., eds. (1980). *Language, culture, media*. London: Hutchinson.
Hartley, John (1982). *Understanding news*. London: Methuen.
Hartman, Paul, & Husband, Charles (1974). *Racism and the mass media*. London: Davis-Poynter.
Höijer, Birgitta, & Findahl, Olle (1984). *Nyheter, Forståelse, och minne*. Ph. D. Diss. Stockholm: Studentlitteratur.
Jones, Linda Kay (1977). *Theme in English expository discourse*. Lake Bluff, Ill.: Jupiter Press.
Knorr-Cetina, K. & Cicourel, A. V. (eds.). (1981). *Advances in social theory and methodology. Towards an integration of micro- and macrosociologies*. London: Routledge and Kegan Paul.
Kniffka, Hannes (1980). *Soziolinguistik und empirische Textanalyse. Schlagzeilen und Leadformulierungen in amerikanischen Tageszeitungen*. Tübingen: Niemeyer.
Kozminsky, Ely (1977). Altering Comprehension: the effects of biasing titles on text comprehension. *Memory and Cognition* 5, 482—490.
Kress, Guenther & Hodge, Robert (1979). *Language as ideology*. London: Routledge and Kegan Paul.
Labov, William (1972). The transformation of experience in narrative syntax. In W. Labov, *Language in the inner city*. Philadelphia, Pa: University of Pennsylvania Press, 354—396.
Labov, William, & Waletzky, Joshua (1967). Narrative analysis: Oral versions of personal experience. In J. Helm, ed. *Essays on the verbal and visual arts*. Seattle, Washington: Washington University Press, 12—44.
Lüger, Heinz-Helmut (1983). *Pressesprache*. Tübingen: Niemeyer.
Mandler, Jean (1978). A code in the node: The use of story schema in retrieval. *Discourse Processes* 1, 14—35.
Minsky, Marvin (1975). A framework for representing knowledge. In P. Winston, ed. *The psychology of computer vision*. New York: McGraw-Hill.
Norman, Donald A. & Rumelhart, David E. (eds.). (1975). *Explorations in Cognition*. San Francisco: Freeman.
Petöfi, János S. (1971). *Transformationsgrammatiken und eine ko-textuelle Texttheorie*. Stuttgart: Athenaeum.
Quasthoff, Uta M. (1980). *Erzählen in Gesprächen*. Tübingen: Narr.
Roshco, Bernard (1975). *Newsmaking*. Chicago: University of Chicago Press.
Rumelhart, David (1975). Notes on a schema for stories. In Daniel G. Bobrow & Allan Collins, (eds.) *Representation and Understanding*. New York: Academic Press. 211—236.
Sankoff, G. (1980). *The social life of language*. Philadelphia, Pa.: University of Pennsylvania Press.
Schank, Roger (1982). *Dynamic Memory*. Cambridge, Cambridge U. P.
Schank, Roger C. & Abelson, Robert P. (1977) *Scripts, Plans, Goals, and Understanding*. Hillsdale, NJ: Erlbaum.
Schlesinger, Philip. (1978). *Putting 'reality' together*. BBC News. London: Constable.
Strassner, E. (1981). *Fernsehnachrichten*. Tübingen: Niemeyer.
Strassner, E. (ed.). (1975). *Nachrichten*. Munich: Fink.
Thorndyke, Perry W. (1979). Knowledge acquisition from newspaper stories. *Discourse Processes*, 2, 95—112.
Tuchman, Gaye (1978). *Making news*. New York: Free Press.
Tunstall, Jeremy (1971). *Journalists at work*. London: Constable.
Wilensky, Robert (1983). Story grammars versus story points. *The Behavioral and Brain Sciences* 6, 579—624.

KIM B. ROTZOLL

# Advertisements

*Basic elements*

Advertisements as discourse must first be recognized as paid, nonpersonal communication forms used by identified sources through various media with persuasive intent. As "paid" communication forms, then, they are different from common variaties of publicity (e. g. a press release), or "public relations" (e. g. a news conference), which are often covered by the media without charge. By "nonpersonal" they are distinguished from forms of personal salesmanship occuring in business establishments or door—to—door. The advertiser is "identified", which again sets this form of persuasive communication apart from various types of promotion and publicity in the form of "news" or "feature" material often carried by the media but supplied by a particular source whose intent is often persuasive (e. g. a "consumer information" specialist on a TV talk show who in fact works for an appliance company). Advertisements are most commonly associated with the "mass media" of newspapers, magazines, cinema, television, and radio, although they frequently flourish in other forms such as billboards, posters, and direct mail as well. And, finally, advertisements are overwhelmingly used with persuasive intent. That is, the advertisers are striving to alter behavior and/or our levels of awareness, knowledge, attitutde and so on in a manner that would be beneficial to them.

Advertising today is a world-wide phenomenon, with the heaviest concentration in the United States. It is important at the outset to recognize that many advertisers use advertisements for many purposes with many different possible effects. For example, within a given country it is common to find what might be considered highly fanciful advertising for consumer goods such as toothpaste, detergents, or soft drinks, and highly technical messages dealing with construction equipment, medial supplies, or computer services. The advertisers themselves can include huge multinational firms, special interest groups, local shop keepers and individuals. Their intents can range from altering behavior to affecting the way people think about a particular social or economic position. The results of their efforts can range from enormously influential to a waste of the advertiser's money. It is not, then, a subject that lends itself to oversimplification.

*The Forms of Advertising*

A very basic sweep of advertising's many faces would reveal at least eight basic forms. They are:

— *Advertising by producers of consumer goods to reach individuals.* This is often called "general" or "national" advertising, because it involves advertising from a single company (the "producer" of the good or service) to an audience over a large geographic area — a region, or perhaps an entire country. Media used may be magazines, radio, television, newspapers, outdoor, cinema, direct mail, transit, etc. The purpose is generally to attempt to encourage preference for a particular brand. (An example would be a typical advertisement for Coca-Cola.)

— *Advertising by producers of consumers goods to reach retailers and wholesalers.* The same companies that attempt to reach individual consumers also often advertise to retailers to encourage them to stock the product that the retailers would then sell to individuals. This is often a very important form of advertising, frequently combined with personal selling, because the competition for retailer "shelf space" is quite strong. Media used would include direct mail and hihgly specialized "trade" magazines such as *Drug Topics, Supermarket News, Farm Supplier,* etc. (An example would be a Tylenol ad directed to supermarket managers.)

— *Advertising by producers of business goods and services to other business.* The makers of goods and services used by other businesses (e. g., fire extinguishers, machine tools, file cabinets, computer systems, basic chamicals, electronic components, etc.) advertise to them in an attempt to secure sales for their particualar brand. Thus, a glass producer may advertise to car manufacturers to use their glass in making the cars the companies sell, while a supplier of typewriters will advertise to businesses to attempt to secure purchase for the companies' *own* uses — *not* for resale. Media used could include direct mail, highly specialized magazines, and newsletters — e. g., *Hydraulics and Pneumatics, Air & Cosmos, Revista Aerea Latinoamerica.* (An example would be Caterpillar Tractor's advertising in a construction trade paper.)

— *Advertising by producers for "public relations" purposes to individuals, special interest groups, and their own employees.* This increasingly prevalent type of advertising is meant to influence key "publics" (e. g. government, the financial community, employees, etc.) on matters of concern to the firm. Consumer and business media are used. (An example would be Mobil Oil's advertising seeking to influence public opinion on a host of energy-related issues.)

— *Advertising by producers of consumer and/or business goods and services in international distribution.* Marketing today is increasingly of a multinational character. So firms distributing their products and services to countries other than their own increasingly utilize advertising to influence appropriate audiences. International giants such as Unilever, Phillips, General Motors, and Procter and Gamble advertise to consumer *and* business audiences around the world. (An example would be a counter card advertising Pepsi—Cola in Russia.)

— *Advertising by retailers to individual consumers.* Retail advertising is among the oldest forms. It emphasizes patronage of a particular store and uses media that reach generally limited geographic areas. Unlike "general" advertising, the message is usually not "Buy this brand" but "Buy *here*." Often the appeal is one of price. (An example woulde be a "sale" advertisement run by a department store in a local newspaper.)

— *Advertising of individuals to other individuals.* Many of the newspapers and magazines around the world carry "classified" advertising, where individuals are attempting to persuade others to buy or trade. This is perhaps the closest modern form of advertising to the traditional "market" or "casbah" where goods and services were bought, sold, or traded between individuals. (An example would be an individual running a small classified advertisement to attempt to sell their bicycle.)

— *Advertising of governments, social institutions, and special interest groups.* This final classification can encompass everything from the Russian government attempting to encourage domestic margarine consumption, to an English labor union attempting to influence the government's position on their strike. In virtually every country this is a growing area for advertising, ranging from "public service" to far more controversial subjects involving abortion or national energy policy. (An example would be the advertising of Population Services International in an attempt to encourage family planning in Sri Lanka.)

*Factors Explaining the Forms of Advertising*

To begin to understand any given advertisement, then, one must first attempt to understand its purpose. It is clear that the intent of, say, an individual attempting to sell a refrigerator through a classified ad does not lend itself to easy comparsion with a multinational corporation attempting to secure brand preference for a snack food with a multimillion dollar budget. We can, then, begin to have some general understanding of advertisements by placing them in one of the eight basic forms just discussed. Each, as mentioned, has *general* purposes, media, and audiences in common.

But, clearly, all retailer advertisements are not alike, nor all messages from multinational firms, etc. In order to clarify still further, it is necessary to realize that any advertiser, from an individual to the loftiest corporate enterprise, confronts both non-controllable (external) and controllable (internal) factors in the potential use of advertising. It is with these conceptual tools, then, that we can begin to understand advertisements as a form of discourse with somewhat greater precision.

*Non controllable (external) factors.* The most obvious external factor is the socio-economic system in which the advertiser finds himself. Generally, advertisements in their total range of forms and functions are found in countries with market economies. Here there is general reliance on individual initiative as a form of resource allocation, thus providing ample room for the self interests of sellers to manifest themselves in advertisements as well as other forms of business initiative. There is, of course, no totally "free" market in the classic *lassiez-faire* sense, but is it clear that, in spite of various regulations and guidelines, the advertiser in the United States has considerable more latitude in media choice, subject matter, and tone than a counterpart in Russia.

Even in countries with relatively similar economic systems, however, there are still often striking differences in the regulations of particular forms (e. g. whether advertising to children is permitted, the advertising of cigarettes, alcoholic beverages, etc.) and media (e. g. no advertising accepted in the broadcast media, or limited to particular time segments, etc.).

One is advised, then, to approach advertisements with some understanding of the expectations of advertising in that particular *culture*. These expectations are, of course, closely aligned with the more general "world view" of the country regarding such fundamental assumptions as the "rationality" of man, the relationship of the individual and the state, etc. Given different assumptions about these core beliefs, advertising's role can be perceived quite differently.

Advertisers are often quite powerless to affect many other factors that may strongly influence the opportunities for their successful use of advertising. The most obvious within a culture is the complexity of the individual. Potential receivers of a typical advertisement are themselves influenced by myriad external (e. g. the presence or absence of other people, the weather, the physical environment) and internal (past experiences, attitudes, the state of health) at any given moment, thus making the probability of successful communication at any given time chancy at best. Advertisers must, as we shall see, make certain assumptions about the particular combination of these factors when they prepare their advertisements. Given the host of potential influences on individual behavior in the absence of, or in addition to, advertising, then, this factor explains one of the most important characteristics of contemporary advertising — the uncertainty of its outcome.

Other non-controllable factors could include changes in the age of the population (e. g. a decline in the birth rate affects the "market" for baby clothes), occupational shifts (e. g. the vast increase in the percentage of working women assures a better reception of advertisements for time-saving products and services), and genereal social norms (e. g. the so-called "sexual revolution" in the United States has resulted in more explicit sexual tone in advertisements as well as more advertising in formerly taboo areas such as birth control products).

General economic conditions affect the opportunities for advertisements (e. g. in inflationary times individuals may tend to redefine "necessities" and "luxuries"), as do geographic factors (e. g. urban-suburban-rural population shifts suggest changing life styles with corresponding interest or disinterest in certain classes of products and services).

Advances in technology also present and withdraw advertising opportunities, (e. g. the invention and virtually universal acceptance of television not only opened a new advertising medium, but drastically changed recreational patterns; the refinement of the computer "micro-processor" has made possible a host of video games, home computer systems, digital watches, pocket calculators and the like, while severely altering the market for conventional watches, adding machines, slide rules, etc.)

Note that none of the factors discussed here as external factors are readily controlled by the advertiser. Rather the opportunities (or limitations) of advertising certain kinds of products and services in certain kinds of ways using certain kinds of media are affected. Thus, to analyze any given advertisement, one needs to ask "What are the non-controllable factors that this message is attempting to respond to?"

*Controllable (internal) factors*, include such questions as: What will be produced? At what price? Where will it be distributed? How will it be promoted? Logically, the kinds of products and services that are offered are determined in part by the "external" factors just discussed. For example, as gasoline prices rise to more typical "world" levels, Americans are now being offered more and more gas-efficient cars. Soccer can readily be promoted in many countries of the world, whereas it is still somewhat difficult to "sell" in the United States. So-called "convenience" foods may be eagerly received in some countries, but in others may be considered wasteful and extra vagant.

Clearly, how a product or service is priced affects how advertising is used, if it is used at all. In some countries, "generic" brands use little or no advertising and rely on very low prices. In some cases advertising can be used to promote prices (e. g. in typical grocery store or discount store advertising), but in others (particularly with many consumer goods sold by manufactures), advertising is used to *avoid* price competition — to suggest, implicitly or explicitly, that the *brand* rather than the price should be the deciding factor (e. g. with many virtual parity products such as cigarettes, beers, soaps, etc., as well as generally regarded "status" products such as liquor, certain types of clothing, cosmetics, etc.).

Where a product or service is offered can, of course, affect the extent of advertising as well as its content. If a product is distributed "nationally," then certain types of media (e. g. network television) and certain types of appeals (e. g. somewhat more heterogeneous to span regional differences) are more likely to be used than with local distribution (e. g. with newspapers and more localized appeal).

Advertising is not, of course, the only form of promotion available to a firm or individual. Personal selling may be far more effective than advertising with many business or technical products and services (e. g. computer systems), and some types of sales promotions (e. g. contests, "point-of-purchase" signs) may be used with (or instead of) advertising.

Thus, the choices that individuals or firms have open to them in a general attempt to respond to (and influence) non-controllable factors affect whether advertising will or will not play an important role. As we have seen, it may be one of the leading elements in the advertiser's "marketing mix" (e. g. a $50,000,000 effort to establish and maintain a cigarette brand), or be used largely as a supplement to other forms of promotional activity (e. g. a firm offering basic chemicals advertises to purchasing agents only to acquire name recognition to make the personal salesman's task easier), if it is used at all.

Finally, in the most narrow focus within the contexts already discussed, any advertisement can be considered a "symbol package," reflecting assumptions about the likely motivational elements on the part of the potential "market."

*The Advertisements as a "Symbol Package"*

Human communication is on a conceptual level. We are able to transmit "pictures in the heads" through the use of verbal (predominantly words) and non-verbal (music, art, photography, graphics, gestures, etc.) symbols. Unlike our normal person-to-person symbolic communication forms, advertisements:
— Are overwhelmingly persuasive in intent. For example, the use of information by an advertiser can still be considered a means to the end of persuasion; hence the classic division of ads into informative (presumably good) and persuasive (presumably bad) is both simplistic and wrong.
— Lack immediate feedback. The feedback from most advertisements is inferred, usually in the form of some action taken on the part of the "target" audience. For example, if sales go up, the advertising campaign is seen to be "working." As we have seen, however, the abundance of potential influences on behavior other than (or in addition to) advertising, makes such an assumption more an act of faith than a statement of fact.
— Are, as Boorstin (1974) and others have noted, characterized by repetition. Much manufacturer advertising tends to involve the repetition of the same message (often *ad nauseum* in the broadcast media). Although retail advertising frequently changes daily, repetition — and potential irritation — can be said to be characteristic of many advertising messages.
— Commonly involve hyperbole, "puffing," exaggeration, fancy. Part of this can be explained by the *caveat emptor* character of the market system. Perhaps of greater interest is the idea expressed by Levitt (1971) that advertising serves as a form of "alleviating imagery" for many of us, offering a world far more interesting, glamorous, sinful, alluring, clean, better ordered, and exciting than that we find around us. Thus, we may be seen to welcome the blandishments of advertisements at the same time that we may be annoyed by their repetition, lack of "taste" and the like.

Given these characteristics for virtually all advertising messages, the particular qualities of any one can be further analyzed by considering the advertiser's presumed *strategy* and *technique* .

*Strategy*, basically involves *what* is to be said. This is a decision that can be seen as an end product of many of the non-controllable and controllable factors discussed earlier. For example:

— A manufacturer of a video disc player attempts to "position" it as an alternative to video tape recorder/players as well as other brands.

— A local restaurant attempts to establish itself as a low-cost alternative to "fast food" franchises.

— A manufacturer of drill bits for oil exploration attempts to communicate the field-tested durability of his product.

— An association of sugar producers attempts to establish the case for sugar as a nutritious part of normal diets.

Note that in many of the examples above the same strategic goals could be implemented with forms other than (or in addition to) advertising. The video disc *could,* for example, be promoted through in-store demonstrations, the drill bit through a sales force, etc.

*Technique*, then, involves *how* to say it. As suggested above, a careful reading of non-controllable factors and appropriate allocation of international (controllable) resources often makes it reasonably clear to the advertiser *what* is to be said, based on a deminishing number of options.

By contrast, however, the advertiser faces an almost infinitive number of choices among the verbal and non verbal symbols to implement the advertising strategy. To use the examples above:

— The video disc manufacturer could choose to be extremely informative, with heavy reliance on words and, perhaps, diagrams. He could also elect to emphasize the end product — i. e. the program *on* the video disc — with emphasis on arresting scenes from familiar movies. He could choose humor; or an appeal to self-fulfillment; or an invitation to peer-envy through being on the cutting edge of the new video technologies.

— The supplier of drill bits could use action photography of the bit in action supplemented by test data. He could also choose to have the data dominate, with little or no illustrative support, or gather "case history" information and present his message in first-person format.

— The sugar producers could use clinical evidence, the testimony of celebrities, or credible nutritional sources. They could attempt to debunk "sugar myths" through cartoon humor, animation, or jingles. Their tone could be light — or deadly earnest, even angry.

— The restauranteur could use man-in-the-booth interviews, reproduce his entire menu, feature "specials," concentrate on "atmosphere," the competency of waitresses, or the availability of parking. All of these, in turn, could be implemented through words, pictures, music, sound effects, graphics, or some combination.

With all of this, the advertiser faces the very real possibility of simply being ignored. Or having the symbol package interpreted in ways other than those intended. And, almost always, he will never be entirely sure of the advertisement's contribution to the outcome.

Now, given the complexity of the advertisement, its context and form, it is easy to see how its analysis in terms of communication discourse could follow many avenues. For example, Goffman (1979) and Brown (1981) offer insights into advertisers use of stereotypes in terms of sexual roles and family life, while Rank (1982) has worked with the National Council of Teachers of English Committee on Public Dublespeak to develop tools for "analyzing commercial and political propaganda," etc.

Within this prolific array, let me focus briefly on my interpretation of two propositions from the social-psychological (Rotzoll, 1980) theories of Muzafer and Carolyn Sherif (1969).

*Structured stimulus situations set limits to alternatives in psychological patterning.* This proposition – and the next – examine the potential influence of a major *external* (to the individual) variable – the degree of "structure" in the advertisement. A "structured" stimulus situation may be defined as one that is clear cut, has a definite pattern, is unambiguous, and so on. As a simple example, a drawing of a square is relatively "structured" compared to an ink blot. The simulus situation of typical Protestant or Catholic church service is relatively structured while that of (say) the Quakers and many fundamentalist sects is not.

Now, the propositions suggests that whenever the external stimulus situation is relatively structured, the influence of internal factors (such as our ability to "see what we want to see") will be lessened.

The implications for advertising response are significant. It would seem to follow from the proposition that whenever an ad is highly structured, the opportunity for us to interpret it via our internal factors is limited. Now, an advertising message that is relatively structured would be one that would have a clear, unambiguous message. A structured ad would possibly feature explicitly stated product/service characteristics and expectations. It would make clear what the message is and what action we're supposed to take as a result. Given this type of message then, the possibility of distortion via internal factors is presumably minimized.

The advantages of such an approach are fairly obvious. The small newspaper ad that headlines, "Hemorrhoid Sufferers" is likely to attract precisely who is sought. The "trade" ad that cries "Now, A Profitable Line of Paperbacks for the Small Retailer," signals a particular target. We are all familiar with the so-called "slice of life" approach to broadcast commercials. These are simply mini-dramas occuring in the supermarket, kitchen, garage, picnic grove, or wherever. Typically, the problem is presented, the product introduced, and the problem resolved. There is a little time for character development. These are also frequently the types of advertisements most subject to ridicule. There's little guesswork about "What's going on," or nagging questions about what we are supposed to learn from the message.

There are, of course, other responses to the highly structured message that are *not* so desirable. The straightforward message may discourage us from misinterpreting it but it may also limit its appeal. If we are not concerned primarily with the problems of overly waxy floors, the need for perfection in our morning coffee, or the assurance of masculinity in our cigarette, the highly structured message may be screened out. By its very nature it makes it clear from the outset what it's about and we may simply not be interested. If the message proclaims, "Wonder Bread Builds Strong Bodies 12 Ways," and we are *not* concerned with the nutritional qualities of bread (as compared with, say, its taste), then we may simply ignore the message. Thus, the advertiser utilizing a relatively structured message form runs the risk of limiting his potential audience. The potential customer *recognizes* the message *due* to its structure, but decides "Tha's not for me" because there is so little room for injecting his or own product criteria experiences into the picture.

With a highly structured ad message, then, alternatives in psychological patterning (other than those intended by the advertiser) are limited, simply because the message imposes its clear-cut pattern on the stimulus situation. Whether or not we *respond* to that pattern (clear though it may be) is determined in large part by whether the advertiser's patterning of reality matches our own.

*In unstructured stimulus situations, alternatives in psychological patterning are increased.* Given the psychological tendency toward patterning of experience, and given an external stimulus situation that is *not* clearly structured, it follows that the patterning will tend to be added by *internal* factors. Thus, many reports on unidentified flying objects (U. F. O. s) have described them as "saucer" or "cigar" shaped, apparently as a result of imposing a *known* pattern (structure) on a subject (the flying object) which, to put it mildly, is unstructured, ambiguous, fluid, lacking clear definition, etc. The individual must *bring* the "pattern" to the ink blot, since it has no structure to make a pattern clear. Here, then, the interpretations tend to be subjective, varying from individual to individual. Exposed to Rembrandt's "Man in a Gold Helmet," we all see much the same thing. Exposed to a Picasso, we may *each* have different ideas of the appropriate "pattern."

It follows, then, that relatively "unstructured" advertisements may be interpreted in different ways by different people. The "Un-Cola" campaign for 7-up, for example, required the individuals to "make sense" of many of the messages, to interject their own order, as did the extraordinarily expensive Levis "trademark" effort. Many of the so-called "soft-sell" approaches used by perfumes, cosmetics, beers, liquors — and even some politicians — are deliberately designed to be ambiguous enough so that the individual can impose their own (hopefully positive) structure on the situation.

The advantages and disadvantages of such an approach should be evident. Basically, by allowing room for many interpretations, the advertiser increases the possibility of attracting a wide range of customers, each of whom could potentially find something in the message that could be patterned from their own experiences, etc. Also, to the extent that the effort of patterning is that of the individual, there is potentially a greater sense of achievement, "involvement" if you will, in having "closed" the message structure to some meaningful whole.

The potential pitfalls in response are due in part precisely to the "effort" required. Unless the reward for taking time to induce a pattern seems reasonable, the ad may simply be ignored. The mental question, "What's going on here?" may simply be answered, "Who cares?" Of course, if the *individual* supplies a pattern, it may *not* be the interpretation the advertiser wishes. Misinterpretation of advertising messages has been the downfall of many expensive advertising efforts.

Thus, the response to advertising messages may be influenced by the degree of structure of the advertising message. When the message is relatively structured, the "pattern" is already imposed and the chances for individual interpretation and patterning are diminished. This is the advertising approach frequently associated with the so-called "hard-sell" school. In contrast, as the structure of the advertising message loosens, the patterning is more likely to be supplied by the individual in line with previous experiences, attitudes, and so on. Often interpreted as "soft-sell" this message approach implies a frame-of-reference with internal factors intended to fill in the gaps intentionally or unintentionally left in the message structure.

*Two Examples*

We are advised, then, to approach individual advertisements with these questions:
— Are we certain this is advertising rather than, say, publicity, public relations, promotion, etc.?
— Which of the eight basic forms presented does it seem to represent?
— What uncontrollable (external) factors does it seem to be responding to, or attempting to change?
— What role is advertising likely to be playing in relation to the controllable (internal) factors that the advertiser can manipulate?
— What has the advertiser apparently attempted to accomplish with his advertising? What is his apparent strategy?
— How has he chosen to implement that strategy in his "symbol package?" Based on what apparent assumptions about the motivation of his potential audience?
— Did he choose a predominately structured or unstructured symbol package?

*Example 1: An advertisement for an office computer system.*

— This is clearly an advertisement — identified, appearing in paid space in a business magazine, etc.
— This can be classified as advertising of producers of business goods and services to other businesses.
— The advertisement is a reflection of changes in technology that make the use of computers for even small businesses possible if not mandatory.
— The advertisement is obviously not attempting to "close the sale," but rather impart enough information to generate inquiries which will then be followed up by personal salespeople.
— The apparent strategy of the message is to position the computer as ideal for small businesses.
— The techniques involve the use of a case history, including a toll-free number to facilitate inquiries. The advertiser is assuming his audience to be information-sensitive, thus providing an advertisement heavy on facts.
— The advertiser uses a structured message form, leaving little room for reader misinterpretation. This was apparently based on assumptions about the informations needs of the audience — i. e. they *need* facts in this still evolving (and confusing) office computer milieu.

*Example 2: An advertisement for "fashion" dungarees.*

— It is clearly an advertisement, appearing in paid time on television, with the manufacturer identified.
— It is an example of advertising by producers of consumer goods to individuals.
— It is clearly a response to the cultural drift toward the acceptance of "casual" clothing for all dress occasions.
— It reflects the predominate role of advertising in the "marketing mix" — the advertisement is considered sufficient to stimulate brand preference and "close the sale."
— The apparent strategy is to position the jeans as the height of sensual fashion — clothing that will cause the wearer to be noticed.
— the technique involves provocative "soft rock" music, "new wave" graphics, with quick cuts meant to deliver an overall mood. This assumes the audience is likely to buy the brand for impression, style, "feel," rather than, say, durability. Thus impression is of greater concern than information.
— The advertisement is predominately unstructured, assuming that the ego-involved viewer will make their own interpretation of the pieces and essentially "custom fit" the message to their particular perception of fashion and self.

Advertisements as a form of discourse. Beware of oversimplifications of often highly complex artifacts.

*Bibliography*

Boorstin (1974). "Advertising and American Civilization," In Yale Brozen (ed.). *Advertising and Society*, New York: New York University Press.

Brown, Bruce W. (1981). *Images of Family Life in Magazine Advertising: 1920–1978*, New York: Praeger.

Goffman, Erving (1979). *Gender Advertisements*. Cambridge, Massachusetts: Harvard University Press.

Levitt, Theodore. "Advertising and its Adversaries." Speech to the American Association of Advertising Agencies, May 14, 1971.

Rank, Hugh (1982). *The Pitch*. Park Forest, Illinois: the Counter–Propaganda Press.

Rotzoll, Kim (1978). *What Factors Affect Response to Advertisements?* Urbana: University of Illinois, Department of Advertising.

Sherif, Muzafer, and Sherif, Carolyn (1969). *Social Psychology*. New York: Harper & Row.

W. JOHN HUTCHINS

# Information Retrieval and Text Analysis

*1. Introduction*

All scientists and scholars know that the effective dissemination and reception of new ideas, theories and experimental results and the open dispassionate discussion and evaluation of hypotheses and research findings are absolutely crucial factors in the advancement and intellectual vitality of any field of scientific or scholarly activity. Access to what their fellow scientists and scholars have said and written is essential not only for individual researchers but also for the evolution of that consensus of opinion which represents the corpus of 'knowledge' in the discipline (Ziman, 1968; Popper, 1972). In this communication network the published literature plays a central role. It is virtually a truism that 'scientific knowledge' exists primarily in the documentation of science (journal articles, reports, conference proceedings, dissertations, textbooks, etc.) and only secondarily in the fallible memories of individual scientists. It is also true to say that scientists and scholars exist professionally (i. e. as researchers and thinkers, rather than as teachers or administrators) by and through their contributions to the literature of their subjects and by the influence of their publications on other scientists and scholars. The maintenance of this system requires and has always required effective ways and means of gaining access to and finding out about what has been published, i. e. effective 'information retrieval'.

In essence, information retrieval means the extraction of 'information' of some kind (data, texts, references) form a 'store' (memory, file, database, document collection) in response to an 'informaton need'. The term is now often used for systems which do not involve published or recorded information, such as biological and psychological processes in animal and human memories and computer models of 'human information processing'. This paper is concerned with the more traditional concept of information retrieval, with the problems of handling the written and recorded texts and data of scientific documentation. A general overview of the processes involved is given in figures 1 and 2.

Systems may respond in basically two ways to requests: either by providing the actual data which satisfies an information need, or by providing citations of documents (i. e. details of authors, titles, journals, etc.) which might contain

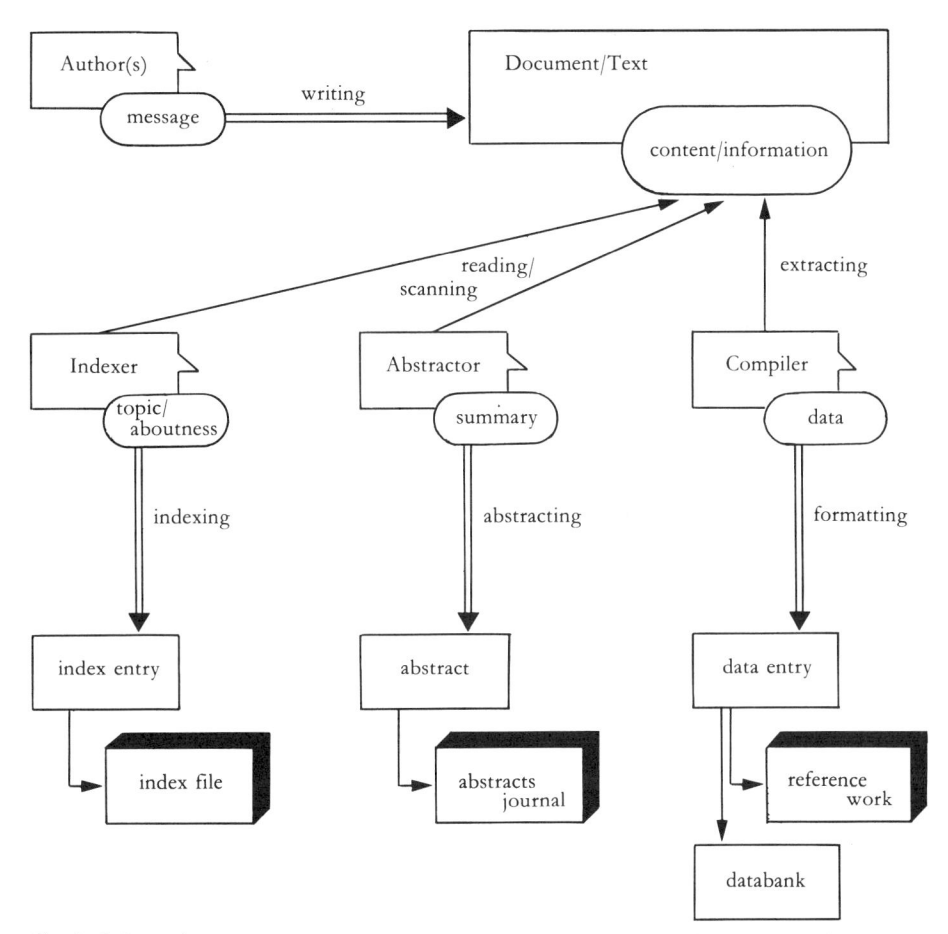

Fig. 1: Information storage

the information sought. The first are commonly referred to as 'fact-retrieval' or 'data-retrieval' systems if they are computer-based; their more familiar printed equivalents are dictionaries, directories, lists of addresses, handbooks of mathematical tables, physical constants, etc. The latter are commonly referred to as 'bibliographic' or 'document-reference' systems; their familiar forms are catalogues, indexes, bibliographies and abstracts journals. Information about the subject contents of documents may be recorded in bibliographic systems either in 'index entries' (individual words or phrases or 'terms' stating the topics treated or mentioned in documents), or in 'abstracts' (brief paragraphs summarizing the essential 'messages' of documents), or in extracts from actual texts (most commonly titles and subtitles, but sometimes longer passages).

Figure 1 represents the processes involved in the production of records or data for information retrieval systems: the writing of texts by authors to express a 'message'; the indexing of texts by indexers to express what they are 'about'; the abstracting of texts by abstractors to express the essence of authors' messages; the extracting of data from texts (and other sources) by compilers of reference works and databases. Figure 2 represents the processes involved in the searching of records and data: the expression of information needs; the formulation of search requests appropriate to the type of record (index, abstract, database); the extraction of information from the system; the evaluation of the information retrieved.

Text analysis and text production are clearly at the heart of information retrieval systems: indexers and abstractors must read and understand the texts they are indexing and abstracting; compilers of dictionaries, handbooks and databases must analyze and arrange ('format') the information to be included; abstractors must write the texts of abstracts; users of systems must express their needs in texts (search requests), and they must interpret the texts retrieved for them. Much of this text processing is not at all peculiar to

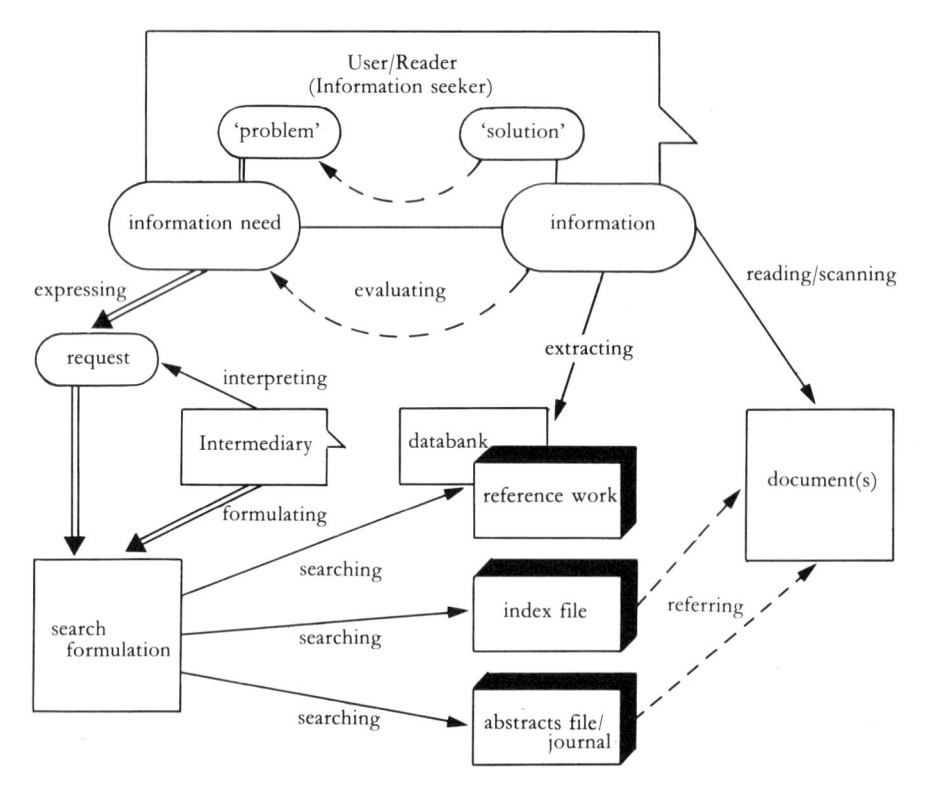

Fig. 2: Information searching

information systems: the ways that indexers, abstractors and information seekers read and interpret documents are no different from those of readers in general; and the ways that abstractors write abstracts and that users express their search requests are no different in essence from those of authors and speakers in general. What is peculiar to information retrieval systems are the processes of summarizing, condensing and extracting texts and the processes of matching search requests against texts (titles, abstracts) or text-like representations (index entries, structured databases) — these are the principal topics of this paper.

An attempt is made to present a unified picture by relating what is known or surmised about human indexing, abstracting and searching to accounts of computer-based systems of automatic indexing, abstracting and searching. Section 2 concentrates on the problems of natural language access to systems, sections 3 and 4 on the analysis of texts to produce indexes and abstracts, section 5 on the 'formatting' of information in data-retrieval systems, and section 6 on the problems of evaluating the results of searches.

## 2. *Searching*

Whether searching 'bibliographic' or 'data-retrieval' systems, users are required to express their information needs as precisely as possible in the form appropriate to the system concerned. It is a difficult task and one which is little understood. There may be four stages (Taylor, 1968): an initial awareness of a 'problem space' (a lack of understanding, a dissatisfaction with current explanations, an anomaly in the data, etc.); a preliminary, informal, partly incoherent expression of a 'need'; a more coherent, rational and considered statement of the kind of information or document which might satisfy the need; and lastly, a search request formulated in the 'language' of the information system.

*2.1.* In the case of non-computerized systems, users generally require the assistance of 'intermediary experts' (e. g. librarians, information officers) to adapt requests and to search systems. Searching indexes, for example, demands knowledge of the way index entries are constructed and how they are to be interpreted if users are to make the most effective use of them. (Index languages have indeed their own semantic and syntactic structures and may be studied as linguistic systems in their own right (Gardin, 1973; Hutchins, 1975).) Searching 'formatted' sources makes equivalent demands on users; they have to understand the structure and meanings of tables (e. g. of statistical data), the norms and conventions of dictionary entries, the formats in which biographical information is presented, etc.

The process of adapting (even 'distorting') requests to the particular requirements of individual information systems is undoubtedly one of the reasons why all too often users fail to find the data or documents that satisfy their needs. What is not always realised is that the very process of producing a coherent statement of 'information need' contributes a certain degree of distortion. By its very nature an information need cannot be expressed precisely and concisely. It may well be plausible to suggest (Beaugrande and Dressler, 1981) that in 'normal' text production speakers and writers have some idea of what they want to say or write, and adopt suitable plans and strategies for putting over their 'messages' — even if they have often to make corrections and revisions when they realise that they have not said or written what they intended. In the expression of information needs, however, the problem is that users do not know precisely what they want at any stage — there is no clear 'message' or 'intention' to go back to, only a vague awareness of a 'problem area'. Requests are inevitably imprecise and approximate, and nobody knows whether they correspond to 'real' information needs or not — hence, in part, the difficulties of evaluating searches (cf. section 6).

*2.2.* Computerized bibliographic systems enable users to search not only the index terms assigned to documents but also natural language texts: the titles and abstracts of documents in nearly all cases, but in some systems even the full texts of documents (e.g. the legal retrieval systems LEXIS and FLITE; cf. Larson, 1977) and as computer storage capacities increase and more and more documents and records become available in machine-readable form (often as by-products of printing/publishing processes) this is likely to be the norm in future systems (Lancaster, 1977). Yet paradoxically, the users of these operational systems cannot formulate requests in 'free' natural language; they must break down requests into individual terms, for which they must provide possible synonyms (or near-synonyms) and alternative spellings, and decide how terms are to be combined (present systems allow only Boolean links: *and, or, not*). Assistance may be provided by manuals and thesauri and also by 'intermediary experts', but what these bibliographic systems clearly need are more 'friendly' interfaces. Considerable research has been devoted to systems which help users to modify and refine searches — mainly by statistical techniques which adjust search formulations (e.g. adding or subtracting terms, substituting more general or more specific terms, etc.) in the light of users' evaluations of a selection of retrieved documents (cf. Rijsbergen, 1979; Bates, 1981). There is now also increasing research activity on systems which accept requests in 'free' natural language, which identify search terms and supply synonyms and alternatives and which enable users to interact with the system during searches. One of the most advanced systems of this kind is CITE (Doszkocs and Rapp, 1979), designed for searching the large medical database MEDLINE; this incorporates not only automatic identification of search terms and automatic construction of search formulae but also interactive modification during searches and ranking of documents according to potential 'relevance' in meeting users' needs.

However, efficient natural language interfaces will not solve all difficulties in searching bibliographic databases. For example, there is the inevitable 'distortion' of users' information needs by the inherent constraints of information systems. Belkin and Oddy (1979) suggest that searching should be based not on (relatively precise) search requests, however 'freely' expressed, but on informal, rambling, loose (even incoherent) statements by users of their 'problem' as they see it and how they think it might be 'solved' (i. e. Taylor's second stage in the expression of 'information need'); such statements would provide an outline 'profile' of search terms to be modified and made more precise during interactive searching. Another problem is the imprecision of bibliographic searches (i. e. too many irrelevant documents retrieved) which may result from failure to take into account semantic and syntactic relationships within document texts. The problem becomes acute if the full texts of documents are searched, since clearly search terms (i. e. individual words) may be found within a document in quite unrelated passages. One approach is illustrated by the research of O'Connor (1975, 1980) on full text searching. Documents are retrieved only if they contain passages of text which both include a minimum number of search terms and consist of 'connected' sentences. Connectivity is determined by the occurrence of connector words (e. g. conjunctions and sentence adverbs) and by the repetition of search terms. For example, in response to 'What are the effects on the ureter of radiation treatment of cancer?' the following passage was located (words corresponding to search terms are italicized):

> Complications of *radiation therapy* for prostatic *carcinoma* are frequent but usually minor. A patient is described in whom localized *ureteral* fibrosis developed following *curative radiation therapy*, which subsequently required a reconstructive operation. (O'Connor, 1980: 233)

*2.3.* Most research on natural language interfaces for database searching has taken place in the context of artificial intelligence work on question-answering systems (i. e. fact-retrieval systems). One of the best known examples is LUNAR, developed by Woods (1977, 1978) to enable geologists at NASA to interrogate a structured ('formatted') database containing results of chemical analyses of lunar rock and soil samples from the Apollo missions. A request such as 'How many samples contain silicon?' is first parsed (by the now familiar Augmented Transition Network parser):

```
S      Q
       NP      DET     HOWMANY
               N       SAMPLE
               NU      PL
       AUX     TNS     PRESENT
       VP      V       CONTAIN
               NP      DET     NIL
                       N       SILICON
                       NU      SG
```

and then converted into a logical format specifying the procedures (e.g. calculations) to be carried out on data from the file. Thus, HOWMANY is interpreted as an instruction to calculate the number of records satisfying the specified conditions (presence of silicon), and to print out the result. However, LUNAR has very limited facilities for user-system interaction. Later systems enable searchers to conduct more or less natural language dialogues — within the subject domain of the database. For example, GUS (Bobrow, et al., 1977) acts as a travel agent booking airflights in California:

> CLIENT: I want to go to San Diego on May 28
> GUS: What time do you want to leave?
> CLIENT: I must be in San Diego before 10 am
> GUS: Would you like P.S.A. flight 102 that arrives at 9.15 am?
> CLIENT: What is the next flight?
> GUS: Air California flight 310 that leaves at 8.30 and arrives at 10.00 am
> CLIENT: I'll take the first one

The example illustrates the handling of complex problems of anaphora: *next flight* refers both to GUS's preceding statement and to the order of flights in the airline guide, and *first one* refers to the order in which flights have been mentioned during this particular dialogue. A number of question-answering systems are able to handle ungrammatical and misspelled requests and to deal with elliptical expressions (e.g. Waltz, 1978) — facilities which are now regarded as essential for 'intelligent' interface systems (Weischedel and Black, 1980).

One system incorporating all these features is the LIFER natural language interface as applied in a highly complex database network providing information for the U.S. Navy (Hendrix, et al., 1978). An illustrative interchange (with comments in parentheses) is given in figure 3. Like most question-answering parsers LIFER embeds considerable semantic information in its syntax — it is a 'semantic grammar'. For example, words like NAUTILUS and DISPLACEMENT are not grouped together in a single Noun category, but treated as /SHIP-NAME/ and as /ATTRIBUTE/ respectively; and, instead of general syntactic patterns such as $NP + VP$, it analyzes in terms such as:

WHAT IS THE /ATTRIBUTE/ OF /SHIP-NAME/

As a result, 'semantic grammars' tend to be domain-specific and not easily transferred to other databases. However, LIFER is more flexible than most — it has been applied also as an interface to a medical database (Epstein and Walker, 1978) — as it has been developed within the context of a large-scale programme of information retrieval research (Walker, 1981) in order to provide natural language access to a variety of different kinds of databases. Increased flexibility and domain-independence is the goal of many current projects; it has been achieved to some extent by Sager's linguistic string parser (section 5.2 below) and by the ROBOT parser (Harris, 1977). Already applied to six different databases of great variety, ROBOT derives its semantic

1. What is the length of the Constellation
   PARSED!                            (= request successfully analyzed,
   (LENGTH 1072 feet)             database being searched)

2. of the Nautilus
   TRYING ELLIPSIS: WHAT IS THE LENGTH OF THE NAUTILUS
   (LENGTH 319 feet)             (= expanded request successfully answered)

3. displacement
   TRYING ELLIPSIS: WHAT IS THE DISPLACEMENT OF THE NAUTILUS
   (STANDARD-DISPLACEMENT 4040 tons)

4. length of the fastest American Nuclear sub
   TRYING ELLIPSIS: WHAT IS THE LENGTH OF THE FASTEST AMERICAN NUCLEAR SUB
   (LENGTH 360 feet NAME LOS ANGELES SPEED 30.0 knots)

5. Who commands the Constellation
       SPELLING − − CONSTELLATION (= correction of misspelling)
   PARSED!                            (= corrected form analyzed)
   (COMMANDER CAPT J. ELLISON)

6. Who commands JFK
   TRYING ELLIPSIS: ELLIPSIS HAS FAILED
   THE PARSER DOES NOT EXPECT THE WORD "JFK" TO FOLLOW "WHO COMMANDS"
   OPTIONS FOR NEXT WORD OR META-SYMBOL ARE: /SHIP-NAME/

7. Define JFK to be like Kennedy
   PARSED!                            (= acknowledges user's definition of 'JFK' as a synonym of KENNEDY, which is already known as a /SHIP-NAME/.)

8. Who commands JFK
   PARSED!                            (= retry of 6 is now accepted)
   (COMMANDER CAPT P. MOFFETT)

Fig. 3: LIFER dialogue

independence largely from utilizing dynamically the structural properties of the database itself during analysis and interpretation. The advent of more flexible and independent interfaces and their application to larger databases promises improved natural language access not only to fact-retrieval systems but also to bibliographic databases.

## 3. Indexing

In bibliograhic systems the index terms associated with documents may either be 'derived' from words or phrases occurring in the documents, i. e. extracted from actual texts, or they may be 'assigned' (selected) by indexers or indexing systems. The selection may be 'controlled' in that only terms appearing in a particular list (an authority file) may be used, or it may be 'uncontrolled'. Index terms for a particular document may, in some systems, refer to the 'topic' of the document considered as a whole ('topic indexing'), or they may, in other systems, refer to any subjects the document may mention so that, taken together, they constitute a kind of 'summary' of the document's message ('summary indexing'). In addition, indexing may be 'user-oriented' in that only those terms are assigned which are expected to be sought for by the particular clients of the system; or it may be 'document-oriented' if general, 'objectively' valid characterizations are intended which are not specific to particular environments.

*3.1.* The indexing done by human indexers is invariably 'assigned' indexing, most often with 'controlled' terms. In systems for the general user (public libraries, general bibliographies) the usual approach is that of 'topic indexing' with a predominantly 'document-orientation'. In systems for specialists and experts (research libraries, specialised bibliographies) the usual approach is that of 'summary indexing' with a 'user-orientation'.

Little is known about how indexing is done; guides and manuals for indexers concentrate on formal properties of index terms and the construction of index entries; they say nothing about how indexers decide what documents are 'about' or how they select suitable index descriptions. In 'user-oriented' indexing it is suggested that they scan texts for particular words or phrases known to be likely search terms in the relevant specialism, i.e. they refer to an internalised check list (Soergel, 1974: 47). As for 'topic indexing' it is suggested that the theme-rheme articulations of paragraph and text structures (cf. Daneš, 1974) provide clues to global topics of dcuments and that these may be related to the 'given' knowledge which authors assume their potential readers have already (Hutchins, 1978). By contrast, in 'summary indexing' the notion of topic appears to be related to the node in a text-linguistic representation of a paragraph (or text) which has most links to other nodes, i.e. generally a noun phrase occurring as subject in more than one sentence and referred to by pro-forms — e.g. *rocket* in the following passage analyzed by Beaugrande and Dressler (1981: 103):

> With a great roar and burst of flame the giant rocket rose slowly at first and then faster and faster. Behind it trailed sixty feet of yellow flame. Soon the flame looked like a yellow star. In a few seconds, it was too high to be seen, but radar tracked it as it sped upward to 3,000 mph.

*3.2* Most experimental work on automatic indexing has concentrated on statistical methods of analysis (Sparck Jones, 1974; Harter, 1978), the general assumption being that frequency of occurrence is correlated broadly with semantic importance. Since the crude counting of word tokens is clearly inadequate (in the passage above, *flame* occurring three times would be ranked higher than *rocket* occurring once), many subtle and complex refinements are employed: e. g. the exclusion of words which occur frequently in the subject field (as well as words frequent in the language in general, such as function words), the truncation of words to bring together morphologically related words (suffix-stripping), the normalisation of frequencies to allow for varying document lengths, the weighting of words appearing in certain 'important' parts of texts (titles, section headings, conclusions), the use of co-occurrence frequencies, and so forth.

In general the terms derived by automatic indexing are 'uncontrolled', but there are exceptions. Klingbiel (1973) and Barnes et al. (1978) describe systems where potential terms are scrutinized against an authority file: some are accepted, some rejected, some replaced by synonyms, others replaced by more general terms. Another form of control is described by Sparck Jones (1971): if two terms tend to co-occur in the same documents then they may be equally effective as search terms for the retrieval of those documents, i. e. they are mutually substitutible (whether or not they happen to be close in meaning and whether or not they happen to refer to similar topics). A good discussion of statistical methods in information retrieval is to be found in Rijsbergen (1979).

*3.3.* Research in automatic indexing has made relatively little use of linguistic methods of analysis. Some limited parsing is found in the systems of Klingbiel (1973) and Barnes et al. (1978), where a simple parser identifies nouns and noun phrases for testing as potential index terms, and in the LEADERMART system (Hillmann, 1968, 1973), where a parser identifies nouns and 'logical' relations between them (from analyses of prepositions, conjunctions and simple phrase structures). However, two projects have been more ambitious: the SMART and SYNTOL systems of automatic indexing.

SMART now uses statistical methods almost exclusively, but in earlier versions (Salton, 1968) there was some semantic and syntactic analysis. Each sentence of a document (or, more often, its abstract) was parsed by the Harvard Predictive Analyzer (a finite-state parser designed originally in the 1950's for machine translation), which produced a basic phrase structure analysis in dependency grammar format. From the parsing were extracted substructures (e. g. subject-verb and noun-adjective links) to be matched against a dictionary of 'criterion phrases'. A criterion phrase was a dependency tree in which each node represented a set of semantically related words (a concept group) and each link a defined syntactic relationship (e. g. attribute, instrument), and which could be treated in subsequent procedures as a single unit. There were considerable problems in establishing the syntactic and semantic conditions for criterion phrases, but there were even more difficulties with the inadequacies of the parser, which notoriously produced either no analyses at all or far too many — and it is not surprising that Salton abandoned syntactic analysis in favour of the then more satisfactory statistical methods.

In certain respects, the analytical procedures of SYNTOL (Bely, et al., 1970) were similar: here too, the parser (context-free) produced a dependency structure from which substructures could be extracted representing pairs of index terms linked by basic relations. These were the 'syntagms' which were combined in networks in order to represent the content of document texts (or rather, document abstracts). It was realised that if syntagms were to be found successfully in searches they would not have to be too specifically defined; in fact they were perhaps made too abstract (eventually only three types of link were permitted) and the analysis program was not powerful enough to convert the semantic complexities of the natural language input into the required abstractness of SYNTOL's syntagmatic representations.

*4. Abstracting*

Research on automatic abstracting has tended to be more ambitious from a linguistic point of view than most research on automatic indexing. The reason is not far to seek: not only must the texts of documents be analysed in some detail, but also texts must be produced (the abstracts) which are coherent syntactically and semantically and which at the same time are reasonable 'summaries' of some kind of the original documents.

*4.1.* The process of 'summarization' is itself highly complex, as we shall see, but it is clear from manuals and guides for abstractors (e.g. Bernier, 1968; Weil, 1970) that abstracts are more than just summaries. Other text types also include condensations of texts, e.g. review articles surveying the literature of a subject, newspaper articles reporting research, handbooks outlining the current 'state of knowledge' in a discipline, encyclopaedia articles, etc. (Bernier, 1970); and abstracts are distinct from these. Two basic types are identified: 'informative' abstracts which include actual results, figures and conclusions from source documents, and 'indicative' abstracts which simply record the fact that certain topics are covered. (The distinction is roughly parallel to that between 'summary indexing' and 'topic indexing'.) To maintain standards and consistency, recommendations and gudelines for abstractors are often very specific: state the purpose of the work reported; give the methods used, the results obtained and the conclusions reached; retain the balance and emphases of the original; convey only what is 'new' information; pass no comments, either favourable or critical; produce a self-contained coherent text within the confines of (ideally) a single paragraph and which might stand as a substitute for the original for some purposes; and so forth. The linguistic complexities of abstracting clearly transcend just 'summarizing' and it is not surprising that they still await investigation.

Summarization itself is complex enough as a linguistic process. Within his general theory of text linguistics, Van Dijk (1977, 1980) has outlined some basic operations. Van Dijk distinguishes between the microstructure of a text (the underlying propositional content of its sentences and clauses, and their connections to each other, in the linear sequence in which they are expressed) and its macrostructure (the semantic representation of the text as an entity, independently of its particular propositional manifestation). Summaries are one way of expressing the macrostructures of texts. Macrostructures are derived from microstructures by the operations of four types of 'macrorules'. Two are concerned essentially with the identification of 'important' propositions: *deletion* operates negatively by eliminating the unnecessary and irrelevant (e. g. detailed descriptions, background information, common knowledge), and *selection* operates positively by extracting the necessary and the relevant (e. g. propositions expressing pre-conditions and data required for the interpretation of other propositions). The other two are concerned with condensation and abstraction: *generalization* constructs general propositions from the semantic detail of microstructural propositions (e. g. from a description of girls playing with dolls, boys playing with train sets, etc. it derives a description of children playing with toys), and *construction* replaces sequences of propositions by single propositions expressing self-contained events or processes ('scripts').

*4.2.* The experience of research on automatic abstracting indicates that deletion and selection are more easily simulated in computer analysis than are the other summarization operations. Initially, researchers attempted to produce 'abstracts' by extracting sentences en bloc from texts on the basis of high frequency words (excluding function words and items of common vocabulary), e. g. Luhn's (1958) pioneering work. The results were neither particularly good condensations nor very coherent texts. Later systems have combined more sophisticated statistical methods (similar to those in automatic indexing) with attempts to use the kind of textual 'cues' which abstractors seem to use. Edmundson (1969) and Rush et al. (1971) employed three types of 'cues': (i) the recurrence of words in titles, subtitles and section headings, or the occurrence of words synonymous with them, (ii) the presence of words such as *significant, impossible, hardly*, which indicate authors' views of the importance of the information presented, and (iii) the location of sentences within paragraphs and sections. Such 'cues' identify potentially 'important' passages — they are in part refinements of Baxendale's (1958) observations on the occurrence of topic sentences in paragraphs and the overt textual marking of important passages. (Similar observations are part of the rhetorical tradition now formalised to some extent in text linguistics.)

Most researchers concede that these procedures should be properly called 'automatic extracting' of sentences; but there have been some attempts to produce coherent sequences, to make some generalizations and so to come closer to 'abstracting' of some kind. Mathis et al. (1973) introduced various refinements into the procedures of Rush et al. (1971): (i) if an extracted sentence contains an anaphoric link to a preceding sentence then the latter is also included in the abstract, (ii) specific references to particular tables, graphs, etc. (e. g. *Table 2, figure 3, the second mechanism*) are changed to general references (*a table, a figure, a mechanism*), and (iii) some extracted sentences are combined by coordinate and subordinate conjunctions. The latter involved limited parsing of candidate sentences to identify noun, verb, and preposition phrases, to locate antecedents of pronouns, and to recognize parallel structures. For example, the two sentences:

> The system exceeded the capacity of its present auxiliary equipment. The system was modified for further testing

could be combined as:

> The system exceeded the capacity of its present auxiliary equipment and was modified for further testing

Obviously, much more is needed than such simple syntactic manipulations if genuine abstracting and summarizing is to be achieved; some indications of the techniques required are to be seen in artificial intelligence, where the concept of 'script' in text understanding appears to be an example of Van Dijk's macro-rule of construction.

*4.3.* Most pertinent in this context is the research of Schank and his colleagues (Schank, 1975) on programs for understanding simple stories on the basis of 'scripts' which outline sequences of events or actions to be expected in particular situations — e. g. the 'restaurant script' outlines the normal action-sequence of calling the waiter, ordering food, being served, eating the food, getting the bill, and paying it. One output of the story-understander is a summary of the story extracted and condensed from the full semantic representation (i. e. a kind of 'macrostructural' output). However, it is now proposed by Schank et al. (1980) that equivalent summaries can be produced by text parsers which do not attempt to understand everything in a text and do not need a complete semantic representation. An experimental program FRUMP (DeJong, 1979) works from 'sketchy scripts' of typical newspaper stories (kidnaps, acts of terrorism, diplomatic negotiations, etc.); it skims through texts looking only for words signalling a known 'script', from which it is able to predict or expect the occurrence of other words or phrases and so build up the outline of the story, i. e. a 'summary' of the newspaper report. FRUMP is therefore only 'interested' in and only interprets those parts of the text which relate directly to elements of a 'sketchy script', the rest of the text is ignored.

Text scanning or 'skimming' is pervasive in many areas of information retrieval: users do not, in general, read in full everything put before them, they scan texts to decide which documents are relevant or worth reading; likewise, indexers and abstractors rarely read the full texts to documents, they scan them for words and phrases indicating general content. Yet 'scanning' has not attracted widespread attention. However, one aspect has been investigated by Keen (1977) in his study, under controlled experimental conditions, of the psychological and (in part) linguistic processes involved in the consultation of printed subject indexes. Obviously, index users do not read every entry; but how are they able to locate entries with the terms they seek? how do they spot entries with related meanings but with terms they had not thought of?

Although the research of DeJong and Schank on text scanning is clearly important, its direct relevance to information retrieval will remain marginal until more work is done on analysing non-narrative texts. Information retrieval is concerned primarily with expository and descriptive texts (scientific papers, research reports, scholarly articles, etc.) which exhibit different structural features from those found in stories and other narrative texts; indeed, it appears that they reflect in their text structure the hypothesis-testing and problem-solving frameworks of the research process itself (Gopnik, 1972; Hutchins, 1977). Some insight may come from text-linguistic analyses of scientific discourse.

## 5. Formatting

Structured databases of the kinds found in question-answering systems (section 2.3 above) are generally compiled in the same way as their non-computerized printed equivalents, i. e. by human effort. The auxiliary processes of sorting, filing and indexing may be automated to varying degrees but not, in general, the basic activities of restructuring text material into formats suitable for searching. As for the intellectual aspects of collating and organising information and data, almost as little is known about them as is known about the psychological processes of indexing and abstracting.

*5.1.* There has been, however, considerable research activity on the problems of representing knowledge in databases, particularly in the field of artificial intelligence (cf. Findler, 1979). Although some of this research has involved the representation of information extracted from texts, there has been little work on the problems of handling substantial volumes of textual material or of integrating information from a variety of texts. In this respect, research at SRI International could be important: one project involves the incorporation of textual material from different sources into a single database, the 'Polytext' project (Walker, 1981) the other involves the conversion of a large database at present in text format into a semantic representation suitable for interrogation by a LIFER-type question-answering system (Hobbs, et al., 1982). The database selected is the Hepatitis Knowledge Base (Bernstein, et al., 1980), a computer-based textbook representing the current consensus of experts in this medical field, compiled and continuously updated by computer conferencing techniques.

5.2. The most substantial research so far on converting natural language material into 'information formats' is the work of Sager and her colleagues (Sager, 1975, 1978, 1981). The team has developed a generalised parser — the linguistic string parser, deriving from Zellig Harris' well-known work in mathematical linguistics — which has been applied to the analysis and representation of medical records in a large database. The automatic 'formatting' of the text takes place in two stages: first, the parser produces a linguistic string analysis of sentences (a phrase-structure, dependency representation which does not distort the original linear sequence); and then, each parsing is segmented into semantic categories appropriate to the content of the text type in question. For example, the following medical record would be 'formatted' as in figure 4:

> Patient first had sickle cell anemia diagnosed at age 2 when he complained of leg pain. He was worked up and diagnosis was made. He was asymptomatic until age 5 when he was admitted to Bellevue Hospital with chest pains. He was hospitalized for a month and released.

Information formatted in this way can be used not only as databases for fact-retrieval (Grishman and Hirschman, 1978) but also as data sources for further statistical analyses and as foundations for 'expert systems' (cf. Bramer, 1981).

Successful formatting depends on the validity of the initial analysis of the 'sublanguage' of the texts to be handled. In any discipline there are semantic constraints on the acceptability of certain statements. In cell biology, for example, the statement *the ion crosses the membrane* would be an acceptable proposition (whether true or false in a particular instance), whereas *the membrane crosses the ion* would be rejected as nonsense. Such observations lead to the establishment of 'sublanguage grammars' consisting of subject-specific classifications of vocabulary (e.g. noun-classes for digitalis texts such as 'cations', 'enzymes', 'cells', 'proteins') and subject-specific syntactic rules (e.g. elementary propositions of the form $N_{ion}$ $V_{move}$ $N_{cell}$, and causal structures of the form $N_{drug}$ $V_{affect}$ (N V N), etc.) These sublanguage categories and structures determine rules of the second stage of analysis and the headings of information formats (i.e. V-MD, V-PART, NORM, SIGN/SYMPT in figure 4.)

5.3. The concept of a 'sublanguage grammar' is obviously closely related to that of a 'semantic grammar' in question-answering systems (section 2.3 above). Many interests converge in the investigation of 'sublanguages', making it a distinct field of research within the general disciplines of text linguistics and computational linguistics (Kittredge and Lehrberger, 1982); information science could also contribute with statistical methods for the automatic classification and differentiation of texts according to subject

| CONJ | PATIENT | TREATMENT | | PATIENT STATE | | | | | TIME | | |
|---|---|---|---|---|---|---|---|---|---|---|---|
| | | INST | V-MD | V-PAT | BODY PART | NORM | SIGN/SYMPT | DIAGNOSIS | P1 | P2 | REF. PT |
| | patient | | first had diagnosed | | | | | sickle cell anemia | | at | age 2 yrs |
| when | he | | | complained of | leg | | pain | | | | (age 2 yrs) |
| and | he | | was worked up | | | | | | | | |
| | | | diagnosis was made | | | | | | | | |
| | he | | | was | | asymptomatic | | | | until | age 5 yrs |
| when | he | Bellevue Hospital | was admitted to | with | chest | | pains | | | | (age 5 yrs) |
| | he | | was hospitalized | | | | | | for a month | | |
| and | (he) | | (was) released | | | | | | | | |

Fig. 4: Information format

content (e.g. in automatic indexing; section 3.2 above). However, it is more probable that 'sublanguage' research will eventually revive interest in linguistics-based approaches to automatic indexing and abstracting.

*6. Evaluating*

The ultimate test of an information retrieval system, whether a bibliographic system or a fact-retrieval system, is its effectiveness in satisfying the information needs of its users. The future role of text analysis procedures in information retrieval can be put in simple terms: can text analysis improve system performance? and, if so, will the improvement be sufficient to justify any additional costs? However, the questions are not at all easy to answer. There are many complex factors involved when users of systems assess the value of the information provided. First, the documents or data retrieved must be interpreted (read and understood), the particular information required must be extracted, and then it must be 'applied' in solving the problem (or anomaly) which prompted the original request. In the case of bibliographic systems there are additional complexities in that users have to decide which documents are likely to be worth reading on the basis of their titles, abstracts and index entries — and these can easily be misleading or misunderstood. There are numerous occasions for mistaken assessments: unfamiliarity with the subject matter, unfamiliarity with the information system and its indexing/abstracting policy, failure to recognise the 'relevance' of texts to actual needs, etc. The problem of 'relevance' has indeed engaged researchers for many years (Saracevic, 1975); and rightly so, as relevance assessment is at the heart of system evaluation in information retrieval. What is being assessed: relevance to a request, to a search formulation, to a supposed 'information need', or to an ultimate 'solution' of a problem? relevance of a document citation, or of a document text, or of a document's contents? relevance as seen by the user, or by the information supplier, or by an independent judge?

With such a complexity of factors it is not surprising that most researchers are convinced that retrieval from bibliographic systems will long remain essentially a probabilistic process. In this context, detailed analysis and representation of document texts is likely to be always of less significance than interactive searching and feedback techniques for helping users to find the documents they think might satisfy their needs. There is also the question of scale: bibliographic systems are necessarily concerned with the gross characterisation of documents within large collections; there appears to be little justification for the detailed semantic analysis of fact-retrieval and question-answering systems. The latter are generally designed for relatively narrow subject domains and for access by expert users requiring precise information. It is research on these systems that most advances in text understanding and text representation have been made in the field of information retrieval, and this is likely to continue in the future. However, it is hoped that this overview has shown that text processing of many kinds is an integral part of all information retrieval systems and that resrach on the understanding of these processes (whether it leads to improved systems, or to computerization, or not) may well contribute something of value in the general field of discourse analysis and text linguistics.

*Acknowledgement*

The author wishes to thank in particular Dr. Karen Sparck Jones for her invaluable suggestions and comments on an earlier version of this paper.

*Bibliography*

    (Notes: * = survey or review article
    ARIST = Annual Review of Information Science and Technology
    JASIS = Journal of the American Society for Information Science)

Barnes, C. I., Constantini, L. and Perschke, S. (1978). Automatic indexing using the SLC-II system. *Information Processing and Management* 19, 107–119
*Bates, M. J. (1981). Search techniques. *ARIST* 16, 139–169
Baxendale, P. B. (1958). Machine-made index for technical literature — an experiment. *IBM Journal of Research and Development* 2, 354–361
Beaugrande, R. de and Dressler, W. (1981). *Introduction to text linguistics.* London: Longman.
*Becker, D. (1981). Automated language processing. *ARIST* 16, 113–138
Belkin, N. J. and Oddy, R. N. (1979). Design study for an Anomalous State of Knowledge based information retrieval system. Birmingham, University of Aston: Computer Centre. (British Library Research and Development Report no. 5547)
Bely, N., Borillo, A., Virbel, J. and Siot-Decauville, N. (1970). *Procédures d'analyse sémantique appliquées à la documentation scientifique.* Paris: Gauthier.
*Bernier, C. I. (1968). Abstracts and abstracting. In *Encyclopedia of Library and Information Science*, vol. 1, 16–38. New York: Dekker.
Bernier, C. I. (1970). Terse literatures, 1: Terse conclusions. *JASIS* 21, 316–319
Bernstein, L. M., Siegel, E. R. and Goldstein, C. M. (1980). The Hepatitis Knowledge Base: a prototype information system. *Annals of Internal Medicine* 93, 169–222
Bobrow, D. G., Kaplan, R. M., Kay, M., Norman, D. A., Thompson, H. and Winograd, T. (1977). GUS: a frame-driven dialog system. *Artificial Intelligence* 8, 155–173
*Bramer, M. A. (1981). A survey and critical review of expert systems research. In *Information Technology for the Eighties*, R. D. Parslow (ed.), 486–515. London: Heyden.
*Damerau, F. J. (1976). Automated language processing. *ARIST* 11, 107–161
Daneš, F. (1974). Functional sentence perspective and the organization of text. In *Papers on Functional Sentence Perspective*, F. Daneš (ed.), 106–128. The Hague: Mouton.
DeJong, G. (1979). Prediction and substantiation: two processes that comprise understanding. In *IJCAI-79: Proceedings of the Sixth International Joint Conference on Artificial Intelligence, Tokyo 1979*, 217–222. Stanford, Ca.: Stanford Univ.
Dijk, T. A. van (1977). Complex semantic information processing. In *Natural Language in Information Science*, D. E. Walker (ed.), 127–163. Stockholm: Skriptor.
Dijk, T. A. van (1980). *Macrostructures: An interdisciplinary study of global structures in discourse, interaction, and cognition.* Hillsdale, N.J.: Erlbaum.

Doszkocs, T. E. and Rapp, B. A. (1979). Searching MEDLINE in English: a prototype user interface with natural language query, ranked output, and relevance feedback. In *Information Choices and Policies: Proceedings of the ASIS Annual Meeting 1979*, 131–137. White Plains, N.Y.: Knowledge Industry Publ.

Edmundson, H. P. (1969). New methods in automatic extracting. *Journal of the ACM* 16, 264–285

Epstein, M. N. and Walker, D. E. (1978). Natural language access to a melanoma database. In *Proceedings of the Second Annual Symposium on Computer Applications in Medical Care*, 320–325. New York: IEEE.

*Findler, N. V. (1979), ed. *Associative networks: representation and use of knowledge by computers*. New York: Academic Press.

Gardin, J. C. (1973). Document analysis and linguistic theory. *Journal of Documentation* 29, 137–168

Gopnik, M. (1972). *Linguistic structures in scientific texts*. The Hague: Mouton.

Grishman, H. and Hirschman, L. (1978). Question answering from natural language medical data bases. *Artificial Intelligence* 11, 25–43

Harris, L. R. (1977). User oriented data base query with the ROBOT natural language query system. *International Journal of Man-Machine Studies* 9, 697–713

Harter, S. P. (1978). Statistical approaches to automatic indexing. *Drexel Library Quarterly* 14, 57–74

Hendrix, G. G., Sacerdoti, E. D., Sagalowicz, D. and Slocum, J. (1978). Developing a natural language interface to complex data. *ACM Transactions on Database Systems* 3, 105–147

Hillman, D. J. (1968). Negotiation of inquiries in an on-line retrieval system. *Information Storage and Retrieval* 4, 219–238

Hillman, D. J. (1973). Customized user services via interactions with LEADERMART. *Information Storage and Retrieval* 9, 587–596

Hobbs, J. R., Walker, D. E. and Amsler, R. A. (1982). Natural language access to structured text. In *COLING 82*, J. Horecky (ed.), 127–132. Amsterdam: North-Holland Publ. Co.

Hutchins, W. J. (1975). *Languages of indexing and classification: a linguistic study of structures and functions*. Stevenage: Peregrinus.

Hutchins, W. J. (1977). On the structure of scientific texts. *UEA Papers in Linguistics* 5, 18–39

Hutchins, W. J. (1978). The concept of 'aboutness' in subject indexing. *Aslib Proceedings* 30, 172–181

Keen, E. M. (1977). On the processing of printed subject index entries during searching. *Journal of Documentation* 33, 266–276

Kittredge, R. and Lehrberger, J. (1982), eds. *Sublanguage: studies of language in restricted semantic domains*. Berlin: de Gruyter.

Klingbiel, P. H. (1973). Machine-aided indexing of technical literature. *Information Storage and Retrieval* 9, 79–84

*Lancaster, F. W. (1968). *Information retrieval systems: characteristics, testing and evaluation*. New York: Wiley

Lancaster, F. W. (1977). Information science. In *Natural Language in Information Science*, D. E. Walker (ed.), 19–43. Stockholm: Skriptor.

Larson, S. (1977). On-line systems for legal research. *Online* 1(3), 10–14

*Larson, S. E. and Williams, M. E. (1980). Computer assisted legal research. *ARIST* 15, 251–286

Luhn, H. P. (1958). The automatic creation of literature abstracts. *IBM Journal of Research and Development* 2, 159–165

Mathis, B. A., Rush, J. E. and Young, C. E. (1973). Improvement of automatic abstracts by the use of structural analysis. *JASIS* 24, 101–109

*Montgomery, C. A. (1972). Linguistics and informations science. *JASIS* 23, 195–219

O'Connor, J. (1975). Retrieval of answer-sentences and answer-figures from papers by text searching. *Information Processing and Management* 11, 155–164

O'Connor, J. (1980). Answer-passage retrieval by text searching. *JASIS* 31, 227–239

*Petrick, S. R. (1976). On natural language based computer systems. *IBM Journal of Research and Development* 20, 314–325

Popper, K. R. (1972). *Objective knowledge: an evolutionary approach.* Oxford: Clarendon Press.

*Rijsbergen, C. J. van (1979). *Information retrieval.* 2nd ed. London: Butterworths.

Rush, J. E., Salvador, R. and Zamora, A. (1971). Automatic abstracting and indexing, II: Production of indicative abstracts by application of contextual inference and syntactic coherence criteria. *JASIS* 22, 260–274

Sager, N. (1975). Sublanguage grammars in science information processing. *JASIS* 26, 10–16

Sager, N. (1978). Natural language information formatting: the automatic conversion of texts to a structured data base. *Advances in Computers* 17, 89–162

Sager, N. (1981). *Natural language information processing: a computer grammar of English and its applications.* Reading, Mass.: Addison-Wesley.

Salton, G. (1968). *Automatic information organization and retrieval.* New York: McGraw-Hill.

*Saracevic, T. (1975). Relevance: a review of and a framework for the thinking on the notion in information science. *JASIS* 26, 321–343

Schank, R. C. (1975). *Conceptual information processing.* Amsterdam: North-Holland Publ. Co.

Schank, R. C., Lebowitz, M. and Birnbaum, L. (1980). An integrated understander. *American Journal of Computational Linguistics* 6, 13–30

*Smith, L. C. (1980). Artificial intelligence applications in information systems. *ARIST* 15, 67–105

Soergel, D. (1974). *Indexing languages and thesauri: construction and maintenance.* Los Angeles: Melville.

Sparck Jones, K. (1971). *Automatic keyword classification for information retrieval.* London: Butterworth.

*Sparck Jones, K. (1974). Automatic indexing. *Journal of Documentation* 30, 393–432

*Sparck Jones, K. and Kay, M. (1973). *Linguistics and information science.* New York: Academic Press.

Taylor, R. S. (1968). Question-negotiation and information seeking in libraries. *College and Research Libraries* 29, 178–194

*Walker, D. E. (1977), ed. *Natural language in information science.* Stockholm: Skriptor.

*Walker, D. E. (1981). The organization and use of information: contributions of information science, computational linguistics and artificial intelligence. *JASIS* 32, 347–363

Waltz, D. L. (1978). An English language question answering system for a large relational database. *Communications of the ACM* 21, 526–539

Weil, B. H. (1970). Standards for writing abstracts. *JASIS* 21, 351–357

Weischedel, R. M. and Black, J. E. (1980). Responding intelligently to unparsable inputs. *American Journal of Computational Linguistics* 6, 97–109

Woods, W. A. (1977). Lunar rocks in natural English: explorations in natural language question answering. In *Linguistic Structures Processing*, A. Zampolli (ed.), 521–569. Amsterdam: North-Holland Publ. Co.

Woods, W. A. (1978). Semantics and quantification in natural language question answering. *Advances in Computers* 17, 1–87

Ziman, J. (1968). *Public knowledge: the social dimension of science.* Cambridge: Cambridge Univ. Press.

ROM HARRÉ

# Persuasion and Manipulation

*1. Introduction*

Surely one of the most pervasive features of non-traditional social orders must be the efforts of some members to persuade and manipulate others. There is one kind of persuasion that has come to dominate all others. Recent studies in the sociology of knowledge have tended to concentrate on the ways features of a social order are reflected in and influence the form and content of what we take to be knowledge, and particularly what we admire as scientific knowledge. But the contrary influence has not gone unnoticed. (Habermas, 1971; Moscovici, 1961). One might sum up the views of many commentators in the principle:

'People strive to become what the best authorities say they are'. This suggests some kind of persuasive force in authoritative pronouncements concerning the nature of man, perhaps a persuasive force that is more potent now than heretofore. The most forceful voice of contemporary authority is that of 'scientist'. Part of my task in this paper is to open up the issue of the rhetorical features of scientific discourse, through which that potency is exerted, and to bring together various insights from the work already done to understand scientific writing as persuasive discourse. But I want to link this more specific interest to some general issues in the theory of persuasion, notably the problem of the correct identification of that which is changed when people have been persuaded or manipulated.

*The Concepts of Persuasion and Manipulation*

Clearly 'persuasion' and 'manipulation' are social psychological concepts. They describe processes of interpersonal action, they imply an asymmetrical direction of influence, and, at least the former, seems to entail the existence of a psychological state or condition, that of being persuaded. The latter also seems to have psychological entailments but they are of a negative kind, namely that the victim of manipulation is unaware of the influences exerted upon him.

Like most social psychological concepts, these are both descriptive and normative in complex ways. In describing the basic form of persuasion Aristotle uses the terms 'orator' and 'hearer', and I shall use them as terms of art to refer to the active and passive role. This use suggests that the theory of persuasion is something to do with discourse and hence that its understanding is, in effect, a branch of discourse analysis. The moral structure of these concepts and of the psychology associated with them is quite complex.

i) In the case of persuasion the moral implications seem to be that while an influence is exerted from 'orator' to 'hearer', the effect on the 'hearer' of successful persuasion will be in the 'hearer's' interests, though these will not exclude those of the 'orator'. But the notion of manipulation seems to be reserved for those cases where the effect of successful manipulation of someone or a group of people will be a change in them that is in the interests of the 'orator', and probably not in the best interests of the 'hearer'. From this it follows that of necessity the concept of manipulation can be applied only to those cases of interpersonal influence in which the persons influenced are unaware of the influence, or at any rate of the interests of the 'orator', since, if they were, one of the conditions of successful manipulation would be violated, that is the condition that the 'hearer' thinks well of the 'orator'.

ii) In the case of persuasion it seems to be implied that the 'orator' is engaging the 'hearer' in some kind of dialogue, at least potentially, and is drawing upon the 'hearer's' powers of rational thought. Though this latter notion is somewhat problematic as it is baldly set down here, and will be refined in a later section, at least it is clear that in persuasion the moral quality of the activity is set by the respect which the 'orator' shows to the 'hearer' by treating him as a person. Aristotle says somewhere that to appeal to someone's reason is to draw upon that part of him that is peculiarly human. According to Kant the very foundation of morality is the distiction between treating a human being as a person and treating him as a thing. In manipulation, since the 'hearer' is not engaged as a conscious and rational being in the discourse the 'orator' is and must be treating the 'hearer' as a thing. In the worst kinds of manipulation the 'orator' hopes to affect the 'hearer' through some kind of causal mechanism.

iii) But there is a more subtle moral issue buried in the psychology of persuasion and manipulation. Aristotle's theory tends to enhance the moral standing of all concerned by emphasizing that 'rhetoric is the counterpart of dialectic', and he supposes that the ultimate persuasive discourse is rational. In the tradition of experimental social psychology, particularly as practised by people working on the supposed phenomenon of attitude change, by behaviour therapists and by cognitive dissonance theorists, there is embodied a certain contempt for their subjects. This tradition presupposes that changes of mind, so to speak, are the effects of causes, effectively subsuming the concept of persuasion under that of manipulation. Indeed, without that subsumption the experimentalist tradition would make no sense, since if the 'subjects' are engaged in a conscious dialogue with the experimenter the experiment is thought to be ruined. People are treated contemptuously, as automata. I shall elaborate this point in a later section, since I want to argue that the moral (and political) presumptions of experimental psychology prevent it addressing some of the most interesting topics of interpersonal research, namely discourse analysis.

In a general I will be trying to show that while concepts like 'persuasion' and 'manipulation' are distinctive morally, the persuasive discourses of the 'orators' engaged in these morally dinstinctive projects have certain features in common.

*Rhetoric*

The study of persuasive discourse is perhaps the oldest form of explicit psycho-linguistics. The theoretical sophistication and the detail of the empirical observations make Aristotle's *Rhetoric* the major text to this day. Since psycho-linguistics, like so much in social psychology, is a reflection of the cultural conventions of an era, one can hardly set about refuting Aristotle's principles and observations, since he both abstracted from and part created the rhetorical practices of a civilization. Our task relative to Aristotle, should be to use his principles and observations as guides to the comparative analysis and recording of our own rhetorical practices. There can be no more universal 'laws' of persuasive discourse that there can be universal principles of good literary style.

There is a serious shortcoming in Aristotle's *Rhetoric*. By and large he addresses the problem of the characteristics and mechanism of effectiveness of the speech of the 'orator'. He is concerned with those occasions in which a person has the right to address a group of others, and to be listened to, apparently without interruption. But much persuasive and even manipulative discourse is dialogue: 'Please!' 'No, I don't want to.' 'Oh, go on, let me.' 'No, stop it.' 'Why won't you? It'll be fun.' etc., etc. He nowhere discusses the properties of that kind of dialogue or of any other. Furthermore, even when an audience sits quietly listening to an oration, be it judge and jury, political constituents, playgoers, and so on, it can hardly be psychologically true that the event is a mere monologue. Considered from the point of view of public speech alone, it seems to be a monologue, but we can be fairly sure that the 'orator's' remarks are being counterpointed by a private discourse of each of the hearers. Aristotle nowhere discusses the interactional effects of the dialogue or rather multiplicity of dialogues that are actually going in the courtroom, council chamber, theatre, etc.

Nevertheless it is worth taking our start by reminding the reader of Aristotle's views on the nature of persuasive discourse. He seems to hold that there are three necessary conditions for persuasion to be successful. It must be 'effected either (1) by working on the emotions of the judges themselves, (2) by giving the right impression of the speaker's character, or (3) by proving the truth of the statements made.' (Book III, 1403b)

But it is not quite right to cite these as necessary conditions, all on the same footing. Aristotle points out that someone who arouses the hostility of his or her hearers, or appears to display a bad or unattractive character, say talks in such a way as to seem shifty or dishonest, is not likely to secure conviction. In the last analysis, though, it is the rationality of the discourse that counts. It is just possible that both the emotional and personality conditions could be violated and a discourse which brought on the contempt of the listeners for one they thought sly, might still, through its impeccable 'logical' structure, actually persuade. So the latter might just sometimes be a sufficient condition.

Aristotle does seem to suggest that where a discourse of defective rationality does persuade through the force of the character of the 'orator' and perhaps the favourable/pleasant emotions aroused by his speech, something morally disreputable has happened.

Dialectic, the theory of correct reasoning, defines what is proper in a scientific discourse. Rhetoric, the theory of effective reasoning, defines what is potent in a persuasive discourse. And this parallelism is thoroughgoing, since as Aristotle says 'Rhetoric is the counterpart of dialectic'. In particular the two prime features of persuasive discourse are the use of examples to prove a point, and the use of enthymemes, compressed stretches of logically connected reasonings, in which commonly understood premises are not mentioned explicitly. But these are the counterparts of features of strict dialect. 'Just as in dialectic there is induction on the one hand and syllogism ... on the other, so it is in rhetoric ... I call the enthymeme a rhetorical syllogism and, the example a rhetorical induction.' (Book I, 1356b)

But why, apart from intellectual piety, should one return to Aristotle for the wherewithal to define contemporary research projects? A glance at recent social psychological textbooks suggests that most psychological work on persuasive influences has merely gone over the ground already tilled by Aristotle himself. (C. f. Gergen and Gergen, 1981.) for instance, it is still the case in the contemporary United States as it was in Ancient Greece, that the personality of the 'orator' is as potent as his actual words in getting others to come round to agreeing with him.

*II. How Scientific Discourse Persuades*

Suppose we call the idea that rhetoric is the counterpart of dialectic, 'Aristotle's Principle'. Then does not that Principle suggest that we should make a psycholinguistic study of persuasive discourse with the structure of the discourse of natural science in mind as its counterpart? Of all forms of contemporary discourse, scientific talk and writing seems to have the greatest power. But to define the principles of a scientistic rhetoric, through the use of which that power could be exploited, we would need to have a clear conception of how scientific discourse proper is constructed. Unfortunately there has been little agreement as to the proper and essential structure of scientific discourse. Some philosophers hoped to find it by the application of the principles of formal logic. The ideal of theory as a deductive structure was shared by both C. G. Hempel (1965) and K. R. Popper (1959). But to take logical entailment as the ordering relation which creates an ideal scientific discourse runs into irresolvable paradoxes. The structure of scientific discourse resists explication in such restricted terms. More subtle analyses in terms of multiple supporting structures of balanced analogies begin to come somewhere near capturing the inner form of the discourse of theorizers. Perhaps a programme for abstracting the rhetorical counterpart from them could be undertaken.

We know now after thirty fruitless years, that scientific discourse is not characterized by any specially compelling logical form. Its persuasive power lies somehow in the relations between elements of the content of discourse, not its form. To get to the heart of the matter two myths have to be given up: one that there is a clearly identifiable realm of fact, given so to speak, by the natural world; and the second, that a purely logical coordination of these 'data' makes up a theory. We have to ask two deep questions: how are facts engendered in experience; and how are plausible theories constructed?

Examination of a wide range of scientific disciplines shows that the persuasiveness of a scientific discourse, its plausibility, derives from the interlocking of a number of analogies. (At one time these would have been called 'models', but the term has been so abused that it is better now to drop it). I will adopt one of Aristotle's principles myself and try to persuade the reader of the correctness of the analysis to follow by using an example. It is deliberately chosen to be hackneyed and very clear and simple.

Step 1: In order for common experience to yield 'facts' some way must be found systematically to abstract significant pattern from the complicated and largely undifferentiated givenness of experiece. In the initial stages of his study of the behaviour of gases Boyle explicitly adopted an analogy. He chose to compare gases to springs, and the famous experiment from whence came the Law, was designed to explore the properties of an 'air-spring'. By asking himself whether air-springs behaved analogously to metal-springs he defined his research project. He found that they did.

Step 2: But Boyle could not say why an air-spring behaved analogously to a metal-spring. *Observation* of air or any other gaseous substance will not give one an answer. We must try to imagine something which behaves like a gas. By studying how a swarm of randomly moving minute material bodies (molecules) would behave later theoreticians were able to show that in the relevant respects they would behave like a gas is known to behave, when studied using Boyle's basic analogy. A swarm of molecules behaves like, that is analogously to, a gas-spring when confined and compressed.

Step 3: But might not these molecules be mere figments of the imagination of theoreticians? Why should we find this story plausible; why should it persuade us? At this point a third analogy appears. Molecules are conceived on the analogy with mechanical bodies, that is ordinary material things whose behaviour in certain respects was charted by Newton. A molecule is not exactly like an ordinary material thing, but is supposed to have many of the leading mechanical properties of ordinary things, such as mass, velocity, elasticity and so on.

Taken together a theory (it is really a theory-family, but that point need not concern us in this discussion), is created out of a coordinated trio of analogies, an analytical analogy, a bahavioural analogy, and what one might call a material analogy. In the example all three are mechanical. There are various more subtle demands that the trio must fulfil to be accounted plausible, but the exploration of those would be an issue in technical philosophy of science. What I have just sketched out above is the content structure that determines the persuasiveness of a theory. Much of what is described above does not figure in textbooks accounts of the kinetic theory of gases, which tend to pick out only the patterns of behaviour of natural things already abstracted by the use of an analytical analogy. (Compare, for instance, the patterns of inheritance picked out by Darwin and others using the idea of 'family'.) Only rarely, and that during the formative phase of the conceptual structure that is going to form a theory-family, are the behavioural and material analogies discussed explicitly. In the case of the gas laws I suppose it was Amagat who first set out the full content of the gas-law theory-family explicitly. Darwin, in his usual masterful way, gave a very full account of the analogical structure of the theory-family we call 'The theory of organic evolution' in the first third or so of *The Origin of Species* (Darwin, 1859). The first part of the book is filled with descriptions of breeding plants and animals in domesticity. The upshot is a kind of formula:

$$\text{Domestic variation} \times \text{Domestic selection} \rightarrow \text{Domestic novelty}$$

As the second chapter develops Darwin leads his readers through a great many examples of Natural Variation and Natural Novelty, the appearance of new species. We are carried along by the narrative to the point at which we seem driven to contemplate another 'formula':

$$\text{Natural variation} \times \quad ? \quad \rightarrow \text{Natural novelty}$$

The force is irresistible, and we make Darwin's great discovery ourselves. The unknown and unobservable mechanism of speciation must be Natural Selection.

But this construction of a concept for an unknown and unobservable process is an example of analogical reasoning, and so the limits of the analogy need to be specified by an explicit statement of the negative component in the analogy relation. Darwin systematically deleted some of the common implications of the term 'selection' from his scientific concept. His deletions include volition, and personification of the forces involved.

Could this structure be used to define strategies of persuasion? The most detailed work on the rhetorical features of scientific writing is to be found in K. Knorr-Cetina's (1981) analysis of the transformation of 'traces of laboratory writings' into a 'published paper'. In the laboratory the discovery of a technique often precedes the formulation of a problem for which it provides solutions. One has to hand solutions, and looks about for problems to fit them to. But when a paper is written up for publication, the technique is 'recontextualised' *as* the *best* solution to 'the' problem. The transformation, usually accomplished in the 'Introduction' to a printed paper, ensures that the mythopoeic 'problem → solution' format is retained, having all the persuasive power of the declaration 'Eureka. Here's a (good) solution to a (pressing) problem!' Knorr-Cetina's work is largely concerned with the rhetorics of small scale scientific writings. The analysis I have proposed is appropriate to larger edifices.

The Darwin text could be used as an exemplar to formulate a strategy of persuasion for large-scale works. The text provides a familiar source of understanding, in the analytical and source models which determine the meaning of the theory they underpin. Of course, they need not be drawn from commonsense understandings. Indeed, Darwin takes some trouble to acquaint his readers (probably many of them being urban dwellers) with the details of rural practices with which they would be familiar only in a general way. However novel the concept of 'natural selection' might be, it is made to appear at a specific nexus in an conceptual network, all of whose other elements are familiar. This does suggest a formal strategy in the construction of persuasive discourse — whatever is novel is to be provided with an *aura* of familiarity by establishing a network of semantic links with existing conceptual structures, links created by familiar figures of speech such as simile and metaphor. In the quasi-technical rhetoric which Knorr—Cetina tries to persuade us to accept her account of the rhetoric of successful scientific discourse, the role of interlocking analogical relations, carried by figures of speech, is to *pre*-contextualize novel concepts, seducing us into accepting them as proper by ensuring that *we already know more or less what they mean.*

I return to a reminder of what I called 'Aristotle's Principle', that 'Rhetoric is the counterpart of dialectic'. In what has just gone before I have tried to set out in some detail the 'dialectic' of one of the most persuasive forms of discourse ever invented, that of the natural sciences. Aristotle's Principle could be used with respect to that in two ways. It could be used prescriptively. Having grasped the inner workings of scientific theorizing by which it secures its power to convince (one should not forget the consequential technical power that it gives us over nature as a second-order of persuasion), one could then set about constructing other discourses in which the balancing structures of analogies at the heart of a scientific theory-family is replicated in other fields, say for instance the political. Or the scheme could be used analytically; that is, when faced with a discourse one might search it for the presence of the kind of triple structure I have sketched above. In either case fascinating research projects in the analysis *and synthesis* of discourse branch out from here.

To test 'Aristotle's Principle' I propose to analyse an example of persuasive, academic but non-scientific discourse. According to the principle the structure of linked analogies that serves to found the persuasive power of a scientific discourse ought to reappear as the ground of rhetoric that appears in the non-scientific discourse. The following passage is selected more or less at random from the theology texts in my college library: Lampe, 1977, p. 101.

'The Cross, as the climactic disclosure of the tragedy of man's resistence to the creative love of God, and at the same time of the invincibility of that love, as the revelation, too, of the perfect integration of human will with the will of God, marks the Christ-event as the focal moment in the outreach of God to man. We can rightly claim that Christ's death, the inspiration of the martyrs who have died in his Spirit, the ground of the Christian's death to the principle of sin, and the powerfully effective symbol of total dedication and obedience to God in the face of hideous evil, compels us to assign this central and decisive place to Christ in the history of the creation of man by God the spirit'.

The phenomenon which requires interpretation and explanation is the Crucifixion. Two reinterpretations are offered — (i) it was the result of man's resistance to God's invincible will; (ii) it was an integration of man's will with God's will. This pair are at first glance contradictory. The analytical analogue is that of an *inter-relations of wills* (Christ's willing his own death in the context of man's resistance to God's will in general). The viability of this interpretation and the appropriateness of the analytical analogue depend upon the underlying structure of theorizing which stems from a source analogue, 'the creation of man by God the spirit'. This creates a theoretical framework in which the explanation of the Crucifixion is developed as 'the outreach of God to man'. Just as the gas laws are interpreted through the analogy of the spring and explained through the analogy of the molecules, so the Crucifixion is interpreted through the 'clash of wills' idea and explained, coordinatively, through the picture of the world and man as created by a personalized spirit. Since God is no more observable than molecules we look to *further consequences* to test our whole structure of analogical concepts. We are offered such confirmatory types of events as martyrdom, resistance to sin, and so on. Once again, the social psychological principle that it is an air of familiarity, even if spurious, that makes persuasion and manipulation possible, is exemplified. We shall find that there ar other ways of achieving this.

## III. Attitudes, Beliefs and Language Games

The notions of persuasion and manipulation suggest the exerting of an influence from 'orator' to 'hearer' primarily through the medium of talk and other semiotic displays. In the first section I examined some of Aristotle's hypotheses as to what properties talk etc. must have to be able to exert the alleged influence. But what is it about the 'hearer' that is to be taken as an effect of the influence? I do not think we can develop an adequate social psychology of persuasion and manipulation, necessary for a properly grounded analysis of persuasive discourse, unless the typical terminus of a persuasive or manipulative influence is properly identified. In this section I try to show that neither attitudes nor beliefs could be affected since they are both reifications of features of discourse. Yet individual cognitive structures are indeed affected. If human thought and action are essentially forms of discourse then the cognitive structures relevant to them are the rules and conventions of proper discourse. My argument is directed to showing how research into this field must be focussed on the nature of those rule-systems and how changes might occur.

The psychology of persuasion has been based mainly on two foundations. The one is the generalization of the commonsense concept of 'attitude' to mean something like a mental set which comes out in both speech and action. Since there was alleged to be a disparity between attitudes as revealed to questionnaires and attitudes as evinced in actions, those that believed that there were attitudes, in the above sense, struggled to improve their methods of 'measuring' these mysterious entities, and to solve the problem of why there were these alleged disparities. The second pillar was the theory of cognitive dissonance. It has proved extremely difficult to get a clear statement of the theory, because of the vagueness of the notion of cognitive dissonance. But on one reading it amounts to the view that if someone is forced to act contrary to their beliefs (as these have been admitted to in a prior study) they will adjust the one to other, the exact direction of the adjustment being a function of various situational factors.

Both theories make the mistake of reading back into the 'human mind' certain attributes of discourse. Because someone says 'I believe that so and so' it does not follow that there is something 'in his head' that is *the* belief. We have to ask about the nature of the whole discourse within which that utterance occurs, its place in an essentially collective activity, that of 'talking about beliefs' or, maybe that of 'persuading someone to change their beliefs by avowing one's own' etc. Not that the way of describing the latter language game should be taken literally. If there is 'anything in the head' it must surely be the rules for playing 'belief' language games. And as Needham (1972) has convincingly argued, there are cultures which do not play those language games. On the naive view, that would entitle us to accuse them of some kind of mental deficit, 'not having beliefs'! One must ask 'What is a contributor to a conversations doing when they avow a belief?' Or in a slightly extended sense of conversation, evince one in action, say by voting, by running away or whatever it might be? I may produce a bit of attitude-talk because I wish to appear polite. I may avow a belief because in my culture circle there is supposed to be a rational framework to thought and action of which one's beliefs form a proper and indeed fundamental part. But in one commonplace language game of uttering beliefs, there is no implication of revealing some inner state of believing. Instead the words 'I believe....' are used to make public acts of commitment to a faith.

If there are neither attitudes nor beliefs, as some kind of mental entities, but rather individual cognitive structures are for the most part made up of sets of ruelves for the playing of all sorts of language games, then the puzzling results of 'experiments' in attitude studies, or in cognitive dissonance manipulations, melt away. There cannot be a disparity between an anvowed attitude and envinced attitude, since each will have its proper place in an appropriate discourse. And it will be collective constraints, not personal cognitions that determine what discourse. And it will be collective constraints, not personal cognitions that determine what discourse it is that is being put together by skilled participants. It seems to me that persuasion should not be thought of as the attempt to change mythical model entities like attitudes and beliefs, but to teach people new rules, the rules of novel forms of speech and action. But I cannot make this point just by virtue of the shortcomings of the two classical theories of persuasion. I must reach it by a proper analysis of the nature of thinking in general, and I must connect it up with the remarks about the study of rhetoric from Part I.

Part of what lay behind the old psychology's attempt to 'measure' mysterious properties or entities such as attitudes, was the Cartesian idea of the world as a kind of double universe, an outer objective, primarily physical realm, set over against an inner, subjective and primarily mental realm. How to get from the former, thought to be unproblematically observable, to the other, hidden forever and on principle, from the prying scientific eye? But suppose that that picture is fundamentally mistaken. What if instead of objective and subjective, outer and inner realms, we had instead public and private discourse? Conversations span the alleged chasm between thought and action, between mental and physical, because the realms of public and private conversations are continuous. Add another thought. In his famous dispute with Piaget, Vigotsky argued that theory and observation showed that children did not individually and subjectively develop cognitive powers, such as the power of speech, which somehow emerged into the public world. On the contrary, their primary activity is always public, and collective. It is to be engaged in a public conversation. Gradually features of this conversation are appropriated by a child for personal use, and one of the ways one does that is to get the trick of talking to oneself, of acting to oneself, of perceiving to oneself. Thinking, planning and imaging are species of talking, acting and perceiving, and it is the latter which are *primary*. By that I mean that it is the properties of the latter, the public/collective activities, that determine the properties of the former, the personal or private/individual activities.

If public and private discourses are both forms of talk, so to speak, then persuasion must have something to do with rules of discourse. My hypothesis is this: provided the rules of the private discourse remain unchanged nothing that the current collective forces on an actor by way of public conversational forms (and the actions that go with them) will create anything other than what is quite properly called 'lip' service. But what about new generations? If Vigotsky (1934) and his intellectual descendents, such as Shotter (1974), are right, the forms of private discourse are appropriated by a young child in psychological symbiosis with his or her mother (or other prime caretaker). Such forms will be very resistant to change, since they will be unlikely to be much affected by the public discourse of adults, in say the political arena. Poles can stay catholic after thirty six years of taking part in a constant public-collective discourse of bureaucratic socialism, because there has been another public-collective discourse over and around the cradles of that unhappy nation, couched in a very different rhetoric. It is from that discourse that the infants appropriate, in Vygotskyean fashion, the forms of their private and personal lives, those we mistakenly call inner.

These remarks are themselves but rhetoric. Is there any clinical evidence to suggest that one acts most strongly in terms of the demands of a privatized discourse?

Clinical psychologists have tried to find out under what conditions behaviour therapy works (that is someone begins to abandon their previous ways of acting). The pioneering work in this field of meta-therapeutic studies was done some time ago by Marks and Gelder (1967). It strongly supports the 'private discourse' hypothesis suggested above. They showed that therapy is effective only in so far as there are changes in the private discourse of the actor, within which the actions in question are set, defined and planned for. If we allow a generous concept of discourse, to include the use of symbolic and iconic modes of representation, as well as privatized talk, the personal conversation, so to speak, is the key to the genesis of action. If it is aborted, so is the tendency to do the things originally complained of, and in so far as it is changed so are the things that people do. More recent work has amply confirmed the original insights of Marks and Gelder. It is the dialogue between public exhortation etc., and private reply that is the heart of the persuasive process. And Vygotsky's insight suggests that the properties of that dialogue come from the forms of public dialogue from which the private forms are appropriated.

*IV. Monodrama.*

A scientific discourse persuades (secures conviction) by virtue of the structure of the tacit analogies through which that which is already known or believed is incorporated into a new discourse. I have argued that to persuade is to get someone to change the rules and conventions by which they control their contributions to a discourse. These remarks make up, as it were, two premises upon which an understanding of manipulation can be achieved.

According to these premises a manipulation will have been successful if someone is forced to adopt a set of discourse-conventions which constrain, amongst other things, what actions and speeches he/she can legitimately perform. The first premise above suggests that this can occur through the power of an analogy (usually tacit) to create a condition under which the novel takes on the air of being already known. In describing the phenomena of 'monodrama' I bring out an example of a mode of manipulation, achieved in and through discourse, which involves both a change in the conventions of the victims's discourse, and is mediated by a tacit analogy. The analogy induces in the victim just that necessary sense of familiarity that allows the modulation in discourse conventions to which he/she has been committed, to be taken as natural.

The original concept of monodrama derives from a theory of theatre (Evreinov, 1927). The characters in a play are seen an personifications of aspects of the mind and character of one person. The plot which apparently treats of the interplay of persons with one another is interpreted as an indirect way of representing cognitive processes and emotional tensions etc. In the simplest form of monodrama the psychology of Freud is used to define personifications of Id, Ego and Super-ego, personalifications of personifications, so to speak. In the nineteen-twenties Evreinov actually wrote and directed stage plays built up around the Freudian theory of the human mind.

The notion can be extended and modified to take in a very particular and subtle way in which one human being can manipulate others, through the forms of his/her speech. Torode (1976) has suggested the importance of studying the organization of the pronouns in the flow of speech, in trying to understand how speech itself can create a form of order. Pronouns can be used to create a kind of imaginary world of persons, which is really the construction of the prime speaker. By joining in a conversation with such a speaker other people become trapped in roles which are not their own, and indeed have no place in the social reality from which they come to the conversation, but are created by the prime speaker. Torode calls these 'Voices'. In the original monodramatic productions the interactions of the 'characters' were predetermined by the given psychology, and in monodramatic criticism, say of melodrama, the characters are interpreted in terms of a pre-given psychological theory. The villian is the Id, the heroine's father is the Super-ego and the hero, the Ego. The melodrama merely displays the dynamical relations between these aspects of the mind.

But the monodrama, in this extended sense, can draw on a wider range of plots, picking up perhaps some of the commonplace events of everyday life. Thus the sentence, "We'll have to see" when used by way of a reply to a request addressed to a single authoritative person, exploits the commonplace episode of 'going away to consult with other authoritative persons whose general decision will be eventually brought back'. For instance, this is the plot of the discourse of Trade Union leaders who, when asked about the prospects of a strike, by some public media-person, reply, 'I'll have to consult my executive (ask my members) etc.' The implication is that the decision will be taken elsewhere and at another time. In exploiting the commonsense plot displayed, for example, in the Trade Union leader's speech, the person who says, 'I'll have to see' conjures up the idea of a group currently not on the scene whose deliberations will decide the matter, and for which the speaker, as spokesman, is not responsible. Thus a dispute about the issue addressed cannot be reasonably begun with the speaker, who is no more than a spokesman. It is no good arguing since the speech form implies that the decision is taken elsewhere by others.

This use of 'we' as a 'transcendental voice', is in sharp contrast to the 'royal we', in which the speaker is appearing as the embodiment of the collective will. The user of a 'royal we' is indeed making the decision there and then, and as such can be addressed. But that decision once made is announced not with the feeble authority of the human individual but with the majesty of one who is the sovereign, the embodiment of the people.

Monodramatic analysis is a form of discourse analysis which must proceed through two distinct stages, one looking for form and the other for content. In the first stage the layout of the personal pornouns in a discourse is to be mapped. But the grammatical categories are inadequate to differentiate, say, a 'transcendental' from a 'royal' 'we'. To complete the analysis, the plot (and sub-plots) must be identified, and the analogues with commonplace episodes and their expected ways of unfolding made explicit. Only when that has been done can the pronouns be identified with their proper 'Voices'. When this has been done the structure of the conversation will often appear quite differently from what it would have done if speeches had been assigned only to ostensible speakers. Any given speaker may speak with one or more of several Voices, and the consequent conversation can be understood only if speeches are assigned to Voices, not to persons. Thus, someone who says, 'We'll have to see, won't we?' is, on one possible monodramatic reading of this utterance, producing a speech 'We'll have to see/' as an utterance of the Transcendental Voice, the off-stage authoritative collective, and another speech '/won't we?' as an utterance of the immediate, on-stage, collective of speaker and interlocutor(s) who are currently in conversation. Those who would have to nod or otherwise signify their agreement to that last query (itself not quite what it seems grammatically) are those who are then and there present to the speaker.

Once one has made the step to reading a conversation monodramatically, that is in terms of the parts assigned by being created in the speech forms of the prime speaker, it becomes fairly easy to identify one of the more subtle forms of manipulative speech. The others who engage the prime speaker in a conversation, on the terms implied in the monodramatic uses of the pronouns, are thereby trapped into playing parts with a cast of characters who are the creations of the prime speaker. They are not appearing as themselves but as players in a scenario (taken from some *other* episode than the one currently unfolding) and as such they must play out the scene, *since they already know the plot*. They have themselves been present playing themselves, in the kind of scenes from which the scenario into which they have fallen, was originally taken.

It is a fairly subtle matter to disentangle what one might call the plots of basic episode types. Once we have a repertoire of these adequately described, then we have the necessary material available to make a start on spotting the analogies to such episode structures that form the basis of the plots of manipulative monodramas. Goffman, alone of sociologists and social psychologists, has tried to see episodes as 'unfoldings', as resolutions of situations, resolutions in which the characters of the persons engaged are to some extend in hazard. But apart from his work I believe we know very little about the commonplace plots of everyday life. Pathological forms of life have been catalogued to some extent, (Berne is perhaps still the most comprehensive) but since ethnomethodology slipped away to studying only the superficial forms of the speech order, without using a prior and supervening sociological analysis (thus cutting itself off from speech-act theory), no detailed studies of story-lines, plots and so on of everyday episodes seem to be being done. But without them we can hardly identify the structure of the pronoun distributions in conversations and other discourses of interchange (courtroom procedure for instance).

Both my major examples could be interpreted as special cases of the rhetorical device of 'relexicalization'. This device is examined in detail in Fowler *et al* (1979) and used in the analysis of a wide variety of persuasive and manipulative discourse. A text is 'relexicalized' by deleting transparent descriptive terms, for instance verbs of action ('studying') and replacing them by opaque terms, for instance abstract nouns ('study'). The manipulative effect is to depersonalize the activity of studying, as something people *do*, and so represent it as a kind of entity. The rules for talking about entities admit of the formulation of questions of ownership, as for example, by a University, questions not admissible if the activity is represented as that of 'people studying'.

From the point of view of discourse-analysis the persuasive power of the sense of familiarity created by analogies and monodramatic Voices playing familiar parts, could be treated as a consequence of 'relexicalization'. In both cases there is substitution of one mode of description for another, such that the new mode provides for inferences and actions respectively, not provided for in the original descriptive conventions.

*V. Psychology as Rhetoric*

Folk psychology presumes a distinction between those cases where people reason, form intentions and work out plans for realizing them, and those where matters are out of their control, for instance, because of witchcraft, madness, biological imperatives, and so on. Obviously, the viability of the distinction is not just practical but also political. Much in recent psychology tends to blur the distinction. Two closely related tendencies can be identified. Psychologists talk and write about reasoning and acting as if it were a causal process. They try to study how people reason by performing experiments. But once the *rhetoric* of experiment-talk has been adopted the experiment-episodes are construed, not as opportunities for people to display cognitive skills, local prejudices, hang-ups, coolness under threat, etc., but as tests of causal hypotheses. In the folk-psychology mode of speech people are represented as autonomous; in the scientific mode they are represented as automata. So to re-describe commonplace events in scientific terms is to assimilate non-causal accounts of the genesis of action to causal explanation. Effectively, this is to deny the reality of human autonomy. Even if people display autonomy in the social events called 'experiments', the use of a scientific *rhetoric* to describe them prevents that autonomy being registered, so to speak. Creative or novel moves in the face of the problem set by the experimenter, must be treated not as authentic free action, but as confirmation or disconfirmation of *a priori* hypothesis. In some cases free action is treated as statistical variation. The experiment, then, and its associated rhetoric, is the expression of an essentially reactionary attitude to social life. Divorced from that attitude an experiment hardly makes sense as a way of studying how people produce social actions.

A vivid example of the effect of scientific rhetoric to create a misleading discourse can be found in J. Turner's (1980) description of the psychological 'mechanisms' involved in discrimination.

> '... intergroup discrimination is probably best conceptualized as a psychological or behavioural continuum which varies from maximal ingroup favouritism at one pole to exact fairness at the other (or through fairness as the mid-point to FAV or outgroup favouritism at the opposite pole). Any specific behavioural tendency or position on this continuum would be reflected in both F and FAV pulls. A perfect correspondence between conceptual variables and operational measures would be as follows: maximal FAV and minimal F would indicate maximum discrimination, minimal FAV and maximal F exact fairness and intermediate values of F and FAV would indicate degrees of discrimination. Thus, FAV pulls

increasing from zero and F pulls decreasing from +12 indicate shifts away from fairness towards ingroup favouritism, whereas the reverse changes indicate the opposite. The important point of this simple analysis is that in half the possible combinations of F and FAV values, the pull of F will be greater than FAV and yet the subjects will nevertheless be discriminating in favour of the ingroup over the outgroup — even if only to a moderate degree. This would only cease to be true if subjects compensated for their FAV responses by displaying an equal degree of A or MJP...'

Instead of describing people reasoning in accordance with principles such as fairness and favouritism the psychology of discrimination is 'scientised' by relexicalization into an interplay of 'forces' ('F' and 'FAV') whose scalar product determines how prejudiced people are against the relevant group.

What would happen if, through the effect of social representations, people begin to think of themselves in the same terms as Dr. Turner thinks of them? If I am right in thinking that belief in one's autonomy is among the conditions for being able to act autonomously, and hence to act contrary to the given imperatives of society, anything which tends to undermine the belief in autonomy will tend to make people more inclined to accept as imperatives, the existing rules, conventions, and interpretations of social action that define the political *status quo*. The spread of Turner's scientific rhetoric would be likely to lead to people adopting something like the passive conservatism of traditional societies.

This example, and many others like it, suggest a general thesis; that social psychology may be nothing more than the rhetorical transformation of folk-psychology through relexicalization into a scientistic vocabulary. While the motive of politically naive social psychologists in adopting the rhetoric may be only to persuade, a careful consideration of its consequences suggests it may have far-reaching and deleterious effects as manipulation.

*Bibliography*

Aristotle (1926). *The 'Art' of Rhetoric*, trans. Freese J. H., Heinemann, London.
Darwin, C. (1819). *The Origin of Species*, Dent, London, (1908)
Evreinov, N. (1927). *The Theatre as Life*, Harrap, London.
Fowler, R., Hodge, B., Kress, G., and Trew, T. (1979). *Language and Control*, Routledge and Kegan Paul, London etc.
Gergen, K. J., and Gergen, M. M. (1981). *Social Psychology*, Harcourt-Brace-Jovanivich, New York, etc.
Habermas, J. (1972). *Knowledge and Human Interests*, Heinemann, London.
Hempel, C. G. (1965). *Aspects of Scientific Explanation*, Free Press, New York.
Knorr-Cetina, K. (1981). *The Manufacture of Knowledge*, Pergamon, Oxford.
Lampe, G. W. H. (1977). *God as Spirit*, Clarendon Press, Oxford.
Marks, I. M., and Geller, M. G. (1967). 'Transvestism and Fetishism', *British Journal of Psychiatry*, 113, 711–729
Moscovici, S. (1961). *La Psycho-analyse, son image et son publique*, Presses Universitaires de France, Paris.
Needham, R. (1972). *Belief, Language and Experience*, Blackwell, Oxford.

Popper, K. R. (1959). *The Logic of Scientific Discovery*, Hutchinson, London.
Shotter, J. (1974). 'The development of personal powers', in Richards, M. P. M. (ed.) *The Integration of a Child into a Social World*, Cambridge University Press, Cambridge.
Torode, B. (1976). 'The revelation of a theory of the social world as grammar', in Harré, R. (ed.) *Life Sentences*, Wiley, London, etc.
Turner, J. (1980). 'Fairness or discrimination in intergroup behaviour?' *European Journal of Social Psychology*, 10, 131–146.
Vigotsky, L. (1934). *Thought and Language*, MIT Press, Cambridge, Mass., (1962).

CEES J. HAMELINK

# International Communication

*The field of inquiry*

Studies and debates on international communication tend to adopt a rather narrow conception of their topic and usually focus on one particular dimension: the international news.
 International communication, however, employs a wide range of formats, contents and carriers and encompasses beyond the news, also entertainment, educational materials, children's comics, women's magazines, electronic databases, advertising, and marketing, as well as mail, telex, and telephone traffic for private or business purposes. The one-sided attention generally paid to the phenomenon 'news' unduly restricts the field of inquiry to only one of its facets. As a result, a serious misrepresentation of the issues at stake occurs. In the total international exchange of information, the news represents a relatively minor part. In the problems caused by today's international communication, the news plays no more decisive role than advertising or computer data flows. By concentrating on the news, the transnational industrial organization of international communication cannot be fully appreciated. Compared to the key actors in international communication (such corporations as IBM, AT & T, General Electric, RCA, and Philips), the leading news agencies (UPI, Associated Press, Reuters and Agence France Presse) are 'small fish' indeed.
 The totality of international communication needs to be the focal point of any serious academic inquiry. Only thus can international communication be understood as integral part of the existing international economic, political, and cultural relations.
 Adopting this broad approach, international communication can be seen as 'the total volume of messages that flow across national borders'.
 These transborder flows may occur from point-to-point (as in telephone and computer traffic) or from point-to-mass audience (as in radio and tv broadcasting).
 The flows carry both data (representations of facts, concepts, objects, events, etc. in unprocessed, but processable format) and information (the data processed into functional format).

Data and information do not transmit facts, events, topics, persons etc. per se, they transmit messages. War activities, criminal behaviour, and physical money do not flow across borders, but messages about war, crime and money.

These messages may be for private or public reception, they may be single or multi-layered.

Transborder messages have different forms corresponding to the intentions of their originators; they may be descriptive, evaluative, persuasive, instructive, fictional, or factual. Descriptive messages are for example newsdispatches. Evaluative messages are for example editorial comments. Persuasive messages are for example commercial spots. Instructive messages can be found in international textbooks. Fictional messages populate international TV drama. International funds transfers are examples of factual messages.

On these messages a chain of operations is performed that can be broadly divided into three stages: production (selection of sources, encoding of messages), distribution (technical tranformation), and reception (decoding and further processing of messages).

The format and content of the messages are inseparably linked to the organizational mode of the production, distribution and reception stages. These show a number of relevant constraints which impinge on the messages.

The organizational mode of message production implies such constraints as internal and external institutional pressures (from clients, competitors, authorities, audiences), and more or less rigid professional norms and standards (e. g. 'news values').

The organizational mode of message distribution implies such constraints as the technical and financial availability of transmission vehicles. Infrastructural facilities for international communication (e. g. telex) tend to charge tariffs that are prohibitive to some message producers (e. g. most developing countries). The organizational mode of message reception implies such constraints as the linguistic, psychological and social capacity for decoding and processing of messages. Comprehension and retention of messages, for example, are constrained by the level of 'communicative competence' of the receiver.

These constraints bias messages through omission or distortion. Their emphasis on certain formats and contents is not random: it stems from the basic structural and functional characteristics which determine the organizational modes referred to above.

*Structural Characteristics*

*Oligopoly*: few large transnational corporations control the majority of transborder message production and distribution (Mattelart, 1976; Schiller, 1973, 1981; Hamelink, 1977, 1983a).

*Hierarchy*: few producers distribute to many receivers via one-way flows (Harris, 1974; Varis and Nordenstreng, 1974): the top-bottom (North to South) flow is decisive.

*Synchronic Mode*: the mode of communicating ist prescriptive: receivers are managed into synchronizing with the messages (Hamelink, 1983b).

*Non-participatory*: management of international communication is left to select social strata: predominantly middle/upper middle class, white, Anglosaxon, and male (Ceulemans, 1979; Clement, 1975; Gans, 1979; Murdock, 1979).

*Privatization*: increasingly control over international communication is with private interests rather than with public institutions (Schiller, 1981).

*Commercialization*: the majority of transborder messages is produced and distributed with commercial interests: the commodity 'transborder message' has become big and profitable business (Schiller, 1981; Hamelink, 1983a).

*Technocratization*: the effectiveness of international communication in increasing tied up with the accessibility of ever advancing technical infrastructures (Hamelink, 1984c).

In addition to these structural characteristics, there are the functional requirements for international communication which will determine its organizational modes. Messages will be largely in accordance with these requirements. Dysfunctional messages will tend to be omitted.


*Functional Characteristics*

*Political*: international communication fuctions as an instrument of foreign policy: diplomats and politicians execute foreign policy through the international media (cf. Kissinger), and media producers act as policy-makers (cf. Walter Cronkite in the Begin—Sadat talks). International communication provides political powerholders with a convenient conduit for the transmission of their selected views on the world.

*Economic*: international communication funtions as conduit for the support of economic interests through the marketing of consumerist values, through the advertising of goods and services, through the exploration of foreign markets, and through the distribution of financial information.

*Cultural*: international communication fuctions as conduit for the transmission of the 'metropolitan' cultural system to 'satellite' countries, thus reinforcing patterns of international cultural dependency which provide the cultural basis for the maintenance of the 'metropolis/satellite' disequilibrium (Hamelink, 1983b).

*Ideological*: international communication functions as conduit for the distribution of messages that convey sets of thought patterns through which the existing international order is legitimized: the 'mind management' (Schiller, 1973) of the 'consciousness industry' (Horkheimer and Adorno, 1969;

Enzensberger, 1974) is a vital operative factor for the provision of legitimacy to the international status quo; international communication contributes to 'the belief that the existing political institutions are the most appropriate for the society' (Lipset, 1963) by producing and distributing those messages that legitimize existing social arrangements and by implication delegitimize alternative arrangements.

The transborder messages thus produced, distributes and received, are not all accessible to academic inquiry. A considerable part is only available for quantitative analysis (mail, telex, or computer data flows), and even this offers occasionally insurmountable problems. Messages that are accessible in their aural, visual and verbal textual manifestations, include the following categories:

newsstory (i. a. dispatches from the international newsagencies),
editorial (i. a. newscommentaries in the international press),
advertisement (i. a. commercials in international broadcasting or magazines),
propaganda (i. a. broadcasts from such stations as Radio Moscow or Voice of America),
fiction (i. a. international TV drama, feature theatrical film, children's comics, short stories in international women's magazines)
instructional text (i. a. in international textbooks).

Messages in these categories use a large variety of discourse types many of which have been described elsewhere in this volume, such as interview, drama, comics, political discourse, scholary discourse, advertising, and propaganda.

*The problems*

Today's international communication poses a number of serious problems, largely stemming from its organizational modes.

Particularly after the Second World War the international flow of messages was expected to bring the nations of the world to a better understanding of each other and to the respect for the sovereignty of individual countries. Meanwhile, sufficient documentation has been amassed to show that the international flow is in fact onesided, ethnocentric, and unequally accessible to the nations. This has motivated developing nations to wonder in how far a better understanding can be achieved as long as their contribution to the flow is heavily curtailed.

The problems this causes can be subsumed under four headings: cultivation, legitimation, synchronization, and differential distribution.

*Cultivation*

The constraints on the production, distribution and reception of messages lead to a particular selection of images on the world. Through omission or distortion (e. g. stereotyping) they cultivate in the receivers a highly inadequate representation of the world.

*Legitimation*

The selected images tend to contribute to the belief that a virtually 'exclusive world' (in which many nations do not really participate) is an 'inclusive world' (to which all nations can equally belong).

*Synchronization*

International communication is the main carrier of the process of cultural synchronization which implies that a particular type of cultural development in the metropolitan country is persuasively communicated to the satellite country. The metropolis offers the cultural model with which the receiving party synchronizes. Cultural synchronization is a massive threat to cultural autonomy and a major support mechanism for present international dependency relations.

*Differential distribution*

International communication strengthens through cultivation, legitimation, and synchronization existing international disparities in the distribution of vital resources. It supports present patterns of international trading and benefits mainly its most powerful actors, the large transnational corporations. Therefore, increases in international communication largely increase the benefits of those who can best afford the utilization of its infrastructures.

*The role of research*

Recent developments in international politics have given the study of international communication a new and forceful impulse. Never before has this field enjoyed so much interest from political, commercial and academic circles.

In 1971, in his bibliography on international communication, Hamid Mowlana cited 1457 studies concerning international communication, although many of these refer to 'an understanding of the develpoment as well as the existence of communication in each others' countries' (Mowlana, 1971). In fact, almost half of the studies cited deal more with national than with international structures.

During the second half of the 1970s both the debate and the study on international communication came to flourish, particulary following the first request for a new international information order expressed in May 1976 at the 'Symposium of non-aligned countries on the information media' in Tunis. Various international fora have subsequently put questions relating to international communication high or their list of political priorities which as a consequence has led to a prolonged series of heated and controversial exchanges. Not only in conference rooms, but also in the mass media. In fact, the media have never before commented so frequently on their own performances.

The work done so far on international communication is certainly not sufficient. It has often been fragmentary, piece-meal, and short range. Moreover, the theoretical models applied in the analysis were borrowed from theoretical perspectives that were themseves far from satisfactiory. No pertinent theoretical framework for the study of international communication has yet been developed and as a result there is continuing dependence on: mass media theories (usually based on obsolete psychological and sociological notions); political science theories on international relations (usually inadequate descriptions of the status quo); and imperialism/dependencia theories (usually too narrowly confined to the transfer of mechanisms).

The analysis has also suffered from a number of conceptual deficiencies and consequently dubious operationalizations. An example is the concept of power which is mainly restricted to the measure of influence on the message receiver through linear relations between stimuli and reponses.

Research that has been carried out on international communication can be divided into work on:

— the structure of message production (e. g. Boyd—Barrett, 1977; Guback, 1969, 1974, 1977, 1979; Schiller, 1973, 1981; Tunstall, 1977; Mattelart, 1976; Hamelink, 1977, 1983a);
— the patterns of message flow (e. g. Varis, 1973);
— the contents of messages (e. g. I. A. M. C. R., forthcoming);
— the impact of messages (e. g. Gerbner, 1970, 1973, 1977; Beltràn, 1978; Contreras, 1976).

In summary, it can be said that pertinent studies are particularly lacking on the content and impact of messages, whereas available material on structures and patterns labours under the shortcomings referred to above. All four categories suffer considerably from their relative isolation. There is presently no relevant theoretical framework providing the linkage between structure, pattern, content, and impact. Such a framework would be needed if academic inquiry in this field is to contribute to the solution of the problems outlined earlier.

*The contribution of discourse analysis*

It deserves serious exploration whether present inadequacies in the study of international communication could be overcome by an interdisciplinary effort that would combine the present (largely) sociological analysis with discourse analysis.

Discourse analysis could study the structure of message production as a complex set of discourse processing procedures. It could go beyond simple gatekeeper analyses and linear notions on the relations between media-control and media-power, and probe into the selection of source discourses, the determinant ideological perspectives, and the mechanisms guiding the encoding process.

Discourse analysis could go beyond the normally applied content analytical techniques which tend to stick to surface forms into the analysis of the linguistic and ideological structuration of the messages. Discourse analysis could provide the 'ideological reading' (Veron, 1971) of international communication.

Discourse analysis could go beyond the perennial linear stimulus-response studies. 'Cause and effect' theories determined the beginnings of mass communication research and are today still alive. Intervening 'blackbox' variables have complicated the theory (such as primary group roles, two-step-flow patterns), but have not fundamentally changed it. There is a history to be written of modifications of the stimulus-response model which would show that inspite of all the added sophistications, the dominant model is still of a one-to-one relationship which prevents the insight that the frame of reference which guides the receiver's reconstruction of the messages is largely created by the cultivation of ideological perspectives to which the message producers contributed themselves. Discourse analysis could study how messages are reconstructed, how new discourses are constructed how differential capacity to decode discourses is functional to the strengthening of particular ideological perspectives, how 'selective perception' does not occur as arbitrarily and individually as much of the literature suggests, and which pertinent correspondencies exist between the encoding and decoding of messages (Hall, 1980).

Discourse analysis in collaboration with the sociological analysis could possibly provide the theoretical linkage between the production, distribution and reception of messages. This would promise insight into the ways in which the structuration of messages and the reinforcement of dominant legitimations relate.

If it is indeed the case that international communication produces and distributes the messages which cultivate an image of the present international order as legitimate in spite of its apparent disparities, then its operative mechanisms need to be well understood in order to be exposed.

As long as flows of transborder messages can bridge the gap between pretense and reality, people can be managed into the acceptance of an international order which in fact excludes them from participation. This touches on one of most complicated problems for (north-Atlantic) bourgeois democracy: the legitimation of a non-egalitarian social order. Formally, the existing social order is 'inclusive' and guarantees equal rights and political participation through elections. De facto, however, this order is 'exclusive': its distribution and execution of decisive power is highly unequally divided.

Any social order needs constant sustenance of its legitimacy. It is crucial that the citizen beliefs that the order fulfills indeed his or her needs. If a social order does not deliver what it promises, this needs exposure. The order needs de-legitimizing.

An important contribution to this can be expected from the uncovering of the ideological perspectives which guide production, distribution, and reception of transborder messages. Based on this insight also the development of counter-interpretations could be initiated. Finally, receivers will need the 'communicative capacity' to validate the messages selected for them and to select the sources from which alternative messages can be produced.

*Discourse examples*

The following examples are textual manifestations of international communication which relate to the problems of cultivation, legitimation, synchronization, and differential distribution.

*Cultivation*

Discourse analysis would probe into the source selection, message structuration, and ideological perspective which guided the images that were cultivated in receivers during such historic events as the opposition against the Shah Pahlavi.

Newsdispatches:

'The Shah of Iran postponed a trip to Eastern Europe today and took command of troops acting to break up demonstrations by thousand of Moslem extremists' (Associated Press, May 12, 1978)

'The Shah's troops advanced steadily and the demontrators-an unlikely coalition of Moslem fundamentalists and leftist activists-scattered in panic' (Newsweek, May 22, 1978).

'Shah also has a broad base of popular support, particulary in the army, and among farmers, and a newly created industrial working class, who have benefitted from land reforms' (TIME; June 5, 1978).

'Moslems of the dominant Shi'ite sect are opposed to the Shah's efforts to modernize... by granting freedom to women and redistributing church lands' (Associated Press, October 29, 1978).

These newsdispatches are selected and processed by US based newsagencies and newsmagazines which in spite of their international distribution cater primarily for their domestic audiences.

The message they cultivate is supportive of US foreign policy at the time and reflects the development paradigm in which modernisation and tradition are seen as respectively supporting or obstructing development. Using as basic moral model the good guy versus bad guy dichotomy of the Western movie, the Shah is presented as the modern leader (equals supportive of progress, equals development, equals 'good') who is troubled and hampered in his efforts by an unlikely collection of traditionalists (equals obstruction to progress, equals hindering development, equals 'bad').

### Editorial

'What kind of government of Iran is imaginable without the Shah? The Ayatollah Ruhollah Khomeini, the intransigent, reactionary Shiite religious leader, wants to set up an Islamic republic run by the mullahs, with women shown their place.

This aging figure is now living in France. Flora Lewis of the New York Times interviewed him the other day. She was obliged to remove her shoes, cover her head and shoulders with a large white cotton square draped so that only the eyes showed, and kneel before the Ayatollah to ask questions. It would be hard to convice us that any modern state as large and economically advanced as Iran could conceivably be ruled successfully or for long by the kind of fanatic priesthood that Khomeini symbolizes' (San Francisco Chronicle, November 10, 1978).

This San Francisco Chronicle editorial follows the same basic pattern as the newsdispatches and cultivates a distorted image of the opposition against the Shah, inter alia through a total lack of understanding for Moslem custom, for the Islamic vision on state-religion relations, and the deliberate blowing out of proportions of such details as the removal of the shoes, the draping with the cotton square, and the kneeling.

The last detail is particulary interesting since, as several pictures show, in such talks also Khomeini would be in kneeling position. The suggested humiliation never took place.

## Legitimation

Discourse analysis would probe into the question how receivers are managed into acceptance of the existing social order as legitimate and even mobilized to actively support it.

### Newsstory

'Women are a most effective political weapon.. they have time, and a great capacity, to develop emotion and mobilize themselves rapidly... Women are most directly affected by leftwing economics and politics which create a lack of supplies in the shops. The women will complain at home and can poison the atmosphere. And, of course, there are the wives of military men and politicans' (Washington Post, January 6, 1974).

The best way of legitimizing the existing order is to mobilize people in active support of it. In several instances (the anti-Allende campaign in Chile is a telling example) women have been exploited as such legitimizing instruments. Full use is made in such cases of the whole gamut of sterotypes through which women tend to be portrayed in the media: emotional, a-political, mainly interested in material goods, unemployed, housewives and spouses.

The media also produce messages about themselves in order to instill the belief that they are dealing with the whole and the real world.

### Advertisement

'Whatever the news, you can count on the Trib's objectivity. Reading the Trib, even for a few days, will show how a daily newspaper can become an indispensable friend, helping you to control and understand the flood of information which engulfs modern life. Refreshingly concise and rigorously fair, the Trib's succint global overview will help you bring the world into focus-politically, culturally and financially.' (International Herald Tribune).

## Synchronization

Discourse analysis would probe into the social model that is exported globally in massive editions. The model of the Cosmopolitan girl and the Playboy man.

### Advertisement

'How do you fit it all in? The job (systems analyst), the husband (TV cameraman), the apartment (three rooms and a garden), the friends (dozens and I can't skimp on *them*), two cats (babies later) and a little modern dance on the side. You are organized, that's how...

very, very organized! My favorite magazine says organized is what makes people like to be around because you don't mess up; it also helps you get more out of life every single day. I love that magazine. I guess you could say I'm that COSMOPOLITAN Girl' (Cosmopolitan)

'PLAYBOY fits the social side of my life, the personal side, the 'me' side, if you will. The side that asks, 'How can my life be more enjoyable, more fulfilling?' And PLAYBOY shows me how in a very classy way. I read it and I relate to it and I'm affected by it. PLAYBOY is the magazine for the man who recognizes how much is out there for him in today's world. And I'm that man' (Playboy).

Advertising is just one example of the many carriers through which the transnational communications industry spreads globally the message about 'the real life'.

Transnational advertising does indeed more than selling products and shaping patterns of consumption, it educates, informs, changes attitudes, and builds images.

Most transnational advertising is done for the largest US based producers of consumer articles and it is executed through a few large advertising agencies. Their main concern is to create a global shopping centre in which the world market consumer can feel at ease. National cultural differentiation is inconsequential to this concern.

The transnational corporation cannot recognize the validity of the autonomous nation state or national culture. Cultural ideosyncracies are inadequate for an effective definition of business requirements. The world has to be seen as 'one market' and essential for this market is the 'model consumer': the Cosmopolitan girl, the Playboy man. Since the world market functions most smoothly with an optimal synchronization of cultural values, the message of transnational advertising is that 'real life' depends upon successfull adaptation to values radiated from the metropolis where headquaters and domestic markets are located.

Massive advertising in developing countries suggests the poor to identify with the rich. The message is that poor and rich are mere incidental categories, basically all have similar access to the 'real life'; it is just a matter of luck whether one can buy the goods, and luck can change.

*Differential distribution*

Discourse analysis would probe into the ways in which the differential distribution of resources is supported, made look self-evident and acceptable.

Newsdispatch

'Surinam's economy relies mainly on the exportation of 7 million tons of bauxite a year, which represents one-tenth of world supplies and provides the government with an estimated yearly income of US $30 million in taxes paid by Alcoa Aluminium Company and other producers. Arron's government has adopted a liberal attitude toward foreign investments in Surinam, mainly North American, which total some US $300 million. Nevertheless Arron has insisted that all new enterprises must obtain participation agreements' (UPI, November 24, 1975).

Since source discourses that were not selected or the message production are also pertinent, compare a part of the statement that Surinam's new premier, Arron, made at the eve of the independence and that was omitted in the UPI dispatch:

> 'We shall not let the riches of our land serve to confer greater benefits on others and leave us poor. Our natural resources and our human energy, the capital we dispose of, will be used exclusively for the economic growth of the whole of the nation'.

Many messages in the international communication traffic support more or less explicit the present differential distribution of people's and nation's access to vital resources. This can be very effectively done through sheer omissions, such as Arron's speech shows.

There is also the widespread tendency in international reporting to unquestioningly announce the positive benefits to be expected from new technologies (such as remote sensing satellites) and to suggest that these benefits will indiscriminately befall to developed and developing countries alike.

Few messages are found on how new technological applications will further discrepancies and aggravate already existing problems. The semantics of international reporting is conditioned by the 'technological fix', for all social problems there are technical solutions.

Next to omission the other crucial device is distortion. The unequal relation between, for example Surinam and the US is made to look very attractive for the poor country. The US transnational corporation is depicted as the key instrument for Surinam's economy: it 'provides' the Surinam government with considerable revenues. Receiving all this tax money, it is only logical that the Surinam government would be 'liberal'.

*Bibliography*

Beltran, L. R. (1978). TV etchings in the minds of Latin Americans: conservatism, materialism and conformism, *Gazette*, 24—1, 61—85.

Boyd-Barrett, O. (1977). The global news wholesalers. In *Mass Media Policies in Changing Cultures*, (G. Gerbner, ed), Wiley and Sons, New York, 13—20.

Ceulemans, M. and Fauconnier, G. (1979). *Mass Media: the Image, Role and Social Conditions of Woman*, UNESCO Press, Paris.

Clement, W. (1975). *The Canadian Corporate Elite*, McClelland and Stewart, Toronto.

Contreras, E. et al. (1976). *Cross-cultural broadcasting*, UNESCO Press, Paris.

Enzensberger, H. M. (1974). *The Consciousness Industry*, Seabury Press, New York.

Gans, H. J. (1979). *Deciding what's News*, Pantheon Books, New York.

Gerbner, G. (1970). Cultural indicators: the case of violence in television drama. *The Annals of the American Academy of Political and Social Sciences*, 388, 69—81.

Gerbner, G. (1973), Cultural indicators: the third voice. In *Communication Technology and Social Policy* (G. Gerbner, L. P. Gross, and W. H. Melody, eds), Wiley and Sons, New York, 555–573.
Gerbner, G. (1977), Comparative cultural indicators. In *Mass Media Policies in Changing Cultures*, (G. Gerbner, ed), Wiley and Sons, New York, 199–205.
Guback, T. H. (1969). *The International Film Industry,* Indiana University Press, Bloomington.
Guback, T. H. (1974), Film as international business, *Journal of Communication*, 24–1, 90–101.
Guback, T. H. (1977), The international film industry. In *Mass Media Policies in Changing Cultures* (G. Gerbner, ed), Wiley and Sons, New York, 21–40.
Guback, T. H. (1979) Theatrical films. In *Who Owns the Media?*, (B. M. Compaine, ed), Harmony Books, New York, 179–249.
Hall, S. (1980). Encoding/decoding. In *Culture, Media, Language* (S. Hall, D. Hobson, A. Lowe and P. Willis, eds), Hutchinson, London, 128–138.
Hamelink, C. J. (1977). *The Corporate Village*, IDOC, Rome.
Hamelink, C. J. (1983a), *Finance and Information*, Ablex, Norwood.
Hamelink, C. J. (1983b), *Cultural Autonomy in Global Communications*, Longman, New York.
Hamelink, C. J. (1983c) *Transnational Data Flows in the Information Age*, Studentlitteratur, Lund.
Harris, P. (1974). Hierarchy and concentration in international news flow, *Politics*, 9–2, 159–165.
Horkheimer, M. and Adorno, T. W. (1969). *Dialektik der Aufklärung*, S. Fischer, Frankfurt, 128–176.
International Association for Mass Communication Research (I.A.M.C.R.) (forthcoming), *The World of the News: the News of the World*, UNESCO Press, Paris.
Lipset, S. (1963). *Political Man*, Doubleday, New York, 63
Mattelart, A. (1976). *Multinationales et systèmes de communication*, Anthropos, Paris.
Mowlana, H. (1971). *International Communication, a Selected Bibliography*, Kendal/Hunt, Dubuque.
Murdock, G. (1979). *Mass Media and the Class Structure*, Centre for Mass Communication Research, Leicester.
Schiller, H. I. (1973). *The Mind Managers*, Beacon Press, Boston.
Schiller, H. I. (1981) *Who knows: Information in the Age of the Fortune 500*, Ablex, Norwood.
Tunstall, J. (1977). *The Media are American*, Columbia University Press, New York.
Varis, T. (1973). *International Inventory of Television Programme Structure and the Flow of TV Programmes between Nations*, University of Tampere, Tampere.
Varis, T. and Nordenstreng, K. (1974). *Television traffic: a one-way street?* UNESCO Press, Paris.
Veron, E. (1971). Ideology and the social sciences, *Semiotica*, 3–1.

# Part II Applications Extensions Critical Approaches

GÜNTER BENTELE

# Audio-Visual Analysis and a Grammar of Presentation Forms in News Programs: Some Mediasemiotic Considerations

> Dedicated to Ivan Bystrina in
> honour to his 60th birthday

*Introductory Remarks*

In this contribution, the question is discussed how mass media and, above all, the content and form of mass media can be analysed using descriptive procedures of semiotics in their widest sense. For this purpose, a programmatic classification of these problems within the boundaries of a *semiotics of mass media* will be presented in the first chapter. In the second chapter, methodological questions concerning audio-visual analysis will be discussed. Using the example "television news", a practical model for analysing audiovisual discourse — e. g., for the reconstruction of media grammars — will be presented on chapter three.

*1. Communication Studies, Discourse Analysis and Media Language*

*1.1 Communication Studies and Media Language*

The scientific analysis of mass communications, known as "Publizistikwissenschaft" in the Federal Republic of Germany since 1945[1], has been preoccupied with sociological, economical and political (that is, macro-social) lines of questioning. Investigations of individual psychological effects of the media were also examined from the very beginning. For a long period of time, products of the mass media were analysed only with the instruments of sociological *content analysis*. During the past ten years however, and not only in the Federal Republic of Germany more and more linguists and literature scholars have begun to use linguistic, literary and semiotic methods to examine the contents and forms used in mass media. This can be seen as a reaction to

---

[1] cf. Bohrmann (1981, 132 ff.); Bentele (1984a).

the neglect of micro-analysis in the traditional social-science oriented journalism and science of communications.

While examining mass media products, one lately confronts a concept which, in spite of its intuitive appeal, is in no way precisely defined but rather serves as a metaphor[2]: the concept of "media language(s)".

Attempting to grasp this concept more precisely, one should differentiate between various levels and phenomea often ascribed to this concept.

a) the oral written language used within the mass media (print, radio, television, film, etc.)[3]
b) the language of the images, covering for example
   − the structure and expressive force of photographs in the newspapers
   − the "language" of film[4]
   − the "language" of television[5]
c) nonverbal behavior of persons appearing in the mass media: e. g., gestures, facial expressions and body motion of journalists or politicians
d) certain symbolic systems and rituals that have achieved their special value through the media: political and military rituals, ceremonies, commemorative events, summit conferences etc.[6]
e) graphic sign systems of simple (e. g., punctuation) or complex (e. g., layout) nature.

Research in all of these fields could be integrated into one unified discipline which I will call "*Semiotics of Mass Media*" (*Mediasemiotics*). Semiotics of Mass Media constitutes a sub-discipline of both communication studies and semiotics. Rather than examining mass communication from a primarily sociological, political, technical or other aspect, it derives its main concepts, methods and goals from information-theory and semiotics[7].

Semiotics of mass media is obviously an *interdisciplinary* endeavour, as are semiotics and communication studies. The following Fig. 1 shows the relationships between communication studies, semiotics, film science, and linguistics:

---

[2] cf. Deer/Deer (1965); Sturm/Grewe−Partsch (1979) and others.
[3] cf. Straßner (1981).
[4] The problem of film 'language' is dealt with only metaphorically and often only very imprecisely in most 'classical' film theories. This problem has been more precisely dealt with since the mid-60's with the help of linguistic and general semiotic theories. Cf. the bibliographies from Eschbach/Rader (1978) and Möller (1983). For this problem see also the recent comprehensive work by Möller (1984).
[5] cf. Schulz (1982); Pross (1982), Hunt (1981).
[6] cf. Pross (1974); Edelman (1972).
[7] cf. Bentele (1981).

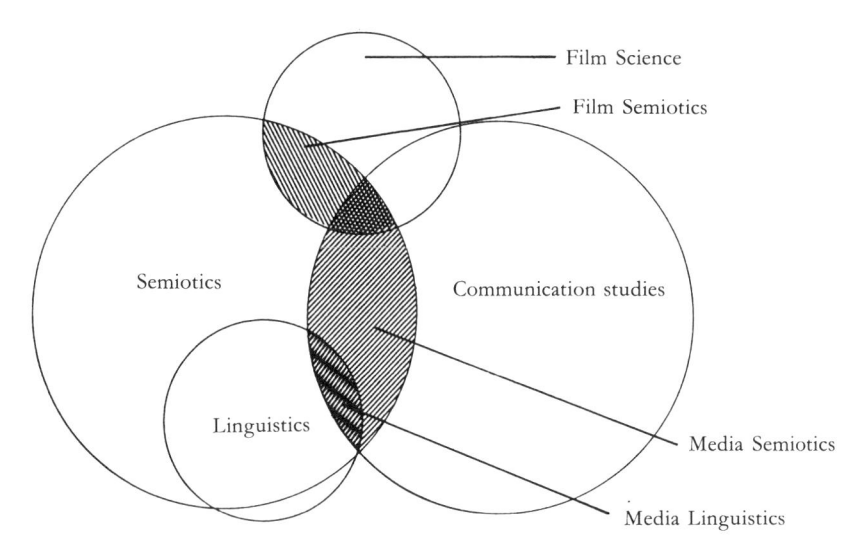

Fig. 1: Relations between different disciplines

*1.2. Some basic Concepts in Mediasemiotics*

In this section a number of mediasemiotic concepts are clarified.

The processes of mass communication normally follow certain *rules*. Because both the manufacturing (producing) and the reception of the products of mass communications are *rule-guided processes* and the rule-systems are of high complexity, one can speak of *codes of mass communication*.

Codes can be conceived of as *ordered sets of rules* or *rule-systems*.[8] Sign producers (journalists) and sign recipients (readers, listeners, viewers, etc.) use these codes without necessarily being aware of their existence. The mastery of these rule-systems can be characterized as *"media competence"* in a similar vein as Chomsky uses the notion of "linguistic competence".

Whereas in natural languages, there is no fundamental difference between competence in producing and competence in understanding sentences (active and passive competence), such a distinction is important in relation to the mass media. The media competence$_p$ (production) of a journalist can be described in general as the capability to master a set of rules necessary to produce media products (texts in their widest sense). This includes the mastery of the rules of craftmanship, often described as "transmission-" or "mediation-competence".[9]

---

[8] cf. Bentele (1984, 127 ff.); Eco (1977, 36 ff.).
[9] Saxer (1979) distinguishes three types of knowledge: 'communicative competence' (i. e. 'journalistic competence'), 'departmental knowledge', and 'reflexive knowledge'. Cf. also Pürer (1984, 336).

Media competence$_r$ (reception), accordingly is the capability of the recipient to perceive and interpret semiotic systems in the media according to a system of rules. Media competence$_p$ and media competence$_r$ overlap and perhaps media competence$_r$ can totally be seen as part of the media competence$_p$.

With the exception of certain codes of perception, these capabilities which can be described as codes, have developed in large part during the past 300—400 years, most rapidly during the past 80 years in the social learning processes and form a cultural tradition transmitted.

Rules and rule-systems are obviously objected to cultural change: rules have disappeared and new rules have formed; the description of these codes must therefore be conducted within their historical context: historical change can be described as the diachronic process of *code-change*.

In contrast to grammars of natural languages, some of which have been codified in written form (starting with Panini grammar), the emergence of *media grammars* is a much more recent development. On the side of the communicator, the acquisition (learning) of media competence has been in large part institutionalized (internships, journalists schools, universities). This is not true with respect to the recipient. The acquisition of mediasemiotic competence on this side is rather a "national learning"-process taking place without "supervisors".

"*Grammar*" can be defined as a system of rules for the combination of certain elements (e. g., simple and complex signs). In this syntax-based concept of grammar, one can distinguish between sentence grammar and text grammar. When simple and complex signs are combined by grammatical means so as to form texts, structures which can be received under situational constraints by recipients endowed with certain cognitive and emotional predispositions and expectations, come into existence.

*Signs* can be defined as *intentional signals* (intentionally produced information-vehicles) which refer to something else. Signals which refer to something else without being intentionally produced, are referred to as *indicators*.[10]

According to Bystrina (1983), one can make a distinction between *primary, secondary* and *tertiary codes*.

Primary codes, that is codes, which must be regarded as primary in both ontogenetic and phylogenetic respects, include *genetic codes* as well as *intraorganismic codes* and *codes of perception*. The rules according to which large molecules are joined and separated in intracellular processes are very "strict". Here, one often speaks of "natural laws", because of the chemical and physical basis of these processes. But even here, "mistakes" are possible: heredity diseases or mutations, for example, can be the results of such mistakes.[11]

---

[10] The concept of 'sign' used here differs from the classical concepts of Peirce and Morris. For a more precise distinction of 'sign', 'indicator' and 'signal' cf. Bentele/Bystrina (1978) and Bentele (1984).

[11] For a discussion of analogies between genetic and human language codes cf. Jakobson (1974); Masters (1970); Eigen (1979).

When plants, animals, and — in particular — human organisms perceive external reality, they also apply to rules. On the one hand, perceptual processes are partly innate (the perceptual apparatus already exists at birth). On the other hand, perception must also be learned. Some rules of perception change ontogenetically, others historically. In this respect, we can speak of *primary codes* to refer to both forms of "ordered" perception.

Our natural languages are also ordered by rules, they involve grammars. The *degree of stringency* of the rules of language is however low in comparison to the invariance of primary codes. Within language codes, the degree of invariability varies as well, declining from the phonological and morphological over syntactic codes to the semantic and pragmatic codes.

Language codes are phylo- and ontogenetically more recent than intra-organismic codes and the codes of perception. Hence the term *secondary codes*.

Pictures (by painters and photographers) are equally produced — perhaps not in the same degree, but still in large part — according to certain rules of individual or general validity. Viewers must master these rules to be able to decipher pictures. Codes of both natural and artificial languages, as well as visual codes can be subsumed under the concept "secondary codes".

Texts and, more so, genres (art forms as literature, film etc.) however cannot be described solely on the basis of (secondary) linguistic rules. The rules of conversation or rules of text construction, for example, in drama, television features or documentaries, all belong to *tertiary codes*. They are built on the basis of primary and secondary codes and are a more recent genetic development. Obviously, the stringency and fixedness, that ist the possibility of deviation, is very different here. Bystrina (1982) referring to Jakobson, therefore speaks of a "Law of Decreasing Stringency" from primary over secondary to tertiary codes.

It must be emphasized that, on all three levels, at least one *syntactic*, one *semantic* and one *pragmatic* dimension exist.

Codes are stored as *patterns* in the human brain, partly as results of genetic programming (especially large parts of primary codes), partly as results of learning processes.

When these code-patterns are activated in signal, indicator, and sign processes, only certain parts of the codes are normally retrieved from memory. By means of the simultaneous retrieval of signal patterns which are also stored in the brain, signs or texts are generated in the process of sign production.

The unintentional *breaking of rules* — i.e., the realisation of text possibilities not provided for by existing codes, enable the historical development of new rules and rule-systems (codes). This phenomenon is particularly important in relation to artistic signs and sign-systems (e.g., film) and other mass media, not defined as art.

There is one other important aspect that needs to be mentioned: at all three levels of primary, secondary and tertiary code processes take on, at least partly the form of *selection* and *combination*. This distinction is based upon the "Two-

Axis-Theory", conceived by Kruszewsky and de Saussure, to account in particular for natural language phenomena. Jakobson (1971) has further developed the "Two-Axis-Theory" to include also non-verbal sign-systems.[12]

*1.3. Codes of the Mass Media: A Typology*

As long as only *print mass media* existed, the sign-systems of writing, layout, drawing and graphics, and, at a later stage, photographics have played the dominating role. Since the appearance and large-scale distribution of *film* and, in particular *television*, motion pictures in conjunction with spoken text have become increasingly important. It would be an immensely interesting scientific enterprise to systematically trace the development of the various media codes from the beginnings of the printed press in the 17th Century to the new telecommunication technologies such as teletext, videotex, cable and satellite-tv, and to integrate this reconstruction into an empirically based theoretical framework. This is, for the present, not a realistic task. In our attempts to provide systematic and precise descriptions of forms and contents of mass-media, we have to settle with classifications, typologies, and partial theories in verbal form, at least for the time being[13]. In some areas it may then be possible to progress to a precise reconstruction of codes (and grammars) or parts there of.

To give an impression of the different roles which codes play at different levels in the *domain of television* alone, I will present a segment of a *code typology* in Fig. 3.

It becomes clear from the code typology that codes with differing degrees of invariance — ranging from international agreements, which are often based on lengthy negotiations and are only valid for limited time periods all the way to the fairly invariant primary codes of perception — can indeed be represented within a unified hierarchy. While the examples relating to the level of partial broadcasting systems refer to broadcasting in general, all lower levels only refer to the program type "news". Of course, neither the various interrelationships between the levels can be represented in this diagram nor the evolution of codes on each level. The higher levels, including the level of the program codes are normally laid down in writing. Laws and broadcasting charters need not be reproduced here. But the reader may find an example of a *program scheme* to be informative, that is, of a macrosyntactical code for the sequencing of different types of programs within certain time units such as days or weeks (Fig. 3).

This sequencing is also based on explicit agreements, its validity lasting only for limited time periods.

---

[12] cf. Holenstein (1975, 142 ff.).
[13] cf. McQuail (1983) as a quite far developed theory of mass communication mostly in verbal form.

| Level | Code Type | Examples |
|---|---|---|
| *World* | international conventions and laws | world information order; International Frequency Treaty; satellite treaties, etc. |
| *individual states and countries* | general laws | basic laws and constitution; civil law codes; § 5 of the FRG constitution |
| *partial system of broadcasting* | laws and treaties on broadcasting | broadcast laws of the German federal states; charters of German Broadcasting Networks (ARD and ZDF) |
| *cultural codes* (in part specific to culture and local systems) | general broadcasting principles (explicit and implicit) | truthful and objective reporting: independence, fairness, right to rebuttal |
| *program codes* | program schemes | program schemes ARD & ZDF and individual stations |
| *tertiary codes* — genre codes | basic principles of individual genres, e. g., news programs | truth and objectivity; actuality; comprehensive and of general interest |
| *tertiary codes* — text codes | thematic codes (selection and combination) | pyramid structure of news programs; foreign and internal affairs; relevance to political and geographical criteria; |
| | codes combining verbal and non-verbal information | synchronicity of text and image; contradiction etc. |
| | textsyntactical codes | sequence of text types (news, report, interview, etc.) and forms of presentation; pyramid structure of a report |
| *secondary codes* | language codes | short, easy-to-understand sentences; quoting source in first sentence; diverse rules of language usage |
| | image codes — motion | codes of editing; syntax of cinematographic properties |
| | image codes — still | framing; visual aids; position of anchorman; diverse image-levels |
| *primary codes* | perception codes | bright/dark; up/down; left/right; color perception; perspective movement, etc. |

Fig. 2: Mass Media Code Typology

Beneath the program code level, codes are normally fixed only in very general terms, sometimes only implicitly. Parts of the secondary (media) *language* codes are also exactly written down, but they are based upon the

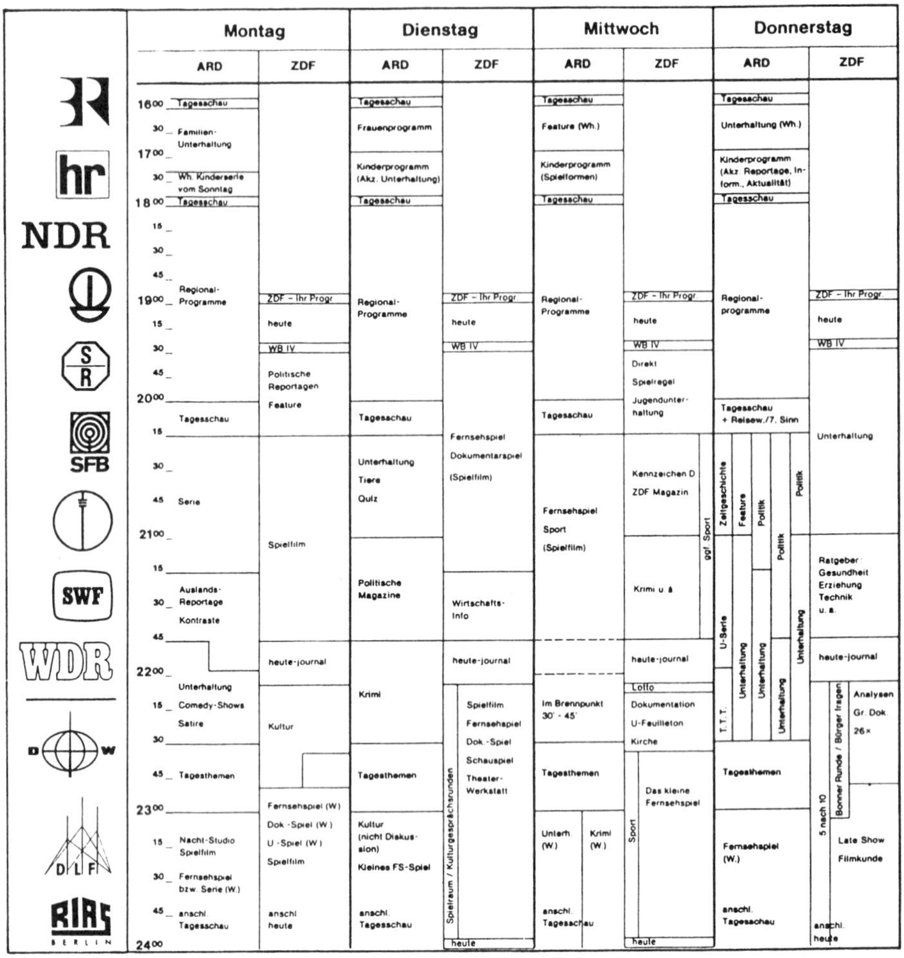

Fig. 3: Programme Scheme of German TV

standard codes and grammar of the country's national language (this aspect could also not be included in Fig. 3). Textbooks for the journalistic profession often include written versions of various text- and genre-codes, image-codes, etc. Textsyntactic codes, in contrast, are often stored only in the minds of newsworkers. On the basis of this outline of some fundamental concepts of a possible semiotics of mass media, I now want to address some *methodological issues* in the analysis of audio-visual products.

This introduction of some basic concepts within the framework of general semiotics was necessary not only to clarify the basis of a potential semiotics of mass media. Many of the concepts can immediately by used as mediasemiotic concepts: primary, secondary and tertiary codes, e.g., play an important role not only within production, but also within reception processes of mass media texts. It was furthermore intended to accentuate a point of view within media research, which does not focus on macrosocially oriented statistical analysis, but rather on microsocially oriented descriptions and reconstructions of rule-systems. Macrosocial and microsocial approaches are surely not seen as contradictory, but as complementary. This problem will be discussed in more detail in the next section.

## 2. Three Main Types of Audio-Visual Analysis[14]: Some Methodological Considerations

Roughly, the analysis of audio-visual programs can be divided into *three main types*: qualitative analysis, (systematic) *content analysis* and *semiotic and structural analysis*.

### 2.1. Qualitative analysis

Qualitative film and television analysis largely consists in the viewing of film and television programs with the goal of underscoring certain noteworthy characteristics such as plots, stylistic elements, actor performance, etc. This is characteristic of both of the various forms of this type of analysis, namely *film criticism* and *film-viewing in educational settings*.

On the basis of short descriptions of content, interpretations and subjective value-judgements are made in ways, which make intersubjectively valid assessments virtually impossible. To be sure, the judgements of film critics are often right-on-the-mark, but only due to the background experience of the individual critic.

The analysis procedures of this first main type of audio-visual analysis are summarized in Fig. 4.

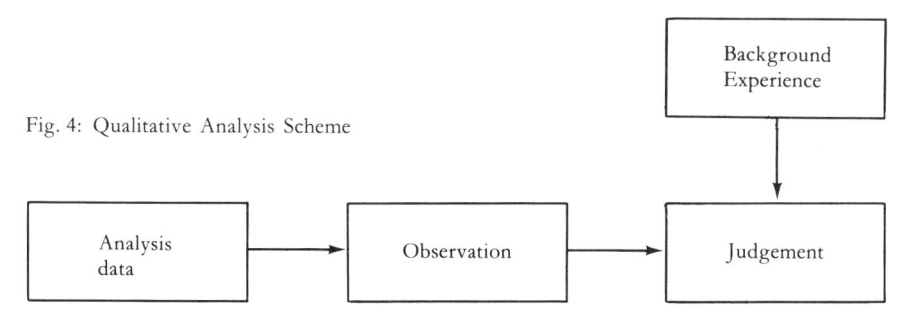

Fig. 4: Qualitative Analysis Scheme

---

[14] Since we are dealing here with film and television programs, the more precise concept of 'audio-visual analysis' is sometimes replaced by the term 'film and television analysis'.

Abstracting from the idiosyncratic differences between individual film critics (more or less systematic; more or less intersubjectively reconstructable), *educational film presentations*- e. g., *film discussions* in classroom situations — can be distinguished from film critisism in so far as the categories of analysis are more clearly and explicitily defined than in the case of most film critics. The type of film analysis that has been offered within literature and theater science in the last several years[15] often represents a mixed form, uniting characteristics of the first main type (low level of intersubjective reliability of descriptions and value judgements) with characteristics of the third main type and partly of the second main type. It is more common here to use protocols of parts of the materials.

## 2.2. Systematic content analysis

Systematic content analysis of film and television programs proceeds in a series of steps, as each other content analysis, working with other type of material:

a) *observation* of the materials
b) development of a more or less comprehensive *category scheme*, according to particular problems and line of questioning.
c) *coding* of the materials on the basis of a number of intermediate procedures, such as pretesting, coder training, successive improvement of category schemes, etc.
d) *evaluation* of the coded data, *analysis* and *interpretation*.[16]

This method of analysis is especially suited for the analysis of large data samples — e. g., television news programs over a period of weeks, stylistic characteristics of American feature films from 1930 to 1940,[17] etc. Operationalized by means of a category scheme which relates to the issues to be investigated, only a small amount of information is normally "retrieved" from each tv or film program and subjected to analysis. In the best case, the data thus retrieved reflect exactly the data needed to answer the specific research-questions applied to the sample of texts. This method has the advantage of a high degree of intersubjective control. Another advantage is the possibility of examining large amounts of data and text materials. But, depending on the overall issues to be adressed, content analysis has disadvantages as well; e. g., most content-analysis procedures are too "wide-meshed" to allow a detailed line of investigation. Another disadvantage is that content analysis

---

[15] cf. Albrecht (1979); Silbermann/Schaaf/Adam (1980); Faulstich (1980); Hickethier/Paech (1979).
[16] See the time-lapse diagram of content analysis in Merten (1983, 312 ff.), as well as the detailed description of the uses of content analysis in Früh (1981).
[17] cf. Salt (1974); Salt (1976), Salt (1977).

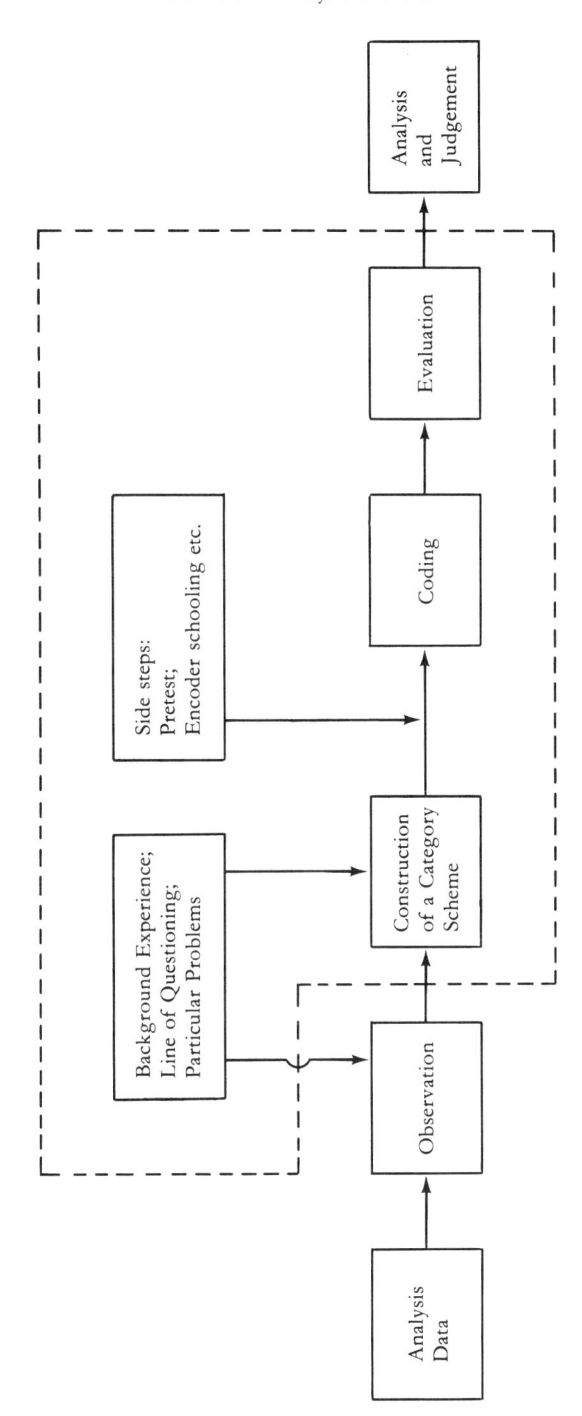

Audio-visual Analysis and Grammar of News Programs    169

Fig. 5: Content Analysis Scheme

normally focusses only on the frequency of distribution of certain variables. Coding procedures within content analysis are based on a relatively simple concept of semantic processes: the possibility to unambiguously identify certain perceivable signs as words, sentences, text fragments, images, action-sequences — and technical characteristics such as panning, zoom etc. is taken for granted. It is assumed that *definite meanings* can be assigned within the coding process. Results of reliablity tests, however, which probe for inter-coder-reliability show the limits of these possibilities. An agreement of 0.75 to 0.8 often is considered as sufficient reliablity.

Relations between individual elements, that is, syntactic relations at the level of sentences (microsyntax) or texts (macrosyntax) have, so far, rarely been examined using content analysis techniques.[18]

A highly simplified schematic representation of systematic content analysis of audiovisual materials is given in Fig. 5.

It is obvious that, in comparison to qualitative film and tv-analysis, a number of *additional steps* are involved in this type of analysis. They range from explications of the questions in research to the operationalization of categories to the coding and evaluation of the materials. "Objectivity" is made possible by the intersubjective reconstruction of each step in the analysis and, thus, of the results.[19]

*2.3. Semiotic and structural analysis*

A great number of analysis procedures can be subsumed under the concept of *semiotic and structural film and television analysis*. The emphasis in each case is placed on the possibility of intersubjectively reconstructable *structural description* of film and television programs. Methods used include, among others, the classificatory procedures such as that developed by Metz (1972) which examines types of syntagmas in feature films, and its extension by Fledelius (1979). Classificatory procedures based on literary studies methods e. g., (Knilli/Reiss, 1971), as well as various procedures developed in linguistic text analysis and applied to audio-visual materials can also be included here.[20]

The choice of the term "semiotic" for this type of analysis procedures is motivated by the *disciplines* within which they have been devised: literature studies, linguistics, and general semiotics. They all adress linguistic and "hyperlinguistic" sign systems.

Semiotic procedures differ from qualitative film and television analysis in that film and television programs are not interpreted directly, but rather first transcribed or translated into written *protocols*. It is obviously impossible to

---

[18] For new approaches in content analysis cf. Rosengren (1981).
[19] cf. the concept of 'objectivity' in content analysis discussion in Lisch/Kriz (1978).
[20] for that type of analysis see also Williams (1976); Bellour (1979); Nichols (1979); Heath (1975) and others.

transpose all of the information contained in an audio-visual product to a written form, that is, include it in a protocol. The transcription of dialogs and monologs for example, is commonly reduced to a reproduction of the main parts of the text. Written versions of oral speech in "average" protocols are little more than the text itself. Neither paralinguistic features, e. g., intonaton and other suprasegmental markers, nor performance features such as pauses and non-verbal elements of communication (gestures, facial expressions and body motion) are transcribed. Overall, transcriptions of visual elements normally include events (action-sequences which, together, constitute the narrative structure) as well as props, landscapes, buildings, etc., which are considered relevant. Cinematographic properties, e. g., camera-angle and camera-movements, framing, shot-length, and, occasionally, the construction of the filmic space, are also included in the common type of protocols.

On the basis of such protocols and certain additional, *contextual and formal relationships* in the materials, direct analyses and interpretations of certain plot elements (the simplest form of film analysis), or *structural descriptions* are worked out. For example, certain formal devices such as shot-length and focal-points can be summarized in "shot profiles" (Kuchenbuch 1978, 22 ff.), The following illustration (Fig. 6) is an example of a *shot profile* of a sequence of shots in the "Tagesschau" program, which is used here for demonstration purposes.

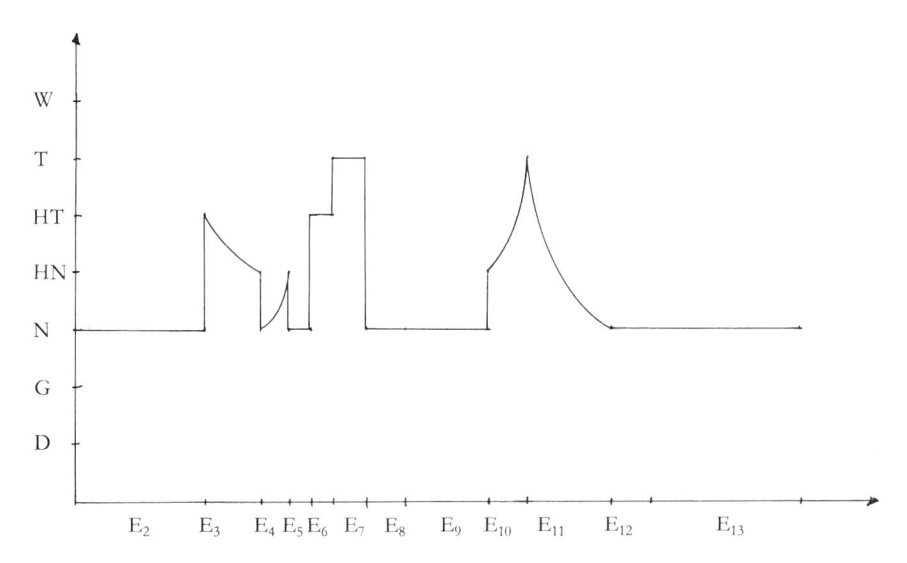

E = Einstellung (shot); W = Weit (extreme long shot); T = Totale (long shot); HT = Halbtotale (medium-long shot); HN = Halbnah (medium shot); N = Nah (medium close-up); G = Groß (close-up); D = Detail (detail)

Fig. 6: Shot profile (Sequence 2 of "Tagesschau" cf. Fig. 10)

172     G. Bentele

Whereas in this shot profile the shot-length and camera-distance are correlated by means of a diagram, it is also possible to correlate other cinematographic properties. Besides shot profiles of this type, a number of other types of structural descriptions are currently in use: Kuchenbuch (1978, 30 ff.) for instance shows *sequence-diagrams* which order sequences at several levels, linguistics for example often use *tree diagrams* to represent syntactic structures. Overall, *structural descriptions* are the main focus of structural and semiotic analysis of audiovisual products. A basic scheme of a semiotic and structural analysis is given in Fig. 7.

```
┌──────────┐     ┌──────────┐     ┌──────────────┐     ┌────────────────┐
│ Analysis │ ──▶ │ Protocol │ ──▶ │  Structural  │ ──▶ │  Analysis and  │
│   Data   │     │          │     │ Description  │     │ Interpretation │
└──────────┘     └──────────┘     └──────────────┘     └────────────────┘
```

Fig. 7: Basic Scheme of a Semiotic and Structural Analysis

It should be noted that only the *main types* of analysis procedures can be described here and that the description itself is somewhat simplifying. There are more differentiated sub-types in each of the main types and above all, there are *mixed types*. The analysis procedure of Albrecht (1979), for example is a combination of elements from systematic content analysis elements with semiotic/structural film and television analysis. Each main type and most sub-types have their use and legitimation in differing contexts — school, adult education, science, etc. It would certainly be mistaken if one wanted to evaluate the different analysis procedures according to only one standard of quality. The choice of analysis procedure is highly dependent on the goal and context of the analysis. In classroom instruction, it is obviously impossible to conduct exact systematic content analysis. Vice versa, a qualitative analysis usually is insufficient where scientific goals are pursued. It is more appropriate, to see the procedures as *complementary*, not as alternative.

In the last chapter, a *special type of semiotic film and television analysis* will be presented. It differs in several respects from the (simplified) main type. No exhaustive analysis and evaluation of news programs is intended, at least not in this article. The procedure will go, however, beyond the main type in attempting to reconstruct a *partial grammar* of television news. The focus here is the reconstruction of that part of the *textsyntactical codes* which relates to the *visual forms of presentation*. A further difference from the main type of semiotic film and television analysis is the fact that two distinct steps of concretion of protocols are employed. The distinction between the two can be summarized as *"macro-protocol"* versus *"micro-protocol"*.

The basic scheme of this kind of film and television analysis is given in Fig. 8.

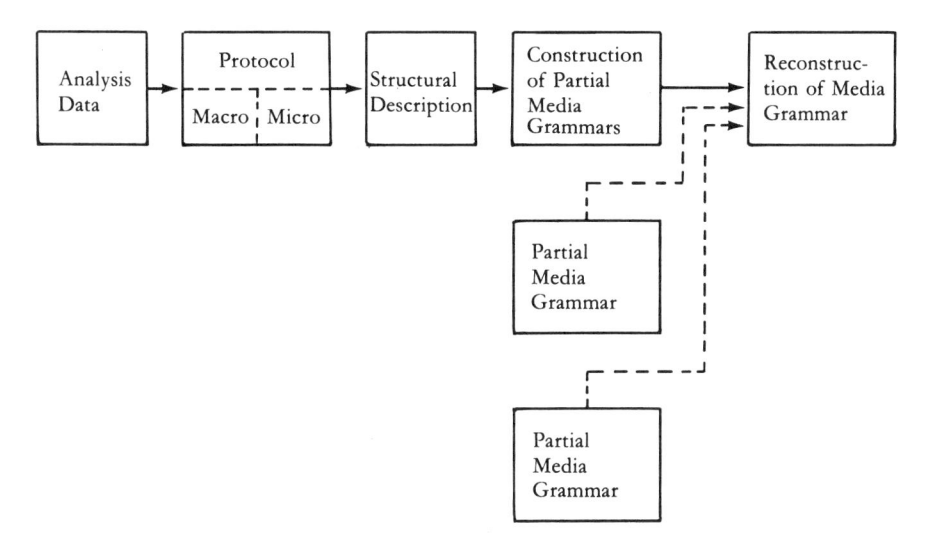

Fig. 8: General Scheme of a Special Type of Semiotic Film and TV-analysis

The following demonstrates the analysis of *one* television news program. It will then become clear that through the analysis of larger program bodies, more and more partial grammars can be reconstructed. It should be possible to reconstruct a sufficiently significant and informative "television-news-grammar" in a *non-metaphorocal sense* by analyzing a sufficiently large sample of programs. *"News grammar"* can be regarded as a small segment of a *television grammar*, which, in turn, constitutes a part of *media grammar*.

*3. Semiotic Analysis of a Television News Program and Reconstruction of a Partial Grammar*

The materials on which the analysis is based, is the main edition of the "Tagesschau" — daily news review — on January 10, 1983. "Tagesschau" is (along with the news magazine "Tagesthemen") the only news program of the ARD (Channel I) of the West German television network. It is broadcasted each night between 8.00 and 8.15 p.m. and competes with "Heute" ("today"), the news program of channel II, the Second German Broadcasting System (ZDF), which is broadcasted from 7 to 7.20 p.m.

*3.1. First Step of the Analysis: Viewing of the program*
The program is viewed several times to gain a general impression and to possibly compare it with other news programs of the same day.

## 3.2. Second Step of the Analysis: Assembling a Macro-Protocol

A so-called "macro-protocol" of the program is assembled which comprises the following columns:

| | |
|---|---|
| 1st column | *Sequence number.* A sequence is normally defined as a correlated succession of shots. In the extreme case, a sequence may consist of one shot. |
| 2nd column | *Length of sequence* (in seconds) |
| 3rd column | *Number of shots per sequence* |
| 4th (main) column | *Forms of presentation.* Forms are coded by letters or graphic symbols. Depending upon the degree of specifity of the description of presentation forms, the main column can be further subdivided into a number of subcolumns. |
| 5th column | *Camera movements.* The camera movements are protocolled. The exactness of these occurrences in time is relatively small, due to the scale of the image. |
| 6th column | *The beginning of text.* The text beginnings in each sequence is specified. |
| 7th column | *Supersequence number.* A supersequence is a sequence of sequences, correlated by a theme. In television news, a sequence is normally defined as a single thematic presentation which itself has a certain structure. |
| 8th column | *Short description of the supersequence.* A thematic label is normally sufficient. |

The boundaries of the sequences are marked by *horizontal lines*. It is important here that the size of the intervals between boundaries matches the recorded time (in seconds). This *iconic form of presentation* shows at a glance not only the relative length of individual sequences and supersequences, but thereby also indexes the *relevance* of the themes. Compared with the lenght of thematic sequences, the order in which thematic sequences are presented in the news, is certainly an even more important indicator of the relevance, assigned to a given theme. The iconic representation of sequence duration in protocols appears to be necessary for the analysis of topical television reporting, but would likely also improve the analysis of feature films.

Fig. 9 shows the *macro-protocol* of the 'Tagesschau' program:

## 3.3. Third Step of the Analysis: Construction of a Micro-Protocol.

A micro-protocol comprises the following columns:

| | |
|---|---|
| 1st column | *Number of shot* |
| 2nd column | *Length of shot* (in seconds) |
| 3rd column | *Script/Graphics* |
| | Fade-ins, subtitles, visual aids, and related features are noted. Also included is the complete transcription of written texts occuring in the image. |
| 4th (main) column | *Cimatographic properties* |
| | The main column is normally divided into a number of sub-columns. The example shown here gives the camera-distance, the camera movements and the camera-perspective. The individual devices can be identified by letters as symbols. |

→

Zeichenerklärung: NS = Nachrichtensprecher (news speaker); Gr/F = Graphik/Foto (graphics/photograph); FB = Filmbericht (news film); $S_{off}$ = Sprecher$_{off}$; Int = Interview; St = Statement; S = Schwenk (pan); Z = Zoom; SS = Supersequenz

175

| Sequence number | length (in sec.) | number shots/sequence | presentation forms | camera movement | text beginning | number of super-sequences | |
|---|---|---|---|---|---|---|---|
| 1 | | 1 | | | | $SS_1$ | Vorspann |
| 2 | 17 | 1 | ‖⋮ | | Guten Abend ... | | |
| 3 | 26 | | ⋮ | $S_l \to Z_{on}$ $Z_{off}$ | Auf der CDU-Prä ... | | |
| 4 | 20 | 2 | × | | Herr Geißler, ... | $SS_2$ | Geißler/ |
| 5 | 23 | 2 | ⋮ | $Z_{off}$ $Z_{on}$ | Das SPD-Präsidium ... | | Wahlkampf |
| 6 | 35 | 2 | × | | Halten Sie ein ... | | |
| 7 | 15 | 1 | ‖⋮ | | Gegen Aufrüstung ... | | |
| 8 | 33 | 6 | ⋮ | | Entspannte Bezie ... | | Neujahrs- |
| 9 | 25 | 1 | ○ | | etc. | $SS_3$ | empfang |
| 10 | 27 | 4 | ⋮ | | | | Honecker |
| 11 | 27 | 1 | ‖⋮ | | | $SS_4$ | Möllemann |
| 12 | 25 | 1 | ⋮ | | | $SS_5$ | Mertes |
| 13 | 25 | 1 | ⋮ | | | $SS_6$ | London/ Moskau |
| 14 | 10 | 1 | ‖⋮ | | | | |
| 15 | 30 | 3 | ⋮ | $Z_{on}$ $Z_{off}$ | | $SS_7$ | Vogel/ Moskau- besuch |
| 16 | 22 | 1 | ‖⋮ | | | | |
| 17 | 93 | 9 | ⋮ | $S_r$ $S_l$ $F_{on} \to S_r$ $Z_{off} \to S_l$ $Z_{on}$ $S_t \to Z_{on}$ $Z_{on} \to S_{ri}\ Z_{on}$ | | $SS_8$ | Israel/ Libanon |
| 18 | 33 | 1 | ⋮ | | | $SS_9$ | Drachme/ Abwertung |
| 19 | 27 | 1 | ⋮ | | | $SS_{10}$ | BSP −1,2% |
| 20 | 30 | 1 | ⋮ | | | $SS_{11}$ | Lambsdorff |
| 21 | 10 | 1 | ‖⋮ | | | | |
| 22 | 90 | 15 | ⋮ | $Z_{off}$ $S_r$ $Z_{on}$ $S_t$ $Z_{off}$ | | $SS_{12}$ | Deutscher Wald |
| 23 | 38 | 1 | ⋮ | | | $SS_{13}$ | CDU/FDP- Ausländer |
| 24 | 22 | 1 | ‖⋮ | | | | |
| 25 | 78 | 13 | ⋮ | $Z_{on}$ $Z_{off}$ | | $SS_{14}$ | Herzschritt- macher- Prozeß |
| 26 | 18 | 1 | ○ | | | | |
| 27 | 27 | 1 | ‖⋮ | | | $SS_{15}$ | Trimming |
| 28 | 8 | 1 | ⋮ | | | | |
| 29 | 60 | | ⋮ | | | $SS_{16}$ | Wetterkarte Hamburg |

NS  Gr/F  FB  $S_{off}$  Int.  St

Fig. 9: Macro-Protocol of "Tagesschau" (10. 1. 1983)

| number of shot | length (in sec.) | written and graphic elements | camera distance | camera movement | camera angle | description of the image | remarks to sound | (spoken) texts |
|---|---|---|---|---|---|---|---|---|
| E$_2$ | 23 | *Schrifttafel:* CDU Vorwürfe SPD *Untertitelung:* Sprecherin: Dagmar Berghoff | N | — | n | Sprecherin Dagmar Berghoff rechts unten; Schrifttafel links oben; blauer Hintergrund; rote (CDU, SPD) und schwarze Schrift | Nachrichtensprecherin | Guten Abend, meine Damen und Herren. CDU und SPD haben sich heute gegenseitig schlechten Wahlkampfstil vorgeworfen. Die Sozialdemokraten nahmen vor allem die jüngsten Angriffe von CDU-Generalsekretär Geißler aufs Korn und sprachen von unerträglichen und ehrabschneidenden Äußerungen. Die CDU ihrerseits hielt der SPD vor, mit unwahren Aussagen vorsätzlich Wählertäuschung zu betreiben. |
| E$_3$ | 10 | *Untertitelung:* Reporter: ROLF SCHMIDT-HOLTZ | HT HN | S$_l$ Z$_{on}$ | n | CDU-Präsidiumsmitglieder u.a. Blüm, Geißler, Albrecht Kamera fokussiert Geißler Politiker begrüßen sich | Rep./ O-Ton-Hintergrund | Auf der CDU-Präsidiumssitzung heute morgen ging es um seine Wahlkampfäußerungen vom Wochenende in Ludwigshafen. Dort hatte Geschäftsführer Geißler |
| | | | | | | | | zugeschlagen … |

E = Einstellung (shot); N = Nah (medium close-up); HN = Halbnah (medium shot); HT = Halbtotal (medium-long shot); S$_l$ = Schwenk$_{links}$ (pan); Z$_{on}$ = Zoom$_{on}$ (zoom); Rep. = Reporter; O-Ton = Original-Ton; n = normal

Fig. 10

5th column   *Image description.*
Here, all 'talking heads' (anchorman, politicans, etc.) and all special actions, props, buildings, scenery, etc, are listed. Also identified are all visible objects relevant to the analysis. Elements of the image composition (location of persons in the picture, spatial relations between 'talking heads' and objects etc.) are also marked.

6th column   *Sound.*
Relevant information for the analysis of sound (original language, background noise etc.) can be noted.

7th column   *Forms of presentation*
(See the description within chapter 3.2.)

8th column   *Text.*
The entire spoken text presently (without reference to intonation or other paralinguistic features) is transcribed.

Due to the limited space, only a few shots of the second supersequence of the news program (Tagesschau) can be presented in Fig. 10.

*3.4. Fourth Step of the Analysis: Structural description*

A *structural description* for each sequence is now produced on the basis of both types of protocol. The structures are displayed in tree-diagrams. The criteria for segmentation (i.e., branching) include *visual presentation forms, shot boundaries* and certain *content criteria*. Content criteria are only be used when the content itself obviously marks off a supersequence. For example, the branching on the right side of supersequence No. 8 ($SS_8$) is not only motivated by presentation form, but also by the content-related fact that the text refers to two different political parties.

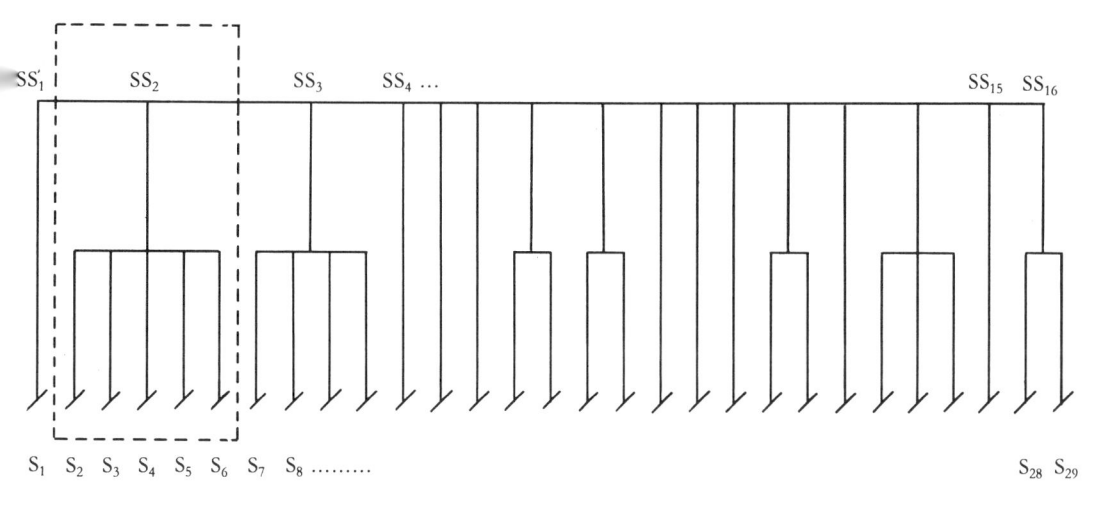

Fig. 11: Structure of the "Tagesschau" program

(S = sequence; SS = super-sequence)

178  G. Bentele

The total structure of the 'Tagesschau' program is represented in Fig. 11. Note that, only individual supersequences and sequences are recorded, individual shots are ommitted at this level.

The tree-diagram demonstrates the hierarchical structure of each super-sequence, beginning at the lowest level of individual shots ($E_1 \ldots E_n$). Supersequence No. 2 (hatched in Fig. 12) can be presented as follows:

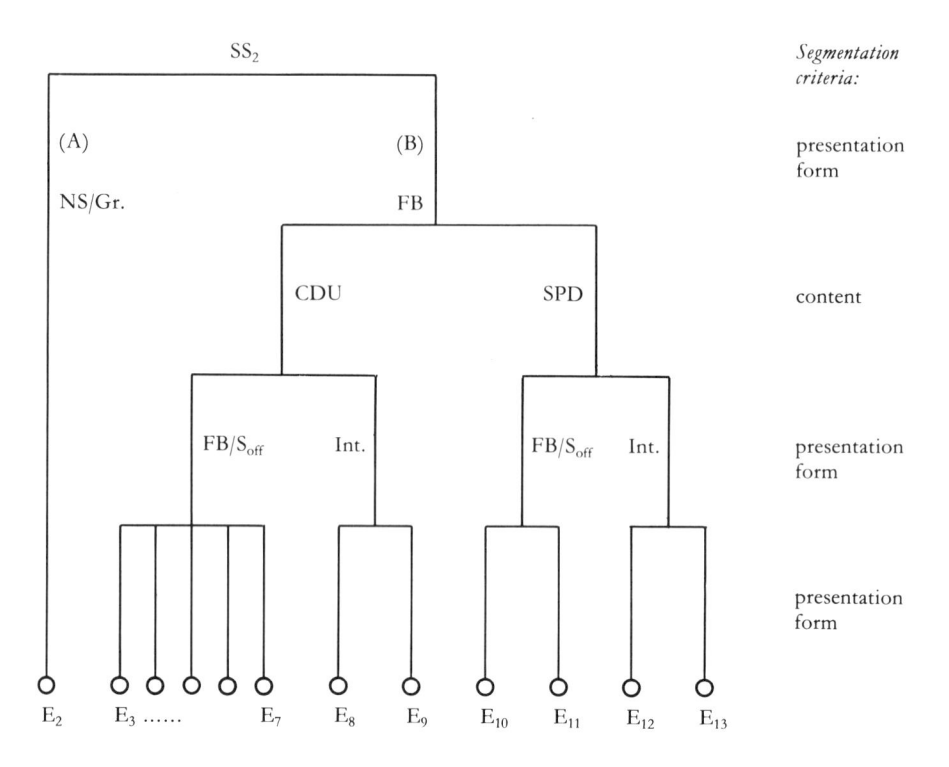

Fig. 12: Structure of super-sequence, no. 2

Audio-visual Analysis and Grammar of News Programs 179

Further examples are the structures of supersequences No. 4 through No. 8:

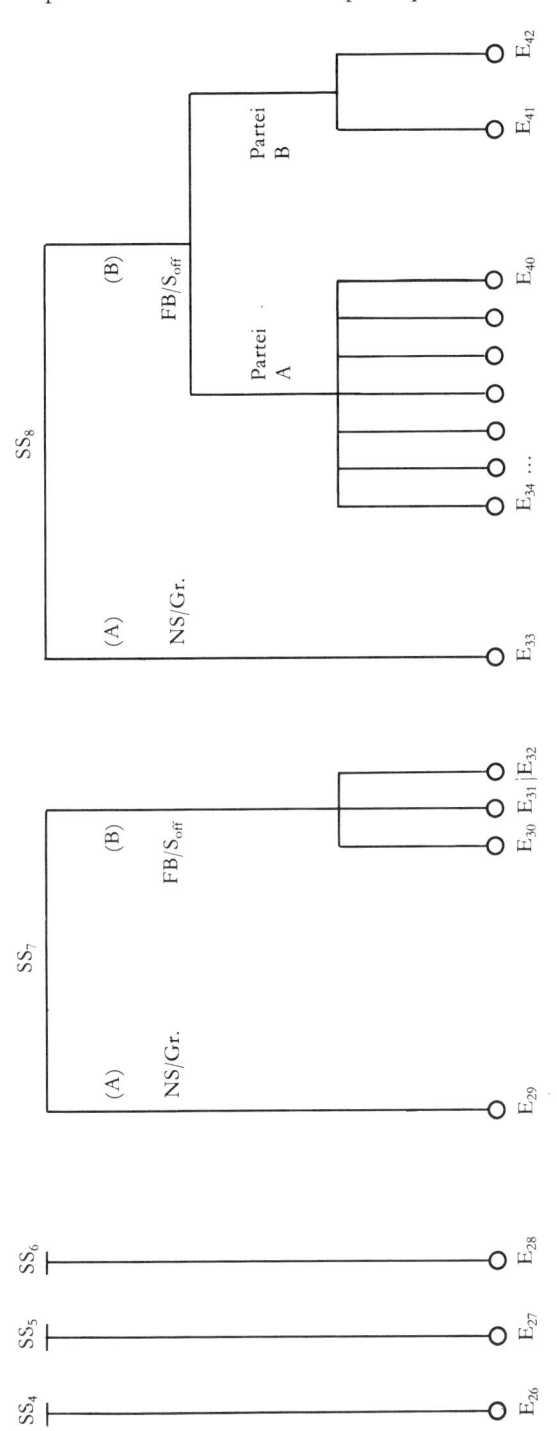

Fig. 13: Further examples for super-sequence structures

## 3.5. Fifth Step of the Analysis: Reconstruction of Partial Media Grammars

In the next step of the analysis, the structural description of each supersequence can be combined with the micro-protocol, as in Fig. 14. The 'top-down-protocol' matches the temporal progression of the supersequence, and it is therefore necessary to turn the structural description upside-down.

These structural descriptions which are derived from the protocol, form the basis of a simple *constituent structure grammar*. Constituent structure grammar is a well suited device for the reconstruction of the syntax of presentations forms within supersequences. It does not in itself describe the total text-syntax of news programs. For that purpose, semantic codes of relevance, for instance, would have to be taken into account, involving criteria of actuality, thematic relevance, geographic relevance, etc. How these codes can be described and integrated into the model of 'news factors'[21] are issues that need to be addressed in future mediasemiotic research. On the basis of protocols and structural descriptions of four news programs, the following partial grammar of presentation forms can be reconstructed in Fig. 15.

Rules (3), (5), (6), (7) and (8), for example, generate supersequence No. 2 from presentation forms. Rules (2) and (5) generate supersequence No. 4, 5 and 6. Rules (3), (5), (7), and (17) generate supersequence No. 7.

These examples should suffice to clarify the principle guiding the reconstruction of the grammar. It must once again be emphasized that we are not dealing here with a total grammar of television, but with a sequence grammar of presentation forms by means of constituent structure grammar.

An independent *discourse analysis* of the reconstructed news diagram based, for example, on van Dijk (1983) is also possible. It appears, though, as if the results of a discourse analysis of the same materials yield a structure which is fairly independent of the syntax of presentation forms. At a certain level, however, the elements of discourse analysis are likely to correspond to the categories of visual presentation form. This is not only the case at those points where structural descriptions follow content criteria, but also whenever *certain categories* of the *superstructure* (van Dijk 1980, van Dijk 1983) are expressed through different presentation forms. For example, when 'episode' and 'commentary' (van Dijk 1983, 37) are visually distinguished. *Commentaries* are normally spoken by commentators who are visible in the picture while they speak. *Episodes*, in contrast, are mostly represented by correspondent reports and news films etc. The category of 'consequences' could also be distinguished from the category 'events' on the basis of differences in presentation forms. 'Consequences' are often explained by a correspondent or news announcer (anchorperson) who is 'on camera', whereas 'events' are visually supplemented by news film.

---

[21] cf. Galtung/Ruge (1965); Schulz (1976).

| number of shot | written and graphic elements | camera distance | camera movement | camera angle | description of the image | remarks to sound | (spoken) texts |
|---|---|---|---|---|---|---|---|
| E$_2$ | Schrifttafel: CDU Vorwürfe SPD Untertitelung: Sprecherin: Dagmar Berghoff | N | — | n | *Sprecherin* Dagmar Berghoff rechts (unten) Schrifttafel links (oben); blauer Hintergrund rote (CDU, SPD) und schwarze Schrift | Nachrichten-sprecherin | Guten Abend, meine Damen und Herren. CDU und SPD haben sich heute gegenseitig schlechten Wahlkampfstil vorgeworfen. Die Sozialdemokraten nahmen vor allem die jüngsten Angriffe von CDU-Generalsekretär Geißler aufs Korn und sprachen von unerträglichen und ehrabschneidenden Äußerungen. Die CDU ihrerseits hielt der SPD vor, mit unwahren Aussagen vorsätzlich Wählertäuschung zu betreiben. |
| E$_3$ | Untertitelung: Reporter: ROLF SCHMIDT-HOLTZ | HT ↓ HN | S$_1$ Z$_{on}$ | n | CDU-Präsidiumsmitglieder u. a. Blüm, Geißler, Albrecht K fokussiert Geißler (begrüßen sich) | Rep. + O-Ton (HG) | Auf der *CDU-Präsidiumssitzung* heute morgen ging es um *seine* Wahlkampfäußerungen vom Wochenende in Ludwigshafen. Dort hatte Geschäftsführer Geißler |
| E$_4$ | | N ↓ HN | Z$_{of}$ f | O$_1$ | Kohl (wird begrüßt) | Rep. + O-Ton | zugeschlagen. Die SPD hatte er der „Mietenlüge" bezichtigt und auf sie das Brecht- |
| E$_5$ | | N | | | Stoltenberg, Vogel, Kiep (begrüßen sich) | usw. | Zitat gemünzt: „Wer die Wahrheit kennt und sie Lüge nennt, ist |
| E$_6$ | | HT | | | weitere Präs.mitglieder sitzen an e. Tisch | usw. | ein Verbrecher." Das CDU-Präsidium hat sich heute hinter die Kritik |
| E$_7$ | | T | | | der ganze Tisch ist im Blickfeld | usw. | Geißlers an der SPD gestellt. Der Wahlkampf kann hart werden. |
| E$_8$ | | N | | n | Geißler links, von hinten Reporter rechts, von vorn | Rep. | Herr Geißler, halten Sie ein Fairness-Abkommen noch für sinnvoll und glauben Sie, daß es auch angesichts Ihrer Äußerungen noch dazu kommt? |
| E$_9$ | Untertitelung: CDU-Generalsekretär GEISSLER | N | | | Geißler links/Mitte, von vorn, spricht nach rechts | Geißl. | Ich bin für ein Fairness-Abkommen, aber gleichzeitig für die Einrichtung einer Schiedskommission, die das Fairness-Abkommen überprüft und vor allem die Möglichkeit hat, die Behauptungen der Parteien auf ihren Wahrheitsgehalt zu untersuchen. Darauf kommt es entscheidend an. |
| E$_{10}$ | | HN ↓ T | Z$_{of}$ f | U$_{ex}$ | SPD-Fahnen und Fahnenstangen (rot/gelb) (SPD-Schriftzug lesbar) | Rep. | Das SPD-Präsidium bezeichnete heute abend die Angriffe Geißlers als „maßlos". Die Union werde wohl nervös angesichts |
| E$_{11}$ | | T ↓ N | Z$_{on}$ | | SPD-Fahnen; Z auf Lichtwürfel (gelb/rot) mit SPD-Schriftzug | Rep. | des nahen Wahltermins und unsicher, so *erklärte ein SPD-Sprecher*, wegen des wachsenden Vertrauens, das dem Kanzlerkandidaten Hans-Jochen Vogel entgegengebracht werde. Hin und her — daher die gleiche Frage an die SPD: |
| E$_{12}$ | | N | | | Glotz rechts (oben), von hinten; Reporter links von vorn | Rep. | Halten Sie ein Wahlkampfabkommen und die Einrichtung einer Schiedsstelle für den Bundestagswahlkampf für sinnvoll, glauben Sie, daß es dazu kommen wird? |
| E$_{13}$ | Untertitelung: SPD-Bundesgeschäftsführer GLOTZ | N | | U$_1$ | Glotz rechts/Mitte; von vorn | Glotz | Ich bin für fairen Wahlkampf wie Bundestagspräsident Stücklen — ob dazu ein Abkommen hilft — kann man skeptisch sein, aber man kann darüber reden. Eine Schiedsstelle werden wir nicht machen, denn das ist normalerweise nichts anderes als eine Art Lautverstärker, eine Art Resonanzboden für solche schrillen Äußerungen wie die, die Geißler in jedem Wahlkampf mal tut, und wir wollen ja nicht noch ein zusätzliches Podium schaffen, auf das die Wadlbeißer draufgestellt werden. |

Fig. 14: Detailed Protocol of a Super Sequence (SS$_2$) of "Tagesschau"

$G = \{V_N, V_T, \{TS\}, R\}$
$V_N = \{TS, SS_{1-n}, A, B, NS/Gr, FB, I, St, ...\}$
$V_T = \{E_{1-n}, S, Gr\}$

(1) TS → $SS_1 + SS_2 + SS_3 + SS_4 + ...... SS_n$
(2) SS → A
(3) SS → A + B
(4) SS → B + A + B
(5) A → NS/Gr
(6) B → $FB/S_{off}$ + Int + $FB/S_{off}$ + Int
(7) $FB/S_{off}$ → $E_1 + E_2 + E_3 + ...... E_n$
(8) Int → $E_1 (It_v + Ir_h) + E_2 (It_v)$
(9) B → $FB/S_{off}$ + St + $FB/S_{off}$
(10) St → E
(11) St → $E_1 + E_2 + E_3 + E_4 + ...... E_n$
(12) B → $St_1 + St_2 + St_3$
(13) B → $S + Gr_1 + S + Gr_2 + S + Gr_3$
(14) B → A' + B'
(15) A' → S
(16) B' → $E_1 + E_2 + E_3 + ...... E_n$
(17) B → $FB/S_{off}$

*Explanation:* G = Grammatik (grammar); $V_N$ = nichtterminales Vokabular (non-terminal vocabulary); $V_T$ = terminales Vokabular (terminal vocabulary); TS = Tagesschau; R = Menge von Regeln (set of rules); SS = Supersequenz (super sequence); A, B = abstraktes, nichtterminales Symbol (abstract, non-terminal symbol); NS/Gr = Nachrichtensprecher mit Grafik oder Foto (anchorperson with graphics or photographs); $S_{off}$ = Sprecher im off (commentator/off); Int = Interview; St = Statement; FB = Filmbericht (news film); E = Einstellung (shot); S = Sprecher (reporter); Gr = Grafik (graphics); It = der Interviewte (the interviewed person); Ir = der Interviewer (the interviewing reporter); $It_{v/h}$ = der Interviewte, von vorn (v) oder hinten (h) aufgenommen (the interviewed person, camera in front or behind)

Fig. 15: Partial Grammar of Presentation Forms in German TV-News

*Conclusion*

At the beginning of this article, some basic concepts of a mediasemiotic approach were introduced. Mediasemiotic studies mainly focus on the phenomenon of "media languages". The precise description of media languages requires different methods that are not commonly used within communication studies: reconstruction of rule-systems and description of text-structures are mainly focused on within this perspective of media-research.

Reconstructive procedures are aimed not only at the analysis of mass media *texts*, but also at the processes of production and reception of mass media forms and contents. Reconstructive procedures usually work with a lower amount of data material than is common in statistically oriented procedures. Nevertheless they can be subjected, to the same extent, to intersubjective control as the usual methods within social sciences.

The mutual relationships between three main types of audio-visual analysis (qualitative analysis, systematic content analysis and semiotic/structural analysis) were discussed in section two. Each type of analysis has its own advantages and disadvantages, depending on the aims of analysis and its context.

In the third section, an analytic procedure was introduced, which allows the reconstruction of partial grammars of news and other media programs. Presentation forms (or presentation modes) constitute a formal pattern, which functions as a "skeleton" of the news program and enables the "filling in" of different content-complexes, i.e. themes, and are thus comparable to the function of syntax in natural languages. Because of the relative independency of this pattern, it is independently reconstructable as a rule-system, and it is therefore possible, to speak of a *grammar of presentation forms* in news programs. This grammar constitutes an important component of the tertiary codes of news programs and therefore a component of the mass media codes in general.

It would be worthwhile, to reconstruct the grammars of presentation forms of other programs in a similar way. Moreover, the textsemantic and textpragmatic codes could be reconstructed by applying textlinguistic methods of description. Not only intercultural and comparative studies of the same program type, but also the correlation of those reconstructed grammars with regularities of the relatively well-known processes of news selection would be interesting tasks for future work in mediasemiotics. With this perspective, the claim of interdisciplinary work, which is often declared, could realized at least in parts of mass media research.

*Bibliography*

Albrecht, Gerd (1979). Filmanalyse. In: Albrecht, Gerd/Ulrich Allwardt/Peter Uhlig/Erich Weinreuter (Hrsg.) (1979) *Handbuch Medienarbeit. Medienanalyse, Medieneinordnung, Medienwirkung*. Opladen: Leske + Budrich, p. 9—42.
Bellour, Raymond (1979). *L'analyse du Film*. Paris: Editions Albatros.
Bentele, Günter/Ivan Bystrina (1978) *Semiotik. Grundlagen und Probleme*. Stuttgart/Berlin/Köln/Mainz: Kohlhammer.
Bentele, Günter (1981). Semiotik und Massenmedien — eine Problemskizze. In: Bentele, Günter (ed.) (1981) *Semiotik und Massenmedien*. München: Ölschläger, p. 15—38.
Bentele, Günter (1984). *Zeichen und Entwicklung. Vorüberlegungen zu einer genetischen Semiotik*. Tübingen: Narr.

Bentele, Günter (1984a). Kommunikationswissenschaft, Kommunikation und Massenkommunikation. In: Modellversuch Journalisten-Weiterbildung (ed.) (1984) *Fernstudium Kommunikationswissenschaft.* Bd. 1, München: Ölschläger, p. 15—57.
Bohrmann, Hans (1981). Kommunikationswissenschaft, -forschung. In: Koszyk, Kurt/Karl Hugo Pruyse (ed.) *Handbuch der Massenkommunikation.* München: dtv, p. 132—137.
Bystrina, Ivan (1982). Ritus, Mythos, Ideologie: Entstehen und Vergehen von Kodes. In: Borbé, Tasso (ed.) (1983) *Semiotics Unfolding,* Vol I Berlin etc.: Mouton, p. 51—59.
Bystrina, Ivan (1983). Kodes und Kodewandel. *Zeitschrift für Semiotik,* 4,1 p. 25—49.
Deer, Irving/Harriet Deer (ed.) (1965). *Languages of the Mass Media.* Boston: Heath & Co.
Dijk, Teun A. van (1980), *Textwissenschaft. Eine interdisziplinäre Einführung.* München: dtv.
Dijk, Teun A. van (1983). Discourse Analysis: Its development and application to the strucuture of news. *Journal of Communication,* Vol. 33,2, p. 20—43.
Eco, Umberto (1977). *A Theory of Semiotics.* London and Basingstoke: The MacMillan Press Ltd.
Edelman, Murray (1972). *The Symbolic Uses of Politics.* Urbana/Chicago/London: University of Illinois Press.
Eigen, Manfred (1979). Sprache und Lernen auf molekularer Ebene. In: Peisl, Anton/Armin Mohler (ed.) (1979) *Der Mensch und seine Sprache. Schriften der Carl Friedrich von Siemens Stiftung.* München: Propyläen Verlag, p. 181—218.
Eschbach, Achim/Wendelin Rader (ed.) (1981). *Film-Semiotik.Eine Bibliographie.* München: Dokumentation.
Faulstich, Werner (1980). *Einführung in die Filmanalyse.* Tübingen: Narr.
Fledelius, Karsten (1979). Considerations about the content analysis of audiovisuals. *Papiere des Münsteraner Arbeitskreises für Semiotik e. V. (papmaks),* No. 8. Münster, p. 5—30.
Fledelius, Karsten (1979a). Syntagmatic film analysis. *Papiere des Münsteraner Arbeitskreises für Semiotik e. V. (papmaks)* No. 8, Münster, p. 31—68.
Früh, Werner (1981). *Inhaltsanalyse. Theorie und Praxis.* München: Ölschläger.
Galtung, Johan, Mari Holmboe Ruge (1965). The structure of foreign news. The presentation of the Congo, Cuba, and Cyprus Crises in four Norwegian Newspapers. *Journal of Peace Research* 1 (1965) p. 64—91.
Hartley, John (1982). *Understanding News.* London/New York: Methuen.
Heath, Stephen (1975). Film and system. Terms of Analysis. Part I. *Screen,* 16, 1, p. 7—77.
Hickethier, Knut (1981). Filmsprache und Filmanalyse. In: *Der Deutschunterricht,* 4 (1981) p. 6—27.
Hickethier, Knut/Joachim Paech (ed.) (1979). *Modelle der Film- und Fernsehanalyse.* Stuttgart: Metzler.
Holenstein, Elmar (1975). *Roman Jakobsons phänomenologischer Strukturalismus.* Frankfurt a.M.: Suhrkamp.
Hunt, Albert (1981). *The Language of Television. Uses and Abuses.* London: Methuen.
Jakobson, Roman (1971). Two aspects of Language and two types of Aphasic Disturbances. *Selected Writings,* II, The Hague: Mouton, p. 239—259.
Jakobson, Roman (1974). Die Linguistik und ihr Verhältnis zu anderen Wissenschaften. In: Jakobson, Roman, *Aufsätze zur Linguistik und Poetik.* München: Nymphenburger Verlagsbuchhandlung, p. 150—224.
Knilli, Friedrich/Erwin Reiss (1971). *Einführung in die Film- und Fernsehanalyse. Ein ABC für Zuschauer.* Steinbach bei Gießen: Anabas.
Kuchenbuch, Thomas (1978). *Filmanalyse. Theorien, Modelle, Kritik.* Köln: Prometh.
Lisch, Ralf/Jürgen Kriz (1978). *Grundlagen und Modelle der Inhaltsanalyse.* Reinbek bei Hamburg: Rowohlt.
McQuail, Denis (1983). *Mass Communication Theory.* London: Sage.
Masters, Roger D. (1970). Genes, Language and Evolution. In: *Semiotica,* 2, 4, p. 295—320.
Merten, Klaus (1983) *Inhaltsanalyse. Einführung in Theorie, Methode und Praxis.* Opladen: Westdeutscher Verlag.
Metz, Christian (1972). *Semiologie des Films.* München: Fink.
Möller, Karl Dietmar (1983). Bibliography of Film Theory. *Film Theory. Bibilographic Information and Newsletter,* No. 1 and No. 2. Münster: Münsteraner Arbeitskreis für Semiotik e. V.

Möller, Karl Dietmar (1984). Film und Sprache. Filmwissenschaft und Linguistik. Unpublished Dissertation, Münster.
Nichols, Bill (1979). The birds: at the window. *Film Reader*, 5, (1979), p. 121–144.
Pross, Harry (1982). Fernsehen als Symbolsystem. Vortrag auf der Jahrestagung der Gesellschaft für Wissenschaftliche Symbolforschung. Kloster Weingarten am 30. 9. 1982. mimeo.
Pross, Harry (1974). *Politische Symbolik. Theorie und Praxis der öffentlichen Kommunikation.* Stuttgart/Berlin/Köln/Mainz: Kohlhammer.
Pürer, Heinz (ed.) (1984). *Praktischer Journalismus in Zeitung, Radio und Fernsehen.* Mit einer Berufs- und Medienkunde für Journalisten in Österreich. Salzburg: Kuratorium für Journalistenausbildung.
Rosengren, Karl Erik (ed.) (1981). *Advances in Content Analysis.* Beverly Hills/London: Sage.
Salt, Barry (1974). Statistical Style Analysis of Motion Pictures. *Film Quaterly*, Vol. 28, 1, p. 13–22.
Salt, Barry (1976). Film Style and Technology in the thirties. *Film Quaterly*, Vol. 30, 1, p. 19–32.
Salt, Barry (1977). Film Style and Technology in the fourties. *Film Quaterly*, Vol. 31, 1, p. 46–57.
Saxer, Ulrich (1980). Wie lernbar ist Journalismus? Probleme der Journalistenaus- und fortbildung. In: Schweizerische Gesellschaft für Kommunikations- und Medienwissenschaften (ed.) (1980). *Journalistenausbildung in der Schweiz*, p. 8–21.
Schulz, Winfried (1976). *Die Konstruktion von Realität in den Nachrichtenmedien. Analyse der aktuellen Berichterstattung.* München/Freiburg: Alber.
Schulz, Winfried (1982). Vorbemerkungen zur Semiotik des Fernsehens. *medien + erziehung* 2 (1982) p. 101–110.
Silbermann, Alphons/Michael Schaaf/Gerhard Adam (1980). *Filmanalyse. Grundlagen – Methoden – Didaktik.* München: Oldenburg.
Straßner, Erich (1981). Sprache in den Massenmedien – ein Forschungsüberblick. In: Bentele, Günter (ed.) (1981) *Semiotik und Massenmedien.* München: Ölschläger, p. 57–74.
Sturm, Herta/Marianne Grewe-Partsch (1979). Prinzipien und Determinanten einer Medienpädagogik. In: *Grundlagen einer Medienpädagogik.* Zürich: Klett und Balmer, p. 23–59.
Williams, Alan (1976). Narrative Patterns in 'Only angels have wings' *Quaterly review of Film Studies*, vol 1, 4, p. 357–372.

CLAIRE LINDEGREN LERMAN

# Media Analysis of a Presidential Speech: Impersonal Identity Forms in Discourse

*1. Introduction*

The broadcast speech of the political head of state is one of the most significant forms of mass communication, the only form of 'direct' communication between the symbol of political power and authority and the people. In the United States, the Presidential speech provides the basic data for news and news commentary broadcasts, which echo or interpret its meanings and significance. These two 'Institutional Voices', the President, and the television journalists who are professionally trained to interpret his message, are two primary sources of public understanding, or misunderstanding, of political reality. The two voices of this 'dialogue' might seem to represent two distinct types of discourse; while political discourse is noted for its persuasive, equivocal and often indirect style, the ideals of journalism are objectivity and a Gricean (1975) clarity of meaning. However, the discourse of both the President, and the journalists 'instant analysis' of it, which I examine here, are extremely indirect.

A model of the discourse structure of the Institutional Voice, the discourse of one who speaks in a dual role, as an individual, who also represents (as the journalists do) or personifies (as the President may) an institution, is described in Lerman (1983a). The significance of identity, the speaker's expression of 'self' in his discourse is not a familiar concept in discourse analysis.[1] The problem of dual identity is present in the speech of all public figures, whose 'I' is fused with a public role and addressed to a mass audience. The inherent paradoxes of Institutional identity are most apparent in non-trivial and in public discourse, such as the data of this study, in which serious propositions are asserted for which the speaker is not responsible, or whose propositional structure creates a level of ambiguity which defies logical analysis. Thus, in the speech analyzed here President Nixon refers to charges

---

[1] Studies of social norms governing pronominal reference to self-and-other (Brown and Gilman, 1960) and of social distance achieved by variation in usage of forms of address (Scotton and Wanjin, 1983) focus on social relations, rather than the speaker's relation to his own propositional utterance.

concerning the integrity of *himself* and his intimate advisors, using the institutional metaphor, 'the integrity of the White House itself'. In the same utterance, 'I' is used for self-reference:

(1) charges [which] raise questions about the integrity of THE WHITE HOUSE ITSELF. Tonight I wish to address those questions.[2]

In the President's speech, the topic, the 'charges of illegal activity ... and cover-up' was transformed to 'the excesses of others'. Through his identity shift to 'we' (the mass audience) the President indirectly asserted his separation from 'others', those responsible for the Watergate:[3]

(2) It is essential that in reacting to the excesses of OTHERS, WE not fall into excesses OURSELVES.

The journalists also avoid first-person + proposition forms of utterance, in relation to Problematic Topics. The effect of their many forms of avoidance is the statement of propositions whose source is either unknown, or someone other than the speaker. The propositions lack not only a resposible source, but often, explicit or literal meaning:

(3) NBC Carl, WE'VE HEARD THE EXPRESSION A GREAT DEAL ... 'CLEAN
NEWMAN HOUSE', The President 'MUST CLEAN HOUSE'. Did he CLEAN HOUSE?
STERN Well, THE BODY COUNT is expected to go a little bit higher ...

This paper proposes some empirically-based rules of impersonal discourse which are derived from the media journalists' analyses of a Presidential speech. The rules provide for a discourse which achieves: 1) the avoidance of direct, personally-responsible statements of fact or opinion, in relation to Problematic Topics (P-topics) and 2) the avoidance of clear or unequivocal interpretation of the meaning of the speech. The data base for this study is three fifteen-minutes programs of 'instant analysis' (three or four speakers on each program) on the major television networks, following President Nixon's first speech on the Watergate crisis.[4] The questions considered in this paper center around the linguistic features of dual and impersonal identity of the journalistic Institutional Voices. I first consider the question, how are complex propositions and the extremely indirect discourse of this Presidential speech interpreted by the media experts? The second general question developed as a consequence of the first, and led to an analysis of the linguistic forms of indirection used by the journalists to distance themselves from direct, personal, responsible statement concerning 'problematic topics' (P-topics) in the Presidents' speech.

---

[2] The text of President Nixon's speech is found in: Judiciary Committee, House, 1974.
[3] FULL CAPS are used to emphasize features under discussion.
[4] Source of the media analysis: Tapes furnished by The Vanderbilt University Television News Archive, transcribed by the author.

## 1.1. The topic of the news analysis

The Nixon speech, the topic of the journalists' discourse, was the first of many Watergate speeches, given, after ten months of Presidential silence, at the first major crisis of the Watergate period. It was broadcast to the nation on the day that President Nixon's chief aides, R. Haldeman and J. Ehrlichman, and John Dean, and his Attorney General resigned (because of pending criminal charges). On the same day, formal inquiry into possible impeachment of the President was proposed in the House of Representatives (N. Y. Times, 1973). The speech is extremely complex; a summary comprised of its central indirect propositions is appended (Appendix 1). The gravity of the occasion was expressed in the introductory remarks of the journalists, immediately following the speech:[5]

(4) ABC SMITH   The President of the United States, speaking about WHAT HE CALLED 'a sordid affair', the Watergate affair ... an affair which COMMENTATORS HAVE SAID MAY constitute the greatest threat to the authority of his office since THE TEAPOT DOME SCANDALS of the 1920's.

(5) CBS   THIS IS Roger Mudd in Washington, where President Nixon has just concluded his, uh, first — — extensive talk on the Watergate scandal, WHICH MANY ARE CALLING, now, his seventh crisis.

## 1.2. The format of the television 'News Special'

A major Presidential speech, and the analysis which follows are unique news events in American commercial television. The two most powerful 'Institutional Voices' monopolize all of the commercial channels; the President presents a formal monologue, and the leading television journalists, departing from their usual frames, engage immediately in spontaneous analysis and discussion of the speech. The solemnity of the event is indicated by the absence of commercial interruptions or sponsorship, a sacrifice of profit which is usually restricted only to major crisis reporting. The format is well established; a 'moderator' or 'anchor man' makes a general statement, introduces his colleagues, and then interviews the other reporters.

---

[5] SYMBOLS USED IN TRANSCRIPTION:
   ...   materials deleted within an utterance
   :     indicates intervening conversation omitted
   —    a longer pause than a comma or period
   u    indicates a short filled pause, shorter than 'uh'
   //   a juncture between two rule-governed elements in a sentence
   ///  Mark a focus, topic, or person shift, within an utterance.
   [ ]  Enclose material not in the text.
Full capitals mark linguistic forms under discussion.
Punctuation reflects the rapid tempo of the speech, i.e., the absence of punctuation shows absence of normal pauses.

## 2. Some rules for impersonal discourse

The data suggest several (unwritten) traditions of the discourse of television journalism, which could be stated as rules or maxims. It is assumed that these 'rules', like any linguistic rule are beneath the conscious awareness of the speakers; that they are part of a repertoire of, in this case, skills in indirection, and general 'sociolinguistic competence' (Hymes 1974). The degree to which the rules reflect professional journalistic training, or explicit media directives, or simply, the acquired Institutional Voice of news reporting, transferred to analysis, is unknown, and is not my interest. Rather my interest is with the broader linguistic question, 1) the specific linguistic devices through which personal identity is deleted or disguised in the journalists' discourse 2) the types of indirect and ambiguous communication which result from the impersonality of media discourse style.

The rules are inferentially evidenced by the data of the discourse and the regularity of occurrence of several types of indirect propositions which conform to the general rules. The effect of the Rules of Impersonality is the achievment of a discourse in which many speakers express opinions, interpretations and value judgments concerning P-topics, for which they have no personal responsibility. The first rule is well known, and applies to the structuring of the media event itself:

> RULES FOR IMPERSONAL, INDIRECT DISCUSSION OF PROBLEMATIC TOPICS.
>
> Rule I: PRESENT ALLS SIDES. OFFER MULTIPLE ACCOUNTS, by several reporters, insuring that if Rules and II and III are violated, there will be a 'balance' of views presented on the program.
>
> Rule II: STATE A P-TOPIC IN A FORM WHICH CLEARLY STATES THAT IT IS NOT THE REPORTER'S OPINION.
> (This rule is shown in (3), (4) and (5) above.)
>
> GENERAL PROHIBITION:
> Avoid the use of 'I' or personal pronouns with P-topics.
>
> GENERAL POSITIVE RULE: In stating a P-topic, cite other(s).
> 1. Directly quote others, or report others' speech.
> 2. State the P-topic as an O-topic (known to everyone). Use such forms as 'People are saying' etc.
>
> OTHER ACCEPTABLE IMPERSONAL FORMS:
> 3. State a P-topic as a question.
> 4. State a P-topic in non-literal or obscure language, such as metaphor.
>
> Rule III: If the speaker uses a personal identity token, such as 'I' in association with a P-topic, it must be combined with metaphor, or other indefinite forms of reference, or with one of the devices of Rule II.
>
> Rule IV: A-topics (facts known only to the speaker) may be stated only if they meet the criteria of 'fact'. Speaking of A-topics risks expression of personal opinion. Non-'fact' A-topics must he transformed, using Rule II or III)

The avoidance by all of the speakers of first-person, direct or literal statement concerning P-topics is the principle underlying virtually all of the indirection in the text. In (3) (4) and (5) above, some applications of Rule II are seen. In (4), for example, distancing from self is achieved by citation of an O-topic, (known to everybody, or the topic of 'others') plus direct quotation, and metaphor. These are linguistic markers of indirection which are in common use in naturally-occuring indirect discourse (cf. Lerman 1981) and in this text. They often cluster together, reinforcing the distancing. I shall discuss data illustrating the prevalence and effect of each of these rules, separately, for clarity, though they are logically inter-related and often co-occur, and function as interdependent elements and in the indirect communicative system.

## 2.1. Rule I. The constitutive structure of the media analysis

Many of the traditions and constitutive features of media news reporting and analysis seem designed for confusion rather than clarity of public understanding of political events (see Lerman 1983a). The implicit claim of 'instant analysis' is that it *can* provide an immediate, meaningful interpretation of the event it follows. In the informal conversation among several expert analysts, many perceptive analytic points are offered. However, there is no coherent development, quite the contrary. In the interchange of views and disagreements, the strands of meaning, as well as any possible 'sense' of the President's speech, are lost. This form of analysis has the effect of a Robert Haldeman maxim, concerning White House media strategies for P-topics: 'Turn it all into a puzzle.' (Lerman 1981)

In the three fifteen-minute instant analyses of the President's speech, each network provided, not one coherent voice, and an intelligible and personally responsible 'sense' of the speech, or an interpretation whose logic could be followed, but three or four established experts. Following the model of the nightly news, the analysis produced a kaleidoscope of fragmented topics; unlike the news, the analysis provides *many* accounts or interpretations of the facts at issue, as well as a variety of opinions. In accordance with Rule II, the opinions referring to P-topics are usually not those of the speakers, but of absent 'others'. In accordance with Rule III, P-topics are discussed in metaphor or other forms of indirect discourse, which like metaphor, depart from the level of declarative, explicit, or 'logical' statement. The discourse of both Institutional Voices, the President and his analysts, is constrained by the traditions of their respective institutions, towards impersonality (speaking in role) and indirection, the values which the rules above promote.

## 3. The effects of Rule I. The many interpretations of indirect discourse

In this section, the discourse effects of Rule I are examined, through the experts' discussion of one of the few recurrent topics in their discourse, the President's indirect statement concerning 'responsibility'. Rule I and the others have a complementary relationship; Rule I states a fundamental tenet of all television public affairs discussion: present at least 'two sides'. This principle, in itself, would be sufficient to insure the absence of a clear understanding of a topic.

The general answer to the question, how do the experts interpret or summarize complex propositions and indirect discourse, is simple. With the exception of one major proposition, the three groups in this sample did not attempt any general analysis of the indirect propositional text, summarized in Appendix I, and therefore, did not interpret the central argument of the speech. Samples of the President's identity-shift argument are shown in (1) and (2) above; the journalists ignored the identity and topic transformations which are central to the global topic of the speech, the innocence and rectitude of the President. It is well known that indirection, even at the sentential level, is difficult to understand, and the failure to understand the sub-text is not surprising. Rather, it shows one pragmatic, functional value of the indirection which is so prevalent in serious discourse; auditors tend to ignore that which they do not understand. This media analysis was an acid test of skill, which placed the analysts in the 'normal' hearers' position. As is often the case in crises, they did not have advance copies of the text, a fact mentioned only by Schorr, on CBS.

Only one network moderator, Edward Newman, attempted a summary of the text, focusing on the 'factual' section of the speech, from which the indirect and central propositions were excluded, or if referenced, transformed. Newman's brief summary began with a familiar authoritative tone:

(6)    'The main points of the speech were these: It was not until March of this year that he realized that some members ... *might be involved in the Watergate affair.*'

The phrases italicized below are stated twice in Newman's summary:

(7)    *nobody in his Administration was involved* in the Watergate affair. He asked the people *not to lose faith* in the system. He also said it was essential that the country *not be distracted* from the vital work ...

This form of paraphrase deprives the propositions of their syntactic context and discourse meaning. The summary claims that Newman's statements and the President's words *are* coherent facts, and that the sense of the speech is here presented. The form, and especially (6) obscures completely the line between the journalist and the speaker and confers the status of 'a fact of the news' on the words cited. Mr. Newman did not include in his summary, nor did he or his colleagues discuss the intricate propositional argument concerning 'responsibility' or 'blame', which was the textual focus on the other networks.

## 3.1. *The interpretation of an indirect proposition*

With the exception of Newman and the NBC program, the journalists' textual analysis focussed on one central indirect proposition, which seemed to symbolize for them the puzzle of the indirect level of the speech. The meaning of the President's statement concerning 'responsibility' was a recurrent topic for discussion, on CBS and ABC. The many, and contradictory interpretations offered, which were not resolved on either program, show the effect of Rule I. The value of the indirect, ambiguous proposition in avoiding speaker commitment can be seen in the variety of interpretations which this single (compound) proposition produced. The speaker may make a statement concerning a Problematic Topic; he may be required to speak on this topic, and does so. Yet, the multiple potential meanings of the proposition create a new topic: 'What did the President mean?' The President's statement uses the form of a logical syllogism; there is good reason why its logic was bewildering to the journalists, as I will show in the analysis of its propositional structure. The end of the previous proposition (paragraph 24 in the speech), is shown, as it caused some confusion to the analysts:

(8)  [I will NOT place the blame on subordinates ... who may have done wrong in a cause they deeply believed to be right. (24)]

(9)  IN ANY ORGANIZATION, THE MAN AT THE TOP MUST BEAR THE RESPONSIBILITY.
That responsibility, THEREFORE belongs here, in this office. *I accept it.* (25)

Most analysts agreed in their immediate recognition of (9) as the central statement in a long (twenty-seven minute — 3,000 word) and very complex speech. They were unable to reach agreement as to its interpretation. (Contrasts in interpretation are printed in full capitals.) The CBS moderator, in his introduction, clearly misinterpreted (8) and (9):

(10) ... The President tonight, uh, talked not so much about details of Watergate.
MUDD  HE DID this evening TAKE THE BLAME — HE CALLED IT THE RESPONSIBILITY — for the Watergate scandal. He said to do otherwise would be cowardly — ...

Mudd's statement was corrected by a senior journalist, Daniel Schorr, in response to Mudd's first question:

(11)  THE PRESIDENT DID, indeed, ACCEPT THE RESPONSIBILITY, IN A
SCHORR  RHETORICAL SENSE, for what happened, because he is the President, BUT DID NOT ACCEPT THE BLAME. (He gave very little indication of where he would apportion that blame.)

Schorr correctly perceived the identity paradox; the President, speaking as 'I', accepts 'it'. His generally correct solution was lost, ignored in the polyphonic discourse. The last sentence in (11) is unwarranted by close analysis of the text. The direct, declarative style of (10) and (11) and the simple clarity of direct discourse contrast with the usual rule-governed journalistic style.

On NBC, 'responsibility' was omitted from Newman's summary, but raised by Richard Valeriani, in response to Newman's first question:

(12) NEWMAN  Dick, I THINK / / it's FAIR to say that before the President's speech tonight, / / THE SITUATION WAS OUT OF HIS CONTROL. By virtue of his speech tonight, has he BROUGHT IT UNDER HIS CONTROL?

(13) VALERIANI  I THINK / / the idea that the President himself ASSUMED FULL RESPONSIBILITY, uh, for the Watergate affair, MAY HELP TO BRING IT UNDER CONTROL.

Valeriani added 'full responsibility', and a third interpretation. His serious factual error was not recognized; his interpretation of 'responsibility' was mentioned only once more on NBC.

Rule III is used above, in the 'I' + metaphor statements. In (12) 'fair'ness also mitigates 'I'. By contrast, (14) below uses direct speech for statements favorable to the President.[6]

On ABC, the answer to the first question produced another variant, which agrees with (13) as to the importance of the presumed 'acceptance'. Some of the President's assertions of innocence, which are part of the chain of inferences denying responsibility are stated, without apparent awareness of their meaning. Though the question is raised by a few analysts, the journalists are, in general, surprisingly unaware of the absence in the text (9) of the complement for a transitive verb, of basic syntactic logic:

(14) JARRIEL  First of all, Howard, the President ACKNOWLEDGING RESPONSIBILITY FOR THE WATERGATE ACT, although he again said that he did not know of it beforehand, he did not know of a cover-up, he was misled by his staff, but certainly, TAKING THE RESPONSIBILITY UPON HIMSELF, to me was a very major step.

The varied and (with the exception of Schorr (11)) incorrect expert recall and interpretation of what the President said exemplifies why a public exposed to television journalism can also be remarkably ignorant or confused concerning public affairs. To the complexity of the President's speech is added the many conflicting, and often authoritatively-stated views of the experts as to its meaning. The conditions imposed by Rule I, the very structure of the discourse, preclude the time and reflection necessary for understanding the paradoxes of the speech.

## 3.2. The analysis of the complex proposition

The simplest way to understand the structure of a complex proposition (or any ambiguity) is to reduce its possible meanings to a direct, declarative

---

[6] The double stroke (//) is used to emphasize rule-governed elements, here the 'I think + metaphor form.

paraphrase.[7] Had the President wished to accept personal responsibility, he could have said, unequivocally:

> [I accept full responsibility for the Watergate burglary and for the cover-up.]

In this direct sentence, another important ambiguity in the text, the complement of 'responsibility', what the speaker is accepting responsibility 'for', is relatively clear.

One form of coherence in discourse is characterized by the relationship between sequential propositions (van Dijk and Kintsch 1983, Hobbs 1979). That is only to say that successive utterances are presumed to assert a logical relationship to each other. This assumption is very strong in the categorical syllogism, such as (9) or in any complex proposition. The paradox and seeming double meanings, of (9) arise from its linkage of a generic sentence, which states a general truth, or even a moral truth:

(9)    IN ANY ORGANIZATION, THE MAN AT THE TOP MUST BEAR THE RESPONSIBILITY.

as the sole reason for a statement which uses a personal identity form:

> That responsibility, THEREFORE belongs here, *in this office*. 'I accept IT.'

On analysis, there is no ambiguity in (9). The implication of the logical argument is not obvious, though the logical implication is clear and unambiguous: logic, institutional custom and honor are *the only reasons* for the 'acceptance', an interpretation which was skillfully caught by Schorr (11). Therefore, the speaker does not *personally* 'accept it'; he even specifies the institutional location of responsibility, 'here, in this office'. Moreover, through deletion in the second term [responsibility: for what?] he does not define what 'it' is.

Generic sentences can indeed be 'very tricky and treacherous' (Thomason 1970) (cf. Geis 1984, Zadeh 1983). Generic forms or universal, categorical statements are a significant source of distancing from personal responsibility or explicit meaning; several are listed together in Appendix I. The linkage of the generic and the personal actually (and inherently) asserts, a YES—BUT—NO proposition (Lerman 1983b):

> [YES, I accept it. BUT—NO, I am not personally responsible. (Because of the general principle I cite, as the basis for acceptance.)]

*3.3. The continuing puzzle of the President's 'responsibility'.*

On two of the networks, the puzzle of the 'responsibility statement' was a question repeatedly and inconclusively raised in the talk, in brief isolated utterances, often embedded in a longer utterance, and dropped. Many of these

---

[7] Though this practice now seems obvious, it was suggested to me by John Gumperz (personal communication) some years ago.

statements are direct in form; the President's statements in the speech are knowledge, 'fact' shared by the speakers and the public, and 'facts' may be referred to directly. On CBS, Eric Severeid, the senior journalist present, offered in clear language a statement of the problem, and a candid admission of inability to understand, introduced by a Rule II clause, invoking others:

(15)  What is going to be talked about here a great deal and argued about and dissected
SEVEREID ... // is THE DIFFERENCE BETWEEN BLAME AND RESPONSIBILITY. HE DOES NOT TAKE THE BLAME for any of this, BUT THEN HE SAYS, HE ACCEPTS THE RESPONSIBILITY. I don't know what these words mean in that context.

NBC continued to ignore the paradox:

(16)  Well, it's very noticeable ... Although he said that HE ACCEPTED RESPONSI-
NEWMAN BILITY FOR IT, HE ALSO SAID VERY CLEARLY HE DID NOT WANT TO SPEND ANY MORE TIME ON IT.

On ABC, Smith, the moderator, gave an interpretation concerning blame which is not literally justified by the text, except, and this is often the case in the analyses, that it catches a 'gist' of the paradox. The indirect text did specify blame (See Appendix 1).

(17)  But unfortunately, the President has spoken in terms so rhetorical of, uh,
SMITH 'RESPONSIBILITY STOPS HERE, BUT BLAME IS ELSEWHERE' – – and NO INDICATION OF WHERE THAT ELSEWHERE SHOULD BE.

These fragments of the 'responsibility' discussion show some of the varied interpretations concerning one of the few identifiable recurrent topics in the media analysis. The examples (7–17) provide some sense of the confusion effected by Rule I.

*3.4. Covert propositions and sequencing patterns*

Below are examples of indirect or covert propositions stated by the journalists. In response to an open question about 'responsibility', Jarriel combines Rules II and III, and states 'others' questions and inferences concerning the topic. Though shielded by O-topicalization and metaphor, the P-topic of 'cover-up at the very top' is raised:

(18)  Tom, YOU SAID IT IS NEW TO YOU THAT HE TOOK RESPONSIBILITY.
SMITH Did he have any other choice?

JARRIEL I THINK NOT. // The thing has just CLOSED IN ON HIM ... THE EVENTS HAVE in effect CORNERED HIM ... WE // still don't have the specifics, which MOST PEOPLE ARE ASKING FOR AND MOST PEOPLE ARE DEMANDING, // in terms of which of these people were involved, and how, and who authorized this operation and WAS THERE AN ATTEMPTED COVER-UP AT THE VERY TOP. [Rule II.]

The moderator, as is common, changes focus, away from the sensitive, general statement of the P-topic, to a specific P-topic.

Smith: = ~ And why did the President learn only on March 21st ...

Two of the ABC journalists collusively speculate on the meaning of responsibility, discussing a Naval model. They raise, and immediately drop, the P-topic of the penalties of 'responsibility', 'court-martial'.

(19) JARRIEL   You mean, as a captain of a ship is responsible for anything that happens on the ship?

RATHER   He's the one who is court-martialed.

JARRIEL   Right.
[topic shift by next speaker]

In order to appreciate the confounding effect of Rule I, it is necessary to realize that all of the data shown in this paper is spoken in the rapid tempo of the usual news broadcast. Further, the usual speaker-turn is brief, and the next speaker seldom develops a P-topic. Focus shift by the next speaker or the moderator is a very general practice, shown in Smith's shift = ~ above (18). The moderator often chooses a next speaker, or next question, who provides a balance, or to change the topic, after a P-topic has been raised in acceptable form, as is shown in (20):

(20) SMITH   [calling on next speaker] Sam Donaldson —

Donaldson:   Howard, it was NOT A SPEECH THAT MANY PEOPLE ON CAPITOL HILL HOPED TO HEAR. // They hoped to hear // a much more substantive speech as to the President's investigation ... I FEAR, AND I SAY THIS WITH NO PLEASURE, THAT HIS CRITICS on Capitol Hill and throughout the country, the PEOPLE WHO ARE TERRIBLY CONCERNED THAT THERE WAS A COVER-UP IN THIS CASE, // will not be satisfied with what they heard tonight.

Smith:   (choosing next speaker) Bill Gill --

Gill:   I have a little different concept of what he was trying to do there ...

The rules seem to require that the journalists express opinions by implication, creating a discourse that is as complex and indecipherable as the President's speech. The problem with indirect propositions is not only that no one is 'responsible' for them, but also that they are not open for examination or discussion, merely alluded to. The most sensitive P-topics, such as (18–20) are usually dropped; the next speaker shifting topical focus, or the moderator intervening.

*4. What is a 'fact' of the news?*

The Rules of Impersonality cited in this paper reflect the 'objective, depersonalized' values of the profession of journalism, and show the paradox and the dilemma of 'analysis' from which personal expressions or opinion are barred. The principle of journalistic neutrality is a controlling ideal which proscribes 'interpretation'. Reporting is restricted to 'the facts of an event' and to neutrality or the presentation of 'another side' (Westley, 1972:75), whether the 'facts' concern a war, a natural disaster, a political campaign, or political or economic 'facts'. 'Neutrality' concerning political authority in the United States means, in effect, the absence of partisan bias concerning the two major political parties. Reporting of the Watergate crisis, or any political scandal affecting one the major political parties is a litmus test for journalistic ideals; inevitably, 'the facts' or charges are detrimental to one political party.

Though the profession of journalism places a high value on 'objective reporting of fact', the question of what is 'fact' and what is 'opinion' is, in itself, a well-recognized problematic in other fields of inquiry. 'We don't make the news, we report it' is a frequent claim. 'I have no opinion.' (Jim Lehrer, National Public Radio, 6—1—84) expresses the honored principle of neutrality expected of reporters and even of news analysts. Daniel Schorr expressed these professional values, at the beginning of the CBS analysis program.

(21)    ...It may be very hard, TO COME DOWN TO THE FACTS AND SUB-
STANCE of the Watergate case, and yet we conceive that to be our job.

The value of 'objectivity' is expressed in texts or discussions in the field. A typical statement, from a text (Blake and Haroldsen, 1975:53)

Objective journalism means presenting the FACTS of an event as it actually happens. It is an accurate, balanced, fair presentation of the FACTS, one UNTAINTED BY PERSONAL BIAS or outside influence.

In this section, I consider the types of data which are treated by the journalists as 'facts', and thus, referred to in direct discourse forms, which includes the journalistic use of personal pronouns, the offering of personal opinions, and other forms proscribed with P-topics. Several categories of 'fact' can be identified, by regular patterns of direct usage in the three networks. With this background established, the contrastive discourse referring to P-topics and the functions of Rules II and III can be better understood:

| FACT | P-TOPICS |
|---|---|
| Favorable or sympathetic observations of the President's demeanor, plans, or future. | Negative observations. |
| | Reference to crimes, problems or present or future difficulties. |
| The words of the President's speech. | Opinions not related to 'fact'. |
| | Inferences. |
| Past events or statements known to all, which relate to the other categories of fact. | Generalizations referring to any of the above. |

This chart indicates that there are two categories of data in this text. 'Facts' are favorable observations relating to the President and the future, or matters of general knowledge. Labov and Fanshel's (1977) concept of 'O-events' (known to everyone) serves as a useful metaphor to designate this category, of generally accepted and undisputed 'fact' in a given discourse. In this discourse, Labov and Fanshel's typology fits very well: A-events (facts known only to the speaker) or D-events (disputed), which I term A-topics and P-topics, respectively, describe critical variables which govern discourse rules. I use the term, O-topics, because 'events' are not central to this discourse about discourse; direct and indirect usages focus on topic. The importance of the categories describing fact is their privileged status in the journalistic discourse: the grammatical rules I have cited do not apply to 'fact'. The journalists use direct discourse, express opinions, and do not employ Rules II and III, in speaking of facts.

*4.1. O-topics, knowledge reporters share with the audience, and matters of common knowledge are 'facts'*

O-topics, which have been reported in the press, and are indisputable 'facts' are reported, like the speech itself in narrative accounts, without attribution of source:

(22)         He's lost his two main aides. He's lost his Attorney General.
JARRIEL   uh I don't know whether he's communicating with his uh, u, once chief advisor, John Mitchell.

*The words of the President's speech are facts*

The words (or the recalled words) of the President's speech are O-topics; matters of common knowledge. The 'tone' of the speech, the data of the President's speech, and its propositional omissions are analysed and interpreted by the journalists, in direct discourse, often using the form 'he said'.

(23)      One could assume FROM HIS TONE that he regards John Dean as in some way
SCHORR   culpable.

MUDD     But HE DIDN'T SAY what he was culpable OF.

SCHORR   But he didn't say what he was culpable of — He has left the greatest question unanswered.

*4.2. Positive and sympathetic impressions of the speech are facts*

The category of 'fact' includes the experiences which the journalists share with the audience, such as the 'view' of the President on television during his speech, or a general impression of his demeanor. These facts are reported in first or second person, and direct discourse, as long as they are supportive or sympathetic towards the President, and do not refer to P-topics:

(24)       Tonight, I THINK there's a brand-new Nixon, a man very humble and and, uh
JARRIEL   sharply changed himself, because of this traumatic experience which has uh, which
ABC       has occurred with his Administration.

JARRIEL   Instead we see a conciliatory attitude. Now, I SUSPECT that he has made the decision to try to have this reflected in his staff, once he gets it reorganized.

CBS        I THINK the atmosphere may change in a much larger respect. . . . Then, we
SCHORR   may see a whole lot of other (positive) changes as a spill-over from Watergate.

*Contrastive usage for fact-non-fact, within the utterance.*

Contrastive usage, for O- or P-topics is shown in Mudd's statement, below. His first sentence, concerning an O-topic is direct, like those above. Within the same utterance, the shift to a P-topic co-occurs with a switch to indirect discourse, using metaphor to summarize, or generalize the crisis (a P-topic). Mudd also quotes directly the President's own metaphor, 'our Cambodia', introducing another speaker into his discourse, departing entirely from direct, explicit, speech, and in the case of the quotation, from use of his own words.

(25) MUDD CBS    Tonight, WE WITNESSED a, uh, shaken President. He did not exhibit the normal confidence that we associate with his u, television appearances. / / / And obviously, the President is uh IN SOME HEAVY WEATHER, TRYING TO uh COME OUT OF uh WHAT HE CALLED RECENTLY, uh, 'OUR CAMBODIA'.

P-topics (the difficulties of the President and his party) are often metaphorized, even in the 'favorable' comment context.

(26) RATHER    But I WOULD GUESS / / that if that kind of [positive] attitude continues, uh, that the President is going to u, / / GO A LONG WAY TOWARDS TAKING HIMSELF AND HIS PARTY OFF THE HOOK.

*4.3 The transformation of P-topics to 'facts'*

It is important to clarify what is considered 'fact' here, because the Rules for Impersonality or indirection either: 1) transform a P-topic into an O-topic, through identifying it as a statement of other(s), and therefore general knowledge, or 2) obscure the meaning of the propositions, through metaphor and other vague forms, or transform it from a direct declarative form, primarily through the use of question.

*4.4 Questions referring to O-topics are facts*

In discourse, questions, whether information-seeking, or answered by the speaker, or rhetorical, provide a form in which the speaker may state, or propose, a proposition without seeming to do so, and without responsibility for the embedded proposition of the question (see Lerman 1981). Using the 'facts' of the President's words in the speech, the analyst can introduce relevant events, in question form. Below, Smith explores the President's claim that he 'didn't know' about Watergate. ('Mitchell' refers to the Former Attorney-General, whose office was directly involved in the Watergate burglary.):

(27) SMITH    Is it conceivable that Mr. Mitchell went in the end of June, submitted his resignation, and didn't tell the President? Is it conceivable that Mr. Haldeman never told the President — that nobody told the President? —

In question form, the credibility of the facts of the President's speech may be challenged. The Impersonality Rules do not permit the speaker to state directly the inferences offered by the question, which we can paraphrase as:

(27')  [I do not believe that Mitchell and Haldeman did not tell the President.] Or, [I believe that Mitchell and Haldeman told the President.]

The questions may introduce additional factual information, which is logically linked to an O-topic, the words of the President. The often unanswered questions may state speaker's opinion or interpretation, indirectly. The question form provides ambiguity, that is, hedges the relationship of the speaker to his proposition, as well as to the factual status of its content.

(28) RATHER  Now, on the one hand, the President says that he was 'appalled'; if he was in fact appalled, then why did he have his Press Secretary come out and say, well, this was 'a third-rate burglary'? Even as late as the Fall of last year, uh, attack, from the White House itself, the *Washington Post?*

Or, the adequacy of the 'facts' stated in the speech may be questioned, as below. The questions focus on very specific facts, and in this context, raise questions which appear to be restricted to the credibility of the President's account.

(29) SMITH  And why did the President learn only on March 21st of this year, that's the first date he gave that he knew about this thing — that it involved members of his Administration.?

Several prohibitions shown in the rules are circumvented by the question form. The referents of the questions are O-topics, and very specific O-topics. They are a hybrid form, or a double O-topic, the facts of the speech, (O) and the topics of the questions are published facts, also known to all (O). The 'wh' forms (28, 29) avoid the use of personal pronouns; they are rarely combined with clauses using 'I'. Rule III is honored, Rule II observed. These questions are rarely, if ever, answered; they provide a thread of indirect inferences, questioning 'fact', which is balanced in the media analysis by 'positive' statements of fact, in direct style.

By contrast, an information-seeking question may concern a P-topic, and state a generalization, indirectly, in metaphor. The addressee may, as in (30) refuse to answer, and invoke, very often, Rule II:

(30) NEWMAN  ... By virtue of his spedech tonight, HAS HE PROUGHT IT UNDER HIS CONTOL?

VALERIANI Ed, I think THE ANSWER to that MUST COME FROM OUTSIDE THE WHITE HOUSE ...

As will be shown in the next section, the information-seeking question very often metaphorizes P-topics (following Rule II.4).

*5. The metaphoric generalization*

The simplest device that language provides for avoiding clear, unequivocal meaning is the substitution of metaphor for literal, explicit reference. A distinctive form of distancing from personal expression is to state a proposition in metaphor; specific meaning is obscured, and, having said nothing literal, the speaker is as free of 'personal' responsibility for his words, as if he had quoted another. Rule II.4, 'state a P-topic in non-explicit language, such as metaphor' is often followed. 'When in doubt or pressed for time, metaphorize.' accurately describes its usage. The frequency with which metaphor occurs in the media analysis program is unexpected, and seems difficult to reconcile with the 'fact-oriented' values of journalism, discussed above, except as a direct consequence of the restrictions on explicit and literal statement, which follow from the Rules of Impersonality.

Metaphor is the most common form used for the discussion of P-topics. In the context of discourse about a Presidential speech concerning an unprecedented Presidential crisis, the metaphoric proposition provides a natural refuge from literal statement, and a form for the generalization of the crisis.

The first questions on the three networks, and many others, employed metaphor to generalize a difficult P-topic. See (12—13) and (30).

(31) ... And obviously, the President IS uh IN SOME HEAVY WEATHER; trying
MUDD to COME OUT OF uh what he called recently, uh 'OUR CAMBODIA' ...

Question I'd like to ask Dan (Schorr) ... uh, whether or not the speech tonight uh answers enough of the unanswered questions that uh the President uh CAN WEATHER THE STORM.

Daniel Schorr's reply, (21) was a rejection of the metaphoric question.

(21) ... It may be very hard, TO COME DOWN TO THE FACTS AND SUBSTANCE of the Watergate case, and yet we conceive that to be our job.

Lakoff and Johnson (1980) have shown the prevalence and the conceptual significance of metaphoric *isolated sentences* which are in common use in our culture: that collocations of the metaphors (or idioms) in which we speak of time, or argument, and so forth, reveal 'the way we think about' their referent. My own research has shown the prevalence of metaphoric propositions in the context of naturally-occuring discourse, and their specific usage for reference to 'what it is difficult to state', central, problematic and affective topics (Lerman 1981a, 1983b). The conditions of the news analysis program, the spontaneous analysis of a complex speech given in a crisis, and the hazard of saying the wrong thing, are those which favor metaphor. Even so, its prevalence in the news analysis marks a salient contrast between usage and the objectives of the profession.

Thus, the frequency of metaphoric usage, on three separate programs, among a rather large number of journalists, is surprising. The most distinctive use of metaphor is for reference to a P-topic, following an 'I' statement. Rule II. proscribes the use of 'I', and it is rarely used, and is used in combination with P-topics primarily in the combination with metaphor, according to Rule III: 'Personal identity tokens ... must be combined with metaphor or other indefinite forms.' A few examples are shown below; many others are found in the data cited:

(32)  I THINK, for at least for a while, it may TAKE THE HEAT OFF.
I THINK NOT. THE THING HAS JUST CLOSED IN ON HIM. ...
I THINK what the President has done, he's BOUGHT SOME TIME.
I THINK he'll see if the critics will BUY Richardson.
I THINK the idea that ... MAY HELP TO BRING IT UNDER CONTROL.

'I think' preceding *positive* statements about the President, in direct style, the unmarked form, is not metaphorized, nor neutralized by use of any other Rule of Impersonality.

(33)  Tonight, I think there's a brand-new Nixon ...

In the discussion of P-topics, the personal pronoun + think' may be neutralized in other ways. 'I think' + Negation + an O-statement: [Rule II.]

(34)         I DON'T THINK // ANYONE is bringing into question ... the integrity of the
RATHER      White House ...

The metaphors used by the journalists are in common use; they convey 'meaning' which is qualitively different from the literal, or the factual. Metaphor is used to compress and summarize a complex of presumably well-known meanings, yet nothing literal is said. Some characteristic uses of metaphor are shown below.

Metaphors are used in the moderator's introductions, to summarize the situation. The summary metaphor serves as the predicate for a first question. The metaphoric question usually is answered in repetition of the metaphor

(30)         Dick, I THINK // it's FAIR to say that ... THE SITUATION WAS OUT OF
NEWMAN       HIS CONTROL. By virtue of his speech tonight, HAS HE BROUGHT IT
             UNDER HIS CONTROL?

VALERIANI ... Obviously, THE PURPOSE ... IS TO BRING THINGS UNDER
             CONTROL. ... I THINK // the idea that ... MAY HELP TO BRING IT
             UNDER CONTROL.

The use of one metaphor often leads to others. In his answer, Valeriani added another, repeated from the President's speech:

(30)         The fact that ... may also help RESTORE FAITH IN, IN THE SYSTEM.

On ABC, the introduction characterized the Watergate affair by reiterating the President's words, and by use of an established metaphor, which symbolizes governmental corruption:

(4)          The President of the United States, SPEAKING ABOUT WHAT HE CALLED
SMITH        'A SORDID AFFAIR', ... may constitute the greatest threat to the authority of
ABC          his office since THE TEAPOT DOME SCANDALS of the 1920's.

As is shown in these examples, what is metaphorized in serious discourses fits somewhat into Labov and Fanshel's (1978) category of 'D'-events, i.e., 'disputed events, their term for central 'events' in a given discourse. I use the term, 'P-topics' to refer to a more general category of difficult, problematic topics, whose importance in these texts in not related to 'disputes', but to their linkage to the President's guilt or innocence, and to the discourse conventions of media journalism. Without exception, the referents of metaphors are P-topics; the associated implications of many are of crisis. Metaphors which summarize, such as 'clean house' are the type in common use here. The figurative level of communication permits generalizations whose literal statement may be impossible, or proscribed, or quick reference to topics whose explicit statement may be dispreferred, for a variety of reasons.

A metaphoric question may receive an explicit reponse, directed to the literal meaning of the figure. 'Clean house' in this context means, roughly 'to remove from their positions all those connected with the Watergate coverup':

(3) NEWMAN NBC   CARL, we've heard the expression a great deal, in the last day or so, 'CLEAN HOUSE'. THE PRESIDENT MUST CLEAN HOUSE. Did he CLEAN HOUSE?

STERN   Well, the BODY COUNT is expected to go a little bit higher. Originally, Senate investigators had about twelve or thirteen names on their list ... Mr. Kleindienst was on nobody's list. That leaves about three or four suspects still working in the Administration, two at the White House. ...

## 5.1. Metaphoric monologue

In spontaneous conversation, the 'metaphoric message', a long monologue constructed around a chain of related metaphoric predicates, identifies extremely stressed discourse units, crisis centers of conversation, associated with marked hesitations. (Lerman 1981, 1983a). Finding metaphoric monologue (with minor hesitations) in media discourse is unexpected. Two factors seem relevant to the concentration of metaphors here. The metaphoric question often gets a metaphoric response, and there is a tendency to continue in a linguistic form, especially in spontaneous talk, once it is initiated. In these metaphors, the speakers make many related statements which they could not make in explicit language, a further factor for perseveration of the form. The other factor is the time pressure of the media event; metaphor provides a kind of short-hand, an economical form which suits the brief turns that are customary. A literal portion of the response is deleted (. . .).

(35) MUDD   Now, just Politically, DO YOU THINK // that this was a, uh, speech that will uh, TAKE THE HEAT OFF Republicans? Dan — Rather —

RATHER: CBS   I THINK, // for at least for a while, it may TAKE THE HEAT OFF ... the very fact that he went on television and finally g-gave the appearance, at least, of doing something, I THINK // will TAKE THE HEAT OFF of him for a while ... Now, THE FINAL TEST is going to be: Is he LEVELING WITH the American people? Does he LEVEL WITH the American people? ... if he does, then the Republican Party will be OFF THE HOOK. If not, then they're going to be in a lot of trouble for a long time to come.

(36) SMITH   Tom, You said it was new to you, that he took responsibility. Did he have any other choice?

JARRIEL:  I THINK NOT. // THE THING HAS JUST CLOSED IN ON HIM. ... THE
ABC  EVENTS HAVE IN EFFECT CORNERED HIM. His staff ... have gradually GROUND TO A HALT at the White House. HIS CREDIT, both, uh, at home and abroad, HAS JUST SLIPPED VERY SHARPLY. ... only when these problems REACH THE BOILING POINT has he actually MOVED, and whether or not he can TAKE THAT BOIL OFF is something else ... and was there an attempted COVER-UP AT THE VERY TOP?

The propositional content of the metaphoric monologues is high, yet Rule III permits discussion of P-topics in the figurative, non-explicit level, whose 'fuzzy semantics' (Zadeh, 1983) provides a privileged communicative register (Lerman, 1981, 1983b). As in the data above, propositional metaphors are primarily predicates. The typical metaphoric sentence is a dummy or fuzzy subject, often an impersonal pronoun, or metaphor, plus a metaphoric predicate, as seen in:

> THE THING // HAS JUST CLOSED IN ON HIM.
> HIS CREDIT // HAS JUST SLIPPED VERY SHARPLY.
> IT // MAY TAKE THE HEAT OFF.

Or the question form, may avoid 'the subject' entirely:

> AND WAS THERE AN ATTEMPTED COVER-UP AT THE VERY TOP?

However, the functions of metaphor (or any linguistic form) in use in naturally-occurring discourse represent a 'possibility distribution' (Zadeh, 1983), whose seeming limits expand with the size of data base. The rich allusiveness of nominal metaphors is shown in 'body count' or 'Watergate' or 'the Teapot Dome Scandals'. In the context of the patterns of usage of metaphor in this text, 'I think', (which 'usually' functions as a hedge, limiting or restricting the proposition to which it is linked) seems here to serve to give the *illusion* of expression of personal opinion, preceding a fuzzy metaphoric statement.

## 5.2. *Unawareness of metaphor*

Only one journalist responded, and to only one of two striking metaphoric propositions in the President's speech:

> We must MAINTAIN THE INTEGRITY OF THE WHITE HOUSE. There can be no WHITEWASH at THE WHITE HOUSE. (39)

Dan Rather, of CBS, dissected the first part of the first metaphoric proposition, stating an obvious and minimal interpretation: the literal referent of the common institutional metaphor, 'the White House' was the Nixon Administration, or the President himself. There was no response by his colleagues to Rather's analysis:

(37)  Also, he said that we must protect the integrity of the White House, I DON'T THINK // ANYONE is bringing into question here the integrity of the White House or the American Presidency, which has been well established over two hundred years. WHAT WE ARE TALKING ABOUT is the integrity, again, of the Nixon administration.

The unawareness of speakers of the grammars they use seems to be attested by the extensive use of metaphor by skilled and responsible journalists who believe that they are conveying objective, factual analysis. Schorr and Severeid, two senior and respected 'deans' of television news at the time, are exceptions; their speech was for the most part, direct and clear; therefore, they are not much represented in this analysis. It is also evidence of unawareness or the 'low codability' (Brown and Lenneberg, 1954, Chafe, 1980) of metaphor that the President's stated theme of his speech, which used the institutional metaphor, was not otherwise discussed:

> The inevitable result of these charges ['of illegal activity and cover-up'] has been to *raise questions about* THE INTEGRITY *of* THE WHITE HOUSE ITSELF. Tonight, I WISH TO ADDRESS those questions. (paragraph 3)

*6. Speaking through the words of 'others'*

The lack of coherence or clarity of the media analysis rests on one factor which is independent of the large number of speakers who are present, and the frequency of topic shift. Rule II: 'Avoid speaking of your own opinions with regard to P-topics' effects the exclusion from a speaker's utterance of personal identity forms, and the creation of an impersonal style. The journalists rarely speak as themselves, in their own words, with reference to P-topics. Problematic topics are referenced, facts and opinions about them are offered, by the citation of others, the words or opinions of identified, or often, unidentified, generalized absent speakers. Considering the time constraints, of five or fewer minutes for each speaker, a bewildering number of absent speakers are introduced into the talk. Considering the assemblage of analytic talent gathered for the 'news special', the absence of insights and analysis claimed by the speakers themselves is a paradox.

Rule II requires deletion of the speaker from propositions referring to P-topics. Citation of others 'validates' an opinion or a question about a P-topic as 'news', fact, and if the others are generalized, as in 'Many people . . .' the concern or opinion is further legitimated, distanced from personal expression. Direct quotation of another's words, and question, which transforms the declarative sentence, are the other major linguistic forms for compliance with Rule II.

The casual, interview-conversation is personal in style; the speakers are addressed by their first names, which are known to the mass audience. They are informed and influential 'opinion-makers' and their personal analysis and opinions are seemingly sought by the moderator.

(38) Gentlemen, uh, what do YOU KNOW that YOU did not know 27 minutes ago?
SMITH . . .

and acknowledged at the close of the program:

SMITH    WELL; thank you very much gentlemen (clears throat) for YOUR REMARKS about the President's speech, which we 'ave just listened to here on this network.

The facade of personal identity is negated by regular patterns of distanced, impersonal utterance, selectively employed, with relation to P-topics. The prevalence of Rule II (and the other rules) is shown, not only directly, but indirectly, when it is violated: by self-correction or by cooperative (or collusive) intervention by another speaker. As I have discussed (Lerman 1983a) a tension inherent in the discourse of the mass media is that between the simulation of personal identy, in 'the media Institutional Voice', and the constraint or prohibition of the expression of personal views or opinion. Rule II creates, and typifies the credibility problem common to impersonal discourse. Despite the manner of introduction of P-topics, the audience knows, at some level, that the speaker is, in fact, selecting facts and however convertly, expressing opinions.

The excerpt from (4) below is one of many examples of 'other' statements. The moderator begins by directly quoting, in an unmarked manner, the words of the President, 'this sordid affair', referring to the Watergate crisis. The next clause is a typical form in which the speaker states a proposition, invoking another speaker or unidentified source, hedged, below, with a modal, 'may'.

(4)    ... an affair which COMMENTATORS HAVE SAID MAY // constitute the greatest threat to the authority of his office since the Teapot Dome scandals of the 1920's.

In Labov and Fanshel's terms (1977), these propositions claim to be of the O-event (known to everybody) type. Like the President's complex, generic sentence proposition, (9) they permit the speaker to actually make a statement for which he claims no personal responsibility. The P-topics which follow the 'other' citation usually offer an opinion, as in (4). They often refer to the involvement of the President in the cover-up of the Watergate, or to other matters relating to responsibility or guilt.

The following examples show forms of the 'citation of the other' propositional types

Others' expectations are cited:

SMITH    I know that EVERYONE HOPES that that ugly word, 'impeachment', will not be heard again, or will not have to be heard again. But we are in one of the great crises of the Presidency in history.

Donaldson    Howard, it was NOT A SPEECH THAT MANY PEOPLE ON CAPITOL HILL HOPED TO HEAR. THEY HOPED TO HEAR a much more substantive speech...

MANY PEOPLE HOPED TO HEAR him say that he would appoint a Special Prosecutor...

Questions of fact are presented as inevitable:

NEWMAN    Now, THE QUESTION IS BOUND TO ARISE: Who does the President believe, misled him?

Questions are 'justified' as expressing the interests of 'others':

NEWMAN    Dick, one point that I think EVERYBODY WILL BE INTERESTED IN, arose when the President said in effect, that he had been misled...

RATHER    ...THE CENTRAL QUESTION THAT WE CAME HERE TONIGHT WITH — — the one THE FOLKS along Fennel Creek and the Heights OUT IN MY NEIGHBORHOOD are asking is // 'Who did it?' And the President has not yet answered that question... I THINK WE have to give him the benefit of the doubt...

While it is to be expected that reporting of the views of others is one task of the journalist, and the natural style of those who speak ordinarily as Institutional Voices, the force of Rule II is evidenced by the regularity with which P-topics are raised as 'others-topics', and conversely, by the journalists' avoidance of direct statement of P-topics.

*6.1. A case of rule violation*

Violations of the rules are associated with other marked deviations from the usual patterns of discourse. In the spontaneity of the discourse, the mitigative terms accompanying the few 'I' + P-topics (in brackets) express speaker 'awareness' of rule-violation:

(20)     I FEAR, AND I SAY THIS WITH NO PLEASURE... [impeachment]

(40)     MAY I RAISE A VERY HORRIBLE SUBJECT [the President's own credibility]

One of the most direct, and most natural forms of speech is the use of 'I' by the speaker. In this text, the language behavior associated with the personal pronoun is marked. The logic of the impersonality rules is that the most proscribed form of speech is that of Rule IV, a special case of Rule II.

> Rule IV: A-topics (facts known only to the speaker) may be stated only if they meet the criteria of 'fact'. Speaking of A-topics risks expression of personal opinion; non-'fact' A-topics must be transformed, using Rule II or III.

The sequencing pattern of the special news reports is smooth and unstressed. Turns are usually rather short, topic changes or interruptions by the moderator are accepted by the analysts, who are accustomed to speaking together, and whose interactive synchrony is well attuned. They are professionals, trained in and paid to 'reason together', and they do it gracefully. An exception to the general rule of short turns and relinquishing of topic is found in one long sequence (of less that one-minute's duration) in which one speaker (Sam Donaldson, ABC) flouts Rule IV. He persists in attempting to discuss a fact, which is finally revealed to be an 'A-event' (Labov and Fanshel 1977), that is, a fact based on his own personal experience and knowledge. The fact he wishes to raise may also be, as he claims, (40:3) below, an 'A—B event', known to all of the reporters. The fact (40:8) is also a 'P-topic', and perhaps a disputed topic.

The fact is the claim of a White House witness (in the Watergate investigation) which contradicts the President's statements (in the speech) as to when he knew of the cover-up. Therefore, as Donaldson stated in introducing the topic, it relates to a maximally-sensitive P-topic, 'the problem of the President's own credibility' (40:1). As I have discussed, the President's statements in the speech have the status of fact; were Donaldson not wanting to raise an A-topic, the rules allow introduction of other information relating to 'fact'.

I have shown examples of topic or focus-shift by the moderator, in response to atypically expressive journalist statements (18, 20); these are usually successful. In this sequence, Donaldson persists through a long turn in attempting to communicate what he obviously regards as an important fact. The rules for impersonality provide a spectrum of alternative forms for approved reference to P-topics, and Donaldson tries to state his 'fact' in several different conforming ways. All of his attempts at conformance to the rules can be seen to be less direct that his norm-violative final statement (40:8). The problem, the cause of this sequence is that (8) is not only a P-topic, but an A-topic; a rare and proscribed type in this discourse. There is no apparent way to authenticate personal knowledge, whose source must be kept confidential, except by using 'I'. In the speaker's various attempts, and the interruptions of others, the force of Rule IV can be seen.

The numbered utterances below (40:1—7) are units of a sequence which continues despite an interruption and topic change by the moderator (5). The persistent speaker, after a second interruption (7) and an hiatus, returns, at the end of the program, and only then reveals directly the A-topic (8). He is again interrupted (9), and the program ends.

Having violated Rule IV, by first-person introduction of a P-topic in (40:1), the speaker shifts within his utterance, validating his personal form, as it were, by adding the mitigation of 'others' in (2). (2) claims that (1) is an O-topic, adding a qualification 'whether they know anything or not'. (40:1—4) are one continous turn. Shifts in 'person' are marked by (//).

(40) DONALDSON

| | | |
|---|---|---|
| First person + P-topic | 1 | MAY I RAISE A VERY HORRIBLE SUBJECT, and that is the problem of the President's own credibility and involvement, if any, in the cover-up. // |
| Others Rule II.2 | 2 | PEOPLE ARE SAYING THIS IN THIS COUNTRY; whether they know anything or not is another point. IT'S BEING SAID. // |

The speaker now introduces, as an A—B topic, with a qualifier, the A-topic of (8). He also reports the speech of others.:

| | | |
|---|---|---|
| Second Person + Other's Speech Rule II.1 | 3 | We know, // OR AT LEAST I THINK WE KNOW // that SOME OF THE PEOPLE who have been mentioned in this case ARE PREPARED TO SAY that THEY WENT TO THE PRESIDENT EARLIER THAN MARCH and suggested to him that he hadn't been told the truth -- that there were people on his staff who were involved. |
| 'I' + A-topic Rule IV flouted | 4 | I KNOW FOR A FACT that the Ervin Committee on the Hill is GOING TO PURSUE THE SUBJECT OF THE COVER-UP, not just the burglary. And pursue it till it is convinced that it has gone to the very last man. |

The speaker is interrupted only when he violates Rule IV using the only possible form to cite personal knowledge which has been obtained by 'leaks' on the Committee; therefore a source cannot be cited. Smith's interruption focuses on another aspect of the P-topic, the Watergate burglary, stated in acceptable form.

SMITH  
CHANGES  
TOPIC —  
OTHER  
Rule II.1

5  Sam, I've got here in my hand a United Press REPORT OF A SPEECH THAT SENATOR GOLDWATER'S MADE tonight... He said he would expect impeachment proceedings if it is shown that President Nixon knew about Watergate bugging case beforehand.

Donaldson rejects the topic, but emulates the form (Rule II.1), citing 'others' questions (Rule II.3) focused on his own A+P topic. The violation here is novel, Rules II.1 and II.3 de not permit accusatory questions from *unidentified* others, nor hypothetical quatation of the President's presumed words:

Others +  
Question

6  Well, THE QUESTION THAT PEOPLE ARE RAISING NOW IS NOT THAT, but // DID HE know afterwards? DID HE [the President] HELP IN THE COVER-UP by indirection, not by actively going about concocting stories for people, but by simply saying, 'I don't want to hear any evil. I don't want to see any evil'?

At this point Tom Jarriel interjects, citing the President's expectations [Rule II], changing the topic to the recurrent, and unresolved puzzle concerning the meaning of 'responsibility'.

INTER-  
RUPTION

7  After the remarks tonight, I DON'T THINK HE WOULD BE OVERLY SURPRISED // if impeachment proceedings uh should be initiated against him.

Jarriel's second sentence can be seen as a reminder to Donaldson of a legitimate topic, the President's actual words, from the speech, and of Rule IV. He offers also a 'balance', a positive view, of the President's 'responsibility'

II.1  I read that in his remark that, uh, 'Who is responsible? I am responsible.' ... He is taking a large share of the responsibility, not for having directed himself or having had advance knowledge of criminal acts ...

Jarriel cannot be presumed to object to the topic of the President's involvement in the cover-up, which he himself stated in others + question form, (Rule II.1 — 3) earlier in the discussion.

(18)  ... MOST PEOPLE ARE ASKING FOR AND MOST PEOPLE ARE DEMANDING, in terms of ... who authorized this operation and was there an attempted cover-up at the very top?

Jarriel's interruption is successful (perhaps because Donaldson has attempted almost all of the possible rule-conforming forms). He and Rather return to the 'responsibility' question, a portion of which is shown in (19). However, just before the program ended, speaking rapidly, and concisely, with an introduction which asserts a relevance claim, Donaldson finally makes his statement, as a bald A-topic. He ignores Rule IV, stating his personal knowledge of the account of a witness who claims, on the basis of first-hand knowledge, that the President is lying. This fact was not yet public knowledge; the 'man' is obviously John Dean, 'a man directly involved' as the President's legal counsel and the story was a big news story. In his brief, extremely clear and direct statement, Donaldson also makes claims for the importance and accuracy of the fact he is reporting:

Donaldson  8  We were talking a moment ago about . . . whether or not Mr. Nixon knew
Rule 4         earlier than March 21st, now I TALKED WITH A MAN DIRECTLY
flouted        INVOLVED in the Investigation, AND WAS TOLD THREE TIMES, and
               asked him to repeat it the fourth – THAT HE PERSONALLY WENT TO
               THE PRESIDENT IN FEBRUARY, and told him that the White House
               staff was involved, 'We'd better do something.'

Howard K. Smith interrupts, and makes a closing statement:

INTER-      9  WELL, THANK YOU VERY MUCH GENTLEMEN (CLEARS THROAT)
RUPTION        FOR YOUR REMARKS ABOUT THE PRESIDENT'S SPEECH, which
II.2           we 'ave just listened to here on this network. I know that EVERYONE
               HOPES // that that ugly word, 'impeachment', will not be heard again, or
               will not have to be heard again. But we are in one of the great crises of the
               Presidency in history. This is Howard K. Smith, for my colleagues at ABC
               News, Goodnight.

The pattern of (40) is consistent. Rule IV. violations are terminated by another speaker (40:5 and 9, and seemingly, 7). In the earlier interruptions, and even in the last (9), the interrupters offer a model for Donaldson, of rule-governed forms, which he accepts in (6). Each interruption provides a balance of positive-negative statement concerning P-topic. The clustering of impersonality devices for maximally-sensitive P-topics is shown in (6) and (18); which both use other-citation + question (Rule II:1, 2 and 3). The episode illustrates the general finding, the association of multiple distancers with sensitive P-topics.

(40:1–7) gives a sense also of the complexity of the journalists' discourse analysis, the lack of coherence, the focus and topic switches mentioned previously. This segment takes less than a minute of time; there is only one direct statement, not governed by the Impersonality Rules (4). (40:1–9) shows the complementarity of Rule I, the constitutive rule of the discourse, and the other rules which govern the journalists' actual speech. The interactive enforcement of compliance with the rules, the moderators' and colleagues' terminating of breaches and creating 'balance' is often subtle, merely part of the routine of turn-taking (19–20), because it is not challenged. In this case of persistant rule-violation and attempts at compliance, the reciprocal function of the two levels of the rules *in vivo* can be seen.

*6.2 Conclusion*

The Rules of Impersonality that I have proposed are based on regularities of speaker use of linguistic forms referring to problematic or difficult topics in a television analysis of a crisis speech. They show a spectrum of 'acceptable' choices the speakers may make, forms of impersonal and therefore indirect statement of propositions referring to Problematic Topics. The data shows that these conventions of journalistic analysis create a discourse which is closed. Closed, to speaker responsibility for his utterance, through citing others (Rule II) or through the fuzziness of metaphoric meaning (Rule III). *The effect of the Rules is a discourse whose sense or meaning is obscure, and is closed also to the comprehension of the mass audience. This seems an unfortunate paradox for mass communicators, and for their publics.*

The Rules, and the generalizations of this paper should be understood as 'dispositional' generalizations *(Zadeh, 1983)*. Dispositional generalizations are not absolute, *but describe processes and relationships which 'preponderantly', or 'often' or 'almost always' obtain, in a complex system characterized by elastic constraints. The Rules are not mutually exclusive, nor are their boundaries sharply defined.* The unfamiliarity that most of us share with the journalists, of the linguistic processes we use for indirection may make a simple system seem complex. We 'read' and intuitively understand and use indirection, which serves many purposes in communication. However, there is a genuine conceptual problem in linguistic fields which have focused on surface representations of meaning, and on the sentence as the unit of analysis, in understanding the centrality of indirection, the equivocal and ambiguous and obscure forms of communication of natural, serious discourse; or, utterances which have their meaning *only* in the context of the discourse, or, one should say, the many levels of discourse context. The association of indirection with Problematic Topics in the media discourse shows the importance of explicit understanding of the processes of indirection, for analysis of naturally-occurring discourse. The processes of impersonality discussed in this paper include some of the same linguistic forms, associated with central, indirect propositions in the private Nixon White House Conversations (Lerman, 1981).

The notion of a 'system' of various linguistic forms which represents possible, interchangeable ways of achieving a general purpose, indirect, impersonal or obscure speech, is also unfamiliar. Yet, if we examine only one element in the system, such as question, or other-attribution, we can understand only 'usage', not how the system of language itself works, and is used in indirect discourse. By charting several elements in a system, we can perceive the inherent qualities of linguistic forms, elaborated by their use in the reality of discourse.

A further conceptual problem in understanding indirection is unawareness of the structural duality of linguistic form. That is, that the impersonality markers identified here may be used, in an 'unmarked' way, for their direct functions: such as quotation, for clarification concerning the source of relevant facts, or question, in direct discourse, to seek information. The system I have outlined, and the rules, which are stated in positive form represent some of the linguistic choices speakers observe (no doubt, unconsciously) in the statement of impersonal propositions.

A possible further confusion is that most of the markers which delete the speaker from his utterance operate on the nominal, the 'subject', which is the 'natural' location for speaker-deletion. However, metaphor functions primarily at the predicative level. Therefore, metaphor may be used with 'I' forms, and another type of 'impersonal' discourse is achieved. Question is another variant; the speaker is only implicitly present in a question; and the propositions of question are embedded, not explicit.

It seems a useful task for discourse analysis to make explicit the understanding of customary discourse practices of the mass media. Of course, I have selected out of a large text, fragments, which cannot give a complete view; there are many direct and clear units of the text. Yet, the structure of the discourse itself, [Rule I] is inimical to coherent transmission of information or opinion. The use of the impersonal style of discourse for central Problematic Topics adds levels of difficulty to comprehension, assuming that Rule I did not preclude coherence and sense. As is often the case in discourse, there is multiple reinforcement of the Rules for Impersonality, at many levels.

Despite the public consumption of television news reporting in the United States, every survey reveals a public which is largely ignorant or confused about recent historical events, or current events. The practices discussed here provide several explanations for the public confusion or ignorance, any one of which would be sufficient. These customs were no doubt established to promote the impartial and objective transmission of the news; are valid goals for journalism, or any other professional discourse, even though we recognize them as realistically, unattainable. The continuation of these practices is no doubt customary and unreflective, and not designed as a disinformation system. In a previous paper, I have discussed rather commonly understood general constraints on mass communication (Lerman 1983a) and the inherent lack of authenticity of the media 'Institutional Voice'; we can hope that the attention of discourse analysts to defineable problems in the form may effect change. The practices discussed here are very interesting because they seem to stem from genuine, if unreflective, ideals of journalism, without awareness of the communicative difficulties they create. They are, to some considerable degree, remediable.

## Bibliography

Blake, R. H. and Haroldsen, E. O. (1975) *A Taxonomy of Concepts in Communication.* New York: Hastings House.
Brown, R. W. and Gilman, A. (1960). The pronouns of power and solidarity. In *Style in Language*, T. Sebeok (ed.) 253–276. Cambridge, Mass: MIT Press.
Brown, R. W. and Lenneberg, E. H. (1954). A study in language and cognition. *Journal of Abnormal and Social Psychology* 49, 454–462.
Chafe, W. L. (1980). The deployment of consciousness in the production of a narrative. In *The Pear Stories*, W. L. Chafe (ed.) 41–55. Norwood, N.J.: Ablex.

Geis, M. L. (1984). On semantic and pragmatic competence. Paper given at the Georgetown University Roundtable, March 1984.
Grice, H. P. (1975). Logic and conversation. In *Syntax and Semantics, v. 3 Speech Arts*, P. Cole and J. L. Morgan (eds.) 41–58. New York: Academic Press.
Hobbs, J. R. (1978). Why is discourse coherent? Technical Note 176, SRI International, Menlo Park Ca. 94025.
Hymes, D. (1974). Ways of speaking. In *Explorations in the Ethnography of Speaking*, R. Bauman and J. Sherzer (eds.) 433–451. Cambridge: Cambridge University Press.
Judiciary Committee, House (1974). *Presidential Statements on the Watergate Break-in and its Investigation*. Washington, D:C.: Government Printing Office. 14–18.
Labov, W. and Fanshel, D. (1977). *Therapeutic Discourse*. New York: Academic Press.
Lakoff, G. and Johnson, M. (1980). *Metaphors We live By*. Chicago: University of Chicago Press.
Lerman, C. L. (1981). *A Sociolinguistic Study of Political Discourse: The Nixon White House Conversations*. Ph. D. dissertation, University of Cambridge.
Lerman, C. L. (1983a) Dominant discourse: The institutional voice and control of topic. In *Language, Image, Media*. H. Davis and P. Walton (eds). 75–103. Oxford: Blackwell.
Lerman, C. L. (1983b). The functions of propositional metaphor in the Nixon Conversations. Paper presented at the Linguistic Society of America Annual Meeting, Minneapolis.
Lerman, C. L. (1983c). Analysing discourse: A method for the analysis of distancing. Paper presented at the International Conference of the Association for Literary and Linguistic Computing, San Francisco. (To appear in *the Journal of the ALLC*.)
New York Times Staff (1973). *The end of a Presidency. Chronology 1968–74*. New York: Holt, Rinehart and Winston.
Scotton, C. M. and Wanjin, Z. (1983). Tongzhi in China: Language change and its conversational consequences. *Language in Society* 12, 477–494.
Thomason, R. H. (1970). *Symbolic Logic: An Introduction*. London:Macmillan.
Westley, B. H. (1972). *News Editing*. 2nd ed. Boston: Houghton Mifflin.
van Dijk, T. A. and Kintsch (1983). *Strategies of Discourse Comprehension*. New York: Academic Press.
Zadeh, L. A. (1983). A fuzzy-set-theoretic approach to the compositionality of meaning: propositions, dispositions and canonical forms. Memorandum No. UCB/ERL M83/24, Electronics Research Laboratory, University of California, Berkeley, Ca. 94720. (to appear in *The Journal of Semantics*).

*Appendix 1*

EXCERPTS FROM THE INDIRECT TEXT
President Nixon's address to the nation, April 30, 1973 (2.719 words)

Showing the association of distancers with *central propositions and themes* in the discourse, and the co-occurrence of markers.

The central, indirect propositions were identified by the method of 'analysis of distancing' (Lerman 1981, 1983c). This method elicits the indirect propositions of the text, which is then the basis of analysis. The major propositions of the sub-text are shown below. The indirect message is achieved through speaker identity shifts, from 'I' to 'WE' — to the Institutional Role, of moral leader. The identity shift is the mechanism for Topic Transformations. The 'charges' (2) are transformed to 'campaign excesses' (40–41–42), of which 'all' have been guilty. The media analysis largely ignored the indirect propositional level of the speech, except for the 'responsibility' statement (25).

The distancing markers are listed: domniant markers (or Themes features) are shown in the right margin. Other distances are listed, following the propositions. Numbers in parentheses indicate paragraph number in text. Symbols used are shown in note 5.

UTTERANCE VERBS: express the speaker's relationship to his utterance, and often precede central propositions.

| | | |
|---|---|---|
| CON-<br>TEXT<br>OF<br>SPEECH | I WANT TO TALK TO YOU tonight from my heart on a subject of deep concern to every American. [Utterance verb] | (1) |
| | some of my closest friends and most trusted aides ... have been charged. ... charges of illegal activity and charges that responsible officials participated in efforts to cover-up that illegal activity. | (2) |
| | The *inevitable*** result of these charges has been to *raise questions about the integrity of* THE WHITE HOUSE ITSELF.** [+ Normalization + Institutional Metaphor* + evaluative adjective*] | |
| TOPIC | Tonight I WISH TO ADDRESS those questions. [Utterance verb] | (3) |
| WE<br>were<br>deceived | new information then *came to me* ... suggesting that *there had been an effort to conceal* the facts ... FROM YOU AND FROM ME. [Nonagentives, First use, 'I' + You] | (6) |

Questions: Implicit proposition: I — We don't know.

| | | |
|---|---|---|
| | How could it have happened? Who is to blame? | (17) |
| | ... Who then is to blame for what happened? | (21) |
| Virtue | THAT (the easiest course) WOULD BE A COWARDLY THING TO DO. // I will NOT place the blame on subordinates ... who may done wrong in a cause they deeply* believed to be right. [Generic sentence + Negation + Intensity marker*] | (23, 24) |
| Responsi-<br>bility | IN ANY ORGANIZATION, THE MAN AT THE TOP MUST BEAR THE RESPONSIBILITY. // That responsibility, THEREFORE belongs here, *in this office*. // *I accept it*. And I pledge* to you ... [Generic sentence + 'I' + Syllogism + Utterance verb* + Imperative] | (25) |
| WE | *It is essential* // that WE place OUR FAITH in the system. [Imperative clause] | (26) |

214   C. L. Lerman

WE —         *It is essential* // that in reacting to the excesses of OTHERS,
'OTHERS' WE not fall into excesses OURSELVES. [Imperative clause +
             Negative + parallel structures]                           (27)

WE           It is also essential // that WE NOT be so distracted by events
Duty to      such as this [Watergate] // that WE neglect the vital work before
World        US, before this Nation. ... at a time of critical importance to the
             world. [Imperative clause + Negation]                     (28)

'I'          I MUST now turn my full attention ... to LARGER duties ...
LEADER       I OWE it to this great office ... I OWE it to you ... to my
Future       country. [+ Imperative modal]                             (30)
WE           WE MUST MAINTAIN the integrity of *the White House**  [+
Virtue       Imperative Modal + Institutional Metaphor*]
             There can be NO *whitewash* at the White House.* [Institutional
             metaphor* + Metaphor + Negation]                          (39)

WE           WE MUST reform OUR political process. ridding it not only of
Virtue       violations of the law, but also of the ugly mob violence. ... [+
             Imperative]                                               (40)


Establishment of Shared Guilt. Topic Transformation: 'Charges' are defined as 'campaign excesses'.

BOTH         BOTH OF OUR GREAT PARTIES have been guilty of such
ERRED        ('INEXCUSABLE CAMPAIGN') TACTICS in the past.    (41)

ALL          ... The campaign excesses that have occurred ON ALL SIDES
ERRED        ... sobering demonstration of how far this false doctrine can take
             US. [+ Nominalization + Universal term]                   (42)

ALL          The lesson is clear: AMERICA, in ITS POLITICAL
Were         CAMPAIGNS, MUST NOT AGAIN FALL INTO THE TRAP
Trapped      of letting the end, however great, ... justify the means. [Generic
             sentence + Institutional metaphor + Imperative Negative Modal]
                                                                       (42)


Moral and World Leadership Established. Time shift, to future.

             I URGE leaders of BOTH POLITICAL PARTIES ... ALL OF
             YOU ... to JOIN in working ... to ensure that FUTURE
             ELECTIONS will be ... free of such abuses. ... MY goal. I
             ASK YOU TO JOIN ME in making it America's goal. [ALL
             + ME + Utterance verbs]                                   (43)
             ... in the wisdom of [American] leadership ... lies the only* hope
             for millions* of people throughout the world ... for peace and
             freedom. WE MUST be worthy of that hope. I ask for your

prayers, to help me ... to be worthy. ... God Bless America. And God bless each and every one of you. [Generic Sentence + Imperative modal + intensity markers* + blessing][1]  (44)

---

[1] Paragraph 44 was omitted from the official text.

THEO VAN LEEUWEN

# Rhythmic Structure of the Film Text

*1. Introduction*

There was a time when few works of film theory failed to discuss the role of rhythm in film. Rhythm was seen as the 'lifebreath' of film, as that which 'turns a succession of separate shots into an organic unity' and 'infuses images with life and cohesion' (Peters, 1964, p. 138). Detailed attention was given to what constitutes film rhythm, to its aesthetic and communicative potential, to its role in film perception (cf. e. g. Eisenstein, 1943, 1963; Chartier, 1946; Balasz, 1952; Martin, 1962; Peters, 1964; Mitry, 1963).

More recently the study of film rhythm has been all but abandoned. Since the publication of Mitry's *Esthétique et Psychologie du Cinéma* (1963), little if any original thought has been contributed to the subject. Textbooks continue to repeat, in one form or another, the brilliant but one-sided insights of the Soviet-Russian theorist-filmmakers of the 1920ies, turning what once was theory into conventional wisdom, and rarely testing it against films other than those described in the classic literature. If film rhythm is mentioned by modern, semiologically oriented film theorists, it is to elucidate some other problem rather than to contribute to the study of film rhythm itself (cf. e. g. Metz, 1971, pp. 166—167).

This paper, building on my research on intonation and rhythm in speech (Van Leeuwen, 1982), attempts a critique of the conventional approach to the study of film rhythm, and proposes an alternative — an approach which not only provides a method of analyzing the rhythmic structure of film sequences, but also, it is hoped, opens up new ways of theorizing the role of rhythm in film communication and new ways of segmenting film texts for the purpose of structural analysis.

*2. Film rhythm and film cutting*

*Potential cutting points*

If one view of film rhythm dominates film theory it is the view that film rhythm is *created* by the filmmaker, more specifically by the film editor:

> ...rhythm stems from the succession of shots according to their relation in terms of *duration* (or rather of the viewer's *impression* of that duration, created both by the actual duration of the shot and by its dramatic impact) and of *size of frame* (the closer a shot, the greater its psychological impact) ...
>
> (Martin, 1962, p. 143, *my tr.*)

It is a view which sees film rhythm as resulting from an alternation between what could be called 'upbeat' and 'downbeat' shots, shots which are rhythmically accented (and hence have greater perceptual conspicuity and 'psychological impact') and shots which are not. The perceptual conspicuity which causes the shot to be perceived as 'accented' is seen as created by the director's or photographer's choice of size of frame, and by the editor's manipulation of the duration of shots: film rhythm is articulated by the technical manipulation of the material.

But the material thus manipulated, the profilmic event, is already rhythmic: film rhythm begins with the rhythms reproduced on image- and soundtrack (the speech rhythm of dialogue or narration; the rhythm of the accompanying music; the rhythms of extended sound effects: footsteps, ticking clocks, shrieking gulls, the rhythmicality of the actors' movements) — it is these rhythms, separately or in combination, which originate and determine the filmic rhythm. Rather than that film editors impose their rhythm on the images, the images and sounds impose their rhythms on the editors, restrict them as to where and how the film can be cut and the sound effects positioned ('layed'), furnish the *potential cutting points* for which the good film editor is said to have a 'feeling'.

Two elements of the profilmic rhythm determine the location of these potential cutting points: rhythmic accent and rhythmic juncture. I will discuss and exemplify each in turn.

*Rhythmic accent.* Rhythm always involves cycles, cycles which consist of an alternation between successive sensations of accentedness and non-accentedness, and these cycles repeat themselves with time intervals perceived as equal (*perceptual isochrony*). The accented and non-accented stimuli differ, usually, in duration, intensity and/or other discriminable features — the contrast between them is that between long and short, strong and weak, tense and lax, active and dormant, etc.

But even when the accented and non-accented and stimuli are not measurably different a sensation of rhythmic alternation will be perceived: listening to a series of absolutely identical and isochronously spaced click noises, so psychological experimentation has discovered, people will, at regular intervals, hear one of the clicks as stronger than the others, despite the fact that the perceived difference has no physical counterpart (Allen, 1975).

The isochronous spacing of accents, too, is a perceptual effect rather than an objective reality: when the durations of successive cycles are not equal, as is often the case in speech, they will nevertheless be perceived as such: rhythm is imposed by perception (cf. Lehiste, 1973).

The film excerpts of which transcriptions are appended to this paper provide examples on which potential cutting points are realized as well as examples in which they are not. Thus in the *Latin American Rhapsody* excerpt (appendix 2) the first three cuts occur on the accented notes of each 2-bar melodic phrase of the music. In the *North by Northwest* excerpt (appendix 1) a cut occurs on the main accent of a rhythm group in the dialogue (i.e. on the word 'Wait'). Other speech accents, however (e.g. the accent on the word 'Please') are not used as cutting points.

*Rhythmic juncture.* A second category of potential cutting points is formed by the boundaries of the rhythm groups in the profilmic rhythm. These rhythm groups constitute the higher level rhythm units into which the rhythm cycles are organized. The junctures between them, occurring generally after maximally 7 or 8 cycles, are marked by a momentary interruption in the isochronous spacing of the accents, a pause in the speech, a rallentando in the body movements, an organ point in the music, etc. Following the junctures the regular alternation starts up again, though in the case of nonstylized body rhythms and ordinary speech the tempo may no longer be the same — in contrast to, for example, music and dance, such speech and body rhythms are characterized by frequent tempo changes.

The transcribed excerpts provide some examples of cutting points coinciding with junctures in the various profilmic rhythms. Thus the first two cuts of the *North by Northwest* excerpt (appendix 1) coincide with the junctures between the rhythm groups in the dialogue. In the *Hotel du Nord* excerpt (appendix 3), on the other hand, the first shot continues after the first rhythm group (enclosed in square brackets) has concluded. The absence of a cut makes the rhythmic boundary no less marked: the slowing down of the rhythm of the footsteps, the commencement of the prostitute's dialogue, the end of the camera movement all contribute to the realization of the rhythmic boundary, and participate, in this way, in the film's rhythmic structure.

*Initiating rhythms*

As there may be (and usually is) more than one profilmic rhythm, editors are faced with the problem on synchronizing the various profilmic rhythms — at least insofar as these have not been recorded simultaneously and synchronously, or been postsynchronized, as music often is. To do so, the editor chooses one of the profilmic rhythms as an *initiating rhythm* and subordinates to this rhythm the other profilmic rhythms.

The *Latin American Rhapsody* excerpt (appendix 2) shows this process at work. The music track provides the initiating rhythm. The shots have been trimmed in such a way that the various incidental body movements reproduced on the film (head and arm movements, glances) coincide with the rhythmic accents of the music. The *Hotel du Nord* excerpt (appendix 3) uses body movement as the initiating rhythm. A sound effect (the whistle) is placed in synchrony with these movements, on a rhythmic accent.

An initiating rhythm will usually continue to determine the cutting points throughout a sequence, even when the initiating element itself is momentarily absent. Thus the dialogue in the *North by Northwest* excerpt (appendix 1) continues to structure the film rhythm even after the actors have ceased to speak: the rhythm set up by the isochronous spacing of the nuclear accents in the third line of the transcript ('Wait' and 'Please') determines the timing of the cut to the point-of-view shot of the station hall. The cut occurs on a 'virtual' dialogue accent, and this accent gives the shot extra salience, stresses it, so to speak.

Another virtual accent occurs a moment later, in the same excerpt, but this time it is not accompanied by a cut. It *could* have been, but the editor chose, instead, to emphasize the moment of indecision, the moment at which nothing happens, the hesitation of Eve — and, as it happens, this 'nothing' is of great dramatic importance in the film.

## 3. *Natural and stylized rhythm*

Much of the literature on film rhythm suffers from a confusion between natural and stylized rhythm, between rhythms such as occur in everyday speech and body motion, and rhythms such as occur in metric poetry, music and dance, rhythms on which a form of patterning, a metric organization of the expression matter is superimposed.

Eisenstein (1963) has been influential in discerning a separate category of 'rhythmic editing', defined in terms of regular variation in the duration of shots. More precisely: he distinguished between metric editing, which involves only the patterning of shot durations, an abstract play with duration, an attempt to create 'visual music', and *rhythmic editing* in which the regular variation in duration is accompanied by an equally regular variation in the content of the shot. A similar treatment of 'rhythmicality' as a category apart, a kind of 'special effect' or 'aesthetic ingredient', occurs at times in the linguistic literature on rhythm and intonation. Crystal, for example, marks as 'rhythmic' stretches of speech in which the organization of the rhythm approaches meter (1969; also Crystal and Davy, 1969).

Natural and stylized rhythm have in common that accented moments (syllables, gestures, notes, etc.) recur with time intervals perceived as equal, and that other, unaccented syllables, gestures, notes, etc. may intervene between the accents. In both, the regular occurrence of accented moments is, from time to time (after up to 7 accents), interrupted by some kind of momentary disturbance of the rhythm (pause, slowing down, change of tempo, etc.) which marks the transition between rhythm groups. Each rhythm group thus contains a number of rhythm cycles which, each, consist, obligatorily, of an accent, and, optionally, of a number (maximally 7 or 8) of unaccented moments. Each rhythm group further contains a *nucleus* — an accent perceived as more salient than the others, and usually found at one of the extremities of the group. Finally, in both natural and stylized rhythm, the rhythm groups combine to form what could be called 'rhythm paragraphs', the junctures between which are marked by more salient suspensions of the beat than those between rhythm groups.

The difference between natural and stylized rhythm is that in stylized rhythm some form of patterning is superimposed on the rhythmic cycles — apart from the obligatory accented syllable or dance step or drum beat, the cycles all contain the same specific numer of unaccented syllables or dance steps or drum beats, and/or on the rhythm groups — each rhythm group containing the same number of rhythm cycles, and/or on the rhythm paragraph — each paragraph containing the same numer of rhythm groups. In addition the tempo is likely to be constant.

The and/or's above already indicate that there are degrees of stylization. In the *North by Northwest* excerpt (appendix 1), for example, equal intervals space the nuclear accents of the rhythm groups in the dialogue. By cutting after each rhythm group and manipulating the duration of the intervening pauses, the editor has in fact imposed a degree of stylization on the natural rhythm of the actors' speech — on the level of the rhythm group, not on that of the rhythm cycle or the rhythm paragraph.

Nevertheless, to ascribe 'rhythmicality' only to film sequences in which this kind of stylization occurs, is to deny the rhythmic basis of all (even the most mundane) films. By virtue of reproducing natural speech, a news broadcast, to mention just one not so 'artistic' example, is also rhythmic. No doubt the desire to see film recognized as an art, on a par with poetry and music and ballet, has influenced classic film theory too much here.

*4. Is visual rhythm possible?*

Another confusion from which much of the classic literature on film rhythm suffers is that between rhythm cycles and rhythm groups. It results from the tendency, already noted, to regard the shot as the basic element of film rhythm and to see cutting as constitutive of that rhythm inasmuch as it creates an alternation between 'strong' and 'weak', 'accented' and 'unaccented' shots.

This view overlooks the fact that shots are generally much longer in duration than the syllables, dance steps, musical notes, etc. to which they are thus compared. Rather than a quarter of a second, shots generally last between 2 and 40 seconds, although shots as short as an eighth of a second and shots as long as 10 minutes do occur. The duration of shots, then, is closer to that of rhythm groups or rhythm paragraphs than to that of the elements of the rhythm cycle.

Regarding shots as the basic elements of film rhythm has had another consequence: it has caused film theorists to try and isolate the features of 'accented' shots which lend them the prominence that features like pitch and intensity lend accented sounds. We have already seen how size of frame has been singled out as one such feature. The initial rhythm paragraph of the *Latin American Rhapsody* excerpt (appendix 2) in fact displays precisely this kind of 'visual rhythm', this alternation in size of frame (Medium Long Shot/ Close Shot/ Medium Long Shot/Close Shot). Yet, the rhythm of the paragraph is undoubtedly initiated by the music. The visual alternation at best provides an additional way of setting off the rhythm groups against each other, of marking their boundaries.

It is not easy to tap the beat of visual rhythms, to dance to the tune of silent images — unless, perhaps, these images are very short, almost empty of content, mere light flashes. After the radical 'visual music' experiments of Richter, Ruttman, and others, in the 20ies, experimental filmmakers have almost always found it necessary to support their abstract visual rhythms with music (cf. discussion in Mitry, 1963, pp. 329–346). But in the theory, which has, by and large, concentrated on the image track, this has not always been recognized.

## 5. *The function of rhythm*

Two approaches to the function of rhythm are most common in film literature, the 'expressive' and the 'psychological' approach.

The 'expressive' approach holds that a film or a section of a film has the 'rhythm' that expresses its mood and theme. An example:

> ...a slow rhythm may give an impression of yearning (as in certain sequences of *The Red*), of sensual immersion in Nature (*The Earth*), of powerlessness before a blind destiny (the final sequences of *Les Rapaces*), of the hopelessness and monotony of the search for simple human contact (*L'Avventura*). A fast, nervous, dynamic rhythm gives an effect of anger (as in the flashes of indignant faces and clenched fists in *Potemkin*), of speed, of feverish activity ...
> 
> (Martin, 1962, p. 142, *my tr.*)

However, it is tempo, rather than rhythm, which thus enhances the mood of the scene. The *North by Northwest* excerpt (appendix 1) provides an example: as the scene becomes more tense, with Eve's line 'Wait a minute ...', the tempo increases. The *Hotel du Nord* excerpt (appendix 3) slows down after the climactic moment, when it has become clear that Jean, after all, has not committed suicide.

The 'psychological' approach allies film rhythm to the fluctuations of the viewer's attention. A fairly typical example:

> ...while we look at a shot, there arrives a moment of maximum attention, the moment during which we grasp the full significance, the *raison d'être* of the shot: a gesture, a word, a movement propels forward the action or the theme. Thereafter attention decreases and if the image is allowed to linger on the screen, boredom or impatience will set in. If, on the other hand, every shot is cut at exactly the moment attention begins to wane, to be replaced by another shot, the attention will remain tightly stretched at all times, and we say that the film has rhythm. Film rhythm is not a relation between the duration of shots, it is a relation between the duration of each shot and the fluctuation of the attention which it sets up and sustains. What matters is not the abstract temporal pattern, but a rhythm of the attention...
> (Chartier, 1946, p. 29, *my tr.*)

There is much insight in this passage, but Chartier, too, can conceive of film rhythm only in terms of cutting. The attention curve he describes can in fact be maintained also by sound effects, words, or gestures which are positioned on accented moments *within* shots: what the viewer needs is not so much a new shot as new information, whether presented within the shot or by a new shot.

Following an approach developed in my research on intonation and rhythm in speech (Van Leeuwen, 1982, ch. 2), I would like here to discuss the function of rhythm under the headings of *ranking* and *grouping*.

*Ranking*. Ranking is the process of making certain elements in a chain prominent at the expense of others. These elements — whether they are syllables, or musical notes, or body movements — are made prominent by virtue of their rhythmically accented position, although their prominence may be enhanced in various other ways — in the case of sound, by increasing pitch or intensity or duration; in the case of movements by increased force or extent of the movement — but for such an element to occur on the beat of the rhythm remains sufficient condition for it to b e perceived as more prominent that the other elements in the chain. Objective, measurable prominence is not necessary.

This perceptual prominence also ranks the elements of the chain in terms of their semantic importance: what is rhythmically made to appear prominent will be perceived as more important, more worthy of attention than what is not — regardless of whether it is more important in some objective sense. Thus, by placing a word, a gesture, a sound, a camera movement on a moment rhythmically privileged by the initiating rhythm, the editor can make it salient, draw the viewer's attention to it. In the case of speech, psycholinguistic experiment has demonstrated this: experimental subjects react more quickly to accented syllables than to unaccented ones, and retain them in memory for a longer time: their attention focusses on the accented moments at the expense of the unaccented moments (Cutler and Foss, 1973; Martin, 1972; Nooteboom *et al.*, 1976)

*Grouping.* Grouping enables rhythm to provide 'frames' for the elements of the structure of the text. In connection with intonation, Halliday has defined the 'tone group' as 'a move in the speech act' (1967, p. 30). In my view rhythm, rather than tone, it the *sine qua non* of grouping — if it were not, grouping could not occur in whispering and monotone speech. I would nevertheless like to borrow and broaden Halliday's definition for my present purpose and define rhythm groups and rhythm paragraphs as 'moves in the filmic act' — be this 'act' a dramatic or a thematic act.

The rhythm group is such a 'move' at a relatively 'micro' level — a move in the gradual unfolding of information, perhaps, or a move of deliberately withholding information, in order to create suspense. The second rhythmic paragraph of the *Hotel du Nord* excerpt (appendix 3), for example, contains a series of distinct dramatic moves, each further augmenting the suspense, the sense that something is going to happen, but none disclosing any new information. The structure of the first rhythmic paragraph of the *Latin American Rhapsody* excerpt (appendix 2), on the other hand, is thematic: the successive 'moves in the thematic act' all provide examples of a general category, the category of 'mothers and children'.

The rhythm paragraph is a 'move in the filmic act' too, but situated at a higher, more 'macro' level. Thus the second rhythm paragraph of the *Hotel du Nord* excerpt (appendix 3) constitutes a move similar in kind to those constituted by its component groups: a move of withholding information to create suspense. The first rhythmic paragraph of the *Latin American Rhapsody* excerpt (appendix 2) is also similar to its component groups, forming an item in a larger 'catalogue' as one of series of rhythmic paragraphs which all exemplify one aspect of the broader category encapsulated by the line 'Land of a thousand faces...' with which the sequence of which it is part opens.

It is not my aim here to enumerate the different kinds of 'move in the filmic act' possible. I merely want to suggest that rhythmic grouping segments the text, at the level of perception, into units which are not only rhythmically but also semantically coherent. Without meaning anything itself, rhythm is nevertheless a necessary condition for meaning ('It don't mean a thing if it ain't got that swing'). For this reason I believe that the segmentation of film texts for the purpose of structural analysis should be based on the rhythmic structure of the film, rather than on its *découpage* ('segmentation') into shots.

### 6. *Postscript: a method for the rhythmic analysis of film sequences*

It is perhaps useful to summarize here the method of rhythmic analysis proposed in this paper. I will present it in the form of a series of discrete steps, during each of which just one element of the rhythmic structure is analyzed and marked on a transcript.

*(1) Initiating rhythm*

The first step is to consider which aspect of the image track and/or the soundtrack provides the initiating rhythm of the sequence. In the case of the examples appended to this paper this posed no problems. The *North by Northwest* sequence contained no music and very little action; the *Latin American Rhapsody* sequence had no dialogue or narration and only incidental body movements, but the music was foregrounded throughout; the *Hotel du Nord* sequence contained neither dialogue nor music. It is, however, possible that two rhythmic carriers operate simultaneously, and in this case a decision needs to be made: should both rhythms be taken into account, or is one subordinated to the other? The following considerations cover all the cases I have come across so far. When (synchronous) dialogue is accompanied by action, the two rhythms are naturally coordinated, and should both be taken into account. In the choreographed sequences of musicals, dance films, etc., music and action are similarly coordinated. If dialogue is accompanied by music, the relative levels will provide the answer — and one should also consider whether or not the music has been composed after completion of the editing: in this case dialogue or action would have provided the editor with an initiating rhythm.

*(2) Transcription ot the initiating element(s)*

This decision made, the relevant aspect of image and/or soundtrack can be transcribed. I have chosen to render action verbally, rather than by means of some kinesic notation, which, in my view, would have complicated the reading of the transcripts unnecessarily.

*(3) Rhythmic accents*

The syllables (in the case of dialogue), notes (in the case of music) or gesture descriptions (in the case of action) can now be divided into those that are accented and those that are not. This is done 'auditorily': the analyst asks herself/himself which notes, gestures, syllables she/he perceives as somehow more prominent, more forceful that other notes, gestures or syllables in their immediate vicinity. The rhythm (tapping to the beat of the tentatively established accents) should be the determining factor. It is helpful to repeat to oneself the dialogue (sing the melody, mentally rehearse the actions) and to base the marking of the accents on this, checking the result by reviewing the fragment. I have marked the accents by underlining the accented syllables and gesture descriptions — in the case of music the accents fall regularly on the first (in the case of a 4/4 time signature the first and third) count of every bar.

*(4) Rhythm groups*

Tapping the rhythm of the accents, one should, at the boundaries of the rhythm groups, find a pause, a slowing down of movement, music or speech, a change in tempo, a break in the phrasing of the music, or some other similar phenomenon. In each case the rhythmic regularity is momentarily perturbed, and a series of movements (notes, words) felt by the viewer/listener to belong together, comes to an end. The boundaries are then marked with a double slash (//) and the rhythm groups enclosed in square brackets. A single slash before each rhythmic accent within the rhythm group divides the group into rhythm cycles.

*(5) Nuclear accent*

Comparing the relative prominence of the accents *within* each group, the accent perceived as the most prominent is marked as the nucleus of the group. I have done this by printing the relevant syllable or gesture description in capitals and encircling the nucleus. The 'tail' of these circles serves to facilitate relating the position of the nucleus to other, concomitant phenomena, written underneath the transcriptions.

*(6) Rhythm paragraphs*

Reviewing the successive rhythm group boundaries, one finds, from time to time, a boundary which appears to be more definitive, more salient, and which is likely to be manifested by a longer pause, or a more considerable slowing down of the tempo. These boundaries, then, are the boundaries, not only of rhythm groups, but also of rhythm paragraphs. I have indicated this by enclosing rhythm paragraphs in double square brackets.

*(7) Rhythm sequences*

A similar procedure can be followed to establish the boundaries of the next higher order rhythm unit, the rhythm sequence. However, at this level content factors (a change in location, or a hiatus in filmic time) will probably be more indicative of the boundary than purely rhythmic factors.

*(8) Subordinated elements of the image and soundtrack*

Below the transcription of the initiating rhythm(s) one can add other relevant phenomena which are subordinated to the initiating rhythm, for example camera movements which begin and end on rhythmically privileged moments, or words, sound effects, gestures (insofar as they are not part of the initiating rhythm) which are positioned on rhythmically determined moments. Cuts, dissolves and other shot transitions also belong to this category. Cuts I have indicated with I, dissolves with X. The sign Φ therefore designates a cut falling on the nucleus of a rhythm group.

*(9) timing*

The perceptual isochrony of rhythm cycles corresponds, in the case of complex stimuli, only roughly to measured time, and is, to some extent, a product of human perception. Objective duration should not, therefore, play a role in determining the locus of the rhythm accents and the junctures between rhythm groups. To give a rough idea of the duration of rhythm groups on the one hand, and shots on the other hand, I have nevertheless included some timings in the transcripts. They were obtained from the second counter of the Steenbeck editing bench on which the transcripts were prepared.

*Appendix 1*

*Transcript of excerpt from Hitchcock's North by Northwest (1959)*

The excerpt immediately precedes the famous scene in which Thornhill (Cary Grant) is attacked by a cropduster plane. Prior to the excerpt Eve Kendall (Eva Marie Saint) has told Thornhill when and where to meet a mysterous

# Legend

| | |
|---|---|
| ♀ | nuclear accent of rhythm group |
| I | cut between two shots |
| X | dissolve between two shots |
| Φ̃ | cut on nuclear accent of rhythm group |
| /.../ | rhythm cycle (R.C.) |
| [...] | rhythm group (R.G.) |
| [[...]] | rhythm paragraph |
| [[[...]]] | rhythm sequence |
| CS | close shot |
| MCS | medium close shot |
| MS | medium shot |
| MLS | medium long shot |
| LS | long shot |
| VLS | very long shot |
| OS | over shoulder |
| POV | point of view |

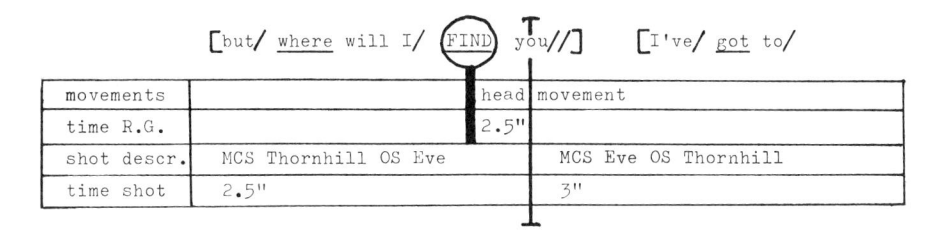

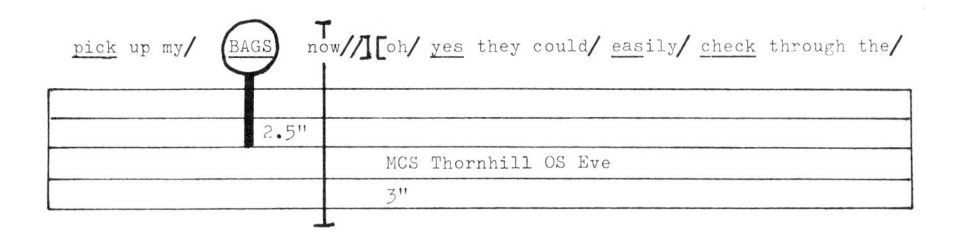

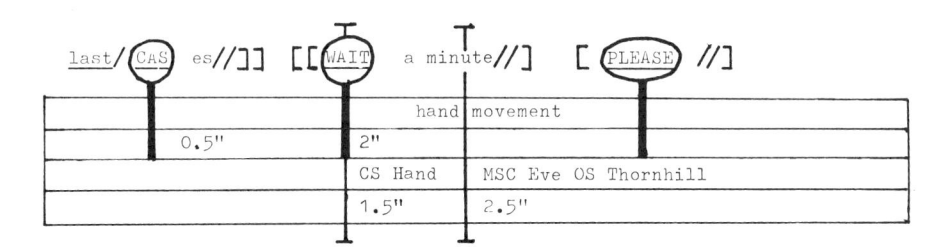

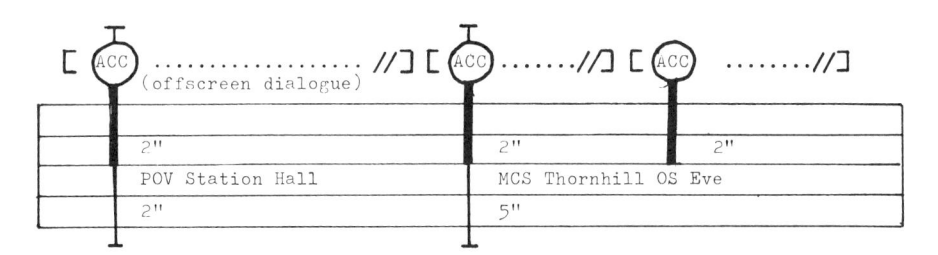

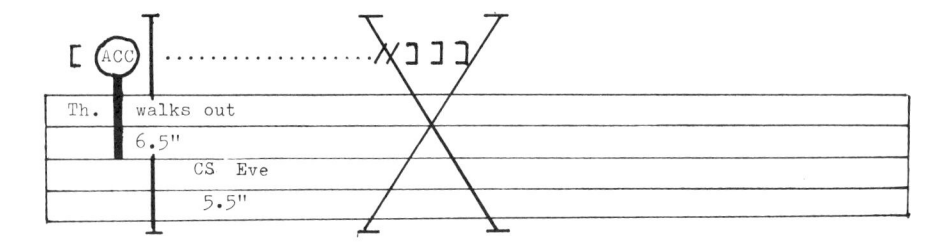

Rhythmic Structure of the Film Text 227

[but/ where will I/ (FIND) you//]   [I've/ got to/

| movements   |                      | head movement          |
|-------------|----------------------|------------------------|
| time R.G.   |                      | 2.5"                   |
| shot descr. | MCS Thornhill OS Eve | MCS Eve OS Thornhill   |
| time shot   | 2.5"                 | 3"                     |

pick up my/ (BAGS) now//][oh/ yes they could/ easily/ check through the/

|   |       |                      |
|---|-------|----------------------|
|   |       |                      |
|   | 2.5"  |                      |
|   |       | MCS Thornhill OS Eve |
|   |       | 3"                   |

last/ (CAS) es//]] [[(WAIT) a minute//]  [ (PLEASE) //]

|   |      | hand movement |                      |
|---|------|---------------|----------------------|
|   | 0.5" | 2"            |                      |
|   |      | CS Hand       | MSC Eve OS Thornhill |
|   |      | 1.5"          | 2.5"                 |

[ (ACC) .................//] [ (ACC) ......//] [ (ACC) ........//]
        (offscreen dialogue)

|                  |                      |    |
|------------------|----------------------|----|
| 2"               | 2"                   | 2" |
| POV Station Hall | MCS Thornhill OS Eve |    |
| 2"               | 5"                   |    |

[ (ACC) ................../x]]]

| Th. | walks out |
|-----|-----------|
|     | 6.5"      |
|     | CS Eve    |
|     | 5.5"      |

man called Kaplan. What Thornhill does not know is that Kaplan does not exist and that the meeting is a trap: instead of meeting Kaplan he will be attacked, and Eve knows this. The excerpt shows Thornhill about to set out on the journey. At the last moment Eve seems to have second thoughts. 'Wait a minute', she says, 'Please.' But then she decides against warning him. The short tense moment passes. Thornhill leaves to board his train.

*Appendix 2*

*Transcript of excerpt from Latin American Rhapsody (1964)*

*Latin American Rhapsody* is a Philips sponsored travelogue, professionally crafted, but without particular artistic merit. The excerpt follows shortly after the beginning of a sequence which opens with the unremarkable line of narration 'South America, land of a thousand faces ... 'This line neatly labels what is to follow: shots of people's faces, and of the 'faces' of the land. The excerpt consists of two sub-sequences from this larger structure, one showing mothers and children, alternately seen in close up and in a wider shot which encompasses also the setting, and one of land- and cityscapes. Further, similar sub-sequences follow the excerpt, until a line of narration, accompanying a long panning shot, concludes the sequence.

Cf. p. 226 for an explanation of the notation and the abbreviations used.

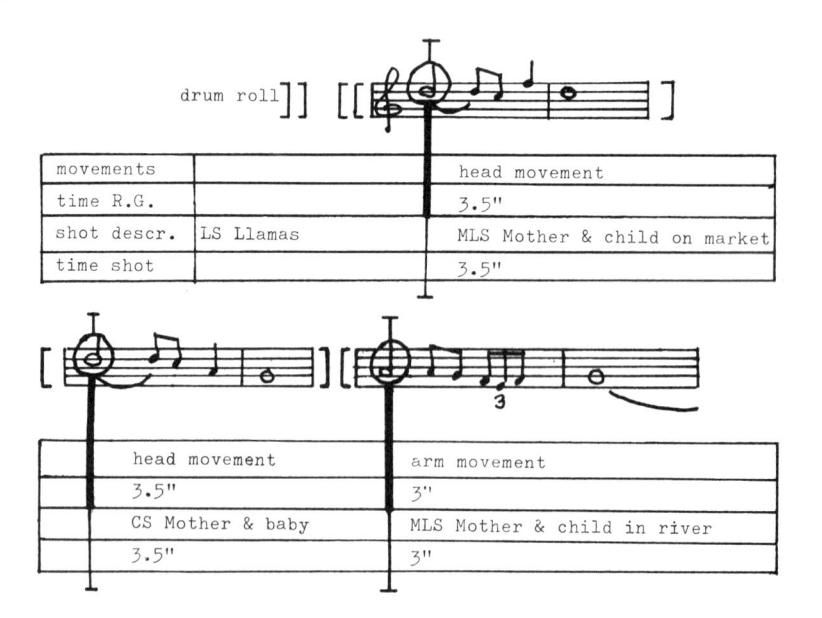

| movements     |           | head movement              |
|---------------|-----------|----------------------------|
| time R.G.     |           | 3.5"                       |
| shot descr.   | LS Llamas | MLS Mother & child on market |
| time shot     |           | 3.5"                       |

| head movement    | arm movement                |
|------------------|-----------------------------|
| 3.5"             | 3"                          |
| CS Mother & baby | MLS Mother & child in river |
| 3.5"             | 3"                          |

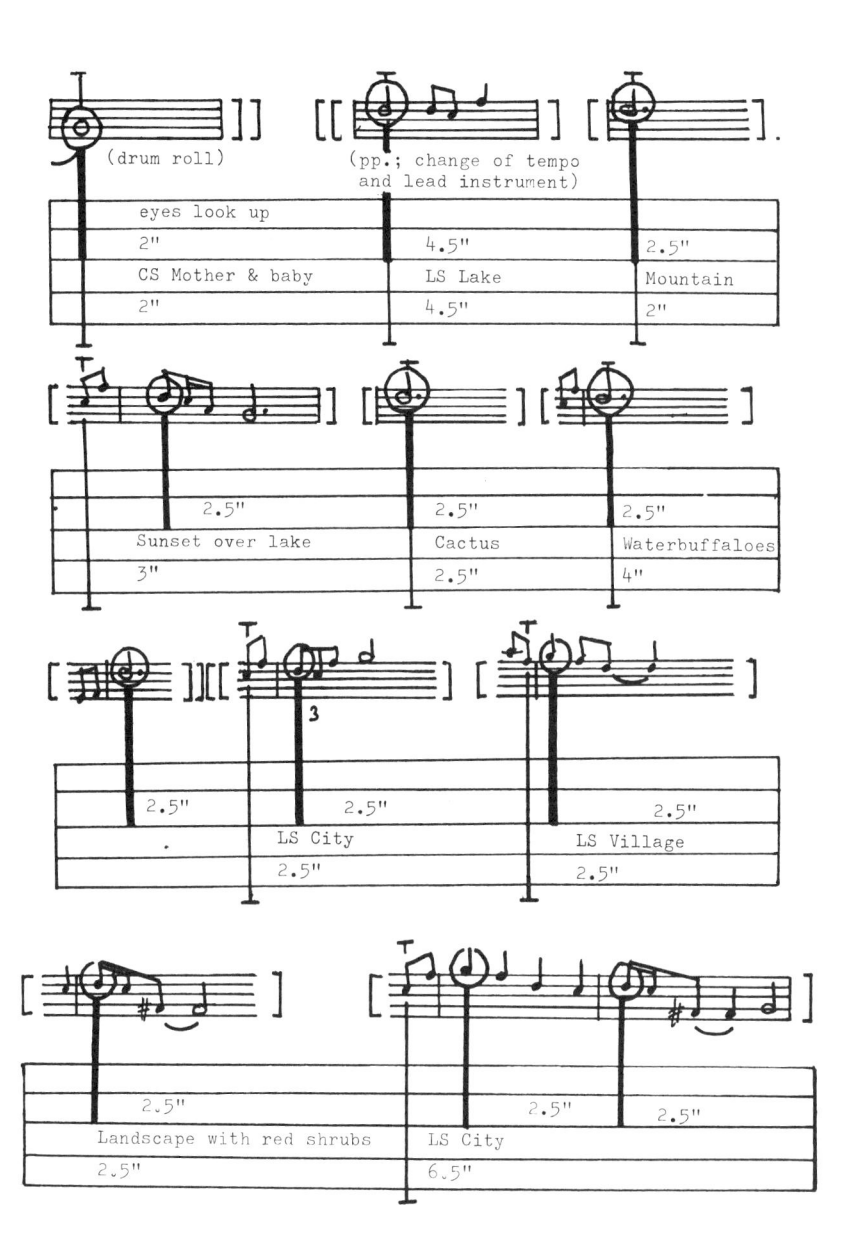

Rhythmic Structure of the Film Text     229

| | | |
|---|---|---|
| eyes look up | | |
| 2" | 4.5" | 2.5" |
| CS Mother & baby | LS Lake | Mountain |
| 2" | 4.5" | 2" |

(drum roll)  (pp.; change of tempo and lead instrument)

| | | |
|---|---|---|
| 2.5" | 2.5" | 2.5" |
| Sunset over lake | Cactus | Waterbuffaloes |
| 3" | 2.5" | 4" |

| | | |
|---|---|---|
| 2.5" | 2.5" | 2.5" |
| | LS City | LS Village |
| | 2.5" | 2.5" |

| | | |
|---|---|---|
| 2.5" | 2.5" | 2.5" |
| Landscape with red shrubs | LS City | |
| 2.5" | 6.5" | |

230    T. van Leeuwen

*Appendix 3*

*Transcript of excerpt from Marcel Carné's Hotel du Nord (1938)*

A highly dramatic incident immediately precedes the excerpt: Jean (Jean-Pierre Aumont) and his girlfriend Renée (Annabella) have made a suicide

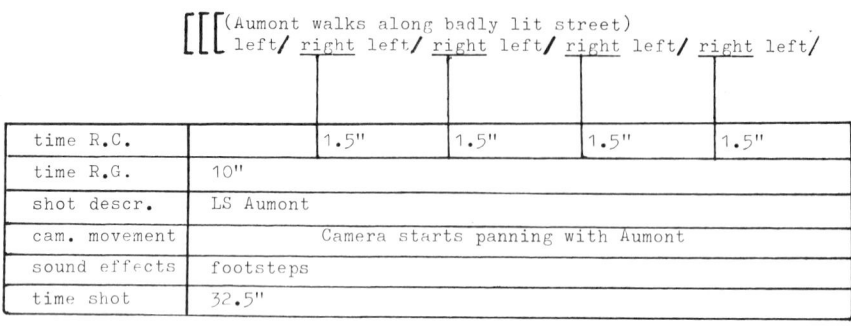

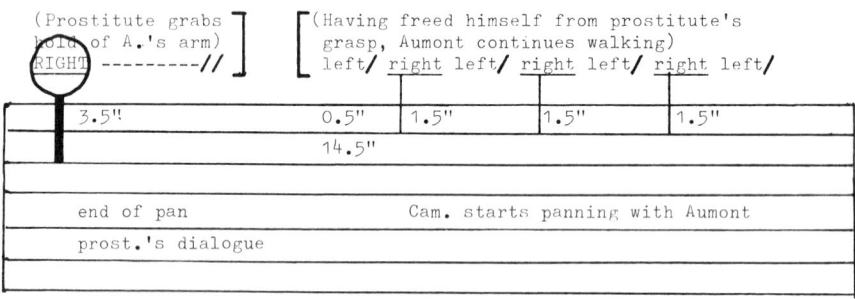

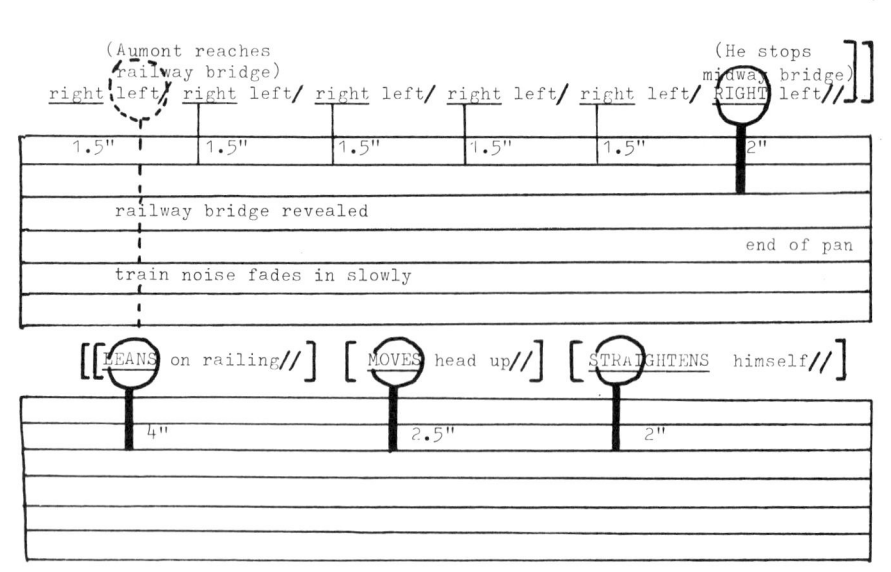

[[(Aumont walks along badly lit street)
left/ right left/ right left/ right left/ right left/

| time R.C. |  | 1.5" | 1.5" | 1.5" | 1.5" |
|---|---|---|---|---|---|
| time R.G. | 10" | | | | |
| shot descr. | LS Aumont | | | | |
| cam. movement | | Camera starts panning with Aumont | | | |
| sound effects | footsteps | | | | |
| time shot | 32.5" | | | | |

(Prostitute grabs hold of A.'s arm)  [(Having freed himself from prostitute's grasp, Aumont continues walking)
RIGHT --------//]   left/ right left/ right left/ right left/

| 3.5" | 0.5" | 1.5" | 1.5" | 1.5" |
|---|---|---|---|---|
| | 14.5" | | | |
| end of pan | Cam. starts panning with Aumont | | | |
| prost.'s dialogue | | | | |

(Aumont reaches railway bridge)    (He stops midway bridge)
right left/ right left/ right left/ right left/ right left/ RIGHT left//]]

| 1.5" | 1.5" | 1.5" | 1.5" | 1.5" | 2" |
|---|---|---|---|---|---|
| railway bridge revealed | | | | | end of pan |
| train noise fades in slowly | | | | | |

[[LEANS on railing//]  [MOVES head up//]  [STRAIGHTENS himself//]

| 4" | 2.5" | 2" |
|---|---|---|

Rhythmic Structure of the Film Text    231

pact and locked themselves into a hotelroom. Jean has shot Renée, but has been prevented from shooting himself also by a knock on the door. He has escaped the hotelroom via the balcony and now walks along badly lit streets, a picture of gloom. He stops on a railway bridge, obviously intending to

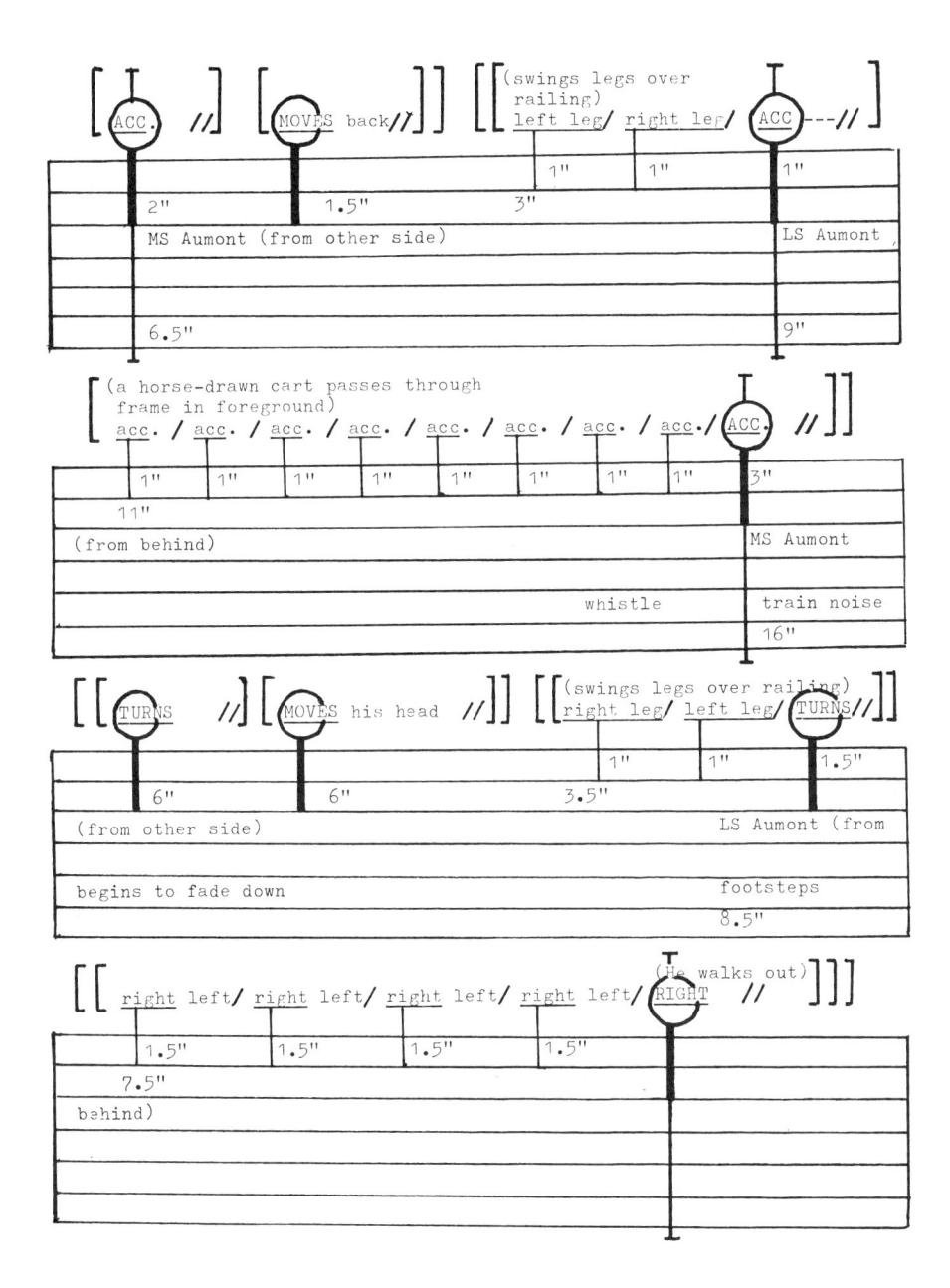

[ ACC. // ] [ MOVES back // ] ] [ [ (swings legs over railing) left leg / right leg / ACC ---// ] ]

| 2" | 1.5" | 3" | 1" | 1" | 1" |
|---|---|---|---|---|---|
| MS Aumont (from other side) | | | | | LS Aumont |

6.5"                                                          9"

[ (a horse-drawn cart passes through frame in foreground) acc. / acc. / acc. / acc. / acc. / acc. / acc. / ACC. // ] ]

| 1" | 1" | 1" | 1" | 1" | 1" | 1" | 1" | 3" |
|---|---|---|---|---|---|---|---|---|

11"
(from behind)                                                 MS Aumont

                                            whistle       train noise
                                                          16"

[ [ TURNS // ] [ MOVES his head // ] ] [ [ (swings legs over railing) right leg / left leg / TURNS // ] ]

| 6" | 6" | 3.5" | 1" | 1" | 1.5" |
|---|---|---|---|---|---|
| (from other side) | | | | | LS Aumont (from |

begins to fade down                                        footsteps
                                                           8.5"

[ [ right left / right left / right left / right left / (He walks out) RIGHT // ] ] ]

| 1.5" | 1.5" | 1.5" | 1.5" | |
|---|---|---|---|---|

7.5"
behind)

throw himself before an onrushing train. Just as he has climbed over the railing, and as the train has nearly reached the bridge, a cart drawn by a white horse passes trough frame, rather close to the camera, obscuring him from view. When it has passed the scene is enveloped in a cloud of steam from the train, and the sound is deafening. Only after the steam has begun to clear away do we discover that Jean has not jumped. He climbs back over the railing and returns in the direction from which he came — to give himself up.

Apart from a brief and almost inaudible solicitation on the part of a prostitute, in the beginning of the excerpt, there is not a word of dialogue. Cf. p. 226 for an explanation of the notation and the abbreviations used.

*Bibliography*

Allen, G. D. (1975). Speech Rhythm: its relation to performance universals and articulatory timing. *Journal of Phonetics* 3: 75—86.
Arnheim, R. (1958 [1938]). *Film as Art*. London: Faber.
Balasz, B. (1970 [1952]). *Theory of the Film*. New York: Dover.
Bettetini, G. (1973). *The Language and Technique of the Film*. Den Haag: Mouton.
Chartier, J.-P. (1946). Art et réalité au cinéma. *Bulletin de L'IDHEC* 4.
Classe, A. (1939). *The Rhythm of English Prose*. Oxford: Blackwell.
Crystal, D. (1969). *Prosodic Systems and Intonation in English*. Cambridge: Cambridge University Press.
Crystal, D. and Davy D. (1969). *Investigating English Style*. London: Longman.
Cutler, A. and Foss, D. J. (1973). The importance of lexical item stress for lexical access. Paper presented at the 44th Annual Meeting of the Midwestern Psychological Association, Chicago.
Eisenstein, S. (1943). *The Film Sense*. London: Faber.
Eisenstein, S. (1963). *Film Forum*. London: Dennis Dobson.
Fraisse, P. (1956). *Les structures rhythmiques*. Paris: Erasme.
Fraisse, P. (1974). *Psychologie du rhythme*. Paris: Presses Universitaires de France.
Halliday, M. A. K. (1967). *Intonation and Grammar in British English*. Den Haag: Mouton.
Lehiste, I. (1973). Rhythmic Units and Syntactic Units in Production and Perception. *Journal of the Acoustical Society of America* 54: 1102—1104.
Martin, M. (1962). *Le Langage Cinématographique*. Paris: Editions du Cerf.
Martin, J. G. (1972). Rhythmic (hierarchical) versus serial structure in speech and other behaviour. *Psychological Review* 79: 487—509.
Metz, C. (1971). *Langage et Cinéma*. Paris: Larousse.
Metz, C. (1972). *Essais sur la Signification au Cinéma*, tome II. Paris: Klincksieck.
Mitry, J. (1963). *Esthétique et psychologie du cinéma*. Paris.
Nooteboom, S. G., Brokx, J. P. L. and de Rooy, J. J. (1976). Contributions of Prosody to Speech Perception. *IPO Annual Progress Report* 11: 34—54
Peters, J. M. (1964). *De Montage bij film en televisie*. Haarlem: Focus.
Pudovkin, V. (1949). *Film Technique and Film Acting*.New York: Bonanza Books.
Spottiswoode, R. (1935). *A Grammar of the Film*. London: Faber.
Van Leeuwen, Th. J. (1982). *Professional Speech: Accentual and Junctural Style in Radio Announcing*. Unpubl. MA thesis, Sydney: Macquarie University.

JOHN HARTLEY AND MARTIN MONTGOMERY

# Representations and Relations:
# Ideology and Power in Press and TV News

*1. Introduction*

In this paper we seek to explore in some detail the signifying practices of a variety of media, through textual analysis. In undertaking these analyses, we acknowledge a substantial debt to the structuralist and semiotic enterprises, but we seek to supplement this tradition in two main ways. First, we draw on relatively recent work in linguistics to sharpen and clarify our sense of the way in which meanings are produced in text. Second, we attempt to show how specific textual features may be understood to invoke 'extra-textual' cultural relations of ideology and power. In particular, we argue that media journalism often operates with a *Manichean*[1] view of the world: events are constructed in terms of *binary oppositions*, a primary opposition being between 'US' and 'THEM', 'HOME' and 'FOREIGN'.

*2. Two Modes of Signification: The Representational and the Relational*

The production of meaning in the media is not a purely linguistic matter — for one thing, a substantial component of the signification is not strictly verbal. Nonetheless, linguistic processes are heavily implicated in even the most visual media, like television. Accordingly, we have found it useful to draw on a distinction current in linguistics between the way utterance (or text) renders the world of objects, persons, events and processes on the one hand, and the way in which that same utterance sets itself into relation with a recipient (reader, viewer or hearer) on the other. Utterance not only 'constructs reality' in a determinate and selective way; it also organizes the relationship between speaker and hearer along specific lines. The distinction is put in various ways in linguistics: 'ideational' v. 'interpersonal'[2]; 'propositional

---

[1] Both Eco (1981) and Laclau (1980) have drawn attention to the way in which popular discourses may revolve around fundamental oppositions.
[2] The terms figure importantly in the work of Michael Halliday. The most relevant source for them is his thoroughgoing attempt to theorise the relationship of language to social structure in *Language as Social Semiotic*.

content' v. pragmatic orientation'[3]; 'constative' v. 'performative'[4]. However, because these available terms refer exclusively to verbal language we would like to introduce a further pair to capture the distinction between two modes of signification, designating them as representational and relational respectively. We apply these terms broadly, not just to speech-based utterance or text, but to semiotic activity generally. As in the case of verbal utterance, both modes of semiosis are typically present at one and the same time in any act of signification — the process of constructing and representing 'a reality' is one that simultaneously implies relations with 'a recipient' of a particular type.

## 3. Culture, Signification and Text

The distinction allows us to mediate between two separate moments of analysis — the cultural and the textual.

On the one hand we have the sphere of the 'cultural', where relations of *power* — of dominance and subordination — are established, maintained and contested around fundamental social divisions such as gender, age, class, ethnicity; and this by means of the production and circulation of specific *ideologies*. On the other hand, we have the sphere of the 'textual'. Texts signify by virtue of the way in which they articulate together signs selected from an array of signifying systems. We hypothesize, in fact, that some of the available systems are more oriented towards the representational, others to the relational. For example, in subsequent sections we discuss some of the vocabulary selected in particular texts as a way of considering their mode of *representation*. And features such as deixis, mode of address, camera- and narrative-point of view, the interplay of picture- and sound-tracks etc. are discussed in order to explore the *relational* dimension.

| CULTURE | SIGNIFICATION | TEXTUAL REALIZATION |
| --- | --- | --- |
| IDEOLOGY | REPRESENTATIONAL | selections in vocabulary, etc. |
| POWER | RELATIONAL | selections in deixis, camera point-of-view, etc. |

Fig. 1: A schematic representation of the two basic modes of language and discourse.

---

[3] See Van Dijk's (1977) examination of the distinction between semantics and pragmatics and the relation of both to discourse.
[4] See Austin (1962).

The distinction, therefore, between representational and relational modes points our analysis in two directions — towards specific features of the text on the one hand, and towards wider cultural processes on the other; these we may schematize as follows: (Figure 1).

*4. Representational and Relational Illustrated: Four Texts on Poverty*

In order to illustrate some aspects of the distinction we would like to comment briefly on four journalistic accounts of the conditions of the poor, published between 1860 and 1931. Short extracts from the four accounts are reproduced as Appendix 1, though we shall also refer to sections other than those reprinted.

*4.1. Representations*

The accounts from which the extracts are drawn have one curious feature in common, irrespective of whether or not they attack the conditions under which the poor live. They quite typically draw on a polyglot eschatological religious vocabulary composed of elements such as 'Lazarus', 'Elysium', 'paradise', 'heaven', 'hell', etc. Given the dreadful conditions of the poor, 'who can wonder that the public-house is "the *Elysian field*" of the tired toiler', queries the *Pall Mall Gazette* (1883). On the other hand, the *Daily Mail* (1911) refers to a particular workhouse at Camberwell as nothing less than a 'Poor Law Elysium on this side of the *Great Divide*', in an article that enumerates 'the creature comforts of the penniles man in the Camberwell *Elysium*'. The same article links inhabitants of the workhouse to Lazarus — 'the spectacles provided for *Lazarus* are perfectly rose-coloured, you see. The atmosphere is quite serene and akin to golden'. Somewhat surprisingly a similar reference to Lazarus surfaces in Orwell's 'The Spike' (*Adelphi Magazine*, 1931), though here inflected very differently:

> Old 'Daddy', aged seventy-four, with his truss, and his red, watering eyes: a herring-gutted starveling, with sparse beard and sunken cheeks, looking like the corpse of *Lazarus* in some primitive picture.

This, of course, is only one kind of strand in the vocabulary of such texts, with variable histories for its individual elements (the invocation of Elysium, for instance, seems a particularly Victorian gesture), and a variable prominence in the texts it surfaces in. In broad terms, however, such a vocabulary serves to represent the conditions of the poor in a particular way — as produced by blind fate, impersonal justice or the wickedness of the poor themselves — and thence to represent a determinate range of responses, from Christian charity to punitive regulation. This clearly helps to close off certain modes of explanation and action. Poverty is a fate ascribed to people, either blindly or on the basis of their own fecklessness. It is not explained as a condition produced by a particular social system. Particular selections in vocabulary are thus part of particular modes of representation doing particular kinds of ideological work.

*4.2. Relations*

The same texts, however, shift markedly in the kinds of relation they adopt to their readership, and the way they position the reader with respect to the conditions described.

Sometimes they issue explicit instructions to the reader:

> *Imagine* a space of about thirty feet by thirty.
> (Appendix 1: ANINAW)

> *Imagine* yourself in this very perfect poverty palace, and *see* how ... your life goes.
> (Appendix 1: TWD)

Such instructions may relate to acts of visualization, and in this respect they can be seen as closely connected with devices that make reference to a scene as if it were immediately present to the reader:

> *Here are* seven people living in one underground kitchen ...
> *Here* lives a widow and her six children ...
> (Appendix 1: TBCOOL)

> *Here is* peace, another world ... *Here* you shall have rest and ease.
> (Appendix 1: TWD)

In these cases, it is noticeable how it is both the proximate demonstrative ('here' rather than 'there'), and the present rather than the past tense which have been selected. Consequently, the depicted scene is rendered in a way that makes it immediate rather than remote in time and space. As a counterpart to this strategy the reader my be directly addressed and occasionally included within the scene:

> *You* have to penetrate courts ... *You* have to ascend rotten staircases ... *You* have to grope your way
> (TBCOOL)

> *You* ring the gate bell, pass the porter's lodge, and the burden of the fiscal problem drops lightly from *your* ahoulders ... Here *you* shall have rest and ease ... Just something to occupy *your* mind, but no task work — for *you* have come to an age when *you* are entitled to sit in the light ...
> (TWD)

In addition to drawing the reader into the scene by direct address (YOU) the reader may be drawn into the argument by direct question:

> In what palace can you find such refreshing spotlessness as your eye rests upon here? On what floors are to be found such freshly gleaming tiles? Where are there brighter walls? Where a more cheerful light?
> (TWD)

> Who can wonder that every evil flourishes in such hotbeds of vice and disease? ... Who can wonder that young girls wander off into a life of immorality, which

promises release from such conditions? Who can wonder that the public-house is the 'Elysian field of the tired toiler'?

(TBCOOL)

An alternative emphasis is to construct a first person narrator into the scene:

No language with which *I* am familiar is capable of conveying an adequate conception of the spectacle *I* then encountered ... *My* bedfellows lay ... *my* appalled vision took in thirty of them. ... Many of *my* fellow casuals were awake.

(ANINAW)

After breakfast *we* had to undress ... *We* stood shivering. ... The filtered light ... lighted *us* up ... what potbellied, degenerate curs *we* looked.

(Appendix 1: TS)

It is worth noting, however, a subtle difference between the first person of the James Greenwood text (ANINAW) and that of the George Orwell text (TS). Greenwood uses first person singular, Orwell first person plural. This enables the Greenwood narrator to preserve some distance between himself and his fellow casuals — the narrator is kept separate from the collectivity which 'they' constitute. In the Orwell text this distance is narrowed by the use of the inclusive 'we'. The narrator is no longer separated from the collectivity constituted by the tramps, though there are occasions when the distance returns, e. g.:

When I arrived *twenty tramps* had already washed their faces. *I* gave one glance at the black scum on top of the water, and decided to go dirty for the day.

(TS)

In general, then, these fragments exemplify a range not only of responses to the conditions of the poor, but they also activate different axes of connection between narrator, depicted scene or event, and reader. The different dynamics at work can be schematized in Figure 2:

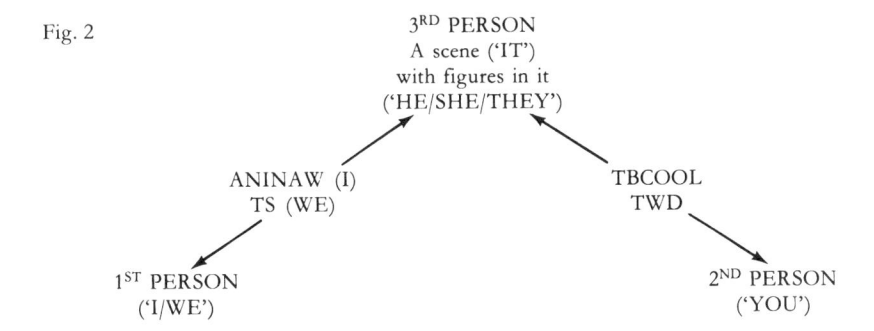

Fig. 2

```
                        3RD PERSON
                        A scene ('IT')
                        with figures in it
                        ('HE/SHE/THEY')
                       ↗              ↖
          ANINAW (I)                       TBCOOL
          TS (WE)                          TWD
         ↙                                      ↘
    1ST PERSON                              2ND PERSON
    ('I/WE')                                ('YOU')
```

In relational terms, whilst ANINAW and TS tend to activate a circuit between first and third person, TBCOOL and TWD tend to operate along the axis between third person and second person. At the same time, it also happens to be the case that both TBCCOOL and TWD, partly as a function of the direct questions and commands adopted by each, are more insistent in the way they actively engage with the reader. In fact, although it cannot be established on just the texts cited here, we would claim that there has been an overall historical shift in the way press journalism sets itself into relation with a readership. The mode of relation exemplified by TBCOOL and TWD, with its direct address to the reader and its direct question and command, is difficult to find in contemporary newspapers outside of certain types of press advertising:

> Just imagine what it's like to have remote control on your garage door. You simply press a button from inside your car — and drive right in.

> The question is, is your bank balance enough? The answer probably yes. You can have a beautiful, colourful 4-pieces suite for as little as £ 350.

This historical shift is not really a matter of texts being more or less overtly 'manipulative' or 'persuasive'; rather it is the case that specific representations are set in play along particular circuits which open up for readers different kinds of possibilities for their alignment with and response to texts. And, as we shall see later on, the rather different semiotic characteristics of television mean that TV news introduces yet further possibilities.

Given the distinction between the representational and the relational in any act of signification, we would like now to examine the *representational* dimension in a more thoroughgoing way by reference to a particular front page of the *Sunday Express*.

## 5. *'The World'* as Represented by the Sunday Express

The page in question is from the February 8th 1981 edition of the newspaper, which is reproduced as Appendix 2. For the purpose of this account we shall concentrate primarily on the editorial text, and not attend, for example, to advertisements, cartoons, photographs or to design features such as layout etc. At first sight, then, we are confronted by a mixed bag of separate news stories, in which each typographically bounded section of the page constitutes a separate text. The separate stories can be rank ordered, on the basis of length and on the basis of the size of the typeface used in the headline[4a], thus:

---

[4a] Some slight differences exist between the newspaper page reproduced here and the original one analysed.
The analysis presented here refers to the front page of an early (Welsh) edition of the Sunday Express of 8/2/81 (VERSION A). However, the copy of this page that we submitted for publication proved inadequate for reproduction. In search of a reproducible copy we contacted Express Newspapers, who supplied the version reprinted here (VERSION B). This late (London) edition, however, turned out unexpectedly to be different from the early (Welsh) edition on which the analysis was based; but it is now the only reproducible copy available. The small differences of wording and story position that affect the analysis are as follows:

| | |
|---|---|
| (1) CUT PRICE RUSSIANS CASH IN ON SHIP STRIKE | ['russians'] |
| (2) TORIES TO FORCE SPLIT ON LABOUR | ['tories'] |
| (3) NKOMO MAN MURDERED IN BOMB BLAST | ['nkomo man'] |
| (4) KIDNAP BOFFIN EXECUTED | ['kidnap boffin'] |
| (5) DRINKS BAN SUCCESS AT BIG MATCH | ['big match'] |
| etc. | |

On looking more closely, however, it is possible to identify features that appear as a kind of continuity between and across the separate stories. We shall try to trace this continuity, particularly through vocabulary or lexis, which we shall examine in detail in relation to the first four stories (though the analysis can be extended to the remainder of the page including the anchoring text for the news-photo).

*5.1. Lexical items, semantic fields and vocabularies*

Certain lexical items seem to dominate the stories on the page, partly through their relatively frequent occurence. The items BRITAIN/BRITISH, for example, occur some thirteen times in all, scattered across a range of separate stories. The lexical item 'britain' and the cognate item 'british' may be considered members of a set of lexical items (such as 'france/french', 'greece/greek', 'russian', 'american', 'basque', 'zimbabwe', 'scots', 'welsh' etc.) which map the semantic domain of NATIONS/NATIONALITIES, in much the same way as items such as 'red' 'blue', 'green' etc. map the semantic domain of COLOUR. In fact members of the lexical set mapping the NATIONS/NATIONALITIES domain occur in excess of fifty times, with instances spanning most of the texts on the page. We may call these items the *nationality vocabulary*. There seem to be at least two other vocabularies which cross-reference the separate stories. There is an *oppositional vocabulary* mapping the semantic domain DISPUTES. Examples are items such as: 'disagreement', 'debate', 'row', 'split', 'breakaway', 'confrontation', 'squabbles', 'clashes', 'rivalry', 'dispute' etc.; and also their antonyms such as: 'conciliation',

---

(i) Differences in headline wording, thus;

| VERSION B | | VERSION A |
|---|---|---|
| "Tribal Clash Fears after Murder of Nkomo Man" | was previously | "Nkomo Man Murdered in Car Bomb Blast" |
| "Execution Shocks Spain" | was previously | "Kidnap Boffin Executed" |

(In each case the text of the news story remains identical.)
(ii) Inclusion/exclusion and positioning;
One small story ("Drinks Ban Success"), discussed in the analysis and in the next footnote, disappeared completely. Another small story, headlined "IRA Blow up Ship", which had previously occupied the minor position currently taken by the Nimmo story at the foot of the page, was developed and given greater salience to become "British Coal Ship Sinks — IRA Threat".
It was now late in the publication stage — too late it seemed to rewrite the analysis to take account of the small changes. We do, however, comment in more detail on their significance in the light of our analysis in the next footnote.

'settlement' and 'arbitration'. Then there is a *violent death vocabulary*, for example 'execute', 'murder', 'killed', 'shot', 'execution', 'death' etc. The *oppositional vocabulary* is particularly interesting in the context of the page as a whole, inasmuch as it is used to characterize a relationship between *two* parties, nations, factions or persons, and it is only, and always, so used. These items always mediate between two terms, and the terms are thereby placed in a relationship of opposition to one another. Hence, LABOUR v. TORIES, RUSSIANS v. BRITISH, FOOT v. RODGERS etc.

## 5.2. *The oppositional vocabulary and the organization of texts*

Each of the four topmost texts in the hierarchy of stories may be seen to be structured around a basic opposition. This basic or primary opposition, however, often becomes the ground for a secondary or derived opposition, involving another term already in play. In other words each primary binary opposition *frames* or subsumes a secondary binary opposition. Thus: RUSSIANS v. BRITISH frames EMPLOYERS v. UNIONS ['russians']. These framings occur in each of the four texts, so that we can represent the basic polarities and their relationships as follows: (Figure 3):

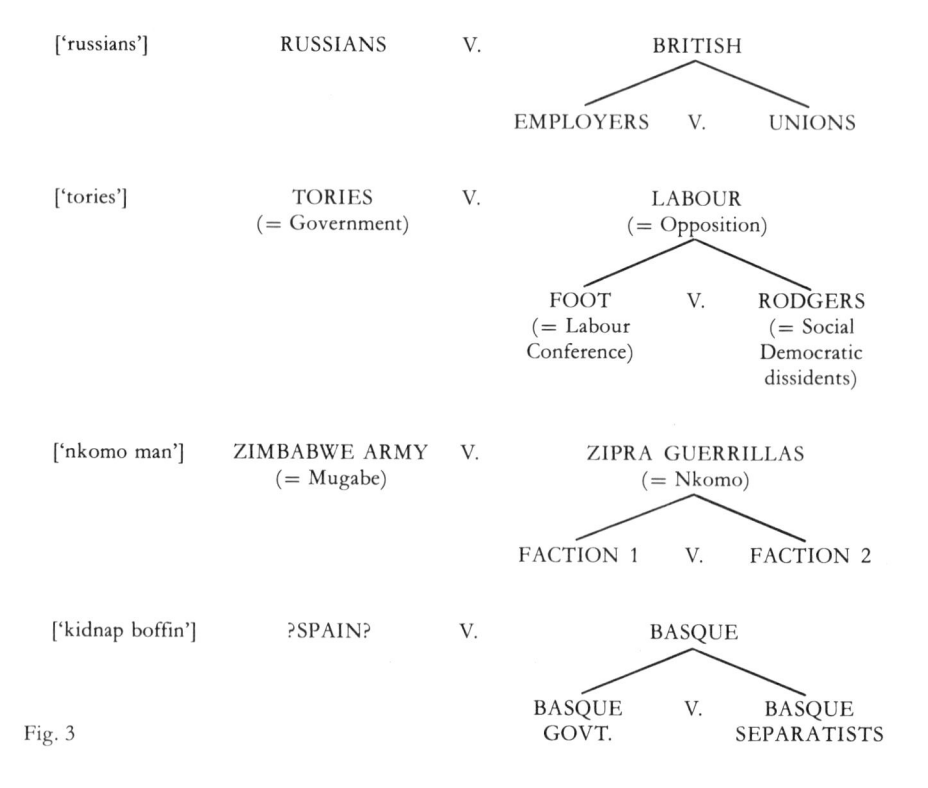

['russians']      RUSSIANS      V.      BRITISH
                                        ╱      ╲
                              EMPLOYERS   V.   UNIONS

['tories']        TORIES         V.      LABOUR
                  (= Government)          (= Opposition)
                                        ╱      ╲
                                  FOOT     V.    RODGERS
                                  (= Labour      (= Social
                                  Conference)    Democratic
                                                 dissidents)

['nkomo man']   ZIMBABWE ARMY   V.     ZIPRA GUERRILLAS
                (= Mugabe)              (= Nkomo)
                                        ╱      ╲
                                  FACTION 1  V.  FACTION 2

['kidnap boffin']    ?SPAIN?    V.      BASQUE
                                        ╱      ╲
                                  BASQUE    V.   BASQUE
Fig. 3                            GOVT.           SEPARATISTS

*5.3. Homologies and supra-textual unity*

The basic unity of the texts of these four stories is displayed not only in the way the various vocabularies cross-reference them, but also in the way they share a common structure based on binary oppositions. Thus, it is not only 'surface' features (vocabulary) that link the separate stories, but a single 'deep' or 'underlying' structure, which is best expressed by means of the concept of *homology*.[5] If there are four terms, A, B, C and D, and if the relationship between A and B is taken to be equivalent to the relationship between C and D, then the totality of relationships may be stated simply as A is to B as C is to D. The formal notation for this is:

$$A : B :: C : D$$

Where the third and fourth terms are derived from the second term (B), then the following notation may be used:

$$A : B :: b1 : b2$$

It is in fact this notation that most exactly expresses the deep structure *within* individual texts:

$$\text{RUSSIANS : BRITISH :: employers : unions}$$
$$\text{TORIES : LABOUR :: foot : rodgers}$$
$$\text{etc.}$$

The former notation, on the other hand, can be used to express the structural homology that exists *between* the separate stories. Thus:

$$\text{EMPLOYERS : UNIONS :: TORIES : LABOUR}$$
$$\text{foot : rodgers :: mugabe : nkomo}$$
$$\text{etc.}$$

Using the concept of homology and its formal notation, it is possible to represent structures both within and between the top four stories in the page's hierarchy as is shown in Figure 4.

Figure 4 does more than display homologies within and between texts. As one proceeds from left to right along the homologies, a transition is effected from domestic to foreign news which corresponds exactly with a division between, on the one hand, 'peaceful means for the conduct of conflict', and on the other hand, 'violent means for the conduct of conflict'. Simultaneously the *oppositional vocabulary* becomes more pronounced and the *violent death vocabulary* makes its appearance. Accordingly, it would seem that these stories are subject to one basic, organizing homology, which can be stated as follows:

DOMESTIC : FOREIGN :: PEACEFUL MEANS : VIOLENT MEANS

---

[5] The concept is drawn from the work of Lévi-Strauss. See especially 'The structural study of myth', in Lévi-Strauss (1968). Accounts may also be found in Leach (1976) and Culler (1975).

242    J. Hartley, M. Montgomery

A:B ⎯⎯⎯⎯⎯ DOMESTIC—[A] ⎯⎯⎯⎯⎯ : ⎯⎯⎯⎯⎯ FOREIGN—[B] ⎯⎯⎯⎯⎯

T1  RUSSIANS:BRITISH::employers:unions                                                  ['russians']
         (EMPLOYERS:UNIONS::TORIES:LABOUR)
T2  ['tories']       TORIES:LABOUR::foot:rodgers
                         (FOOT:RODGERS::MUGABE:NKOMO)
T3  ['nkomo man']              MUGABE:NKOMO::faction 1:faction 2
                                     (faction 1:faction 2::SPAIN:BASQUE)
T4  ['kidnap boffin']                      SPAIN:BASQUE::basque govt:separatists

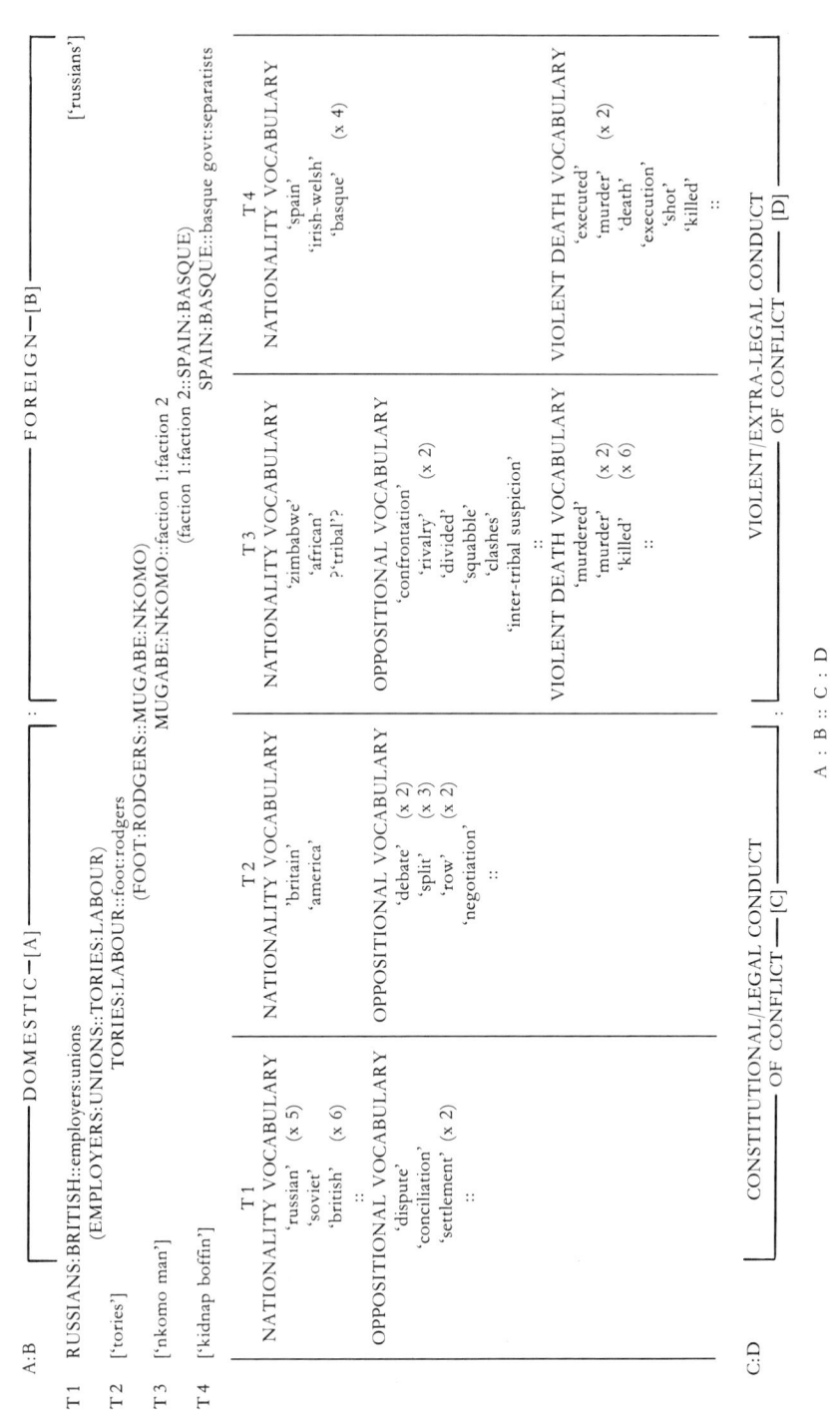

|  | T1 | T2 | T3 | T4 |
|---|---|---|---|---|
| | NATIONALITY VOCABULARY | NATIONALITY VOCABULARY | NATIONALITY VOCABULARY | NATIONALITY VOCABULARY |
| | 'russian'      (x 5) | 'britain' | 'zimbabwe' | 'spain' |
| | 'soviet' | 'america' | 'african' | 'irish-welsh' |
| | 'british'      (x 6) | | ?'tribal'? | 'basque'     (x 4) |
| | :: | | | |
| | OPPOSITIONAL VOCABULARY | OPPOSITIONAL VOCABULARY | OPPOSITIONAL VOCABULARY | |
| | 'dispute' | 'debate'    (x 2) | 'confrontation' | |
| | 'conciliation' | 'split'     (x 3) | 'rivalry'    (x 2) | |
| | 'settlement'    (x 2) | 'row'      (x 2) | 'divided' | |
| | :: | 'negotiation' | 'squabble' | |
| | | :: | 'clashes' | |
| | | | 'inter-tribal suspicion' | |
| | | | :: | |
| | | | VIOLENT DEATH VOCABULARY | VIOLENT DEATH VOCABULARY |
| | | | 'murdered' | 'executed'     (x 2) |
| | | | 'murder'    (x 2) | 'murder' |
| | | | 'killed'    (x 6) | 'death' |
| | | | :: | 'execution' |
| | | | | 'shot' |
| | | | | 'killed' |
| | | | | :: |

C:D ⎯⎯ CONSTITUTIONAL/LEGAL CONDUCT ⎯⎯ : ⎯⎯ VIOLENT/EXTRA-LEGAL CONDUCT ⎯⎯
              OF CONFLICT —[C]                    OF CONFLICT —[D]

A : B :: C : D

Fig. 4: Four-term homologies within and between four Sunday Express front-page news stories

Stories that we have not so far included explicitly in this analysis do in fact make sense in terms of the basic homology. The fifth story ('big match') makes little sense as a news story in and for itself, for it is concerned essentially with a non-event: 'police ... reported ... no trouble'. However, the fact that there was *no violence* between Scots and Welsh supporters is traced directly to the introduction of *new laws* (the police 'had distributed leaflets to fans explaining the terms of the new laws'). Conflict is thus newsworthily resolved without violence by means of law, and an otherwise enigmatic little news story becomes intelligible as an elliptical form of the homology underlying other stories on the page.[5a]

---

[5a] The story that appeared in VERSION A (the early edition) of the Sunday Express front page ran as follows:
DRINKS BAN SUCCESS
AT BIG MATCH

Scotland's new law banning alchohol
from sports grounds stood up well
yesterday to the first major test
when Scotland's international rugby
team entertained the Welsh at
Edinburgh.
Police on duty at Murrayfield
reported virtually no trouble as
thousands of good-humoured Welsh fans
left the stadium after seeing their
team lose by 15 points to 6.
Before the match police outside the
ground distributed leaflets to fans
explaining the terms of the new laws.
Under the criminal justice (Scotland)
Act, which became operative last
Sunday, it is now an offence "to
attempt to enter a ground carrying
a drinks container or have any such
container in your possession inside
the ground."
One senior police officer on duty
at the stadium said: "The sobriety
of the crowd has been remarkable."

---

Although our comments adequately enough accounted for its presence as an elliptical form of the homology (viz. 'peace at home through due process of the law') in which the foreign dimension has not been realised, we did point out its enigmatic status in reporting essentially a non-event. In the light of these comments it is significant that it was precisely this story that was dropped from the late edition. Even more significant, however, are the transformations that take place to fill the gap left by its exclusion. The story "British Coal Ship Sinks — IRA Threat" was formerly a short note headlined "IRA Blow up Ship". Its new prominence and new headline only serve to confirm and accentuate the outlines of our existing analysis, inasmuch as increased salience is given to the vocabularies of 'nationality', 'division' and 'violence'. It would certainly

Violence does, of course, occur within the United Kingdom, and newspapers including the *Sunday Express* report it. At first sight it would seem that such events might challenge the basic homology, which locates violence as *foreign*. But there is some evidence to suggest that the homology is at least as powerful a news value as 'the facts' themselves, since there are important ways in which it is preserved in the face of 'home' violence. The Troubles in N. Ireland, for example, are frequently exempted, as it were, from the concerns of mainstream British politics simply by representing them as 'across the water' — literally foreign. Even when politicized violence actually occurred on the British mainland, in Bristol, London, Liverpool and elsewhere, the homology was preserved in certain newspapers by representing the rioters as 'black youths', or as set up by *agents provocateurs* from 'outside' the affected areas. The *Daily Express* even went so far as to implicate the Russians. Such violence, then, is presented as ethnic or foreign in its origins.

The theme of violence as alien to the British political process (whether it's the case or not) is not merely a feature of newspaper discourse, It has, of course, a central place in the ideology of parliamentarism itself. For instance, then Prime Minister Edward Heath enunciated the basic homology HOME : FOREIGN :: PEACE : VIOLENCE in a ministerial broadcast after the 1972 miner's strike:

> In the kind of country we live in there cannot be any 'we' or 'they'. There is only 'us'; all of us. If the Government is 'defeated', then the country is defeated, because the Government is just a group of people elected to do what the majority of 'us' want to see done. That is what our way of life is all about.
>
> It really does not matter whether it is a picket line, a demonstration or the House of Commons. We are all used to peaceful argument. But when violence or the threat of violence is used, it challenges what most of us consider to be the right way of doing things. I do not believe you elect any government to allow that to happen and I can promise you that it will not be tolerated wherever it occurs.
>
> [cited in Murdock, 1973, p 157]

---

appear to bear out the point made in the next paragraph of our commentary concerning the treatment of events in Northern Ireland, which are handled as if they were outside of, and marginal to, mainstream British politics: effectively they are displaced to the 'foreign' side of the homology.

Changes in the wording of the other headlines are also of interest. One change accentuates further the vocabulary of division ("*Tribal Clash* Fears after Murder of Nkomo Man"). The other accentuates the nationality vocabulary ("Execution Rocks *Spain*"). Both, of course, preserve elements of the violence vocabulary ("Murder" & "Execution"). We can see, therefore, that the changes are all in the direction of confirming and accentuating the homology delineated in our analysis of the earlier edition. It may be too bold a claim to suggest that our analysis of VERSION A predicted the direction of the changes in VERSION B. But the underlying homology revealed in our analysis of VERSION A seems to have provided an implicit logical deep structure for the transformations that produced VERSION B.

The corrolary of this position is, of course, that when 'violence or the threat of violence' occurs, it originates not from amongst 'us' but from the outside, from 'them'.

## 6. Positioning the Viewer: Relational Dimensions of Television News

Having reached a point where it seems that the *representational* mode of signification in the newspaper we have looked at produces a distinction between 'we' and 'they' identities, we turn now to the other mode of signification we outlined at the beginning of the paper, namely the *relational*. Here too, however, we are interested in pursuing the 'we'/'they' distinction, but this time we shall concentrate on the textual strategies that orient the position from which the newsworthy events can be viewed. In other words, we want to see if the construction of 'we'/'they' identities is compounded by implicating the reader or viewer in the process, orienting the relations between narrator, depicted scene or event and reader in such a way as to align the reader on one side or the other of the distinction. For this purpose we shall move from newspaper news to television news, and here it is necessary to introduce an important modification to the schematic model of the relational dimension that we suggested in section 4.2. (Figure 2). Television news exploits one of the most distinctive features of TV in general, namely the representation of people, and in particular of peoples' faces, expressive features and eyes, in the process of narration. But whereas by established convention TV and cinema fiction rarely make use of direct eye-contact with the camera/viewer, television news has instated this form of address at the centre of its textual strategy. Thus, without verbalizing it, television news operates on a direct first person ('I') to second person ('YOU') axis, in the form of the newsreader's relation to the viewer. Thus we can revise our earlier (print based) model thus: (Figure 5):

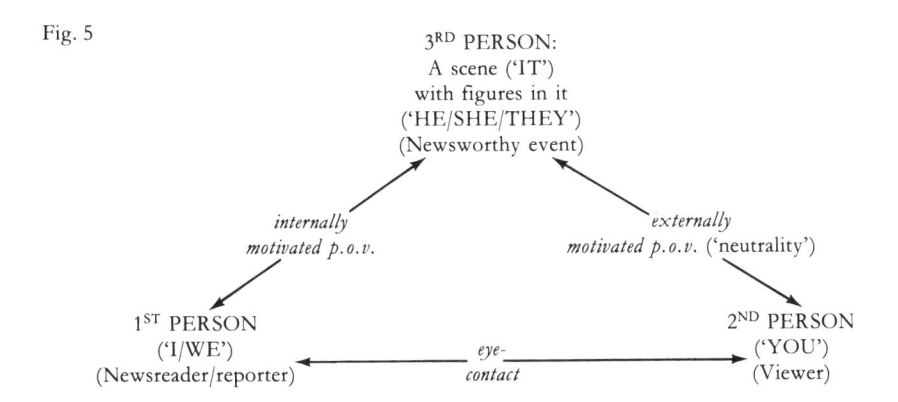

Fig. 5

3ᴿᴰ PERSON:
A scene ('IT')
with figures in it
('HE/SHE/THEY')
(Newsworthy event)

*internally
motivated p.o.v.*

*externally
motivated p.o.v.* ('neutrality')

1ˢᵀ PERSON
('I/WE')
(Newsreader/reporter)

*eye-
contact*

2ᴺᴰ PERSON
('YOU')
(Viewer)

Television news, then, activates a full circuit between first, second and third persons, being able to address the viewer 'over the heads' of the newsworthy people or events depicted. But it can do this without the intrusive questions and commands that characterized the texts on poverty; eye-contact alone establishes an 'I'/'YOU' axis between newsreader and viewer, without, apparently, any unwanted editiorializing interventions.

However, television news is not simply a matter of newsreader addressing viewer. Beyond this basic relation are (at least) two other kinds of relation that TV news has to accommodate in its routine practices. These are 'extra-textual' relations, and it so happens that they make mutually exclusive, and thus contradictory, demands on TV news. The first is what we may call TV news's *institutional* relations. Foremost among these is the statutory requirement laid on broadcasters that TV news be 'impartial'. That is, events must be narrated without the news adopting the point of view of any one faction, party or person. The second relation, which we may call *formal*, contradicts the first because news cannot escape the television/cinema codes of visual representation that is uses. To put it bluntly, the first problem newscamerawork faces is *where to put the camera*. In fiction-filmmaking, a conventional distinction has arisen between what are known as 'p. o. v.' (point of view) shots and neutral shots. A p. o. v. shot is one that shows the scene or characters from the point of view of one of them. Often the p. o. v. is visually *motivated* by including part of the observer's figure (shoulder, side of head) seen from behind, in the frame. Such shots are often used to show dialogue between two characters, with the p. o. v. of each seen in alternate shots. The viewer is thus positioned *as* the character whose p. o. v. is shown. However, the viewer is not limited to this point of view, since that of several different characters may be shown, as well as 'neutral' shots. Hence, during the course of a film, the viewer achieves a kind of composite point of view; one which is privileged over the p. o. v. of any one character since the viewer knows more, from more points of view, than anyone on the film. In fact, television/cinema codes position the viewer as that 'point' from which all the different characters, scenes, actions and plot developments are *intelligible*,[6] and this totalizing position is denied to the characters themselves.

This discussion leads us to two conclusions about news-camerawork. First, the conventionalized distinction between p. o. v. shots and 'neutral' shots does not stand up to close inspection. *All* shots have a point of view, whether it is *internally* motivated by the placing of a character, or *externally* motivated by the positioning of the imaginary observer (viewer). Furthermore, shots that are presented as 'neutral' are unable to stand alone — they are only ever seen in contrast to p. o. v. shots. Thus, at the very least, 'neutral' shots signify 'a-point-of-view-which-is-not-that-of-the-participants'. When set against other

---

[6] See Ellis (1982), Chapter 5.

shots that do offer a participant's point of view, such 'neutrality' becomes, ideologically, very productive.

Second, news-camerawork 'solves' the problem of where to put the camera in a very similar way to the way fictional conventions have dealt with it. That is, the news also constructs an *imaginary viewer*, positioned as it were 'behind' the camera, from whose point of view the partial and disjointed fragments of picture, sound and story can cohere into intelligibility. As in fiction, there is no point of view from *within* the news where it all makes sense — none of the *institutional* personnel (newsreader, correspondent, reporter etc) and none of the *accessed* characters whose faces and voices appear in the news are in a position to see the whole. Indeed, all the people who are seen, and all the textual deployments of sound, picture and sequence are *subordinate* to the imaginary viewer, who thus takes the place of the omniscient author/narrator of realist novels.

It is this point that we can begin to sense the inevitable contradiction between TV news's *formal* relations and the *institutional* relations mentioned earlier. For news has to be impartial, that is, to narrate events *without* a point of view. Since, as we have seen, that is impossible, there is a contradiction between (required) impartiality and (unavoidable) point of view. The construction of an imaginary viewer as the point of intelligibility actually makes matters worse. This is because, in the first place, there is no viewer at the point(s) of production who can offer advice on what an appropriate p. o. v. might look like — broadcasters work to a *fictionalized* image of the viewer. Second, there is no unified point of view among those who actually watch the news at the point(s) of consumption. Quite the reverse, in fact.

Nevertheless, the news institutions have not only accepted the requirement of impartiality, but (even in the face of widespread doubt and criticism) they continue to assert that they have achieved it. Thus the news is presented with an assurance that not only is it *intelligible* to the viewer, but also that it is *true*. So the contradiction we have been discussing is *erased* in the relation the news proposes with its viewers — the *type* of intelligibility that is offered textually 'escapes' the problem of p. o. v., since it is the only point of view that allows of no alternative — the point-of-view-of-impartiality, namely truth.

*7. Looking at Television: Some Analytical Procedures*

In view of television's familiarity, and the apparently seamless unity of its signifying components (sound, picture, sequence etc.), it is sometimes hard to know where to start an analysis. On the one hand an attempt to be specific can result in over-descriptiveness, which is especially to be guarded against with TV since there is so much material to describe — even a transcript is highly selective. On the other hand, an attempt to make general points can lead to over-abstraction, which can easily be refuted by thinking of an exception to the model proposed.

We have tried to take account of both the poles implicit in this. We have certain analytic preoccupations which we shall bring to bear on the news — these are not warranted by any one bulletin. But we shall limit the tendency to abstract generalization by making any general points *through* the specificities of a particular text. We have found two very simple strategies that allow us to take some analytic cues from the object of analysis itself.

*7.1. Comparison*

Television news is conventionalized, but its conventions are not fixed or essential, but relative, contingent and subject to change. Thus comparison of the way its semiotic resources are mobilized in one part of a story, or in respect of one set of people, as against others will enable us to see where *significant differences* arise from the news, rather than arising 'naturally', as it were, from the event depicted. But the comparisons we have chosen to make are partly motivated by the specific story itself — in another story it might be more fruitful to compare quite different conventions, aspects or resources.

*7.2. Reversal*

In this paper, we are concerned in general with 'we/they' identities, and in particular with the problem of point of view — how a relation is proposed and established between text and viewer. In this context we have again had to be mindful of the relativity of television dixcourse. So in order to discover whether there are systematic differences in the point of view from which different people or events are represented, we have simply reversed some element which seems significant to the point of view at that moment. Visually, such elements may be the camera point of view; verbally it may be 'we' and 'they' pronouns. Reversing 'they' pronouns to say 'we' may show that some participants in an event simply don't make sense as 'we', whilst others do.

*8. 'Here at Home': A Television Domestic News Story*

The whole of the remainder of this paper will be referring to one story taken from the BBC *Nine O'Clock News* of 1 February 1979.[7] A transcript of the story, which lasted eight minutes and forty seconds, is given as Appendix 3. It was the second item of that particular bulletin, being preceded by a foreign affairs story from Tehran about the return of the Ayatollah Khomeini from exile. In the transcript we have shown how the story was divided up into

---

[7] Further information and analysis of this story may be found in Hartley (1982), Chapter 7.

seven sections, of which two (sections IV and VI) were film reports. We shall be concentrating largely on these two sections. Overall, the story used 32 different shots, and these are enumerated and described in the transcript — we shall refer to particular sequences by reference to their shot number.

## 9. Camera Point of View

The first, or at least the most obvious, means by which the viewer is positioned in respect to the event is through what we can call the 'plot' of the story as a whole.

### 9.1. Plot

The plot is a simple affair of cause and effect. It is initiated verbally (shot 1):

> Here at home the dispute by public service workers is still spreading.
> 
> (cause)
> 
> Half the hospitals in England and Wales and some in Scotland can now open their doors only to emergency cases.
> 
> (effect)

Both the film report sections (IV and VI) reiterate this cause-effect movement. They open with almost identical shots (9–11 and 19–20) showing the picket lines of strikers (cause), and then spend most of their time on the effects on patients and medical staff. Whilst these effects are being shown visually, the voice-over commentary *ascribes* causes to them, as in shot 13/14:

> Only two cooks were allowed to remain, so lunch was a little late today for nearly 300 young patients ...

This over shots of nurses and a young boy (patient?) trundling foodt-rolleys into a lift.

Hence, it follows, the *cause* of the event is the negative action initiated by the strikers; its *effect* is on medical staff and patients.

### 9.2. Internal and external point of view

Within the cause/effect plot, the camera is used to establish point of view in different ways for the different participants. As far as the picketers are concerned, we can establish the point of view (p. o. v.) of the shots of them by reversal: this can be done by asking whether the camera p. o. v. is that of the strikers themselves. For this to be so we would have to see the scene from their p. o. v.; that is, we would have to look *out* of the picket line (across the street or into the entrance), or else we would have to look *inside* the picket line, sharing the talk and seeing the faces of the others there. Such shots would, in fact, differ considerably from what we are shown (shots 9, 10, 11, 19, 20). These are all filmed from a distance outside the picket line, usually from across a road, and we only ever see the picketers as a collectivity, in longshot, and not as individuals. These shots, then, display an *external* p. o. v., orienting the viewer along the 3rd person — 2nd person axis ('THEY/YOU') [see Figure 5 above]: the p. o. v. is the *viewer's*.

Turning to the film sequences showing the effect of the action inside the hospital the p. o. v. is different. They are framed more tightly that the shots of the pickets, so that we see less people at a time on screen, usually no more than two, and we can identify more of their facial and expressive features than we can those of the strikers. Participants move towards the camera and even past it (shot 13), including it within their action. These shots, then, display an *internal* p. o. v., orienting the viewer along the 3rd person — 1st person axis ('THEY/WE'). This positions the viewer *as* one of the participants, and is comparable to 'proper' p. o. v. shots in cinema.

## 9.3. *Deferential and unmotivated camera movement*

A further set of differences that adds to differences in point of view is that associated with movements of the camera itself, as opposed to the participants moving in the frame. Here again the differences are organized about the strikers on the one hand, and the patients and medical staff on the other. Where there is camera-movement in the shots of the picketers, it is *unmotivated* by their movements. We see reframings from close-ups of details (an entrance sign, a placard, a banner) to longshots of the nearby pickets. If we compare this with the shots of patients and medical staff, it is clear that in these the camera movements *are* motivated by action. The camera is *deferential*; it follows the action of the people in shot, usually by panning. The only shots in the 'effects' sequences where this doesn't hold true are those that show inanimate objects (rubbish, shot 16; equipment, shot 22).

It may be argued that the differences we have noted are determined by the fact that the two sets of shots are *literally* 'outside' and 'inside' buildings, and that this explains the differences. But there are also shots showing effects, this time on patients, which are exterior shots. In both film reports, these are the last shots, and in both the camera is deferential — it follows the movement of a man and a child (shot 17) and of a baby and car (shots 29—30). In both there is subject movement towards the camera, which pans to follow it, and although the framing of the first remains relatively wide, we see the child gazing intently at the camera. In the second, the child is carried towards us by a nurse, and then handed into a woman waiting in a car. At this point the framing is quite tight, and we can hear the nurse saying 'bye-bye, mind how you go'. We hear the car door close, and the motor as it drives away. Thus these exterior shots are both from an internal p. o. v. and differential in their camera movement.

## 9.4. 'THEY' and 'WE'

We may, in summary of this section, set out how the relational dimension of the camera point of view has sorted the strikers and the nurses/patients into a they/we opposition:

> THEY : WE
> CAUSE : EFFECT
> EXTERNAL P.O.V. : INTERNAL P.O.V.
> UNMOTIVATED CAMERA MOVEMENT : DEFERENTIAL CAMERA MOVEMENT
> LONG/WIDE FRAME : MID/CLOSE FRAME
> STRIKERS/PICKETERS : NURSES/PATIENTS

## 10. Narrative Point of View

Whilst the pictures are busy sorting out the strikers from the nurses and patients, the verbal component of the film reports is adding its own relational dimension to the story. In short, it too offers a point of view from which the viewer can make sense of the story. Once again, it is possible to use the strategy of reversal to try to identify a narrative point of view. Here is a version of the opening sequence of section IV (shots 9–12). But what we have done is to reverse the 'they' pronouns and cognates, and the names, to read 'we' instead. What we're looking for is any strain to the syntax, or any disruption of the popular idiom in which the voice-over is delivered.

> *We* didn't give much warning about *our* strike — just five minutes' notice. *We* then walked out to join the picket line and stayed out for four hours. Now further action in other departments of the hospital is planned [*by us*], though *we* claim the children themselves won't suffer.

The two most striking misfits are the agentless passive 'is planned', which is very hard to render with a 'we' agent; and the 'we claim', which is idiomatically suspect. Beyond this, a 'we' identity that made such a point out of giving little warning before walking out and staying out would be representing itself as a bloody-minded identity, to say the least.

After an interview with a union shop steward, the film returns to voice-over. Once again we can reverse the narrative p.o.v. (shots 13–14):

> Inside the hospital the disruption was more than just the minimum *we* had promised. Only two cooks were allowed to remain [*by us*], so lunch was a little late today for nearly 300 [of] *them*.

There is a reiterated agentless passive ('were allowed'), and further oddities are the unconventional way 'we' announce that we have broken our 'promise', and the numerical disproportion of 'two cooks' and 'nearly 300' of 'them'.

If we move on to section VI, the voice over its opening shot (19) can also be reversed:

> *We* refused to supply any cleaners, because *we* say that's not part of *our* emergency service.

Apart from another bloody-minded refusal, the 'we say' seems ill-fitting because it is a hang-over from the reported speech of the original, and is unlikely in direct speech. But it does enable us to ask exactly whose speech was being reported. In the original the 'speakers' are given as 'this hospital's strikers', but it is hardly likely that they actually *said* what is imputed to them here — the idiomatic turn of phrase 'they say' not only resists reversal into a 'we', but is strictly speaking inaccurate too. Thus it cannot easily be understood from a 'we' p. o. v.

If we compare these points of view of the strikers with those of other participants, we can see if there are any significant differences. In section IV, the strikers are followed narratively by 'senior nursing staff' (shot 15), and once again we can reverse the p. o. v.:

> *We* had to help out sorting dirty linen from the wards; it took up much of *our* valuable time.

Here the oddity is actually in the original — this idiomatic phrasing fits a 'we' identity so well that the original's it took up much of their valuable time' is the surprising version. In section VI there are further references to medical staff (shots 21—2 and 24):

> Every day *we* [doctors] treat up to a hundred patients who are suffering from everything from cuts and bruises to heart attacks and appendicitis.

> Until unpaid volunteers like her came along, *we* [the nurses] had to dust and vacuum.

These too fit easily into an idiomatically plausible 'we' form, as do references to the patients, which can be found in shots 27—30.

A 'control' of our revesal strategy can be derived from the bulletin. The union shop steward interviewed in section IV (shot 12) actually uses 'we' forms throughout his answers. If we turn these into 'they' forms, the results can be compared with the voice-overs directly:

> Yes *they* can guarantee . . . *they've* told the unit administrator that if, during *their* action, children were at risk, *they* would immediately leave the picket line and go in and help. . . . *They* believe *they've* shown responsibility . . . *they've* been traditionally a very passive workforce, and *they* hope that by workers at this world famous hospital taking action it will bring public sympathy to *their* side.

In view of the marked difference between this and the voice-over presentation of the strikers, and the differences between them and the medical staff and patients, we feel entitled to conclude that the narrative point of view confirms the camera point of view by sorting out these two classes of participants into 'they' and 'we' identities. Thus, the viewer is positioned differently in respect of the strikers than in respect of the doctors/nurses/patients, and cannot so easily adopt their point of view.

*11. Picture and Sound Track Relations*

These separate components of picture and sound work in their own ways, as we have seen, but they also work together, and this provides a further, distinct area of analysis. Here, however, it is neither easy nor necessary to hold on to a hard and fast distinction between *representational* and *relational* dimensions of the text, since both are implicated. In general, TV news conforms to the realist relationship between picture and sound tracks. That is, each is taken to motivate the other, and the sounds heard are understood as being *synchronous* ('in sync') with the picture. Thus, ambient sound is confined to that which occurred at the moment of shooting — TV news does not avail itself of the possibilities offered by music, wild-track sound etc., as a rule. Ambient sound itself may be significant, but it is subordinate to voice-over commentary, so it tends to get faded up and down according to the VO's prior claim to audibility.

The apparent mutual motivation of picture and sound in TV news is very important ideologically, not because it actually occurs, but because it doesn't. The paradox is voice-over commentary, which benefits from the genre-expectation that picture and sound are synchronized, even though it is in fact quite separate in origin from the footage it comments on. Voice-overs are not *unmotivated* by the picture/ambient sound, but they are *external* to them, and just as voice-overs are always more audible than ambient or sync sound, so they claim a 'higher' level of correspondence than mere synchronicity. Because they 'helpfully' explain the pictures, voices-overs both encourage and benefit from the viewer's sense that there is a *unity* of picture and sound. This 'unity' is then cashed in ideologically, as it were, since the explanations appear to arise 'naturally' from the pictures with which they are united.

*11.1. The construction of 'seamless unity'*

Section VI (shots 21—24 offers a good example of the way the relations between picture and sound track are handled in practice to produce an effect of apparently seamless unity. The sequence opens not with voice-over commentary, but something even more imperative; that is, the reporter on screen, facing the camera and addressing his remarks directly to the viewer. He signals his presence deictically (shot 21): '*This is* the hospital's accident and emergency department . . .'. As he speaks, in longshot, we can observe the difference between what he says and what we see. He says: 'It's normally the busiest place in a hospital', whilst we are looking at empty beds and absence. What happens next is *representationally* quite simple (it's a story of emptiness, caused by industrial action), but *textually* it's quite complex. The reporter tells us, looking directly at us (shot 21):

> Every day doctors treat up to a hundred patients who are suffering from everything from cuts and bruises to/

At this point there is a picture-edit to shot 22, and we go from direct address to voice-over commentary. The picture changes to a piece of equipment, behind which is a chart headlined THE TREATMENT OF CARDIAC ARREST. The picture itself is mute (there's no ambient sound). And the voice-over is saying:

/heart attacks and appendicitis. But since yesterday it's been completely empty./

The picture changes again, to a wide shot of an empty ward. Once again the emptiness is signified by a presence, this time of a nurse who walks across (and so defines visually) the space in front of the camera. The voice-over continues (shot 23):

/The hospital authorities closed it down because of a lack of/

Another picture-edit reveals an active ward, shown in diagonal longshot, so we glimpse a patient with nurse at the bedside in the left foreground, and more patients in bed in the right background. In the middle (middle-distance and mid-screen) is a woman vacuuming between the beds. The camera zooms in to find her in mid-shot. Meanwhile the voice-over is saying (shot 24):

/clean wards to go after their treatment here. . . .

At this stage the voice-over is of ambiguous status, since it is not voice-over 'proper', but a continuation of the words we have seen the reporter addressing directly to us. But we are shifted progressively away from that context by the succession of picture edits, each one of which is 'explained' or *anchored* by what he says. Thus, 'heart attacks' = cardiac arrest machine (though we don't see the more mundane equipment used for 'cuts and bruises'); 'completely empty' = an empty ward; 'clean wards' = a ward being cleaned. But that 'clean' is a point at which the picture-sense and the verbal-sense go out of sync. The voice-over is telling us about a 'lack of/clean wards', but the picture cuts to a cleaner working in a full ward. This corresponds to a 'narrative enigma'[8], setting up a kind of suspense that will be resolved later. Meanwhile, the voice-over signals the *difference* that exists at this point between the picture and sound tracks by the final phrase: 'after their treatment *here*'. This deictic can only be understood by reference back to the earlier shot of the reporter talking to us directly — 'here' corresponds to the opening 'this is'. As the reporter says 'treatment here' we can hear the sync sound of the vacuum cleaner being faded up momentarily, and by the time he's finished speaking the zoom-in has found Mrs Munns in mid-shot. The voice-over resumes almost immediately, but there has been a change in sound-quality of the reporter's voice — we have gone to 'proper' voice-over. The next stage in the story is the description of Mrs Munns, the volunteer who came along to help. At this point the 'narrative enigma' of a *lack* of clean wards / a ward being *cleaned* is resolved, and picture-sense is reunited with sound-sense. So

---

[8] See, for example, Barthes (1975).

in the space of a few seconds the picture and sound tracks have gone from direct synchronicity (lip-sync) through the overlap of speech and picture (mute cutaway) to sync sound (the vacuum cleaner) to picture-with-sync-sound + voice-over. The *only* point from which this complex interplay of picture sound and speech is *intelligible* is the viewer's p. o. v., and further, its intelligibility depends upon the acceptance of the different elements as comprising a unity. Otherwise the narrative confusion of referring *forwards* to the volunteer, and *back* to the empty emergency department, whilst looking *at* a busy ward could not make any sense at all — it would be unintelligible.

*11.2. The employers: an absent 'THEY'*

Having shown how textually complex the relations between picture and sound can be at a given moment, we can return to the main topic of the story, namely the industrial dispute itself, to see if these relations contribute to its signification. Here the apparent unity of picture, speech and sound is ideologically productive, because there are significant points at which the sense of the speech and that of the picture go 'out of sync'. These are the points when the *employers* are brought into the story. As a matter of fact the employers are never named directly as such, and we never see an employer's representative as we do a representative of the union. Since, apart from the shop steward, we also see strikers, volunteers, patients and nurses, and we hear about doctors, the Government and the Opposition, the absence of the employers is by itself significant. But they do make their shadowy presence felt (shots 16—17):

> Because of the unpredictable / nature of the strike action consultants at the hospital *have been instructed* to admit only emergency cases.

The employers, then, are deleted as agents from the passive 'have been instructed'. Verbally, the 'instruction' seems to flow from the 'unpredictable nature of the strike action' rather than from the employers. Visually, the instruction is signified not by reference to those that issued it, but to its *effect*. Whilst we hear what the instruction 'means' ('it means children . . . are being turned away'), we see a man and child approaching the camera, crossing in front of it to stop at the hospital entrance, where the child continues to gaze back at 'us'. Thus the employers cannot be mapped into any position or point of view with respect to the viewer — there is no point of view to observe an *absent* 'they'.

*11.3. 'The authorities think differently'*

In section VI the employers figure again, but this time we encounter them first not in the context of the strike's effects, but of its ascribed (plot) 'cause'. We are told in voice-over about the striker's reported refusal to supply any cleaners, whilst the picture shows the strikers in question — here there is sense-synchronicity between picture and sound (shot 19). And the next shot opens with a close-up of a banner being held by the picketers, which reads 'NUPE [the union] SAY: EVEN DRAGONS MUST EAT'. This is in fact the closest we ever get to an unmediated presentation of the strikers' own point of view, apart from a placard shown in shot 10 which stated the wage demand ('£60 A WEEK BASIC'). But whereas the placard was shown whilst the voice-over described the striker's actions, and can thus be understood as sense-synchronized, the banner is shown at the very moment when the employers make their very indirect appearance. So the juxtaposition of picture and sound at this point actually gives us:

Picture: EVEN DRAGONS MUST EAT
Sound: The authorities think differently

Although the juxtaposition can hardly be read as showing what the authorities think of NUPE's enigmatic message, there is sufficient force in the conventional assumption of a unity between picture and sound for a correspondence of some kind to be proposed. It seems that the relationship here is one of cause and effect: the strikers cause (cleaners aren't part of emergency service) and the employers are affected (they think differently). Thus according to the relationship between picture and sound it is the strikers who cause the closure of the hospital *directly*, not the 'authorities' whose decision it actually was. Moments later the employers figure again, but this time in the same context as in section IV. Whilst we see on screen the *effect* of the action (empty emergency department and ward), we encounter the employers verbally (shots 22—3):

> Since yesterday it's been completely empty. The *hospital authorities* closed it down because of a lack of clean wards. ...

Thus when the employers figure in the actuality sequences they are displaced *verbally* into 'instructions' and 'authorities', and *visually* into the strike's effects rather than its causes. Because of this, it seems in the end that a point of view *is* established for the employers, who are collapsed into the other groups who are represented as the bearers of the strike's effects: the patients, doctor and nurses. To the extent that this is so, and because they are presented in opposition to the strikers (they think differently), the employers are aligned with the 'we' side of the 'we'/'they' opposition we summarized in section 9.4. above.

*12. Relations between Speakers: Who's talking?*

News is often described as being about events, but it isn't. News is a complex mixture of voices, some of which speak for themselves, whilst others speak professionally. Some of the speakers are 'institutional voices', and others are 'accessed voices'; that is, some speakers are employees of the broadcasting institution (newsreaders, correspondents, reporters), whilst others are accessed by it (these include anyone, from prime ministers to vox pops, who isn't a news-person, but it may include professional voices in the form of 'experts', and these are often broadcasters themselves). The way in which this variety of voices actually appears in the news is complex. They may be present in both picture and sound as they speak, or accessed by sound but not by picture (as in recordings of parliament) or vice versa (as in picket line talk). Otherwise, the things people say may be quoted directly or indirectly, with or without attribution, by the institutional voices. Such quotations may be reinforced visually by being spelt out in a caption, often with an accompanying picture of the original speaker (see shot 2).

Thus it is not always easy, in the course of a news story in which all of these possibilities are deployed in one place or another, to identify exactly *who* is speaking at a given moment, or what relation between the speakers is being proposed. But the multiplicity of voices and speakers does not appear at the time as mere confusion, since each speaker is subordinate to the overall *discursive* unity of the bulletin. At this 'higher' level of unity, the variety of voices contributes to the flow of sense. No matter who is speaking, certain terms, concepts and registers are brought into play, and in the course of the story as a whole they are either taken up, confirmed and endorsed, or set in opposition to others, or left unexploited and neglected. But once such a discrusive 'unity' has been achieved, it is useful to return to its textual sources to see which of the volices, if any, have 'won'. Such *textual* gains and losses may turn out to have *political* implications.

*'Home Help': a discourse of domesticity*

A good example of a 'unity' which transcends the voices that contribute to it but clearly works to the benefit of some of those voices as against others is what we shall call the discourse of domesticity. Along the way, this discourse serves to organize the whole story into a very particular kind of intelligibility. It is first encountered in the very first phrase of the story: 'Here at home . . .'; where 'home' is the *nation*, that which is distinct from *abroad* (which had been signified in this bulletin by the previous story about Iran). Thereafter the discourse becomes increasingly important as the story progresses. First, it *displaces* the more 'obvious' discourse for such a story as this, namely the discourse of industrial relations. Whilst we hear very little about wage claims and conditions of work we do hear quite a lot about dusting and vacuuming. Second, it becomes associated in this story with the very fluid signifier 'help'. In actual fact the word 'help' occurs thirteen times in the story, used by different voices in different contexts to mean different things. But by the end of the story, its meaning has been 'fixed'. Here are the places where it occurs:

1. I asked him: 'where does his duty lie?' Is it towards the patients and the doctors and nurses to *help* them; is he therefore prepared to encourage volunteers to go in ...
2. As far as low paid workers are concerned, they must expect to get a reasonable increase in pay in order to *help* them, and those higher up the pay scale can *help*
3. them to do so.
4. I've told the unit administrator that if, during our action, children were at risk, we would immediately leave the picket line and go in and *help*.
5. Senior nursing staff had to *help* out sorting dirty linen from the wards. It took up much of their valuable time.
6. Jenny Munns left her own housework to *help* clean a priority ward. Until unpaid volunteers like her came along the nurses had to dust and vacuum. What made
7. Mrs Munns answer the appeal for *help*?
8. So I thought, w'll, you know, erm, I'm at home in the morning, [...] probably a good idea to *help* [...].
9. Well, actually, I've been [.] washing up and er *helping* out generally
10. No patients grumbled about the paper plates or having to *help* with the washing up afterwards. And when this tiny baby, only 30 hours old, was discharged from
11. hospital a day early, to *help* relieve the pressure on staff and facilities ...
12. The army was called in to *help* the authorities at London's worst affected hospital, the Westminster.
13. A hospital spokesman, who called the incident 'sabotage', said the army was contacted because other breakdown services couldn't *help*.

The first speaker is Margaret Thatcher, the then leader of the Opposition. Next is the then Prime Minister, James Callaghan (2 & 3). Use (4) is that of the interviewed NUPE shop steward, whilst (8 & 9) are those of both the volunteers. All the other uses are those of different institutional voices: the newsreader (12 and 13); and the two film-reporters (5 from section IV and 6, 7, 10, 11 from section VI). Thus, interestingly, almost every participant who speaks, whether accessed or institutional, uses the word 'help'. That means, of course, that the word itself cannot be assumed to 'belong' to any speaker, party or faction. However, it can be 'captured', so that what 'help' means in the given circumstances is both limited and 'obvious'.

What 'captures' it, in fact, is the discourse of domesticity, which proves to be means by which help can be given to the patients and the doctors and nurses who are affected by the strike. Thus, we hear about (and see) Jenny Munns, who left her own '*housework*', so that nurses wouldn't have to '*dust and vacuum*'. She herself says that what made her answer the appeal for help was a '*neighbour*', and the fact that '*I'm at home in the morning*'. The second volunteer has been helping out 'generally', and with the '*washing up*'. Visually the impression of domesticity is confirmed by Mrs Munns' informal housecoat (not uniform) and by her use of the vacuum cleaner. The reporter goes on to speak of '*paper plates*', and of help with the '*washing up*', about which no-one '*grumbled*', but which we do see in detail on the screen.

This language is not that of an industrial dispute, much less of the political conflict between government and opposition, between Tories and Labour, and between the Prime Minister and the 'irresponsible minority' of strikers, that we heard of at the beginning of the story. Thus 'help' has *displaced* politics, but it doesn't *escape* politics. The first time we heard it was from the lips of Margaret Thatcher, who had used it (shot 4) in the very sense the news eventually establishes for it. She calls for volunteers to help the patients and the doctors and nurses. Conversely, James Callaghan's use of 'help' is in a much more directly political sense. He calls for higher paid workers to 'help' the low paid (presumably though not explicitly by moderating their own wage claims) and he says the low-paid workers must get a pay rise to 'help' them (shot 6). But neither of these senses for 'help' is taken further in the news story. Mr Callaghan's use of the term is discursively 'defeated'. Similarly, the NUPE shop steward offers help from the picket line, but, as we have seen, the drift of the story is against such a positive identity for the strikers themselves. The upshot is not only that 'help' comes to mean domestic help, but that the volunteers who supply it are exempted altogether from any suggestion that — seen from another point of view — their action could be seen as strike-breaking, and they themselves as scabs. In this particular news story, then, the discursive victory belongs to Margaret Thatcher,[9] since her mobilization of a particular sense and referent for 'help' is the one that the news uses, not only as a signifier for the event, but even to structure which aspects of it were selected as newsworthy (i. e. the selection of the volunteers for interview).

A way of testing just how complete this victory has been is to compare the interview with Mrs Munns with that of the NUPE shop steward. Once again, the strategy of reversal will tell us how different they are. For instance, given that the shop steward's reply is about coming off the picket line and 'helping', we can give him the question asked of her:

> What [would make] you answer the appeal for help?

Whereas, we can give her a version of his question:

> Now further action [cleaning] in other departments of the hospital is planned, though [she] claims the [strikers] themselves won't suffer.

Perhaps a more plausible reversal, however, would be of the direct questions we hear in the interviews: What if *he* were asked 'Has it been worth it, coming [out on strike]?'; and *she* were asked 'but surely this sort of action isn't going to gain a lot of public sympathy?'.

## 13. Conclusion: The Politics of Populist Discourses

We began this paper by suggesting that the representional and relational dimensions of news texts would allow us to mediate between textual features

---

[9] See Hall (1983).

on the one hand and wider cultural processes on the other. We think our analysis shows that those wider cultural processes are not merely invoked within textual features, but rather that textual features play an active, political role in cultural relations of power. That is to say, the news is active in the *politics* of sense-making, even when the stories concern matters not usually understood as political (as in the *Sunday Express* front page), and even when it is striving for impartiality (as in the BBC TV news). The common ground between news and political struggles is what we can call popular discourse. The news strives for clarity, both of representation and of point-of-view, and one of the most important means it uses towards this end is populism. Populist discourses (e. g. 'domesticity') and popular idioms (e. g. 'help') are mobilized to make sense of both the world and those who represent different social and political constituencies within it (e. g., both the world and such groups are sorted into WE/THEY categories). However, populist discourses are also the ground upon which politicians seek to cultivate support. Thus, the news enters into unwitting collusion with Thatcherism in seeking to make sense of the public service workers' dispute by means of notions of help and domesticity. For by so doing it allows *its* populism to be 'colonized' or captured by *Thatcherite* populism. Along the way it denies the viewer a position from which it is easy to align with the strikers, to such an extent that in the end *their* discourses (of industrial disputes and pay claims) become *unspeakable*, and the representation of 'volunteers' as scabs becomes *unthinkable*, which must have proved a great 'help' to Mrs Thatcher.

*Bibliography*

Austin, J. L. (1962). *How To Do Things With Words*, Oxford, University Press.
Barthes, R. (1975). *S/Z*, London, Jonathan Cape.
Cohen, S. and Young, J. (1973). *The Manufacture of News: Deviance, Social Problems and the Mass Media*, London, Constable.
Culler, J. (1975). *Structural Poetics*, London, RKP.
Eco, U. (1981). *The Role of the Reader*, London, Hutchinson.
Ellis, J. (1982). *Visible Fictions*, London, RKP.
Hall, S. (1983). 'The great moving right show', in Hall and Jaques, eds. (1983) pp. 19–40.
Hall, S. and Jaques, M. (1983). *The Politics of Thatcherism*, London, Lawrence Wishart.
Halliday, M. A. K. (1978). *Language as Social Semiotic*, London, Edward Arnold.
Hartley, J. (1982). *Understanding News*, London, Methuen.
Laclau, E. (1980). 'Populist rupture and discourse', in *Screen Education*, Spring, 1980, No. 34. pp. 87–93.
Leach, E. (1976). *Culture and Communication*, London, Cambridge University, Press.
Lévi-Strauss, C. (1968). *Structural Anthropology*, Harmondsworth, Penguin.
Murdock, G. (1973). 'Political deviance: the press presentation of a militant mass demonstration', in Cohen, S. and Young, J. (1973). pp. 156–175.
Van Dijk, T. A. (1977). *Text and Context*, London, Longman.

*Appendix 1: Four Texts on Poverty*

*(ANINAW)* James Greenwood, "A night in a workhouse", *Pall Mall Gazette*, 1866.

No language with which I am acquainted is capable of conveying an adequate conception of the spectacle I then encountered. Imagine a space of about thirty feet by thirty enclosed on three sides by a dingy white-washed wall, and roofed with naked tiles which were furred with the damp and filth that reeked within. ... My bedfellows lay ... distributed over the flagstones in a double row, on narrow bags scantily stuffed with hay. At one glance my appalled vision took in thirty of them ...

*(TBCOOL)* "The bitter cry of outcast London", *Pall Mall Gazette*, 1883.

Few who will read these pages have any conception of what these pestilential human rookeries are, where tens of thousands are crowded together amidst horrors which call to mind what we have heard of the middle passage of the slave ship. To get into them you have to penetrate courts reeking with poisonous and malodourous gases arising from accumulations of sewage and refuse ... You have to ascend rotten staircases ... You have to grope your way along dark and filthy passages swarming with vermin.

*(TWD)* "The workhouse deluxe", *Daily Mail*, 1911.

Profound nonsense is written about the Poor Law system; but imagine yourself in this very perfect poverty Palace at Camberwell, and see how, under a benevolent and indulgent Board of Guardians, your life goes. Here you shall have rest and ease; a little digging, perchance; a little cleaning, perhaps; ... In what palace can you find such refreshing spotlessness as your eye rests upon here? On what floors are to found such freshly gleaming tiles? Where are there brighter walls? Where a more cheerful light?

*(TS)* Orwell, "The spike", *Adelphi Magazine*, 1931.

After breakfast we had to undress again for the medical inspection ... It was an instructive sight. We stood shivering naked to the waist in two long ranks in the passage. The filtered light, bluish and cold, lighted us up with unmerciful clarity. No one can imagine unless he has seen such a thing, what pot-bellied, degenerate curs we looked.

262  J. Hartley, M. Montgomery

| STORY SECTION | SHOT NUMBER | TYPE OF FRAMING* | DESCRIPTION OF SCENE, SOUND, MOVEMENT, NAMES | WORDS SPOKEN |
|---|---|---|---|---|
| (I) (40 sec) | 1. | MS No camera movement | Newsreader (Angela Rippon); direct address to camera, eye-contact. | Here at home the dispute by public service workers is still spreading. Half the hospitals in England and Wales and some in Scotland can now open their doors to emergency cases. Apart from the hospitals the strike is affecting more ambulance services and schools, as well as water and sewerage works. In the Commons the Prime Minister urged the hospital ancillary workers to 'go back to work' while negotiations could continue on what he called a 'proper basis'. The Prime Minister also said: |
|  | 2. | Graphic | The quotation reproduced in white-on-red across screen. Words read by newsreader, VO. | It is not acceptable in any community that sick human beings, whether adults or children, should have their food denied them and proper attention forbidden to them. |
| (II) (2 min 30 sec) | 3. | MS No camera movement | Political Correspondent (Rodney Foster); direct address to camera, eye contact. Set left-top, a chroma-key graphic background with line-drawing of Big Ben and the word POLITICS. Superimposed name caption. | To be fair to the Prime Minister he's been among the first to condemn action by what he sees as an irresponsible minority; action which he's already decried as 'totally unacceptable to any decent trade unionist'. But what the Conservatives are so angry about is why his ministers keep insisting that the best way to deal with things is through co-operation with the unions concerned. For the Tories argue that any claim to a so-called 'special relationship' between Labour and the unions has long since been shattered. So as Mrs. Thatcher did again today, they demand firm government action. 'Where's the government in that?' has become the favourite Opposition response to the latest spate of Ministerial statements. And despite Mr. Callaghan's sharp words today about not involving the sick in industrial disputes, Mrs. Thatcher wanted more: |

Ideology and Power in Press and TV News 263

| | | | |
|---|---|---|---|
| 4. | Graphic | Line-drawing lower right of House of Commons with superimposed B/W still of Mrs. Thatcher, left. Name caption – Mrs. Thatcher: Opposition Leader, centre. Mrs. Thatcher's voice VO. | It is precisely because the things which he spoke of are not acceptable, and precisely because many of the tasks could be done by volunteers that I ask him: 'where does his duty lie?' Is it towards the patients and the doctors and nurses to help them? Is he therefore prepared to encourage volunteers to go in, in some hospitals they're working well. Will he make his position clear? |
| 5. | MS | (return to shot 3) | Well, Mr. Callaghan insisted this wasn't a governmental matter; of course, they wouldn't stand in the way, but it must be for the local hospital authorities to decide whether or not volunteers could usefully be employed. Labour MPs are by now of course thoroughly disgruntled with all that's going on, many of them accusing the Tories of political provocation. So a number pressed the Prime Minister to give a clear recognition of the low-paid workers' justifiable case for a decent wage. Mr. Callaghan said all these disputes could be settled straight away by meeting the demands in full. But that was something which should not commend itself to anyone. Nevertheless, he went on: |
| 6. | Graphic | As in shot 4, but picture is of Mr. Callaghan, and caption reads James Callaghan: Prime Minister. The words are in his voice. VO. | As far as low-paid workers are concerned, they must expect to get a reasonable increase in pay in order to help them, and those higher up the pay scale can help them to do so. And I trust there will be a return to some co-operation in these matters as distinct from the, I was going to say free collective bargaining, but it would be more true to say free collective vandalism that's going on now. |
| 7. | MS | (return to shot 3) | Well, a parting shot which did nothing to endear him to his left wing MPs, and certainly these troubles won't go away for the government, with MPs probably having an emergency debate on Monday night. |

\* CU = Close Up;  MS = Mid Shot;  LS = Long Shot

| STORY SECTION | SHOT NUMBER | TYPE OF FRAMING* | DESCRIPTION OF SCENE, SOUND, MOVEMENT, NAMES | WORDS SPOKEN |
|---|---|---|---|---|
| (III) (30 sec) | 8. | MS | (return to shot 1) | The Queen Elizabeth Hospital for children in East London is threatened with a 24 hour strike from midnight. All 103 children there are seriously ill, and union officials have agreed that a limited number of staff will remain on duty during the stoppage. Another children's hospital, the world-famous Great Ormond Street Hospital, experienced two lightening strikes today by porters and kitchen staff. But the hospital authorities were able to keep essential services going for the 260 patients. A report by Christopher Morris: |
| (IV) (1 min 25 sec) | 9. | CU | hospital entrance sign reading CHILDREN | |
| | | reframe to M-LS | picket line gathered round entrance, their voices audible, not the words. | The porters and kitchen staff didn't give much warning about their strike — just five minutes |
| | 10. | CU | placard with wage demand: '£60 week basic' | notice. They then |
| | | reframe | | walked out to join the |
| | | to LS | direct shot of picket line across centre; dark building and NUPE sign above; street with parked cars lower foreground. Ambient sound. | picket line and stayed out for four hours. Now further action |

Ideology and Power in Press and TV News    265

| | | | |
|---|---|---|---|
| 11. | VLS | Same scene, longer shot, traffic passes between camera and picket. | in other departments of the hospital is planned, though |
| 12. | MS | Interviewee (Conway Xavier; NUPE shop steward); set to screen right, looking out of frame-left to unseen interviewer. Superimposed name caption. Lip-sync. speech, with reporter's voice-over. Ambient sound audible. | they claim the children themselves won't suffer. (Xavier, lip-sync.) Yes, we can guarantee, erm, I've told the unit administrator that if during our action children were at risk, we would immediately leave the picket line and go in and help. (Reporter VO) But surely this sort of action isn't going to gain a lot of public sympathy. (Xavier, lip-sync.) We believe we've shown responsibility, um, we've been traditionally a very passive workforce, and we hope that by workers at this world famous hospital taking action it will bring public sympathy to our side. |
| 13. | M-LS pan | Two nurses pulling trolley towards and past camera. Minor camera movement motivated by theirs. | Inside the hospital the disruption was more than just the minimum the union had promised. Only two cooks were allowed |
| 14. | MS pan | Boy (patient?) pushes trolley, pan left to follow, and to reveal nurses and trolleys in lift. Ambient sound. | to remain, so lunch was a little late today for nearly three hundred young patients. |
| 15. | M-CU | Linen bin; hand dips in to gather | Senior nursing staff had to help out |
| | reframe | sheets, camera follows movement, | sorting dirty linen from the wards; |
| | (tilt) MS | finds nurse's face and action. | it took up much of their valuable time. |
| 16. | MS | Grubby workbench with bucket on, | And with rubbish left |
| | pan | camera pans to find rubbish pile. Mute | to pile up in the basement there's a growing risk to health. Because of the unpredictable |

| STORY SECTION | SHOT NUMBER | TYPE OF FRAMING* | DESCRIPTION OF SCENE, SOUND, MOVEMENT, NAMES | WORDS SPOKEN |
|---|---|---|---|---|
| | 17. | LS | Street shot, man and child walk into view and towards camera. They | nature of the strike action consultants at the hospital have now been instructed to admit only emergency cases. |
| | | pan | turn, camera follows as they cross in front of it to entrance. Child gazes at camera while they walk. Camera holds on child at entrance peering back at it. | It means that children awaiting non-urgent operations and treatment are being turned away at least until the present dispute is over. |
| (V) (30 sec) | 18. | MS | (return to shot 1) | It's clear that the Code of Conduct drawn up by the unions to protect emergency services is not being observed everywhere. But the National Union of Public Employees is urging local officials to 'pass the code on' to pickets. However, one NUPE official said tonight their tactics would be to 'put the screws on tighter'. More hospitals are being forced to refuse all but emergencies. Even then there's disagreement over what constitutes an emergency. From the Harold Wood Hospital at Romford in Essex, Philip Hayton reports: |
| (VI) (2 min 45 sec) | 19. | LS | Line of picketers under umbrellas seen across roadway. Ambient sound. | This hospital's strikers refused to supply any cleaners, because they say that's not part of their emergency service. |
| | 20. | CU | Makeshift white banner, handwritten to read NUPE SAY: EVEN DRAGONS MUST EAT | The authorities think differently |

Ideology and Power in Press and TV News   267

|     |                         | Pull-out/pan reveals same picket-line as in shot 19; | and they've closed the hospital to all admissions including |
|     |                         | reframe to LS | |
| 21. | LS<br>No camera movement | camera steadies on long-shot | emergencies. |
|     |                         | Interior longshot shows reporter addressing camera, eye-contact, in empty hospital room with beds visible. Lip-sync. | (Lip-sync.) This is the hospital's accident and emergency department. It's normally the busiest place in a hospital. Every day doctors treat up to a hundred patients who are suffering from everything from cuts and bruises to |
| 22. | CU                      | Mute cutaway to equipment, showing instructions: THE TREATMENT OF CARDIAC ARREST. Reporter VO. | heart attacks and appendicitis |
|     | tilt                    | Tilt down reveals more equipment. | But since yesterday, it's been completely empty. |
| 23. | LS                      | Empty ward; nurse crosses in front of camera. No camera movement. Mute. | The hospital authorities closed it down because of a lack of |
| 24. | LS                      | Active ward; nurse at bedside left. Woman vacuuming centre; sync. sound. Patients in bed right background. | clean wards for patients to go to after their treatment here. |
|     | reframe                 | Zoom in to find and follow movement of woman cleaning. Reporter VO. | (Ambient sound of vacuum faded up momentarily.) Jenny Munns left her own housework to help clean a priority ward. Until unpaid volunteers like her came |
|     | reframe                 | pull out to wider shot showing cleaner emerging into open space. | along, the nurses had to dust and vacuum. What made Mrs. Munns answer the appeal for help? |

268    J. Hartley, M. Montgomery

| STORY SECTION | SHOT NUMBER | TYPE OF FRAMING* | DESCRIPTION OF SCENE, SOUND, MOVEMENT, NAMES | WORDS SPOKEN |
|---|---|---|---|---|
| | 25. | MS | Interviewee, centre, looking out of frame left, hands resting on vacuum handle, ward visible behind. No eye contact, no caption, no camera movement. Reporter's question VO. | Well, I've a neighbour that's been in here, and she's been desperately ill at times, and she comes and does a lot of voluntary work, and yes'day moning she came, and she said there was only three on this ward, and would I be willing to come? So I thought, w'll, you know, erm, I'm at home in the morning, it's probably a good idea to help. (Reporter VO) Has it been worth it coming? (Mrs. Munns lip-sync.) Oh yes, yes, they're so appreciative (laughs), they really are. |
| | 26. | M-CU | Woman propped on bed, looking out of frame-right. No eye-contact, no caption, no camera movement. Reporter's question VO. | (Reporter VO) What have you been doing? (Interviewee lip sync.) Well, actually I've been washing up and er helping out generally. But this morning, I had to have an X-ray, so someone else took over for me. |
| | 27. | CU | Plate with food on it, being prodded with plastic knife and fork. No camera movement | Despite the irritations, morale on this ward was high. No patients grumbled about the |
| | 28. | M-CU | Plate being lifted into shot from washing-up bowl | paper plates, or having to help with |
| | | reframe | pull out and up to reveal two nurses washing up, other figures in background | the washing up afterwards. |

# SUNDAY EXPRESS

FEBRUARY 8 1981 PRICE 22p


# CUT-PRICE RUSSIANS CASH IN ON SHIP STRIKE

By DON PERRY and JOHN KESBY

**RUSSIAN merchant ships are feared to have grabbed a big slice of the world trade normally carried in British ships as the result of the four-week-old seamen's strike.**

With 225 ships of the 1,000- strong British merchant fleet stopped in ports around the world by the strike, the Russian merchant lines are understood to have made special efforts to get their services accepted.

The chief executive of a major British line said last night: "The Russians have a long history of striving to get in wherever they can, often by drastic price cutting.

"I do not doubt that one of the gravest problems of winning back the trade will be the way the Russians will more or less give their services away in order to retain the business.

"They do not have to meet the costs of a Western, free world ship and there is no question of their having to make a profit or go out of business.

"What a greater Russian presence on the world's trade lines means in terms of security and the stability of areas where they take a special interest is for others to assess."

**The Soviet shipping lines efforts to increase their share of the carrying has been particularly noted between** Europe and South America, which Marxists regard as ripe for further revolutions; to South Africa; and on routes between Britain and Europe and the Far East.

**An official of the General Council of British Shipping said last night: "It is now suspected that when this strike is over we shall see upwards of 300 British ships being sold to foreign owners with the loss of up to 10,000 officers and seamen's jobs."**

## Peace talks break down

The situation took a turn for the worse last night when talks between leaders of the shipping employers and the National Union of Seamen at the Westminster headquarters of ACAS, the conciliation agency, broke down after ten hours. Ships supplying oil rigs in the North Sea could now be involved in the dispute, and North Sea oil supplies threatened.

Union leaders were proposing that if the dispute, over pay, is to go to arbitration they will now only accept such a move if it is first conceded that the employers will add some extras to the basic 12 per cent increase already on offer.

Arbitration would then be on the question of overtime pay. The union is demanding overtime pay at time and a half instead of the present time and a quarter.

Some union militants are beginning to press for a new demand that weekend overtime shall be paid at double time.

## The longest 100-yard walk in the world

IT was rush hour. But alone in the normally busy street, its outlines partly obscured by fog, stood just one large vehicle.

All buildings nearby had been evacuated. Police and troops barred entry to the area.

For the vehicle was a petrol tanker. It had 3,500 gallons of fuel aboard. **And concealed somewhere aboard, too, was a bomb.**

Earlier that day, the tanker had been hijacked in Belfast by the I.R.A., and the driver had been forced to park it outside one of the city's main police stations.

**Now someone had to force himself to make the spine-tingling 100-yard walk from the safety perimeter to the tanker; someone had to peer under the vehicle and open the cab door; someone had to climb the ladder and open the caps on the top of the tank: someone had to search for the bomb, and having found it, attempt to disarm it, knowing that it might contain traps never encountered before; and knowing the consequences of one tiny error.**

**The task fell to a man whose official designa**tion in the Army in Northern Ireland was CATO: Chief Ammunition Technical Officer.

CATO at that time was Lieut.-Colonel Derrick Patrick, OBE. The tanker bomb outside the police station was just one of scores of hazardous assignments he tackled.

There were other tanker bombs—though a civil servant cooly announced that the loss of a bomb disposal officer was financially more acceptable than the cost of modifying the vehicles to make them less vulnerable.

**And there was the chimney bomb. To get at this, Colonel Patrick had to climb on the roof of the house. When he was straddled on the ridge, and in the act of lifting the device out of the chimney, it began to tick. . . .**

Colonel Patrick, who died recently has told the story of his fight against the Ulster bombers. His book, **FETCH FELIX**, is a vivid record of the realities behind the almost routine news bulletins from Northern Ireland reporting yet another "incident."

Extracts from **FETCH FELIX** are to appear in the **SUNDAY EXPRESS**, starting next Sunday.

## JOAN KENNEDY'S SPECIAL FRIEND

**JOAN KENNEDY, estranged wife of Senator Ted Kennedy, steps out with her special friend — handsome young doctor Jerry Aronoff. The couple, who U.S. newspapers predict will marry as soon as the Kennedys' divorce goes through, are pictured arriving at the Boston Ballet. It was the fifth occasion that Mrs Kennedy, 44, and Dr Aronoff, 36, have been seen together publicly in the two weeks since she left her husband and moved back to her Boston flat. The wealthy doctor said: "I enjoy Joan's company enormously. I would describe our relationship as 'special friends.' But we have not discussed marriage."**

## Tories to force split on Labour

by KEITH RENSHAW

IN A move to squeeze dissident Labour MPs on the key defence issue, the Tories are to mount a major debate on nuclear weapons in the Commons soon. It could enforce the final Labour split.

Violent disagreement with Labour Conference decisions on Britain's retention of nuclear weapons is one of the top policy reasons for the threatened breakaway by the Social Democrats, who include 11 Labour M.P.s.

Should they vote against the Opposition line in the debate it would be an act of rebellion that would mean instant crisis for Labour and the possible withdrawal of the Labour whip.

That would speed the impending split by forcing the whole nuclear row in the Labour Party out into the open.

The Government's aim in the debate will be to obtain Commons sanction for going ahead with Trident, the successor to the Polaris nuclear submarine, and for accepting American-controlled Cruise missiles in Britain.

### Doubts

The dissidents are not expected to support the Government's Trident programme. The group, including Mr William Rodgers, have doubts about going ahead with it because the cost could eat into Britain's conventional military efficiency.

But the Cruise missile, rejected by the last Labour Conference, is seen as an important undertaking in terms of Britain's continued full effectiveness as a NATO ally.

Mr Michael Foot has also pronounced against Britain accepting Cruise missiles. In a television interview of October 26 he said he would "send them back" if he became Prime Minister.

"I believe that there is every possibility of getting a negotiation with the Russians before then that could prevent them being stationed here at all," he said.

Mr Rodger's comment on that was: "Mr Foot's remarks were a plain statement of unilateralism.

"This is not the view of the Parliamentary Labour Party, and I do not believe it is the view of Labour voters."

So the Tories, confident of their majority in the Commons, are stoking up pressure for the dissidents to stand up and be counted, and for the Opposition to be acutely embarrassed.

The Opposition will be able to amend the Government motion, but a blank rejection of nuclear weapons would produce a revolt.

Cruise missiles, upon which the Commons row is likely to centre, start arriving in Britain and elsewhere in autumn of 1983.

## Our colour magazine gets a big welcome

**THE NEWS that the Sunday Express is to publish a colour magazine with every copy of the Sunday Express from April 12 has met with universal approval from readers and advertisers alike.**

**The Sunday Express is already the most powerful single advertising medium in the country. And now the Sunday Express will offer eight million readers the delights of a free colour supplement every weekend.**

**Advertisers are particularly attracted by the fact that nearly six million of these readers do not read any of the existing Sunday colour supplements. So the Sunday Express colour magazine offers them an unparalleled new advertising opportunity.**

**If you are not already a regular reader, make sure of your order for April 12th.**

## Tribal clash fears after murder of Nkomo man

by MICHAEL TONER

TENSION is running high in Zimbabwe this weekend following the murder in a car-bomb explosion of one of Mr Joshua Nkomo's most prominent supporters, Mr Nelson Marembo.

The murder, which follows a week of confrontation between the Zimbabwe army and guerrillas loyal to Mr Nkomo, adds a savage new twist to the bitter factional rivalry which has divided the Patriotic Front.

Our Salisbury correspondent Paul Richards reports that the feeling in the country is that Mr Marembo was probably killed because of an internal squabble in the Nkomo faction.

But at a time when both Prime Minister Mr Robert Mugabe and Mr Nkomo are desperately worried about the possibility of violent clashes between their respective supporters, the incident could well increase inter-tribal suspicions.

Mr Marembo, a shadow Minister and member of Mr Nkomo's Central Committee, was killed when his car hit a landmine planted in the driveway of his suburban home. His nephew, who was with him was also killed.

The blast was so powerful that it cut the car in two.

### Loyal

Neighbours reported seeing two Africans near the house before the explosion.

Whatever local rumours may suggest about Mr Marembo being killed by his own colleagues, there are bound to be some suspicions that he could have suffered at the hands of the former guerrillas loyal to Mr Mugabe.

However, local sources incline strongly to the view that he was killed by colleagues. Several weeks ago, Mr Marembo apparently telephoned a local newspaper in a state of shock, claiming that his life had been threatened by factions within his own party.

National army units confronted Mr Nkomo's former Zipra guerrillas in Salisbury's Chitungwiza township most of last week, in an attempt to remove them to a remote assembly camp in Western Zimbabwe.

## FISHERMEN BLOCKADE IMPORTS

THE anger of 1,000 fishermen took a positive turn at Grimsby yesterday as they set up pickets to block lorry-loads of cheap Continental fish bound for dockside merchants.

Crews up and down the country tied up their boats and refused to sail until midnight on Wednesday. Thousands of them will join a protest march to Downing Street if their demands for action against cheap fish imports are not met by then.

The Grimsby pickets will block the four dock entrances from tomorrow.

## Royal burial for Queen Frederika

THE Greek Government has agreed to allow the funeral of exiled Queen Frederika to be held at the royal family cemetery in Greece after her death on Friday.

The 63-year-old mother of the former King Constantine died from heart failure after an eye operation in Madrid, where she was staying with her daughter, Queen Sophia.

## British coal ship sinks —IRA threat

from JOHN LEY, Belfast, Saturday

A BRITISH coal ship sank off the Irish coast late this afternoon after being blown up by an IRA gang.

The Liverpool-based Nellie M was rocked by two explosions while anchored on Loch Foyle, about 150 yards off Moville, Co. Donegal.

Masked IRA men had boarded the collier and ordered off the crew before planting explosives.

No one was hurt in the blasts and at first the ship was left only partly submerged.

Army bomb experts stood by to defuse two unexploded bombs still on board, before the Nellie M finally sank in about 30 feet of water.

Troops and police on both sides of the Irish border launched a hunt for the bombers.

One member of the Provisional gang had warned a crewman that in future all British shipping entering Northern Ireland waters would be targets for attack.

A National Union of Seamen spokesman in London refused to comment on the warning.

"We would not want to make any comment until we have had an opportunity of speaking with members of the crew," he said.

The Nellie M is owned by the Coe-Manthorpe Line and managed by S. William Crow Co. of Liverpool. Its vessels supply cargoes of coal, oil and grain to ports in Northern Ireland and Donegal in the Irish Republic.

## Savoy to sell 100 rooms

A third of the famous 91-year-old Savoy Hotel in the Strand is to be put up for sale.

More than 100 bedrooms—let at £55 a night for a single room—are involved and at least one would be buyer—reported to be a property firm—is very interested.

## Sunday Telegraph goes up to 25p

The price of the Sunday Telegraph is to go up by 3p to 25p from next week, it was announced last night.

## Execution shocks Spain

from TIM BROWN

MADRID, Saturday: — A wave of horror rocked Spain yesterday after the cold-blooded terrorist murder of one of the country's leading nuclear engineers.

The body of Jose Maria Ryan, 39-year-old father of five, was found in a wood outside Bilbao.

He had been condemned to death by a revolutionary court of the Basque separatist organisation ETA for playing a major part in the construction of Spain's biggest nuclear power station.

Ryan, whose grandfather was Irish-Welsh, was kidnapped as he left the power station at Lemoniz, near Bilbao, on January 29.

The next day ETA gave the government seven days to order the demolition of the plant, which has already cost hundreds of millions of pounds, in exchange for his life.

Nobody believed the fanatics would carry out the execution of the popular Basque engineer. His wife, Josefa, said throughout that she was optimistic he would be released.

She told her second youngest son, Miguel, six, that Daddy would be home for his birthday party.

But instead ETA took the engineer from his kidnap hideaway, made him walk 200 yards into woods with his hands tied behind his back, and then shot him once in the back of the neck.

ETA said that the murder of Ryan was not an isolated case.

## Journalists halt court move

Journalists on the Sunday Times voted yesterday not to proceed with legal action over the planned takeover of Times Newspapers by Mr Rupert Murdoch.

The journalists were due to begin court proceedings tomorrow challenging the Government's decision not to refer the bid to the Monopolies Commission.

## Nimmo in a desert crash

DUBAI, Saturday: — Actor Derek Nimmo went for a ride across the desert, but finished up in hospital with spinal injuries.

His Range Rover dived 10ft over a sand cliff.

Nimmo and a British company are touring Gulf countries with the play "Say Who You Are" which opened in Dubai last week.

### TODAY'S WEATHER

MOSTLY DRY BUT RAIN IN PLACES

Moon rises 9.22 a.m. Sets [illegible]

Weather Map Page 11

Lighting up Time

5.31 p.m. to 6.57 a.m.

Monday

### SUNDAY EXTRA

"Appalling work load, dear. Nothing but pink forms and vital statistics night and day."

**DO MURRAY AND HIS MATES REALLY WANT BRITAIN TO PROSPER?**

Father Duddleswell played the fiddle at the golden wedding party . . . but the joyful occasion was soon to be overshadowed by tragedy P8 & P9

Singing the leek's praises P20

FASHION
Navy and White gives a nautical look to spring P18

*The love life of Stewart Granger* P6



PHONE STD CODE 01
353 8000


## Admire the craftsmanship in a ladder back.

This classic ladder back chair is part of a suite based on an 18th century design. It's called the Florian and it's hand finished.

The Florian appears on pages 14 and 15 of the Parker Knoll Book of Comfort.

**Parker Knoll**
No one cares more for your comfort.

Sue Black, Dept. SEA Parker Knoll Furniture Limited, P.O. Box 22, High Wycombe, Bucks. [illegible]
Please send me my free copy of the Parker Knoll Book of Comfort.
Name
Address

## Ideology and Power in Press and TV News

| | | | | |
|---|---|---|---|---|
| 29. | LS | Exterior shot; nurse carrying baby towards camera | | And when this tiny baby, only 30 hours old, was discharged from hospital a day |
| | reframe | Nurse and baby approach to MS, pan to follow her movement as she hands baby to woman waiting in back of car. | | early to help relieve the pressure on staff and facilities, his parents shrugged their shoulders (car door slams sync.), did not complain |
| 30. | M-LS | car shown driving away from camera, out of screen right | | and left for home. |
| | reframe | pull out to wider shot. Sync. of car motor | | |
| 31. | MS | (return to shot 1) | | The army was called in to help the authorities at London's worst affected hospital, the Westminster. |
| 32. | still | monochrome still-photo showing army vehicle right foreground, men centre background, wheel propped against wall left. | | An ambulance and a van were found with slashed tyres across the delivery entrance. A hospital spokesman, who called the incident 'sabotage', said the army was contacted because other breakdown services couldn't help. |

(VII)
(20 sec)

CHARLES HUSBAND AND JAGDISH M. CHOUHAN

# Local Radio in the Communication Environment of Ethnic Minorities in Britain

*Communication and Human Rights: An Introductory Statement*

There is a constantly increasing body of literature which is concerned to examine the possible role of information in defending and advancing the human and civil rights of migrants and ethnic minorities. Hujanen (1980) summarised a number of international reports and in particular discussed the role of the mass media in terms of their significance for education, for protecting cultural and linguistic plurality and as a medium for facilitating social change. Under the auspices of a UNESCO funded conference, these issues have recently received further discussion. The final report of that conference included a number of principles, agreed by the participants, which provide a valuable contextualizing statement for this chapter. The final report of the conference stated, inter alia, that:

— Because of their legal status and socio-economic position migrant workers often have poor access to normal channels of communication and, therefore, cannot fully realise their human right to freedom of expression and opinion.
— Mass media and other means of communication can contribute to the promotion of basic human rights, and therefore, it is important to guarantee to migrant workers equal access to and participation in them.
— The right of migrant workers to receive regular information in their own language, covering both their country of origin and the host country is vital.
— Migrant workers should not be seen only as receivers of information or objects of cultural adaptation but also as subjects of communication and cultural creation.

(Hujanen 1984 p. 331)

These 'principles' provide an appropriate set of criteria which should be kept in mind as we attempt in this chapter to sketch the communication situation of ethnic minorities in Britain. Within this overview particular reference will be paid to local broadcasting.

*The Background of Migration into Britain*

Over the last four decades Britain has drawn in a large number of migrant workers to fuel the British economy. As a direct consequence of this demand, and of immigration legislation, there developed in Britain a settled population of migrant labour which had, or acquired, legal rights of settlement, and which has now generated a British-born population of children who are still essentially defined as 'immigrant' by the dominant white community. The experience in Britain of the migrant labour from the Indian subcontinent, from the Caribbean and from Africa, and of their now adult offspring, has been one of ubiquitous white racism which initially was expressed in relation to an opposition to 'alien' immigrants; and is now directed against 'the aliens within'. This racism of the indigenous white population has not only contributed to the location of this section of the labour force at the bottom of the socio-economic system, it has also defined cultural difference in racial terms. The ethnic minority communities in Britain have found that their differing cultures have been stigmatized and used as evidence of 'the reality of racial difference'. Their de jure British status has been effectively denied by the dominant white, and state, definition of them as immigrant. Thus in contemporary Britain the cultural resources of minority communities have become a target of attack by British people and institutions, and have become a crucial vehicle of resistance for these ethnic minority communities. (C. C. C. S. 1982). In such a situation the mass media are a crucial site of struggle for control over the definition of events and the transmission of values (Downing, 1980; Cohen and Gardner, 1982).

It is important that, however briefly, the reader be given some indication of the historical background to immigration and nationalism in Britain since this background is crucial to any understanding of contemporary events. Despite the long history of Britain as a nation state and despite the powerful mythology of British identity one commentator has observed that "the British are clearly among the most ethnically composite of the Europeans" (Geipel, 1969 p. 162). It is certainly true that contemporary Britain exists as the end product of a very long period of history during which time invasion by Romans, Angles, Saxons and Normans was followed by less bloody additions to our population through immigration. Not that this immigration is a central part of the British spontaneous self-image. Britishness is more likely to be defined in terms of the deeds of emigrants — who 'discovered America', 'conquered Africa' and 'civilised India' — than in terms of illustrious immigrants. Nonetheless immigration has been a recurrent feature of British history. It is estimated that in the seventeenth century 80,000—100,000 Protestant Hugenots fled to England; where ironically many assisted William of Orange in his suppression of the Catholic Irish. Whilst, in the mid-nineteenth century the 'clearances' from the land and the famine led to a very large movement of Irish labour into England and Scotland. It has also been estimated that between 1875 and 1914 approximately 120,000 European Jews came to Britain. An account of the background of immigration into Britain can be found in Holmes (1978) and Lunn (1980).

In the nineteenth century Irish immigrants provided an essential labour force which carried out much of the heavy and unpleasant work such as the construction of railways and canals. Again after the Second World War Irish labour came in to meet a demand for labour. Also at that time Poles, Ukrainians and Estonians, who saw themselves as refugees rather than migrant workers, joined the British labour market. From the early 1950s immigration into Britain from the Caribbean increased following the restriction of entry into America. This was followed in the 1960s by a growth of migrant labour from the Indian sub-continent. This 'coloured immigration' as it was ubiquitously called became the focus of growing grassroots racism and political disquiet such that discussion of immigration then, and now, has tended to focus upon the Afro-Caribbean and 'Asian' migrants to the neglect of the Cypriot, Italian, Chinese and other ethnic communities which have developed in post-war Britain. A summary of the process of migration can be found in Braham (1982) and a discussion of aspects of the political response in Husband (1982b) and Hall et al (1978).

The long history of immigration into Britain has a crucial consequence in that it provides a historical precepent for resentment, discrimination and racism being generated within the indigenous population, *and* this same history can be invoked to justify claims to a British tradition of tolerance (Husband 1977, 1982b). As recently as Victorian England there was florid racism against the Irish (Curtis 1968, 1971) and immigration of East-European Jews evoked very real racist anti-Semitism at the turn of the century. Britain is a society with a historically-grounded cultural repertoire of race-thinking (Banton and Harwood 1975; Husband 1982a; and Barker 1981). It is also a nation state with a very powerful myth of its national credentials of liberality and tolerance. Images of Britain as 'the home of freemen', of Britain 'the Mother of Parliaments', the very source and essence of civilised democracy, are essential images of this myth. So too is the notion of Britain as a haven for refugees rooted and legitimated through its very history of admitting immigrants; from seventeenth century Hugenots to twentieth century Vietnamese 'boat people' the historical record is invoked. The exact nature of the policy of admission and the reception experienced by these groups is irrelevant to the myth (see Foot 1965, Husband 1982b); the 'facts' are inviolate. Thus within Britain nation and race are interwoven in a mythologised past, and crucially for contemporary events, the belief in British tolerance is a powerful ideological tool in obscuring the nature and extent of British racism. Indeed discriminatory immigration legislation has been repeatedly presented as a mere legislative expression of a political commitment to "good race-relations" and "a concern for those immigrants already here" (Lawrence 1982; Barker

1981; and Reeves 1984, provide valuable accounts of the many-layered nature of British racial discourse).

The series of Acts of Parliament aimed at restricting the entry of black labour into Britain, and the legitimating arguments which were successfully presented to the white British population, had a critical impact upon the legal rights of black migrants and upon settled black British citizens. The 1962 and 1968 Commonwealth Immigration Acts initially led to a rapid escalation in the rate of immigration as workers sought to avoid controls on their entry. Subsequently these Acts brought cyclical migration to an end, since members of a family returning to their homeland would be very unlikely to be able to be replaced by a relative, who would in turn remit money home. Increasingly, migrant workers found themselves becoming settlers. Therefore, in any discussion of ethnic minority communities in Britain one must take into account how long the community has been settled, and whether they view themselves as migrant workers, settled immigrant British citizens, refugees or British-born citizens belonging to a specific community or culture. Recent books by Phizacklea and Miles (1980), Miles (1982), Rex and Tomlinson (1979) and the Centre for Contemporary Cultural Studies (1982) provide a range of empirical data and theoretical approaches which demonstrate the development and significance of such distinctions.

These same references will also indicate a further crucial feature of the pattern of settlement of migrants in Britain. It is highly localised, by city, and within cities. Thus most migrant communities have a geographical and urban concentration which facilitates the development of social networks and the creation of a culturally-specific infrastructure of institutions and resources. As a recent edition of *Race Today* (May/June 1983) points out this is not true in all instances and does not apply, for example, to the population of Latin American refugees and migrant workers concentrated in London; nor to the Vietnamese refugees of recent years whom the Government have quite deliberately sought to disperse (Edholm et al 1983).

There is not the space to develop an analysis of the nature and location of the very different immigrant populations which exist in Britain, but that difference must be born in mind in relation to everything that follows. Particularly in discussing the communication environment of ethnic minorities who experience racial discrimination as an endemic aspect of their existence in Britain the variation in political consciousness and socio-economic infrastructure of business, political and social networks will be significant both within and between specific communities. Only in relation to real communities, in specific towns, with unique histories of immigration and settlement can the significance of media be adequately understood. As Saifullah Khan (1982) has argued the unique social relations within Britain and with the country of emigration must mediate any understanding of the flow of information and media used. Particularly when these social relations are themselves related to the power relations existing between the dominant white British system and that of the minority community. In this chapter, this ideal will not be met, but should inform all that follows.

*The Significance of the Dominant Mass Media*

*The Press*

Before discussing the significance of local radio as a medium of communication it is appropriate to indicate something of the wider context within which it operates. The British national press has been a significant vehicle for maintaining an essentially white British discourse, it has predominantly reflected white racism, *and* white liberal values; it has an essentially white labour force (Morrison 1975; C. R. E. 1980) and assumes a white audience. They have defined the context within which the ethnic minority media have operated. There is considerable empirical evidence of the 'racial' distortion which has characterised the national press reporting of immigration, and of ethnic minority communities in Britain (Butterworth 1962; Hartmann and Husband 1971; Hartmann et al 1974; Hartmann and Husband 1974; Husband 1975; Evans 1977; Downing 1980; Troyna 1981; Joshua et al 1983).

Hartmann and Husband (1974) demonstrated that regardless of variation in editorial stance the national press between 1963 and 1970 had presented a common definition of what immigration of labour into Britain signified. Their research indicated that the press consensus that Britain had "an immigration problem" was widely taken up by the white populace throughout Britain, regardless of their actual experience of immigrants. The press and the white populace were agreed that the 'problem' was "coloured" immigration. Chritcher et al (1977) also demonstrated that for the provincial press, over a comparable period, immigration had been a major aspect of the reporting of 'race relations', and that immigration was "defined almost exclusively as a problem of control". It is difficult to exaggerate the significance of this definition of the situation being so pervasively central to the reporting of the migration of labour into Britain throughout the 1960s. This focus on "coloured immigration" not only obscured the very large number of white immigrants entering Britain, it also cued the potent racial categorisation and stereotyping which was latent in the white readership. It also signalled to the black communities their marginality in British society, and their invisibility as an audience for the British press. Whilst the settlement of immigrants was highly localised in relatively few conurbations in Britain (Rose et al 1968), the effect of the press coverage was to ensure that everyone throughout Britain was provided with an account of events, constructed in the language of racial categories which were employed within the framework of an immigration crisis. Thus for the majority of white people, Britain in the 1960s was in the midst of a disturbing and threatening immigration crisis.

It would be improper to discuss 'race relations' as a unique phenomenon developing independently of other events or forces in Britain. The emerging definition of Britain's 'immigration problem' occurred in the context of a society which was simultaneously negotiating other stresses. Hall et al (1978) have indicated the significance of the challenge to consensus politics and to the economic fabric of society in that period, and Chibnall (1977) in an analysis of the national press noted the emergence of a society under threat as a linking concept in a variety of stories. The potency of such linking concepts as "the violent society" and "society under threat" lay in their ability to provide a common core of value and emotion in stimulating 'moral panics' (Cohen 1973) in relation to such perceived threats as sexual permissiveness, drug abuse, political violence or — immigration.

Thus, the 'immigration problem' did not emerge in an otherwise pacific society; on the contrary it developed at a time when the social order was experiencing a period of considerable flux. Throughout the 1960s and 1970s the reality of the situation has been characterised by an increasingly explicit racism in response to the settlement of black labour and the growth of black British communities. The very vehemence and explicit nature of racist practices threatened the stable hegemony of white 'superiority' by showing it to be in fact dominance based upon discrimination, prejudice and exploitation. The crucial myths of "rule of law", "freedom of expression", "tolerance" and "justice" which are so central to the British liberal democratic state were being painfully disconfirmed by the reality and extent of state and individual racism. In this context defining events in terms of an "immigration problem" directed attention upon the symptoms of white racism, rather than upon the racism itself. This failure to confront the increasing racism was facilitated by the recurrent invoking of that mythic British tolerance spoken of above. Hartmann et al (1974), Kuepper et al (1977) and Troyna (1982) have all noted that the mainstream British press has continually recorded the liberal and tolerant credentials of Britain as a social democracy. In so doing they have helped to mystify the true nature of British racism. However, in making explicit the 'official' liberal values of British society they have also provided a point of leverage for ethnic minorities who may seek to invoke these official values in support of a campaign for improved conditions and rights within Britain. However, the evidence for the success of such pressure in recent decades is not very positive. (See for example: Hill and Issacharoff, 1971; John, 1983).

Throughout the 1970s immigration remained a major issue within party politics in Britain and provided the context within which neo-Fascist, racist organisations like the National Front could prosper (Walker, 1977). The national press continued to reflect this racist sentiment and occasionally provided flamboyant outbursts of anti-immigrant prejudice; as for example in 1976 with banner headlines announcing unanticipated large levels of black immigration, and sensationalist stories of immigrants living in luxury hotels at local authority expense (Evans 1976).

More recently Troyna (1982) and (1981) has demonstrated that the British national and local press have continued to report events in such a way as to marginalise the equal citizenship of the black British immigrants who entered Britain in the 1960s and 1970s. Particularly he has shown that in the reporting of a fascist and racist political organisation, the National Front, the national press have underplayed the racist core of National Front politics in concentrating upon the challenge to law and order created by the anti-racist opposition to them. In Troyna's words: "Because parliamentary democracy is held to be sacrosanct, and the free expression of opinion is seen as pivotal to the process, the 'freedom' of black people to be protected from the NF's racial insults is consistently overlooked" (Troyna, 1982 p. 274). Troyna concludes that for the national press "blacks exist outside the mainstream of British society". He argues that in the 1970s the underlaying ethos of the national press has shifted from a stereotypical concern with an 'immigration crisis' toward a contemporary concern with 'aliens within' and the consequent threat to 'the British way of life'. This was perhaps best represented in the much quoted statement of Mrs Thatcher who, in 1978 in a television interview noted that it was not easy to get clear figures from the Home Office about immigration but estimated that by the end of the century there would be four million people from the New Commonwealth or Pakistan in Britain. She went on to say:

> "Now that is an awful lot and I think it means that people are really rather afraid that this country might be rather swamped by people with a different culture, and you know, the British character has done so much for democracy, for law, and done so much throughout the world that if there is any fear that it might be swamped, people are going to react and be rather hostile to those coming in. So if you want good race relations, you have got to allay people's fears on numbers ..."

Those white Britons who share such sentiments, and we must assume it is the majority, will not have taken any comfort from the press and television reports of the rioting in major cities of Britain during the summer of 1981. (Joshua et al, 1983; Tumber, 1983). Again the press found it congenial to focus upon conflict rather than to explore its aetiology. The challenge to law and order; the feckless, impressionable mob stirred by outside agitators and acting in simple-minded imitation of each other were the dominant images in the press. Increasingly in the 1980s the British press has been articulating a mechanistic notion of democracy; one in which the "rights of the majority" are presented as being usurped by an intemperate yielding to the demands of minorities. As the strategies necessitated by the need to counter the racism which has threatened the hegemony of white liberalism have developed, there has been an accumulating reaction against the resources directed to this purpose, and to the inevitable implicit critique of the British state's capacity to guarantee freedom and justice to all. Tolerance after all is the exercise of largesse by the powerful toward the oppressed. It starts from the premise that there is something intrinsically intolerable which must be tolerated. Thus the logic of tolerance is the extension of privileges to those who do not legitimately 'deserve them'. In the context of Britain this has fueled a perception of minority communities as ungrateful and essentially insatiable in their demands on the 'indigenous' population. It has fueled a deep-seated cultural racism expressing itself in indignation at the extent to which the 'indigenous population' have been made to bend-over-backwards to accomodate to inflexible and ungrateful 'immigrants'. Where there has been no acceptance of the racism in British society, then antiracist strategies not surprisingly are easily construed as politically motivated, unnecessary and insulting. The British press have been permeated by such opinions and have failed to challenge the logic of such cultural racism.

*Television*

British television has echoed the 'white British' hegemony which has been sketched in the press. Television news and current affairs programmes have tended to reflect the news values and news stories of the national press. (Downing, 1975 and 1980;Freeth, 1982). Tumber (1982) however, details the sensitivity which television journalists have developed in understanding the ways in which they may influence the very events they are reporting. British television drama and entertainment programming has on the other hand tended to ignore the multi-ethnic reality of Britain through the late 1960s to the present. A series of empirical studies demonstrated the relative invisibility of British ehtnic minority characters in television drama and light entertainment. (B. B. C. 1972; Equity Coloured Artists' Committee, 1974; Anwar and Shang, 1982). These same reports have also reported that the few roles which are occupied by ethnic minority actors are often of a minor nature or involve a stereotypical representation of their ethnic groups. Even where innovatory, all-black series such as *The Fosters* or *Empire Road* have temporarily been introduced they have been challenged by black critics as distorting Afro-Caribbean or Asian experience in Britain. (Shabazz, 1976; Gilroy, 1983).

A study of 'The Attitudes of Ethnic Minorities to Television Programmes: with special reference to Light Entertainment and Drama' (Jones and Dungey, 1983) reports that both Asian and Afro-Caribbean young people preferred American-made programmes, and that for example, for Afro-Caribbean boys and girls one of the most popular programmes was *Different Strokes*, an American programme in which two black boys live with a white millionaire and his daughter. Disturbingly, *Mind Your Language*, a British-made comedy series constructed almost entirely from ethnic caricatures, was found to be very popular among Asian boys and girls. This can be seen as an unobtrusive measure of the lack of choice for young people, who as the research indicated, had a preference for programming with ethnically compatible characters. This same study reported the anxiety of Asian parents regarding the potentially harmful effects of television in eroding traditional codes of morality and behaviour; whilst West Indian parents too were critical of television in seeing it as presenting a biased representation of Caribbean life and a view of British life which was biased toward the world of the white middle class.

Both B. B. C. Television and the commercial Independent Television companies now have programmes specifically for the Asian and Afro-Caribbean populations in Britain. The other ethnic minority communities, with the exception of the Welsh, have no such provision. The problem with the B. B. C's *Asian Magazine, Gharbar* (aimed at Asian women), and *Ebony*, and Channel Four's *Black on Black* and *Eastern Eye* is that they implicitly group immigrant communities into categories which may be meaningful to white Britons but are hardly acceptable to the migrant communities. Thus Pakistanis, Bangladeshis, Indians and 'East African Asians' must all share the programming of *Asian Magazine* and *Eastern Eye*; whilst all 'West Indians' interests must be met within *Ebony* or *Black on Black*. Thus what to the white audience may seem like a reasonable gesture toward 'Asians' and 'West Indians' can only be regarded as entirely unsatisfactory by the members of the different ethnic communities who must share an approximate 4 hours of television per week. Not surprisingly, these constraints of time and audience diversity generate painful choices for the producers of these programmes. In the relatively new *Black on Black* on Channel Four it is already the case that the black producer has chosen to go for a format of each programme containing a range of items aimed at keeping a wide audience; rather than doing a different topic in depth in each programme. This model also means that the programme largely responds to popular interests in music, entertainment, and current affairs which are already established in the Afro-Caribbean community. Thus it is serving interests which are already largely catered for through other media, such as records or the ethnic press.

To some extent the emergence of the new Channel Four television station in 1982 after much political and commercial lobbying has acted as a catalyst for ethnic communities to develop their critique of British television. Channel Four was given its franchise on the understanding that it would create high-quality programming to meet the need of a wide range of minority interests; including the immigrant ethnic communities. This, and the stated progressive intentions of management and senior editorial staff created expectations among black producers, journalists and activists which have now resulted in a critique of not only the content of television programmes but also the staffing and management of television. (Saakana, 1982; Freeth, 1982; Cohen and Gardner, 1982). Black activists are no longer seeking better content in programming, they are seeking for better access to power in the institutions. This is reflected in the formation of the Black Media Workers Association

(Morris, 1982) to act as a pressure group for Asian and Afro-Caribbean interests.

*The 'Minority Press'*

The predominance of white British sensibilities which prevails in British television and press is challenged by the extensive range of ethnic minority newspapers which are available in Britain. The number and diversity of ethnic minority newspapers in Britain is matched only by the almost total lack of research, or even descriptive information upon them. In the production of this chapter, search of the abstracts has thrown up an ample supply of reports on North American ethnic minority press, but virtually nothing on the British situation. However, inquiry does indicate that it would seem to be an unlucky ethnic minority which could not find, perhaps with some effort, a paper in its own mother tongue. An article by Anthony Mascarenhas in the *Sunday Times* of April 3rd 1983 reports that:

> "At last count, the Commission for Racial Equality listed 35 Asian vernacular publications in Britain for the estimated 2 million people of Asian origin who live here. there were 9 Urdu papers (one daily), 8 Bengali, 6 Punjabi, 4 Gujerati, 3 Hindi, 2 each in Chinese and Tamil, and one in Telegu, a South Indian language. ... And the Commission does not record at least 20 other papers in Asian languages, mainly belonging to expatriate 'revolutionary' groups."

Not mentioned by Mascarenhas, but also listed by the Commission for Racial Equality are such papers as *The Caribbean Times*, *The Weekly Gleaner* and *West Indian World*, all of which are weeklies serving the West Indian communities in Britain. For a large number of ethnic communities it is also possible to obtain a paper which to some extent reflects their own political or religious preference within their larger ethnic boundary. This would seem to be the case for the Polish and the 'Asian' communities. For example, the Polish communities in Britain have the choice of the *Polish Daily*, the *Polish Week*, a weekly produced to reflect the interests of Polish Catholics called *Sunday* and the Lutheran monthly called the *Evangelical Herald* (all names translated from their Polish original). These papers are produced in London, there is also a Polish language magazine called *Culture* which is imported from Paris. The Estonian communities import a daily paper from Canada. The national papers of several European countries such as Italy, France, Germany and Greece are also available in large cities with migrant populations.

In general the situation in Britain is that there is a considerable range of newspapers which are directed at relatively specific ethnic communities. The diversity of papers and the specificity of their audience also increases dramatically when the probably hundreds of community newspapers, with circulations in tens of hundreds rather than tens of thousands, are added to the total production of ethnic minority newsprint. Given that fact, it is interesting to note the total neglect, or highly peripheral mention given to the ethnic minority press, both national and local, in the many ethnographies of ethnic communities in Britain which have been published over the last three decades.

Since literacy in written English may be assumed to be lower among the first generation of Indian, Bangladeshi and Pakistani settlers in Britain than among the equivalent white population, in terms of occupation and class position, we may anticipate that this population will be smaller consumers of the mainstream national press than their white British, or British Afro-Caribbean contemporaries. This literacy barrier may be a factor which may accentuate any cultural predisposition to consume the relevant ethnic newspapers. In the absence of any published readership surveys this must, however, remain as speculation. Equally, there are almost no empirical analyses of the content of the ethnic minority press. A search of the last five years of *Race Relations Abstracts* revealed only two works: Singh (1979) and Shamsher and Russell (1976) have written on the Punjabi press in Britain. Singh reports that:

> "In order of prominence, the news of political changes in the Punjab appear on the front page and occupy more space, and political news of the central Indian Government takes second place. None of the three papers devotes any space to International and British hard news".

This may have been true of the papers he sampled at the time of writing, it may be that there has been a relative change since. Certainly, Anwar (1980) notes in some detail the role of the 'Asian' press in Britain in dicussing the issues relevant to the different ethnic communities during the 1979 General Election.

The ethnic minority press are regarded by 'informed sources' as serving two general functions for their readers which may vary in relative importance depending upon the specific ethnic community and the particular paper. These functions are to keep the reader informed of events in the country of emigration and to provide a partisan commentary on the experience and concerns of the ethnic community in Britain. Ratcliffe, in a survey of 'Asian' and 'West Indian' respondents in Birmingham noted that: "newspapers provided the major source of up-to-date news from the homeland". (Ratcliffe, 1981, p. 32) Singh (1979) discusses the way in which the Punjabi press has provided a platform for discussing the divisions within the Punjabi communities. His account of the editorial stance of the Punjabi press portrays it as being moderate and placatory toward white society. This is not a position taken by all the ethnic press. *Race Today* for example, is a magazine which presents a radical analysis of British racism and places this in an international perspective. In many British cities there are also small circulation local ethnic community weeklies or monthlies which offer a critical commentary on events in their town and community.

For the ethnic minority press which publishes in Britain there are a variety of problems arising from their small circulation figures, relative to those of the Fleet Street dailies. Advertising agencies have chosen not to advertise traditional consumer products in the minority press on the grounds that their circulation figures are too low, and that their readers can effectly be tapped through the appropriate national paper. Thus the revenue for the ethnic minority press is disproportionately weighted toward the sale price of each issue. This may also be possibly matched by diseconomies in production. With small production runs there are likely to be higher capital overheads per unit. Not least of which may be the fact that the minority language print and setting capital equipment may well be under-utilised through lack of a wide range of publications on a permanent production schedule. However, it would be incorrect to assume that all ethnic minority papers are produced on a shoestring with archaic technology. Mascarenhas for example reports that:

> "Punjabi and Gujerati newspapers have computerised setting and are printed in four colours. Topping them all is *Sing Tao*, a Chinese daily, produced by an expensive facsimile transmission by satellite from Hong Kong to an ultra-modern printing plant on the outskirts of London".

Elsewhere in his article Mascarenhas notes that *Sing Tao* is losing £6,000 per week on this European edition, and that another Chinese daily paper, *Wen Wei Po*, which is part of a powerful Hong Kong group is losing £100,000 per year in Britain. Similar international connections are reported by Mascarenhas as sustaining an Urdu language newspaper, *Nawai Wagt*. He reports that *"Nawai Wagt"* is part of a prosperous chain of newspapers in Pakistan (which) . . . finds it more economical to produce an 'international' edition in Karachi from material telexed daily from London and then flown here for distribution". Clearly then there is a great variation in the financial backing available for different ethnic minority papers.

Distribution may also be a problem with some of the large retail outlets not being willing to stock minority papers (Minority Press Group, 1980). Thus finance is likely to be a fundamental problem for many of the indigenous ethnic minority papers. this may then feed back into a further difficulty in terms of being able to pay, train and retain staff. Ethnic minority journalists and some white members of the National Union of Journalists have for many years been active in making public the inadequate recruitment and training of ethnic minority people in the national press. Thus there has been a limited pool of trained journalists to staff the ethnic minority press. Also for those who are qualified, there has recently been evidence of recruitment of ethnic minority staff by the national media and thus this pool has been tapped, but not necessarily replenished. At a conference of ethnic minority journalists held in 1980 and sponsored by the Commission for Racial Equality, the lack of training opportunities was identified as a major reason for the under-representation of blacks in journalism. As a response to this a one year course for black journalists will start at the Polytechnic of Central London in September 1983. The course, financed by the Manpower Services Commission will provide twenty places of which half will be in radio journalism and half in print journalism. This positive initiative will be interesting to monitor in terms of the extent to which the graduates make a contribution to developing a more professional ethnic press, or become co-opted into presenting a 'professional', and hence white, product in major national and regional newspapers and television companies.

Thus ethnic minority communities in Britain exist within a media environment which is highly dichotomized. They are effectively excluded as a putative audience from the national and regional press, and from television; whilst at the same time those media dramatically impinge upon their experience in Britain. On the other hand the ethnic minority press provide a medium for addressing and reflecting the particular concerns of quite discrete populations. Local radio should be located in relation to these media and other channels of communication, such as theatre, dance, film and political organisations, not discussed here.

*Local Radio:*

*The Background*

Britain is now covered by a network of local radio stations which are controlled by the state British Broadcasting Corporation or by the Independent Broadcasting Authority which is responsible for monitoring the operation of commercial radio stations. The Labour Government in 1966, through its White Paper on Broadcasting enabled the B. B. C. to provide local radio stations with a view to "fostering a greater awareness of local affairs and involvement in the community". The first such station opened in Leicester in 1967; there are now 30. From the late 1950s and with increasing vehemence in the 1960s there was a powerful lobby seeking the introduction of commercial radio to operate outside of the tradition of public service broadcasting exemplified by the B. B. C. Despite strong opposition, with the coming to power of a Conservative Government in 1970, the way was paved for the introduction of commercial local radio. This was facilitated by The Sound Broadcasting Act of 1972 which renamed the Independent Television Authority as the Independent Broadcasting Authority and charged it with the responsibility for providing 'local sound broadcasting services'. As a report by the Local Radio Workshop (1983a) notes: "The definition of what constituted a local sound broadcast was deliberately left loose. There was a technical definition:

'In this Act "local sound broadcast" means a programme which is broadcast ... from a station so constructed and operated as to have a range of transmission limited to that which is sufficient, in normal circumstances, to ensure adequate reception throughout a particular locality';

and one statement about programmes:

'In the case of local sound broadcasting services, that the programmes broadcast from different stations for receptions in different localities do not consist of identical or similar material to an extent inconsistent with the character of the services as local sound broadcasting services'."

(Local Radio Workshop, 1983a p. 29)

Not surprisingly the Local Radio Workshop report observes that commercial local radio broadcasting had been set up "under the loosest possible definition of 'localism' ". The first independent local radio stations went on air in the latter part of 1973 and by the end of 1982 there were thirty eight independent local radio stations, with plans to nearly double that number by the end of the decade.

Before discussing the adequacy of local radio as a medium for communication for ethnic minority communities in Britain we should perhaps first note the extent to which they have proved to be imperfect channels for a rich range of communication in general. In 1974 the Labour Government set up a committee, under the chair of Lord Annan, to 'consider the future of broadcasting services in the United Kingdom . . . '. That committee received much critical evidence on the operation of local radio stations and in its 1977 report observed that a minority opinion on the committee felt that:

"Some members of the Committee think that the prospectuses of these stations cynically set out the bare minimum of public service broadcasting consonant with their being allocated the franchise: and then having got it, the stations flagrantly failed to provide what little they had promised. . . . Too many stations are trying to find the cheapest form of programming which would attract the maximum audience. Since quality programmes are the first to be ditched if the ratings show a decline in numbers listening to them, what is left is not of the standard that our country's public service broadcasting system demands."

However:

"Most (of the Committee) approved of the way in which the I. B. A. had handled the matter. There is an ancient maxim which enjoins us first to acquire wealth and then practice virtue. Too many fearsome regulations in the initial stages can cripple commercial enterprises. We agreed with the I. B. A. that rigid adherence to the terms of the franchise application was not necessarily the right policy. . . . It was up to the (I. B. A.) to ensure that the programming was varied and gave a good service to the locality".

(Cited in Local Radio Workshop 1983a, p. 33)

Thus the operation of commercial local radio was in 1977 judged to be falling well short of the intentions for local broadcasting laid down in the original franchise applications; the majority of the Annan Committee, however, seemed to view this as an acceptable consequence of establishing the commercial viability of these stations. Budgetry constraints have remained a consistent force in shaping the programming strategies of most commercial local radio stations, *and* of the B. B. C. stations. A 1981 survey of the commercial and B. B. C. stations servicing London provided the following conclusions:

> "Our findings clearly illustrate the lack of real substance to most of the programming, in a way that no amount of talk about 'natural programming flow' can dispel. All three stations seemed unable or unwilling to get to grips with London issues in the way that was promised when stations opened: instead they offered what they could produce cheaply and easily — 'local news' from the courts, the police and the fire brigade; studio discussions with 'experts' as a substitute for properly researched programmes; and chat shows with celebrities to promote new books and shows. For the rest it was mainly pop records and a stream of information, useful and otherwise. Our most sympathetic verdict would be that they do not know what else local radio could be doing, but in view of the services rendered so enthusiastically to commercial interests (playing their records, promoting their products and making news bulletins out of press releases) such naivete is hard to credit".
>
> (Local Radio Workshop 1983b p. 10)

It is within this general context of competition for audiences within tight budgeting constraints that the service provided to ethnic minority communities must be judged.

*Local Radio and Ethnic Minorities*

The following discussion of local radio and ethnic minorities in Britain is based upon information obtained through interviews with station personnel in seven local radio stations; three Independent Local Radio stations and four from the B. B. C. local radio network. In each station the people responsible for compiling and presenting the programmes to ethnic minorities were interviewed, as were the members of the station management structure who were immediately responsoble for these programmes. The conclusions drawn here are a preliminary statement for a larger report. (Chouhan and Husband, forthcoming). Whilst this report will be concerned to indicate the very real variation between stations in the extent and form of programming made available, there are still general conclusions which can be presented.

*An integrationist ethos?*

A common feature of all the local radio stations in the sample was the essentially integrationist ethos within which broadcasting for ethnic minorities was conceived. Whilst the station may provide a forum for the expression of the cultural interests of minority communities, it must ideally not exclude the dominant white audience, *or* other ethnic minorities. Stations it seemed should promote general inter-ethnic understanding rather than community solidarity for specific ethnic groups. As a political strategy it is hard to see this as an explicit policy passed down from the I. B. A. or the B. B. C., rather it seems more likely it is the implicit ethos of British broadcasting in general: a fusion of the tradition of public service broadcasting and the emergent multiculturalism of policy formulation in the 1970s. The ideological virtue of multiculturalism is that whilst it allows for the recognition of cultural difference it ignores relations of power and domination (See Bourne, 1980; Carby, 1982; and Mullard, 1982). This philosophy within broadcasting is easily articulated in relation to two independent determining forces: namely the pressure to maintain audience size, and the professional commitment to the maintenance of 'balance'. The significance of these forces can be amply illustrated by examples taken from the interviews. The view that the local radio station must be a neutral medium for communication pre-empts the voice of minority community experience being allowed unmediated expression in, very real ways; for not only is balance between specific programmes required, it also became clear that there are real constraints upon expressing a partisan view. Where integration is the goal, and where alienating any part of a potential audience is professionally and economically impermissible then the suppression of real instances of conflict happily becomes an expression of responsible broadcasting.

This concern with balance and avoiding conflict was apparent in the response of the person responsible for ethnic minority programming in a local radio station with a number of distinct ethnic communities in its local area. The question "What ethnic minorities are the target audiences of particular programmes ..." elicited the following comments:

> "... I think you have to be very aware whenever you have anything to do with the Asian programmes, that the Asian community is not a community; it is a number of sub-groups who get on with each other, or who don't to a greater or lesser extent, and so *unless you are going to be divisive* and say, right, Monday's programme is going to be for Punjab-Muslims; Tuesday's for Punjab-Sikhs; Wednesday's for Gujerati-Hindus you have to try and produce a programme which will be all embracing, which is what we try to do ..."
>
> (emphasis added)

This member of the station management demonstrated a repeated concern with the possibility of local radio programming being divisive within the 'Asian' communities. It was a word which recurred in relation to arguing against using the different community languages in particular programmes and in relation to the necessity of maintaining balanced neutrality in news reporting. Thus the programming consequence of this rationale is a flattening of the diversity among the minority communities in the town, and the reification of an 'Asian' audience whose interests and concerns should be accessible to the white audience.

This situation was replicated by another local radio station where both the programme controller and the producer of a programme intended for the diverse 'Asian' communities in the town demonstrated an explicit concern to sustain harmonious integration. The programme controller expressed this view:

> ". . . we do cover things hopefully for Asians and people from other backgrounds, to get their point across. Not just in specific programmes, but in our general programming. In other words to try and encourage, although we don't see it as our particular aim, we try and encourage integration.. Although we don't set out to do that, but we feel we have a responsibility to let our listeners know about things happening within the community, which without us they perhaps wouldn't know about".

This untheorised expression of policy is qualified later in the interview where in response to the question "In programme production what is the situation regarding the possibility of ethnic minority programmes adopting an explicitly partisan position on local or international political issues?" the programme controller states:

> "Well, it is something we don't do at all. We don't express opinions; wherever possible opinions are not expressed. . . . Our job is to be a neutral pervayor of news and information".

He then goes on to make an extended statement about the station's determination to maintain balanced programmes.

This answer is almost perfectly matched by the answer given to the same question by the programme controller of the station in the adjacent town. On the possibility of explicitly partisan broadcasting the answer given is: "We don't encourage it basically", which is also followed by a statement of the necessity of maintaining balance in broadcasting.

Balance and maximising audience quite adequately accomplish the political purpose of permitting a recognition of cultural difference whilst denying the air-waves as a channel for meaningfully discussing political relations between minority communities, between them and the dominant white society, and between these groups and the original countries of emigration; exactly those relations which Saifullah Khan (1982) identified as central to the experience of minorities within Britain. This may inadvertently leave the reader with the impression that we have illuminated the constraints which are placed upon a large body of current affairs, interview and talk shows aimed at minority audiences. This is far from the case, the major instrument of censorship is the sheer absence of the spoken word. The large majority of ethnic minority broadcasting time is music. Again this is not unique to ethnic minority programming. The Independent Broadcasting Authority has expressed concern at the inadequate proportion of 'meaningful speech' to be found in some station schedules. It is nicely indicative of the vacuity of some broadcasting that such a concept should be invoked.

*The 'problem' of linguistic diversity*

One of the major issues to arise from the interviews is the inability of local radio to respond to the language diversity of the ethnic minority communities within their catchment area. Again the concern with audience size is frequently invoked by both management and individual programme producers in justifying the use of English, or the supposed 'Asian' linguafranca — Hindustani. But also expressed is an anxiety regarding the exclusion of the majority audience, with an implicit sense that this would be resented. What is clear is that "the right of migrant workers to receive regular information in their own language" is not going to be significantly advanced by the current form of local radio broadcasting. The following quotations are all taken from interviews with members of the management of different radio stations and are illustrative of the rationale determining language diversity in broadcasting.

Defending their policy of broadcasting in English one programme controller said:

> "You can do one of two things with this sort of programme. You can either ghettoize it and have it completely separate to anything else that the radio station is doing, and have it completely separate from the rest of the audience; in essence saying to the English-speaking audience — this is not something you're supposed to be listening to. Or, you can broadcast in the English language in the hope that English-speaking people will listen to it and will hear what's going on and maybe understand it a little better. You can ghettoize things too much and its not something which I like to do".

Here we have the integrationist ethos expressed in terms of the evocative imagery of the ghetto as a closed structure excluding the participation of the dominant majority, an interesting conceptual inversion. Immediately this interviewee makes it clear that maintaining the largest possible audience excludes the possibility of broadcasting for a 'minority audience': "If we are broadcasting something, then its got to be as part of a general output, and therefore something which could be of interest to our general audience".

In another town with a population of approximately 40,000 Gujeratis within the 'Asian' communities in the catchment area a member of the management team commented of five one-hour 'Asian' programmes that:

> "I think its also important that all the programmes except one are in English, because we also try to encourage the host community to listen to them. I mean we don't want to say 'this is only for Asians'".

Why not? Well apparently not only out of concern for audience maximization for shortly it is revealed that the one hour not in English is in Hindi, and that "the only reason it is in Hindi is simply because it is a language which most of the Asians will understand . . ." There is in consequence a response from the large Gujerati community:

> "I come under a lot of flak from the Gujerati language groups who particularly want their programmes in Gujerati. But I've decided not to be swayed by that because I think its very divisive, and I think to a large extent its a very political thing, more than something which is genuinely wanted. I think its a way of stamping identity — which I think is important too, but . . ."

Language as a vehicle for ethnic political mobilisation is not a new phenomenon and has been characteristic of a number of political struggles in recent decades (see for example Giles, 1977; Giles and Saint-Jacques, 1979) not least in Wales. Such linguistic demands are here clearly recognised as divisive, and the hope that local radio may provide a forum for articulating and facilitating minority identity is 'political' and hence not to be permitted in the balanced neutrality of local radio.

At another station the programme controller saw the diversity of ethnic communities within the catchment area as inimical to the creation of a station persona. He felt that were a station to do programmes for all of the minority communities then:

> "you are not a very effective radio station. You are a radio station that puts out different programmes and you certainly don't build up any loyalty or any real sense of personality for the radio station. It's just a collection of programmes."

Additionally

> "Do you do it for everyone? Such audiences would not be enough to sustain a radio station either because it would really be getting into what I think is narrow broadcasting. So therefore if you were to put a programme out in Asian, or one in Chinese, one alienates such a vast audience anyway then, that you are really on a hiding to nothing".

We now see the professional concept which believes that a station's identity is more important that the identity of its listening audiences. This interviewee, a few sentences later encapsulated the brutal cultural arrogance which flows from the professional logics of local radio broadcasting in his short phrase:

> "I think its wrong to assume that a collection of minorities is a majority".

*Meaningful Speech!*

In local radio broadcasting it is clear that any minority constitutes a threat to the principle of audience maximisation; indeed two of the seven stations spoke of their scheduling strategy as being based on the notion of programming rather than specific programmes. Hence in the world of 'programming', broadcasting is an unbroken thread of music, comment, competition and news into which 'special interests' are distributed. It is a media variant on bussing: the dispersal of minorities in the hope that the assumed homogeneous majority will be less offended by their existence.

Other stations do have specific programmes for ethnic minorities in their area, ranging over, for example, weekly commitments of nine hours forty-five minutes, two hours forty-five minutes, four and a half hours and five hours. As has already been pointed out, however, within these hours committed to ethnic minority interests the vast majority of programme time is committed to music. As one programme controller remarks of their programmes for ethnic minority communities:

"... the evidence we have is that the Asian programme is a mixture of film music, as ever, and announcements; which is not frightfully adventurous in this day and age — and I think the Afro-Caribbean programme again is very patchy. Sometimes it has some very good, some excellent speech items which are relevant to the community. It tends to rely very much on soul and reggae to get it through, which I am not sure again is the best use of the time they have".

In another station which produces approximately five hours per week for the 'Asian' audience, four of these five one-hour programmes are almost entirely music. In the words of one of the producer-presenters:

"So music is actually the base of the programme, they must have at least forty-five minutes music . . . We play about eight to ten records a day. Say in one hour we have ten minutes advertising and three minutes for news and five minutes for speech, so thats divided. So its nearly forty-two minutes music".

The world of local radio ethnic minority broadcasting is predominantly a mute world of cultural reference achieved through the massage of musical tastes. Music cannot be written off as an insubstantial opiate for minority palates. It clearly has very significant political implications in facilitating group identification (see for example Hebdige, 1979). Yet such an exclusion of the spoken word does permit a strangely circumscribed universe of discourse. It facilitates a symbolic and effective identification with group identity and through lyrics is able to rehearse the shibboleths of group ideology. It is a language of group identification and gesture, rather than of analysis. This is not to say that it is inherently conservative, pop music and reggae would disconfirm such a view. Yet whilst music may confirm identity and challenge orthodoxy it is not a tool which advances analysis of socio-political phenomena at a sophisticated level.

*Resources and Responsibility*

What 'meaningful speech' there is has its own constraints. Firstly, the very great majority of programme producers and presenters of ethnic minority programmes are freelance or volunteers who are fully employed in other jobs. The freelance people are paid as little as under £15 per programme and in some stations they are viewed as volunteers who receive only expenses. They are usually given minimal expenses and no back-up staff of researchers. Hence the resource base for serious current affairs analysis does not exist. Hence our examination of local radio broadcasting for ethnic minorities echoes the previously cited quotation of the Local Radio Workshop (1983b) report which concluded that local radio stations:

". . . offered what they could produce cheaply and easily . . ."

Whilst the budgetry constraints are very real there is a further very significant control on the content of the spoken word, namely station policy. As we have seen balance is heavily invoked in legitimating the control of broadcast material, and we have also seen that the interests of 'the majority' heavily inform the shaping of programme content. In all the stations there is a chain of command in which the ethnic minority producer-presenters are directly responsible to a member of the station management. The interviews indicated that the management felt that proper recruitment, experience and a few salutory 'shots-across-the-bow' seemed to have produced a good working relationship between management and the freelance ethnic minority staff. This was also echoed in the interviews with these producer-presenters, the majority of whom expressed satisfaction with their relation to management. With the absence of security of the freelance staff, and the pull of personal job satisfaction, status or ambition this collusion of professional practice is weighted heavily in favour of management. As one person responsible for overseeing the ethnic minority programmes said of the producer-presenters:

"They can do anything they like within reason as long as they consult me first".

Another person with comparable responsibilities in another station said this of possible conflicts of interest between presenters and management:

"No these things are usually disagreed about before they go out on air. Because if a presenter has something which he feels is a grey area, then he will talk to me about it first. And, if its not something which should go to air then I say no — thats the way it works. The presenters are responsible people, they know what job they have got to do, and they know basically what is right and what is wrong for the particular audience that they are broadcasting to".

The presenters may be 'responsible people' but it is clear from the interviews that their essential responsibility is to the radio station rather than their community. Disputes and grey areas can only be settled on the station's terms. As another station programme controller says:

"The only people that make programmes on this radio station are 'broadcasters', so we don't get problems. I think they understand the issues, or sometimes we have got to lead them a bit, but they understand the issues, they understand what the station demands in terms of content and presentation".

Thus the content of local radio ethnic minority broadcasting is regulated by institutional practices which reflect the dominant white hegemony, and are interpreted and enforced by white management whose experience and sensibilities are more in accord with these interests and values than with the experience of black ethnic minority communities in Britain.

*Conclusion*

To conclude by returning to the recommendations of the U. N. E. S. C. O. conference with which we opened this chapter, local radio is singularly failing in advancing the human rights of ethnic minorities in Britain. As we have seen in the earlier review the national press and television effectively exclude black British and ethnic minority participation, and do not reflect their experience of life in Britain. It might have been hoped that *local* radio would have been able to break this lamentable consensus. Clearly our analysis does not allow such a conclusion. Linguistic diversity is perceived more as a threat than a challenging responsibility at the local level, and hence the possibility of receiving regular information in their own language is currently very circumscribed and may even recede further. The possibility of receiving 'information' in depth is almost entirely pre-empted by budgetry constraints and scheduling strategies. Whilst the local radio stations have facilitated the participation of ethnic minority personnel in programme production and presentation it is as subordinate auxilliaries who are maintained in a state of technical impermanence, regardless of the number of years of continuous work they have given to the station. Local radio broadcasting for ethnic minorities is a continuation of the shallow tokenism which has characterised British social policy over the last four decades.

*Bibliography*

Allen, S. (1982). Confusing categories and neglecting contradictions. In *Black Youth in Crisis*, E. Cashmore and B. Troyna (eds.), George Allen & Unwin: London.
Anwar, M. (1978). *Who Tunes in to What*. London: Commission for Racial Equality.
Anwar, M. (1980). *Votes and Policies*. London: Commission for Racial Equality.
Anwar, M. and Shang, A. (1982). *Television in a Multi-Racial Society*. London: Commission for Racial Equality.
Banton, M. and Harwood, J. (1975). *The Race Concept*. Newton Abbot: David & Charles.
Barker, M. (1981). *The New Racism*. London: Junction Books.
B. B. C. (1972). *Non-Whites on British Television*. London: B. B. C. Audience Research Department.
Bourne, J. (1980). Cheerleaders and Ombudsmen: The sociology of race relations in Britain. *Race and Class* 21 (4), 331–352.
Braham, P. (1982a). *Migration and Settlement in Britain*. Course E354, Block 1, Unit 2: Ethnic Minorities and Community Relations. Milton Keynes: Open University Press.
Braham, P. (1982b). How the media report race. In *Culture, Society and the Media*, M. Gurevitch et al (eds.). London: Methuen.
Butterworth, E. (1966). The smallpox outbreak in the British press. *Race* 7, 347–364.
Carby, H. V. (1982). Schooling in Babylon. In *The Empire Strikes Back*, Centre for Contemporary Cultural Studies. London: Hutchinson.
Cashmore, E. (1979). *Rastaman*. London: George Allen & Unwin.
Centre for Contemporary Cultural Studies (1982). *The Empire Strikes Back*. London: Hutchinson.
Chibnall, S. (1977). *Law and Order News*. London: Tavistock.
Cohen, P. and Gardner, C. (1982) *It ain't half racist mum*. London: Comedia.
Cohen, S. (1973). *Folk Devils and Moral Panics*. London: Paladin.
Critcher, C., Parker, M. and Sondhi, R. (1977). Race in the Provincial press: a case study of five West Midlands newspapers. In *Ethnicity and the Media*, U. N. E. S. C. O. Paris.
Curtis, L. P. (1971). *Apes and Angels*. Newton Abbot: David & Charles.
Dhondy, F. (1983). A future for Britain's black theatre. In *The Race Today Review*. London: Race Today Publications.
Downing, J. (1980). *The Media Machine*. London: Pluto Press.
Edholm, F., Roberts, H. and Sayer, J. (1983). *Vietnamese Refugees in Britain*. London: Commission for Racial Equality.
Equity Coloured Artists' Committee (1974). *Coloured Artists on British Television*. London: British Actors' Equity Association.
Evans, P. (1976). *Published and be Damned?* London: Runnymede Trust.

Foot, P. (1965). *Immigration and Race in British Politics*. Harmondsworth: Penguin.
Freeth, T. (1982). T.V. colonialism. In *It ain't half racist mum*, P. Cohen and C. Gardner (eds). London: Comedia.
Gardner, C. (1981). Black employment in the media. *Multiracial Education*, 9 (2), 69—74.
Garrard, J. A. (1971). *The English and Immigration 1880—1910*. London: Oxford University Press.
Gartner, L. P. (1960). *The Jewish Immigrant to Britain 1870—1914*. London: George Allen & Unwin.
Geipel, J. (1969). *The Europeans: An Ethnohistorical Survey*. London: Longmans.
Giles, H. (1977). *Language, Ethnicity and Intergroup Relations*. London: Academic Press.
Giles, H. and Saint-Jacques, B. (1979). *Language and Ethnic Relations*. Oxford: Pergamon Press.
Gilroy, P. (1982). Steppin' out of Babylon — race, class and autonomy. In *The Empire Strikes Back*, Centre for Contemporary Cultural Studies. London: Hutchinson.
Gilroy, P. (1983). Channel Four — Bridgehead or Bantustan. *Screen* 24 (4/5) 130—137.
Hall, S., Critcher, C., Jefferson, T., Clarke, J. & Roberts, B. (1978). *Policing the Crisis*. London: Macmillan.
Hartmann, P. and Husband, C. (1971). The mass media and racial conflict. *Race* 12 (3). 267—82.
Hartmann, P. and Husband, C. (1974). *Racism and the Mass Media*. London: Davis-Poynter.
Hartmann, P., Husband, C. and Clark, J. (1974). Race as news: a study in the handling of race in the British national press from 1963 to 1970. In *Race as News*. Paris: The U. N. E. S. C. O. Press.
Hebdige, D. (1979). *Subculture: The Meaning of Style*. London: Methuen.
Hill, M. J. and Issacharoff, R. M. (1971). *Community Action and Race Relations*. London: Oxford University Press.
Holland, P. (1981). The New Cross fire and the popular press. *Multiracial Education*, 9 (3) 60—80.
Holmes, C. (1978). *Immigrants and Minorities in British Society*. Harmondsworth: Penguin.
Humphry, D. and Ward, M. (1974). *Passports and Politics*. Harmondsworth: Penguin.
Hujanen, T. (1980). *The Role of Information in the Realisation of the Human Rights of Migrant Workers*, Department of Journalism and Mass Communication, University of Tampere, Finland.
Hujanen, T. (ed) (1984). *The Role of Information in the Realisation of the Human Rights of Migrant Workers*. Report of International Conference, Tampere, June 1983. Department of Journalism and Mass Communication, University of Tampere, Finland.
Hurst, C. (1982). Black bookselling and publishing London. *The Bookseller*, February 20th, 620—624.
Husband, C. (1975). Racism in society and the mass media: a critical interaction. In *White Media and Black Britain*, C. Husband (ed). London: Arrow.
Husband, C. (1977). News media, language and race relations: A case study in identity maintenance. In *Language, Ethnicity and Intergroup Relations*, Giles, H. (ed). London: Academic Press.
Husband, C. (1979). Some aspects of the interaction of British entertainment media with contemporary race relations. In *Entertainment: A Cross-Cultural Comparison*, H. D. Fischer and S. R. Melnik (eds). New York: Hastings House.
Husband, C. (1980). Culture, context and practice: Racism in social work. In *Radical Social Work and Practice*, M. Brake and R. Bailey (eds). London: Edward Arnold.
Husband, C. (1982a), Race, the continuity of a concept. In *Race in Britain: Continuity and Change*, C. Husband (ed). London: Hutchinson.
Husband, C. (1982b). *Race, Identity and British Society*. Course E354, Block 2, Units 5—6: Ethnic Minorities and community Relations. Milton Keynes: Open University Press.
John, E. (1981). *In the Service of Black Youth*. Leicester: National Association of Youth Clubs.
Jones, M. and Dungey, J. (1983). *Ethnic Monorities and Television*. University of Leicester: Centre for Mass Communication Research.
Joshua, H., Wallace, T. and Booth, H. (1983). *To Ride the Storm: The 1980 Bristol 'Riots' and the State*. London: Heinemann.
Katnelson, I. (1973). *Black Men, White Cities*. London: Oxford University Press.

Khan, N. (1980). *Britain's New Arts*. London: Commission for Racial Equality.
Kuepper, W. G., Lackey, E. L. and Swinerton, E. N. (1975). *Ugandan Asians in Great Britain*. London: Croom Helm.
Lawrence, E. (1982). In the abundance of water the fool is thirsty: sociology and black 'pathology'. In *The Empire Strikes Back*, Centre for Contemporary Cultural Studies. London: Hutchinson.
Local Radio Workshop (1983a). *Capital — Local Radio and Private Profit*. London: Comedia.
Local Radio Workshop (1983b). *Nothing Local About It: London's Local Radio*. London: Comedia.
Lunn, K. (ed) (1980). *Hosts, Immigrants and Minorities: Historical Responses to Newcomers in British Society 1870–1914*. London: Dawson.
MASS (1982). *MASS Register*. London: MASS.
McCann, E. (1973). The British press and Northern Ireland. In *The Manufacture of News*, S. Cohen and J. Young (eds). London: Constable.
Miles, R. (1982). *Racism and Migrant Labour*. London: Routledge & Kegan Paul.
Minority Press Group (1980a). *Where is the Other News?* London: Minority Press Group.
Minority Press Group (1980b). *The Other Secret Service: Press Distributors and Press Censorship*. London: Minority Press Group.
Morris, G. (1982). Black Media Workers Association. In *It ain't half racist mum*, P. Cohen and C. Gardner (eds). London: Comedia.
Morrison, L. (1975). A black journalist's experience of British journalism. In *White Media and Black Britain*, C. Husband (ed). London: Arrow.
Morrison, L. (1976). *As They See It*. London: Community Relations Council.
Mullard, C. (1982). The state's response to racism: Towards a relational explanation. In *Community Work and Racism*, A. Ohri et al. London: Routledge & Kegan Paul.
Pascall, A. (1982). Black autonomy and the B. B. C. In *It ain't half racist mum*, P. Cohen and C. Gardner (eds). London: Comedia.
Phizacklea, A. and Miles, R. (1980). *Labour and Racism*. London: Routledge and Kegan Paul.
Postgate, R. and Vallance, A. (1937). *'Those Foreigners'*. London: Harrap
Race and the media. A special issue of *Multiracial Education* 9 (2) Spring 1981.
Ratcliffe, P. (1981). *Racism and Reaction*. London: Routledge & Kegan Paul.
Reeves, F. (1984). *British Racial Discourse*. Cambridge University Press.
Rex, J and Tomlinson, S. (1979). *Colonial Immigrants in a British City*. London: Routledge & Kegan Paul.
Rose, E. J. B. et al (1969). *Colour and Citizenship: A Report on British Race Relations*. London: Oxford University Press.
Saakana, A. S. (1982). Channel Four and the black community. In *What's This Channel Four?* S. Blanchard and D. Morley. London: Comedia.
Saifullah Khan, V. (1982). The role of the culture of dominance in structuring the experience of ethnic minorities. In *Race in Britain* C. Husband (ed). London: Hutchinson.
Shabazz, M. (1976). The Fosters: from embarrassment to insult. *Grass Roots* 4 (8), 10.
Shamsher, J. S. and Russell, R. (1976). Punjabi journalism in Britain: a blackground. *New Community* 5, 211–221.
Sharf, A. (1964). *The British Press and News under Nazi Rule*, Institute of Race Relations. London: Oxford University Press.
Singh, R. (1979). A Study of the Punjabi press in Britain. *The Asian* 1 (12). 7–10.
Sivanandan, A. (1979). Race, class and the state: the black experience in Britain. *Race and Class* 17 (4), 347–368.
Smith, D: J. (1977). *Racial Disadvantage in Britain*. Harmondsworth: Penguin.
Stone, M. (1981). *The Education of the Black Child in Britain*. Glasgow: Fontana.
Tambs-Lyche, H. (1980). *London Patidars*. London: Routledge & Kegan Paul.
Troyna, B. (1977). The reggae war. *New Society* 10th March 1977. Vol. 39, 491–492.
Troyna, B. (1978). *Rastafarianism, Reggae and Racism*. Derby: National Association for Multiracial Education.
Troyna, B. (1981). *Public Awareness and the Media*. London: Commission for Racial Equality.

Troyna, B. (1982). Reporting the National Front: British values observed. In *Race in Britain*, C. Husband (ed). London: Hutchinson.
Tumber, H. (1982). *Television and the Riots*. London: British Film Institute.
Walker, M. (1977). *The National Front*. London: Fontana.

JOHN D. H. DOWNING

# 'Coillons ... Shryned in an Hogges Toord':[1] British News Media Discourse on 'Race'

An analysis of racist discourse in British media has the benefit of a substantial literature, unlike the USA, where — curiously or not so curiously — work in this area has been very meagre[2]. I propose therefore to begin with a rapid overview and partial critique of existing British studies, and then to analyse 'elite' press discourse around a brief but highly significant moment in the British politics of 'race' during the early 1980s: the publication in November 1981 of the government's Scarman Report on the Brixton disturbances of the previous April.

*1. Studies of racism and the media in Britain*

One of the better achievements of British social science over the past ten years in the analysis of 'race' — given also some notable nadirs — has been the work done in this area. It has been demonstrated quite systematically that the obvious intuition is correct, namely that the media daily renew the direct stereotypes and associated ideological clusters — law-and-order, social problems, the colonial past — which box citizens of African, Asian and Caribbean descent into debasing categories. Hartmann and Husband (1974), Hartmann, Husband and Clark (1974), Critcher, et al. (1977), have all carried out surveys which repeatedly document the media definition of black communities as 'problems' rather than as enriching British life, as 'immigrants'

---

[1] The title I have given this chapter is taken from some angry remarks addressed by the Innkeeper to the Pardoner, both of them characters among the pilgrims of Chaucer's Canterbury Tales. The words are taken from the closing lines of the Pardoner's Tale, and readers are directed to them for the full flavour of the exchange. 'Coillons', a term of intimate abuse, survives in the French *couillon*, the Italian *coglione* and the Spanish *cojones*. 'Hogges' means 'of a pig', just conceivably of Celtic origin. 'Toord', however, is indisputably Anglo-Saxon, and turns up later in this chapter in its contemporary spelling, in connection with a policeman's unfortunate accident in the street. The pardoner was one of the least likeable of the pilgrims, making his living by selling fake relics and papal pardons (indulgences). I am not sure we have seen the last of him.
[2] The best analysis by far is by Tom Englehardt (1971), hidden away in a hard-to-find journal. See more recently Stam and Spence (1983).

rather than as contributive members of the body politic. Hall, et al. (1978: chs. 1—4) have drawn attention to the development of a new category, 'mugging', drawn from images of US urban violence, which has the effect of homogenising in white consciousness the varied forms of alienation of young black people born in the UK, and faced with the protracted crisis of the 70s and 80s. Elliott (1972) analysed the production process of a liberal TV current affairs series on racial prejudice, demonstrating the painful distance of the well-meaning programme producers from the daily realities of their subject-matter. Foot (1965) and Butterworth (1967) studied the local press in various parts of the country, and found by and large a depressingly antagonistic presentation of black people. Troyna (1981) found a slightly more mixed picture, with local papers in South East London and in Leicester sharply contrasting with each other. (His analysis of the apparently non-racist local programming in two cities in the same study is not indicative of a wider experience: one only has to think of the intensive use made by fascist groups of phone-in programmes to recognise that he was a prisoner of his methodology in this instance.) Downing (1975) analysed the rarity with which TV asked black people their views on issues directly affecting them, either in Britain or overseas. Husband (1979) drew attention to the role of racist humour in media entertainment and conversation in general, in sustaining racist stereotypes. Downing (1980b: ch. 4) recapitulated a series of these themes, and also dissected the infrequency and inadequacy of media coverage of racial discrimination, the poverty of TV interviewing in this area, and the international dimension of black images in the media.

Most recently Holland (1981) has produced an exceptionally acute analysis of media handling of the racist firebomb attack in London's New Cross in January 1981, Tumber (1982) has produced a monograph on TV handling of the disturbances later in 1981, and Troyna (1982) an account of press presentation of the fascist National Front.

Whatever changes and sophistication may emerge in British media in the future, the fact remains that over a generation most have helped sustain the colonial images of the white elderly, have helped nourish the racist hostilities of economically active whites, and have helped induce white youth into new versions of old untruths. Their impact on black people has yet to be properly analysed. Nonetheless, it remains important to extend the critique of racist media culture into new realms. Building a counter-hegemony of insight and analysis requires a sustained determination, a dogged patience, which professional academics are in a very favourable structural position to sustain. In that spirit I will offer a partial critique of the work done, including my own, not in order to dismiss it but in order to take stock. I shall divide my summary comments into the following categories: audience analysis; the importance of entertainment genres; the experience of black journalists; and contextualising media content in history, in political and economic change, and in ideological and discursive nodes.

(a) *Audience analysis.* The pioneering work was done in this area by Hartmann and Husband (1974), who established the fundamental significance of media for white people as an information source about black people, through the discovery of the homogeneity of reactions between those with high, low and no physical proximity to black communities.

However, the impact of white media on black audiences has been far less studied. This is largely because the analysts have been white, and correctly distrustful of their ability to analyse black responses sensitively. The beginning of an understanding are offered by the Ven. Wilfred Wood's reactions th the media as a conscious black person (1975), and by Tumber's (1982) notes on the anger of young black people at journalists' normal lack of interest in their lives or views. This is a task which could very well be untertaken, not in order to 'leak' the private realm of black communities, but to amplify their unheard anger at the images thrown at them in the media.

'Class' is a further key aspect of audience analysis. Almost all the work done has presumed not only a racially homogeneous audience, but also a class-less one. Although I shall be arguing below that racist discourse is a powerfully unifrying element in Britsh culture, it is still the case that it operates differently for readers of *The Times* to viewers of News At Ten. The fact that the ultimate content is the same does not mean its impact would be the same given an identical form of discourse. These different levels of discourse are sometimes subtle, but nonetheless all the more influential for that. (These remarks also have implications for (b) and (d) below.)

Lastly, it is very positive that the study of black media is being taken up (see Husband's and Chouhan's contribution to this volume). The deduction could easily be drawn otherwise, from a certain silence, that media are merely what impinge on black communities, themselves incapable of independent, let alone combative, mass communication. The fact the major media are very nearly a white ghetto in Britain is not the be-all and end-all of the story.

(b) *Entertainment.* Husband (1979) produced the only real contribution to understanding this aspect of racism and the media, in his contribution noted already. Yet the media are principally used for recreation (including sports and music), so that to dwell on the most cognitive-rational component is a major lapse of those of us who have worked in this area (a lapse I fear that I do not remedy in this chapter). Fantasy, humour, drama, sport: perhaps only social scientists, trained to think of culture as "high", and of art as individual aesthetic thrills, could pass over these quite as casually as we have done. At the same time, a caveat for the statistically minded: this material will never be successfully analysed by chi-square . . .

(c) *Black Journalists.* Few and far between as black journalists are in the major media, they are a unique resource of information on media organisational practices and pretences. Apart from Elliott's study noted already, nothing exists on the organisational dimension of this issue (except for Morrison

1975). It needs exposure, not as a series of racist plots, but as the institutional racism of 'established media custom' operating effortlessly to exclude black concerns from the agenda. (With painstaking disguise, for their professional protection, these journalists can pinpoint with accuracy what white researchers might never see at all.)

(d) *Contextualising*. The historical contextualisation has been done well. The roots of media stereotypes in the colonial past have been given due emphasis and documentation (Husband 1975 and 1982; Barker 1981: ch. 4), so that media images of black people are not interpreted as the instant creations of individually prejudiced imaginations. The contextualisation of images in current political and economic change has been rather harder, with Hall, et al. (1978) being the only ones to try to link new racist themes to base trends in the British political economy. Its problem, which Hall, et al. do not avoid in the body of their book, is that such analysis can degenerate into a series of overly generalised assertions. Nonetheless, attentiveness to shifts in discourse and their relation to other societal develpoments is very important, if only not to be always left arguing last year's or the previous decade's battles.

As regards the contextualisation of media images in the production of discourses, there has developed a whole industry of discourse analysis in general, to the point where the term itself has become ridiculously fetishised. Here I will make one brief explanatory remark. By 'discourse' I mean 'ideology-in-verbal-process-of-construction' (I cannot enter now into its relation with non-verbal communication). In the context of this chapter, the concern will be to establish how the discourse around racism is often displaced in 'elite' media in favour of alternative discourses.

I should like to comment briefly on the bearing of some recent work on this subject. In their different ways, Barker (1981), Husband (1977), Reeves (1983), Gilroy (1982) and Parmar (1982), have all contributed to this debate. Barker has clearly shown the effective operation of apparently non-racist discourses, around 'the British nation' and sociobiology, as racist discourses. Reeves has produced a much more cumbersome account of similar phenomena in politicians' discourse in House of Commons debates over immigration. Husband has explored components of "national" discourse in relation to imperial history and the myth of English tolerance for new arrivals. Gilroy has extended our understanding of how the law-and-order discourse relates to racist discourse from the initial analysis of Hall, et al. (1978), and Parmar has valuably illuminated the interpenetrations between racist and sexist discourse.

What emerges from these studies is the recognition that (1) racist discourse overlaps with many others, which might be argued to overdetermine its existential significances, but that (2) often racism and black people are absent in explicit terms, as though they were *the* great unmentionable. It is as though in certain circles the only crime people will not confess to is racism, the only systematic oppression on British soil that will not be admitted is of black people. Women's oppression, even, will be more readily discussed.

Yet on a little further reflection, we find that this deflection of the issues is far more characteristic of classes grouped around the power structure that it is of others. Liberal members of the former category are perpetually taken aback by the blunt brutality of racist discourse among many white workers. What is grossly in error is to see this as a 'primitive grunt' (John Rex, quoted by Reeves (1983: 75), as compared to the 'articulate' discourses of political figures (Reeves' focus). This judgment represents the imposition of an early Basil Bernstein argument about restricted and elaborated codes on the subject-matter, and arguably emerges from a class-based respect for what often turns out to be politicians' waffle, as contrasted to the straightforward utterances of less circumspect speakers. The significant difference is, on consideration, in effect. The discourse of politicians has legislative consequences.

(The technical communicative skill of Powell's speeches lay in his ability to conduct these two discourses simultaneously. When he said in Birmingham on April 20th 1968, 'Like the Roman, I seem to see 'the River Tiber foaming with much blood' (Smithies and Fiddick 1969: 43), one audience could respond to his classical allusion, but the other instantly caught the basic message: 'foaming with blood.' The former could classify him, as many did, as too highly educated to be really a racist, whereas the latter could take to the streets in his defence because he was speaking for them.)

The reasons for this 'strategic de-racialisation' (Reeves) are important to fathom. I would suggest that a combination of three factors has brought it about in the public discourse of circles of power. One is the Holocaust, from which mercifully now — unforgivably not at the time — all responsible politicians are bound to shrink in horror. The second is the seismic nature of anti-colonial movements across the planet in this century. The third is that in the ongoing contest for global legitimacy, racism in western countries is intensively used by the Soviet bloc as a demonstration of the hollowness of western claims to be real democracies. The charge is impossible to answer, and is likely to be felt in political circles more than elsewhere. The gap between public de-racialisation and private opinions can be seen to be much less in rightwing circles, whether of the Conservative Party in Britain, or of leading political figures (Chirac, Poniatowski and others) in France, than in the centre or centre-left.

In this chapter I shall be focussing on 'elite' readership media. I would only emphasise that the communication lines and the discourse linkages between these circles of power and the great mass of the more plain-speaking population are in place, even if they are rarely so directly fused together as Powell has managed to do on this issue (not, it must be noted, on others). And there lies the nexus: racist discourse, whether direct or inflected, whether pure or — more usually — overdetermined by other discourses, is a great, perhaps the greatest, unifier of British cultures in the contemporary period.

The British discourse of self-definition pivots on it, whether in philosophy or the pub, whether in the psyche or in more superficial exchanges.

*2. The Publication of the Scarman Report*

Government reports of one kind or another get issued all the time, a large number destined only to yellow on shelves. They all tend to be written in the same godlike tone, summoning fealty without ever explicitly demanding it. The reasonable, orderly, decently educated citizen is presumed to be soberly reading them, drawn inexorably by their socratic logic to share their policy conclusions. Of course, different governments produce conflicting reports to bolster their varying policies — but still, each and every one is couched in the same serene tone, seemingly rejoicing in effortless objectivity.

For Lord Scarman, veteran official report writer on conflicts in Northern Ireland, on the 1975 Red Lion Square demonstration in which Kevin Gately was killed by the police, on the 1977 pitched battles outside the Grunwick factory in Willesden, to write the official report on the 1981 events in Britain's cities was his largest assignment to date (since Northern Ireland is never seemingly regarded as part of Britain by the British). How was the customary Olympian judgment to be married to emergency and crisis? Normal blandness clearly would not suffice, yet the whole truth was unlikely to be on the agenda either.

A critique of the Report's text is outside this study's scope, but does not matter too much anyway. Since the volume cost eight pounds, it was its media rendition which constituted the Scarman Report for all but a tiny few. Here we will be concerned with how three 'elite' media presented the power structure's response to substantial political turbulence with a 'racial' dimension. The moment was supercharged: on the one side the police, an ever more dominant branch of the state, the proud symbol of British order; on the other, the resistance of black communities, the Achilles' heel of traditional claims that Britain is a universally fair and humane society. The Report and its media rendition crystallised the power structure's response to the events, and communicated to segments of the classes closest to it (in the case of these three newspapers) that it was still in control of events. In turn, however, these readers were being told what might have to be changed in order to retain that control. (We shall not find constructive realism in the proposals for change, but that is another matter.)

The three media selected were *The Times*, *The Guardian* and *The Economist*. *The Times* continues to be the newspaper most read in official circles for official purposes: the newspaper of record. *The Guardian* is read by that segment of the power structure most likely to support certain reforms and a greater measure of social justice. *The Economist* is read by many economic decisionmakers, and by the more perceptive conservatives in politics.

Together, their readers represent the major strands of thinking opinion within the power structure. (*The Daily Telegraph* represents, with great effectiveness, the block-headed backwoodsmen of the British power structure, for whom thought is often painful: we shall not chip away at them here.)

*3. The Times*

The tenor of two articles *The Times* ran the day before the Report's publication was one of reassurance. Support for the police was reiterated in the one, and in the second the putative radicalism of the upcoming Report was implied to be only a necessary defusing action for the sake of public peace. Readers were being what the Americans call 'orientated'.

*On patrol with 'pig in the middle'*

The apostrophised words bear two allusions. One is to the title of a popular children's game for three, in which one stands in the middle and tries to intercept a ball thrown back and forth by the other two. Being in the middle is pretty tiresome unless you are tall. The second allusion is to 'pig' as an epithet for the police. What the headline indicated, therefore, was the classical 'thin blue line' ideology of the police function: whatever mischief they get up to, whatever outrages they commit, they are still necessary to protect social order.

The staffer, Roger Berthoud, described his two days spent with the Brixton police, in terms which graphically underpinned this ideology. The police were all described in glowing terms: 'Inspector Jane Forbes, the duty officer, takes a series of decisions with impressive crispness in her Stirling accent'; 'Commander Fairbairn, a man of considerable bonhomie and humour who was felled by a brick in the riots, but rose to lead his men again'; 'Chief Superintendent Marsh, a lean, handsome 41-year-old'; 'Superintendent Finlay MacLennan... A soft-spoken Highland Scot, he describes himself as the link man between the police and the community'; PC Brian Elliott... the epitome of the gentle giant and the friendly neighbourhood bobby.'

Here then were these decent human beings keeping the great unwashed in line for the rest of us: '... no area of Britain has a higher rate of mugging, predominantly of white females by black males'; '... they cannot go in without risk to their lives, if few in number, or the danger of causing a riot, if they enter in strength'; 'PC Elliott's luminous niceness 'had not prevented him from nearly being killed in the second July riots'; '... how taxing it is to be exposed daily to some of Western man's least loveable activities. In Brixton that exposure is particularly intense.' The themes of white women being in danger from black savages, of the heroic police caught between doing their duty and being blamed for riots, of even the angel-cop being the target of vicious violence, were enough to frighten *The Times'* readers badly.

Indeed, Berthoud took them into a situation which would undoubtedly cause them to shudder if their gentle persons were to be exposed to it. Driving in a squad car, they came across some black teenagers kicking a white teenager on some vacant ground. Berthoud handled the scene with fastidious tongs, but evident relish. In the process of breaking up the incident, one policeman apparently fell fair and square in some dog turd. Another, rescuing the white youth from the teenagers, 'held on to the object (Irish and reeking of drink) of their attentions.' The smells in the car taking the youths back to the station were lovingly evoked. Black violence and the traditional drunken Irish are potent symbols of the world 'beyond the pale' that the police, society's refuse-disposal agents, keep in some kind of manageable condition on behalf of upright *Times* readers. Wrote Berthoud:

> '. . . they can easily come to see themselves as an under-appreciated oasis of order and discipline in a sea of indifference, hostility and active nastiness.'

How did *The Times'* correspondent refer to the black community in Brixton? We have already noted his repeated confirmation of its violent character. His article never made any reference to any crime committed by a white person in Brixton. One young black woman was 'complimented' in sexist terms: 'a pretty black girl wanting to stand bail for her brother.' For the rest, out came the fastidious, ironic tongs again:

> 'L District, under Commander Brian Fairbairn, whose impoverished kingdom of 10.6 square miles and 250,000 souls (roughly a quarter *"ethnics or descendants" in the jargon*) embraces Streatham (and other areas).' (My emphasis.)

There is no reference anywhere in Berthoud's article to a single grievance, justified or not, against the police.

The black experience of being handled like a conquered, subject population in Brixton in Swamp '81 and during other police forays and 'exercises' too numerous to mention, was not even hinted at in the story.

For *The Times'* reader, then, this piece comfortably confirmed not only the necessity of the police, not only their basic decency, but also the reasons why they might sometimes run amok. If the reader disapproved of their patience running out, then would s/he wish to do their work? These latter implications were never stated, but in the context of a report critical of police behaviour in certain respects due the next day, they did not need to be. The ground was being prepared.

We should not forget however the senior police officials who were also the target-readers of this article, leaders of an ever more influential branch of the state. They too needed reassurance from the rest of the governing class that their interests were not about to be disregarded.

*What makes this judge the one to sort out the mess?*

Lord Scarman's portrait took up considerable space in the second piece. Underneath this headline there was a large photograph of him throwing back his head in laughter in the company of a black cricketer and the cricketer's two children. This was captioned *Lord Scarman among friends: '125 out of 100 for public relations.'*

The headline was clearly designed to begin to let the readership anticipate that Augean stables were about to be cleaned — judiciously. The second half of the caption to the photograph actually came closer to the truth of the matter, indicating that the demonstration of an *image* of official concern ('public relations') with black rights was about as tangible a long-term response as black communities could expect. This subterranean tension in the discourse resurfaced at other points in the article, and probably served to soothe the readership's fears. *Drastic action was to be taken.* But not really drastic. (And not really action.) Again, the skill of the presentation was that this vital dialectic was conveyed without ever being explicitly stated.

The photograph of Scarman with a black cricketer, laughing uproariously, was redolent of a nostalgic perception of *sporting* contests, of a *British* sport exported to the West Indies, of British fair play and judicial rectitude, and of the humorous common humanity of the 'traditional' older generation of West Indians and kindly avuncular Brits. The first half of the caption — *Lord Scarman among friends* — told the reader the Report would in some sense be pro-black, but since he was photographed in this context, *The Times'* readership could more or less rest in peace.

The article's text emphasised throughout Scarman's appetite for trouble-shooting (Northern Ireland, etc), as well as his energetic commitment to a revised legal system for Britain in the shape of a Bill of Rights, with a consequently greater political influence for judges: 'there is a political animal just beneath the judge's robes.' Subheads in the piece were *Religious instinct is very deep* and *'Too committed to particular views.'* Scarman's self-description as 'without using capital letters liberal and radical' was cited. The basic message appeared to be that a very distinguished, potentially somewhat maverick individual was the best person to handle this particular crisis. Not a man for all seasons, but uniquely equipped for this one.

Thus reassured, *The Times'* readers the next day were deluged with material on the Report. What may they be thought to have learned from the deluge about the situation of black people in Britain, or their relation to the police? Or about the relevance of the Report's proposals for reform of the police?

The answer is that the little front page cartoon pierced to the heart of the matter in a way quite untypical of the rest of the coverage. The cartoon showed a police constable walking along, serenely untouched by a copy of the Scarman Report bouncing harmlessly off his high helmet, having been thrown at him like a velvet brickbat from a unknown hand. Political cartoonists are traditionally given licence in the press to dissent somewhat from the editorial line, and this was a classic case in point. It said everything in a nutshell, yet was of course unable to argue its statement.

For the rest, the predominant impression created was of worthy public figures, hands on hearts, insisting on their profound recognition of the truths of Scarman. *The Times* certainly could not be accused of suffering from an overdose of journalistic scepticism in its handling of the matter. All statements were taken at face value, with the exception of the editor of *Race Today* whose arguments were explicitly disvowed in the editorial (see below).

The Report itself was hailed as a masterpiece, dripping with wisdom and accuracy. Not everyone was completely pleased with it, but in the tradition of the moderate centre always being confirmed as correct by its rejection from the fringes, that disagreement simply reaffirmed its acceptability. Let us see how this image was achieved.

*Scarman's plan for racial peace wins wide backing*

With this page 1 lead headline, a consensus was instantly anounced. It was noted that the police were offering 'qualified support' and that the Report had 'disappointed some representatives of ethnic groups' — whether black or Ukrainian was not indicated — but that the government had accepted the Report 'promptly'. After all, qualified support is not rejection, nor is the disappointment of some representatives exactly a reason to bring the curtain down.

Scarman's position was summarised as even-handed: praise for the police, but emphasis on the need to reduce racial tension.

> 'Lord Scarman generally gives praise for a force that 'stood between our society and a total collapse of law and order'.'
> 'We have got to get our three or four societies into one society.'

The first theme is very familiar already, and acts as a leitmotif throughout the discourse. The second is phrased with significant ambiguity, for the word 'society', synonymous with social order in the first remark, slides into a quite different sense in the second. There is a crucial vagueness as to whether racial disadvantage is being addressed (in which case 'two societies' might be used, like Disraeli's 'two nations'), or whether cultural variation is the issue ('three or four' societies indicating Africans, Asians, West Indians, and the 'real' English). Was the target to be tolerance for diversity or a revolution in social justice? Even though the Report referred to positive discrimination in favour of black minorities, *The Times*' report of Scarman's interview with London Broadcasting (November 28th, p. 3) made it clear that by 'positive discrimination' he only meant special education for talented black individuals (more or less in line with the function of the old grammar schools for working class children). The ambiguity in the term 'three or four societies' was not inconsequential.

The other elements of the Report noted on the front page followed carefully the tradition of apportioning blame evenly. The police were blamed for

> 'instances of harassment and racial prejudice among junior officers on Brixton streets, which gave credibility and substance to critics of the police'

(was the latter their real offence?), and for failure to adjust their policies to a multi-racial situation. The community was blamed (by inference only the black community):

> 'The community and community leaders in particular must take their share of blame for the atmosphere of distrust and mutual suspicion between the police and the community.'

Politicians were blamed for not acting more effectively to reduce the 'disease' of racial disadvantage 'threatening the very survival of our society.'

In general, however, the police were commended for their restraint in the riots, in that no one was killed; and furthermore the presence of racism among senior officers was actually denied! (No comment from *The Times*.) Racial discrimination was noted as an offence marked down by the Report for punishment by dismissal from the force in the future, and random lay checks on police stations as another recommendation. 'Institutionalised racism' — never once defined by *The Times* — did not exist in Britain, but 'racial disadvantage and its nasty associate — discrimination — *have not yet been eliminated*' (my emphasis).

Insofar as the Report had a radical appearance, one must suppose that the two policy measures recommended, and the admission of racial disadvantage, were what constituted its radicalism. *The Times*, however, did not raise the reality of racism's pervasiveness in the police force, which would make dismissal for racial discrimination a rather large-scale, not to say problematic exercise. It gratefully accepted that racism was not entrenched in British society, either, and implied its elimination could be just a matter of a little more effort. Minor surgery could remove the cancer: it was not all over the patient's body.

The extraordinary distance of '*The Times*' from the realities it purported to be discussing with such authority was another major aspect of its coverage.

Lay checks on police stations, for example: would the 'inspectors' have enough authority to do their work? How would they know that a bruised, bleeding person in a cell had come by their injuries through police violence? How would they cope with intimidation of victims? The proposal was not a bad one, but '*The Times*' was totally uninterested in the practicalities.

*I'll act swiftly, says Whitelaw*

The second major lead commented on the government's response. The Home Secretary's photograph was captioned *Mr Whitelaw: Promises speedy action*. Specific measures were listed as accepted: more independent police complaint procedures, better police training, greater punishment for 'racially motivated behaviour', the proscription of racist marches. It all sounded crisp, clean and efficient, a little at odds indeed with the impression normally asociated with Mr Whitelaw.

Reading on a little further, however, the text of the article became a little less crisp. The Commons debate was presented as rowdy, almost reflecting the street confrontations it was supposed to transcend:

> '... the roars, growls and grunts from the jungles on both sides of the House ...'

Mr Whitelaw, however, was presented as striding masterfully through the confusion, fully accepting

> 'the discouragement in the report for the concept of hard and soft policing and the emphasis on the duty of the police to apply the law firmly and sensitively without differing standards.'

Neither hard nor soft, but firmly *and* sensitively? — *and* without differing standards? Hugh Noyes, *The Times*' staffer, seemed to find nothing odd in this. It is one of the many confused elements in politicians' discourse (*pace* Reeves 1983) which were simply relayed, not criticised or questioned by the media.

*Police 'between society and a collapse of law and order'*

Page 4 and the facing page were a digest of the Report. Underneath this headline was a large photograph of a riot scene, and a smaller one of firemen putting out a smouldering blaze. Violent disorder — not racial disadvantage — was the privileged theme. On page 4 the major focus was on the evaluation of police tactics during the disturbances in April, and these it overwhelmingly endorsed. The other topics were the Brixton situation, future policing policy, and the classical question of outside agitators. *The Times*, like the Report, made no reference to police rioting or looting of black-owned shops during the tumult.

The ambiguity in the discourse which we noted above resurfaced on this page. Let us examine some instances.

Having detailed Brixton's high unemployment rates, poverty indices, levels of black concentration, *The Times* opined:

> 'None of these provides an excuse for disorder, the report says; however, to ignore *complex* political and social factors 'is to put the nation at peril'.' (My emphasis.)

What is actually so 'complex' about entrenched racism, except how to combat it effectively? Why should any nation be in peril internally, unless its structure is intolerable for segments of its population? Would they not then be excused for rebellion?

The Scarman Report quite often speculated, rather than demonstrated, despite its representation in the media as the last word in authoritative analysis. *The Times* either could not or would not put even a question-mark against these speculations. For instance:

> 'There must be a temptation for every young criminal — black or white — stopped in the streets of Brixton to allege misconduct by a police officer: indeed *the position may almost have been reached* where not to do so is to endanger one's credibility in the eyes of one's friends.'
>
> (My emphasis.)

A truly magisterial speculation. But one which quickly disposes of many complaints against police violence as mere products of teenage fantasy.

Another instance of this solemn acceptance of speculation was related to the media themselves. In the July 1981 disturbances, leading public figures repeatedly claimed the media were provoking 'copycat' riots. The use of this playground epithet by such distinguished citizens as an analytical concept is quite astounding. It can only be understood as a preliminary, futile attempt to exorcise the spectre of urban rebellion, like Mrs Thatcher's public reference on television to the presumed failings of the young people's parents. The media authorities were highly sensitive to the charge, and some even accepted its plausibility (Tumber 1982).

The same absence of understanding of the relation between the disturbances, their underlying causes and the media showed itself in Scarman's Report:

> '... many of them, it is obvious, believe with justification, that violence, though wrong, is a very effective means of protest: for by attracting the attention of the mass media of communication, they got their message across to the people as a whole.'

Again, *The Times* reproduced this statement without comment. But how 'obvious' was it? When Tumber (1982) asked participants their view of the media, there was overwhelmingly anger that the only point at which journalists concerned themselves with black communities was during such disturbances.

The final element on page 4 which requires comment is the 'outside agitators' discourse. In every such disturbance in every country in modern times, someone has been found to claim that agitators, communists, anarchists, terrorists, have been the instigators and cause of the events. In racist discourse, for totally paternalistic reasons, the role of white subversives is a particular example of the same theme. They are necessary to stir up the otherwise disorganized and confused natives. Korda's 1930s colonialist classic film, *Sanders of the River*, carries this theme in the shape of two traitorous whites who sell guns and liquor and spread the rumor of District Commissioner Sanders' death, with chaotic and violent results when Africans and the animal world go on the rampage. Scarman slid some way down this path:

> '... it is possible, though the evidence is not sufficient to warrant a finding, that without the guidance and help of certain white people the young blacks, who were the great majority of the rioting crowds, would not have used the bomb.'

Evidence? One constable who said many of the black participants were strangers. A vicar who said a pub and a newsagent's store were burned down by a group of black men because of police harassment of the black and homosexual communities (and homosexual!? JD). Two local residents in private session who claimed to have seen white men distributing petrol bombs.

Neither what one is led to think of as judicial, nor as journalistic, standards of evidence, seem to have been exactly to the fore at this juncture. The implication of a malign twist to the events imparted by white evil geniuses in turn implied that police behaviour had not been, quantitatively or qualitatively, so lawless.

For example, the Report dismissed as rather silly the black crowd's response to two policemen's handling of a stabbing incident, in which one knelt on the victim's chest to try to stop a punctured lung from filling with blood, and the other insisted on calling an ambulance rather than driving the victim to hospital. Maybe their intentions were of the best. Nevertheless, after so many incidents, as when Michael Ferrera was left to bleed to death over forty minutes in Dalston police station in December 1978, the crowd's reaction was not illogical.

It is at points like these that the hegemonic function of the Scarman report and of its media presentation, is best revealed. New policies are urged, reforms outlined, errors admitted. Yet there is also an intricate tracery of denial of numerous individual instances of police wrong-doing, a fine web of inferences to be drawn that black grievances and experiences have been blown out of proportion.

*'Fair and thorough' report provokes favourable reaction*

On the facing page, some reactions were presented, and proposed police reforms outlined.

A large photograph of Scarman was underneath the headline, showing him smiling and shaking hands with Brixton passers-by, including one black man with a kerchief round the lower part of his face. The photograph was captioned: *Walkabout: Lord Scarman visiting Brixton in July, gathering facts for himself.*

The first section cited varying reactions from four senior police representatives, all of whom accepted the need for more police training. The second section quoted Scarman as saying that some special opportunities would 'have to be given to the ethnic minorities . . . to compete on a level with the so-called host community.' He was also quoted as saying that an 'immense myth about the SPG (ie Special Patrol Group) has developed.' Under a third sub-heading, community leaders were described as *broadly in favour*, even though three out of five quoted, weren't. One was cited thus:

> 'The training has got to be brought up to date. The kind of training they have had was for a society with no blacks living in it, and this causes a lot of misunderstanding, especially with young blacks.'

It is hard to know where to begin to return to terra firma in this quagmire. Police training, as an effective mechanism for change, would have to be conducted with a totally different concept of policing. Simply to extend the period taken, with either a token injection of 'multi-racial understanding' lectures, or (more likely) tactics for how to penetrate black communities' defences, would not alter anything in a positive direction. Anti-racist content would be viscerally rejected as do-gooding claptrap. The structure and operation of policing would be the same, the personnel would be the same. In particular the SPG would be just the same, publicly praised by police chiefs after its terror tactics in Southall in 1979 and elsewhere. There was no realism about these matters in the Report, and none in *The Times*. Other examples of half-digested policy proposals were often to be encountered in its pages.

Scarman made the following conceptually confused statement:

> 'I recommend that the work currently being undertaken in the Metropolitan designed to identify scientific ways in which evidence of racial prejudice can be identified should be vigorously pursued with the support of the Home Office and that the results should in due course be incorporated in at (*sic*) the procedures for selecting new recruits to all police forces."

We will pass over the implied image of Scotland Yard's boffins being in the forefront of the detection of racial prejudice even amongst the most cunningly dissembling individuals, for this cutting edge of committed research is founded on a conceptual assumption which is laughable. Despite its erudition, *The Times* was still identifying racism as an individual ailment, and was dismissing the long history of racist perspectives in British culture. The normalcy of racism in British life seemed never even to have occurred to *The Times* as a proposition to consider.

These tests would be the easiest things to circumnavigate. But no word of scepticism, conceptual or practical, was to be heard from the faithful herald of official tidings.

*The Conclusion*

*We must eliminate society's flaws*

This was a classically liberal expression of the issue. Even in a healthy organism there may at any time arise some flaws. Not that they would be central to its functioning, but they should be tidied up. Is racism such a flaw? Admittedly, Scarman concluded his Report, as *The Times* made clear, with a resounding quotation from President Johnson's 1968 Report of the National Advisory Commission on Civil Disorders, on the pressing need to eliminate slums, discrimination and unemployment in America:

> 'These words are as true of Britain today as they have been proved by subsequent events to be true of America.'

To this extent, more than lip-service was being paid to the *condition* of black minorities in Britain. Yet already *The Times* was consigning its own treatment of reforms in housing, education and employment to one sub-section of this page (page 5). The ambiguity of 'flaws' rather than 'structural problems' allowed this displacement of emphasis to take place quite easily. 'Institutionalised racism' did not exist; racial disadvantage did; it was a flaw; subdivide it into housing, education, education and employment; focus on 'positive discrimination' in education and better police education courses; and anyway *public order* was the real issue. *The Times* rendered its priorities very clearly in its allocation of space.

The page 6 digest of the House of Commons debate on the Report also focussed almost exclusively on its policing aspects. The predominant discourses within which black people have been enmeshed in the British news media are indeed those of 'immigration' and 'law and order'.

*After Scarman: a militant voice of black dissent and the policeman at the centre of the storm*

An article by Darcus Howe, editor of *Race Today*, and a portrait of Sir David McNee, then Metropolitan Police Commissioner, were on the editorial facing page.

Howe's article had an interesting multiple function with in the discourse of *The Times*. On the one hand there is something slightly comic, if authentically leninist, in a revolutionary explaining her/his analysis to *The Times*' readership. From *The Times*' perspective, however, Howe did more than confirm its liberalism. His article provided a boundary point, a clarification of the position to be rejected. No more than 'between the army and the gunman' in Northern Ireland (3) was *The Times* implying a moral equivalence between Howe and McNee through their juxtaposition. The editorial opposite made this clear to any potentially confused reader, rejecting Howe's claim that the Scarman Report was 'whitewash'. His article, then, had a ritual rather than a directly communicative function in the discourse. There was no dialogue — how could there be? — between him and McNee.

The piece on McNee noted his longer career and success in Glasgow. It stressed that he had been brought in as an outsider to Scotland Yard to combat police corruption, described by *The Times* as 'police peccadillos' — if true, hardly a justification for such a careful appointment. He was described as having successfully handled 'racial' troublespots (the Notting Hill Carnival, Brick Lane, Southall), and the staffer suggested that the Report might assist his reforming impulse:

> 'The Scarman Report may be the weapon he needs both inside and outside the force to continue his work.'

---

[3] Lord Hill, BBC Chair, to the then Home Secretary in 1971 about coverage of Nothern Ireland. Cited in Schlesinger (1977: 212).

Which reforms for what purpose might be the question; the answer might be gleaned from McNee's comment after the extreme, almost civil war violence of the police in Southall in April 1979, when the teacher Blair Peach was killed. Of the SPG, the cutting edge of that operation to defend the National Front's right to meet without a counter-demonstration, he said, 'I still back them to the hilt.'

The editorial on page 15 gave the normal designation of approval to the Report, describing it as 'commendably judicious'. It focussed on a series of its recommendations, essentially approving them, but asking whether public violence needed new legislation, and querying the precise meaning of the term 'positive discrimination' as used in the Report. It went on to pronounce that

> 'This government and its predecessors have done too little to redress racial disadvantage, and this government has certainly said too little that might contribute to the removal of a sense of black insecurity ...'

As a tireless campaigner for black rights, *The Times* was in a position of unusual moral authority to level this criticism ...

The editorial concluded with an equation of responsibility for the 'racial' disharmony between black racists and white racists, and urged that the future lay in the hands of decent tolerant people:

> 'Black and white elements make up the community: black and white racists pollute and poison it. The quality, and ultimately the safety, of society depends on black and white citizens working consciously to live in toleration together.'

Black racism certainly exists, but whether it has the determining force in Britain of white racism is a highly contentious proposition. Each time, the black minority was named first, as though its responsibility for racial disadvantage were not only equal with the whites', but even prior — as was its responsibility for improving the situation. Let's be British and nice to each other, *The Times* seemed to say, quite oblivious of the widespread zero-sum perception among white people of the nature of the situation. How can concessions be simply made to black needs, when the racist lobby (*Daily Express, Daily Mail, Sun, News of the World*, fascists, a slice of MPs) will immediately tell white workers that the concession is a direct deduction from their own entitlement? The *impression* was given that nettles were being grasped in all directions, a whole bank of them; the realities of racial oppression (4) in the 1980s were nonetheless continuing unabated.

The next two days *The Times* ran a minor series of articles on the Report. On November 27th, page 2 ran an article which began with Commander Fairbairn's admission that the Swamp '81 operation in Brixton had been a mistake, but that

> 'it had to be borne in mind that young officers were sometimes exposed to insults that were hard to bear.'

---

[4] For a survey of these trends, see Downing (1980a).

So were young black people from the police; was this why Swamp '81 had been mounted? The article went on to cite black reactions from Brixton, Toxteth (Liverpool) and Moss Side (Manchester). It quite fairly represented the power structure's credibility gap among many black people. It was one of the few moments in *The Times*' discourse when it became clear that only the surface had been scratched. Perhaps not surprisingly, it was not given central emphasis in the paper's layout. On page 13, the basic policing theme was returned to, with a section of the Report being reproduced which gave a graphic narrative account of the sequence of events on April 11th 1981:

> 'essential reading for anyone who wishes fully to understand the events of that Saturday, the nature of the disturbances, and the police reaction to them.'

A large photograph was reproduced of three policemen taking an injured fourth to safety, captioned *Cold statistic (Lord Scarman's words): injured officer is helped by colleagues.*

The reiteration of the action-packed dimension of the events inevitably refocussed attention once more away from the racial disadvantage dimension back to the public order dimension. To claim readers would then 'fully understand' what had happened, through a description of how people ran up and down streets, was rather ludicrous. In fact, only the 'thin blue line' ideology stood to be reinforced.

The November 28th item in which Scarman clarified what he had meant by 'positive discrimination' (ie not very much),has already been noted above. The other item that day consisted of four readers' letters. The first was from the Chair of the Greater London Tory Reform Group, mostly supporting Scarman. The second was from a West Indian, asking why Brixton could not have a theatre like Hammersmith or the West End. The third was from a journalist complaining about the price of the Report. The fourth was from a reader who had obviously taken the whole media representation of Scarman very seriously, asking if now people could just 'riot, burn and attack' in support of a grievance. These letters were in some sense worthy of *The Times*' coverage.

Where *The Times* did score, as contrasted with *The Guardian*, was in its effort to quote black responses. Including Howe's article, nine were quoted, three of whom were from Manchester and Liverpool. Only one black response was quoted by *The Guardian*, which was frankly outrageous, even if rather characteristic of the media in general (Downing 1975).

At the same time, with the exception of Scarman, Whitelaw and Hattersley, practically every other person quoted was a policeman (nine in all). To the extent that Scarman himself was serious in his emphasis on racial disadvantage, this was a thoroughgoing misrepresentation of his position. It privileged the policing aspect of the matter to the detriment of all others. The question still hangs in the air: was any other aspect actually at stake for the power structure?

## 4. *The Guardian*

Consideration of the other two newspapers will be much less exhaustive, since the major parameters of official media discourse have already been largely defined. Our task will rather be to note how these other two publications differed from *The Times*. *The Guardian* is a newspaper with a strange, split soul. It runs cautious, stuffy, often pompous editorials. Yet, especially in its inner pages, it also runs irreverent, perceptive, caustic articles and reportage which are the root cause of many of its readers' passionate loyalty.

### *At the root of the problem*

Like *The Times*, *The Guardian* offered a 'day-before' article, but here it was a review-article on a book. The latter was a study of British urban policy in multi-racial areas. Beneath the headline, which also served as caption, was a photograph of two Asian adults walking up a nothern industrial street. It was an unfortunate headline/caption, for two reasons. It seemed to identify the Asians as the root of the problem (though the article certainly did not), but actually identified the policy problems discussed in the article as the crux of the problem of racism (which they were not). The study had been based on six averagely effective local authorities. Its message was that there was great absence of co-ordination between central and local government, with the result that even if Scarman's recommendations were enthusiastically accepted by central government, there would be no reason to suppose this acceptance would translate through into practical action by local government. A reasonable point, but hardly the *root* of the problem.

The reviewer also noted with favour the book's recommendation that responsibility for 'race relations' should be taken from the Home Office and given to the Department of the Environment. Some liberal technocrats in this area have long held this view (cf. Rose, et al. 1969, where the same proposal was made concerning the then Ministry of Housing and Local Government). Now it is true that if responsibility there is to be, probably any British government department, the Ministry of Agriculture and Fisheries say, would be more forward-looking that the Home Office. The fact remains that this assumption — that the fundamental solution to the problems of racial oppression in Britain can be solved through switching government departments' oversight — is incurably optimistic, confident beyond bounds that this is a technical problem amenable to solution by humane civil servants. It is a very shallow analysis posing as a sophisticated 'in-the-know' proposal. For readers who need to feel confident that if the situation really deteriorated, the system would pull a new rabbit out of the hat, this analysis may have been comforting.

On November 26th, the front-page cartoon showed two black youths and one skinhead. One of the former was holding a tabloid with 'Scarman Report' on it, and was saying to the others,

> 'Hey, remember the night last April when you'd been chucked by Sandra, I'd had a row with my bird, Mick was all uptight about Crystal Palace going down and we all just happened to fancy starting a bit of a punch-up . . .'

This represented the trivialisation of sustained grievance and bitter protest. In sharp contrast to *The Times'* excellent cartoon, this one collapsed the whole issue into a 'youth problem', much as Mrs Thatcher and other public figures had suggested. It is a different inflection of the issues to the ones so far observed in this study, but like them it seeks to evacuate the 'race' issue of its sting.

*Whitelaw picks up Scarman challenge*

By this front-page lead headline there was a photograph of Scarman holding his Report, captioned *Countdown to question time. Lord Scarman brandishes his report at a press conference yesterday.* The item carried some brief quotations from the Report, and the comments of Whitelaw, Hattersley, Scarman, McNee and the chair of the commission for Racial Equality (a body always to be boosted if possible, according to *The Guardian*). As with *The Times*, the impression was created at once that most official figures applauded the Report, ant that therefore reforming action would be taken. Unlike *The Times*, however, *The Guardian* would only once offer a couple of lines to a black comment on the Report.

Lesser headlines on the front page covered criticism of the Report from Lambeth Council's leader (*Ted Knight protest at 'no hope' report*) and *The Guardian*'s list of leading topics in the Report (*The list of wrongs and how to right them*). Knight's attack on the Report for not urging much more money to his borough was contested by another councillor, but given implicit support by a black lawyer. The 'list of wrongs' focussed almost exclusively on the Report's police proposals and on Whitelaw's response to them. The key question of racial disadvantage was therefore effectively downplayed, but the impression was given that serious action was underway. (It was, in the shape of 'community policing', of which more in the Conclusions.)

*After Brixton, the need for radical reform*
*Inquiry calls for liaison committee — with teeth*
*The spark that blazed one evening*

These were the heads and sub-heads on page 2. A photograph of a line of police — the 'thin blue line' — was also prominent on the page. The Scarman Report was given its due accolade right at the beginning:

> 'In a thorough and at time brilliant report on the Brixton riots, which is likely to become a landmark in both race relations and police administration . . .'

The account continued with that insistent even-handedness of all such discourses:

> 'Only the establishment of an independent service for the investigation of all reports against the police will *silence* their criticisms.'
> 'The allegation that the police are the repressive arm of a racist state not only displays a complete ignorance of the *constitutional* arrangements for controlling the police; it is an injustice to the senior officers of the force.'
>
> (My emphases.)

But, is the objective of a complaints system to *silence* criticisms? Is the Constitution — not even written — a granite bulwark against the growth of police power? Are senior policemen anti-racist archangels? The ideology of the media as 'fourth estate' was not enacted at all by *The Guardian* in the face of these slippery claims.

A second theme of the page included a two-column blow-by-blow account of the April 11th events, similar to but briefer than *The Times*' excerpt from Scarman's narrative of the street events. As with *The Times*, this served to intensify the law-and-order focus of the discourse.

In general, however, the page concentrated on how far the police should or should not be blamed for inflaming the situation. This contrasted with *The Times*' stress on how they saved Britain from anarchy and collapse. *The Guardian* was a little more detached from the police perspective than *The Times* in this respect. It urged the need for 'radical reforms in police training, recruitment and accountability.' Nevertheless, it was no more practical and hard-headed in its assessment of the feasibility of these reforms than was *The Times*. It took them to be self-evidently effective . . .

*Verdict: not a race riot, but a burst of anger*

This sub-head was at the foot of page 2. It was accurate, insofar as whites were not randomly attacked, inaccurate insofar as blacks were, by the police. For some reason, hardly any disturbance in Britain involving blacks and whites has ever been officially conceded to be a 'race riot'. The term is regularly denied, as if to persist in the view that white racism or black resistance are not really 'British'. We see again the pattern of avoidance already noted: it is always an 'immigration' issue, a 'law-and-order' issue, a 'youth problem'. The item concluded with the Report's assertion, unquestioned by *The Guardian*, that

> 'Whether justified or not, many in Brixton *believe* that the police routinely abuse their powers and mistreat *alleged* offenders. The belief here is as important as the fact.' (My emphases.)

The implication is that even black invention and irrationality and rumor have to be taken seriously, because they lead to trouble, but that no one really knows whether black testimony on the police is to be dignified with credibility. And was the Report also saying that it would be *more* acceptable to mistreat *real* offenders? 'The web of inferences to be drawn that black grievances and experiences have been blown out of proportion' was very visible.

On the rest of page 3, various reactions were sounded, and it was noted that Toxteth community spokespeople were not very impressed with the Report (contradicting *The Times*' account). *The Guardian*'s original contribution lay in briefly noting the reactions of three representatives of radical legal reform groups, all of whom offered telling criticisms of Scarman's proposals for police reform. Why could not this measured scepticism have informed the page one coverage?

*Scarman: at the watershed*

On page 16 the editorial began by acknowledging the panic induced by the 1981 events in some people's minds:

> 'It is hard to overestimate the shock to the British system of seeing those appalling scenes of violence and mayhem in Brixton, and then in Southall, Toxteth and the Midlands. It was as if we were brought to the edge of an abyss, beyond which lay anarchy, the breakdown of law, and social catastrophe.'

The initial public order definition exactly echoed that of *The Times*. What was different in *The Guardian* was its insistence later in the editorial on the causes of the events, its critique of Scarman for leaving the Home Office with a lot of 'wriggling room', and for the weakness of its proposed mechanisms for ensuring police accountability and effective complaints procedures. Unlike many *Guardian* editorials on matters of moment, it avoided pontifical sententiousness. And it concluded by hammering hard at the indissolube link between social reform and police reform. Nonetheless, it had begun with public order: how much distance could really be travelled from this prioritisation?

*A judge to please all the people?*

*The Guardian*'s portrait of Scarman on page 17 covered much of the same ground as *The Times* had done, presenting him as a radical constitutional reformer and very much the man of the hour. He was made out to be an extraordinary hero of the establishment, a combination of intensive and sensitive social researcher, and interventive conciliator. One of his legal assistants was quoted as saying that Scarman was now a leading expert on Rastafarianism:

> 'His research was so thorough that at the end of the day I doubt that there was anybody in Brixton who knew more about their background and religion.'

It *could* have been asked whether an English lawyer was likely to be a credible judge of Scarman's knowledge of Rastafarianism! A further question could have been asked, namely what the lawyer meant by 'anybody in Brixton'? Did he mean Rastafarians, or 'real people' like policemen or social workers?

The apparent need to celebrate Scarman's heroic qualities rather downplayed the sceptical impulse sometimes associated with the newspaper.

On the back page, however, this impulse managed to surface a little in Michael White's regular report on the Commons debate. He was describing Whitelaw's attempts to convince the House he meant business:

> 'The more Willie denied opaqueness the more opaque he sounded. But inexpensive.'

Without being so foolish as to expect the established press to be constantly at the windpipe of the power structure, it would still be encouraging to see its journalists, like White, prompting readers to retain their critical faculties.

Of the two remaining *Guardian* items, one was on page 3 of the November 27th issue, and covered the recognition of his errors by Commander Fairbairn of L Division, who had been criticised by name in the Report. He was frank enough to admit that black recruits for the police were few and far between, because they did not wish to be alienated from their communities. This sober truth raised profound questions about how far even the policing reforms were likely to be viable — but no connections of that kind were made.

The final item was an inside page article by Gareth Pearce on November 31st, written out of her experience as a journalist in the USA during the black rebellions of the 60s, and now a lawyer representing some black activists charged during 1981. Pearce stressed the sharp contrast between the individualistic and *ad hoc* manner in which Scarman had gone about gathering and using evidence, and the painstaking, systematic and properly staffed work which had gone into the U. S. Civil Disorders report of 1968, to which, we may recall, reference had been made by Scarman himself, implicitly in the hope of a comparison being drawn with his own work.

Pearce also made the refreshingly straightforward observation that the very photographs of the police faces as they were lined up or waiting in buses 'told their own story', obviating any real need for lengthy disquisitions on how far they were racist. Without such elementary realism, all the rest of the discourse was likely to be froth and pother. Unkind as this verdict might be felt to be, the evidence so far is substantially in its favour.

## 5. The Economist

*The Economist* usually adopts a rather no-nonsense breezy tone, handling national and international political economy with the confident conviction of those who know where they're going and in any event have enough in the bank to survive a mistake or two along the way. From its perspective, racism and racial disadvantage are defined rather as hangovers from the past, irrational and sometimes ugly manifestations of the baser human spirit which have to be handled politically, but make very little sense economically (except as a brake on economic success). The role of racist ideology in oiling the wheels of the national and international division of labour is either not perceived, or is rejected on a reflex basis. Where racism provokes tumult is precisely the point at which it has to have the cap screwed down on it: the paper likes its workers working, and its workless quiet. But, like *The Times* and *The Guardian*, the daily stuff of the matter is all 'out there' to *The Economist*. It is what you read about or see by chance from your car.

*Scarman: for action now*

In its issue of November 28th 1981, *The Economist* ran its second editorial on the Scarman Report, and a news item on page 25 about the policing aspect of the Report. The editorial expressed itself very forthrightly in favour of police reform and for action to reduce racial disadvantage. On the first it went so far as to say that 'Scarman let (the police) off fairly lightly'. It was their 'imprudent behaviour' which started the Brixton riots, which then spread.

> 'The social background of crime and violence must be directly attacked.' 'This newspaper warmly endorses (Scarman's proposals) not least because they are couched in terms designed to make radical reform acceptable to the police.'

On social reform, it spoke of the

> 'urgent need to do something at last about . . . the difficulties, social and economic, which beset the ethnically diverse communities who live and work in our inner cities.'

It noted the disturbances had been widely predicted by specialists. And it concluded that without

> 'positive discrimination, at least for long enough to start righting the present imbalance, reform and so strengthening of the police will be the mere equivalent of binding the cork tighter on the bottle.'

Let us stand back a moment, putting on one side surprise at the paper's apparent radicalism. What is really being said here? The claim is being made that the solution is in the government's hands, which has the ability and should have the will to take the steps necessary. Racist white workers, racist policemen, the racist lobby, will respond to a tug on the levers of power. Technical action from on high will be quite sufficient — a flick of the rudder. 'The main question' was whether Whitelaw would act on the Scarman recommendations, since he had already been defeated on prison reform (by his right wing). But if he could vault this hurdle, nothing stood in his way. This technocratic view of the matter was reinforced by the editorial's reference to the Home Office as the appropriate agent in this regard, being responsible both for the police and for co-ordination 'in this area'. '*In this area*': the problem was a discrete one, responsibilities were clearly defined, fortunately focussed in one department — what else remained to worry about? There was not in evidence even *The Guardian*'s scepticism about the Home Office.

We see, once more, despite the encouraging firmness of its commitment to change, that self-same distance in *The Economist* as existed in the other two papers, from the *substance* of the matter.

*Scarman's stronger and better police*

The page 25 news item carried a small photograph, also reproduced on the contents page, of a young black man being led away with his head under the vice-like arm of a policeman, his face contorted in pain and fear. The captain read *Off to jail, and the complaints board*, implying that there existed *adequate* redress for the victims even if the whole business was being roughly and clumsily handled. Again, the distance was unnervingly far between appearance and reality in *The Economist*'s perception of the matter.

The item began with the customary bow to Scarman's

> 'judicious and beautiful written report on last spring's riots in the seedy multiracial inner London suburb of Brixton.'

(Out came those fastidious tongs again the exquisite Report contrasted with the seedy multi-racial suburb.) Curiously, the writer claimed the Report had not blamed people, only 'arrangements' (hardly the impression given by *The Times* or *The Guardian*). It did interpret Scarman's 'restraint' as politically motivated:

> 'Lord Scarman seems to take the view that if you treat people politely, they are more likely to do what you want.'

Like *The Times*, it considered the Report valuable material for those policemen and politicians who did not want a repeat performance.

However, it was much less sententious about racism in upper levels of the police force than the other two papers had been.

> 'Scarman denies (ho, hum) that any senior police officers are racially prejudiced.'

It seemed that only *The Economist* could afford to poke fun at that absurdity. It also took the view that

> 'outside Britain most of this might seem a catalogue of clichés. That it seems radical in London is odd enough. But it will be resisted, by some conservative policemen and some conservative politicians alike.'

At the same time, the article listed without sceptical comment the list of proposals for police reform, including police community 'consultations', more black recruits, the merits of longer training *per se*, and the screening out of prejudiced police, to be 'eliminated if they show signs of racial prejudice'. Yet if this last wouldn't work in *The Economist*'s own staff, why would it work in the police force? (It seems that middle class white people cannot face their own racism, happy as they may be to pinpoint it in the police or the working class.)

The piece ended with the kind of declamatory rhetoric to which we have by now grown accustomed:

> 'Attacking the roots of social and racial deprivation will demand all-party political drive in central government and money for schooling and work programmes. But every employer can do his stuff now by hiring young blacks as Britain comes out of the recession.'

'Coillons . . . shryned in an hogges toord' does not seem an overly unfair description of this blithe fiat. Where was the actual likelihood of *any* of this happening?

## 6. Conclusions

Discourse about 'race' in these media of the dominant classes was clearly a very contradictory process. It was neither fantasy purely, nor reaction purely, and certainly was not limpid truth. A hero was manufactured in the shape of Lord Scarman, but the weight of his remarks in these media about racial disadvantage was much less than the weight of this disquisitions about the police.

There was a pronounced *lack* of scepticism concerning the workability of his proposals for police reform. And there was a positive correlation between ringing declarations in favour of social reform in *The Times* and *The Economist*, in particular, and the spottiness of their normal concern with the rights of black communities.

We might summarise *The Times*' presentation as focussing overwhelmingly on the public order aspect of the Report, secondarily on the favourable public reactions of leading figures to the Report, and finally on the character of Lord Scarman himself. *The Guardian* was also concerned about law and order, and Scarman's style as a conciliator, but balanced these somewhat with a readiness to ask awkward questions about the police and a certain emphasis on the continuing realities of racism (on which it has a better record that the other two newspapers analysed here.) *The Economist* seemed to be in a hurry to get the whole thing rationally settled and so to proceed with business as usual.

Examination of their discourses shows how difficult it is to generate content categories to summarise each article, which do not do violence to the actual material and its discursive contradictions. An attentive reading of *The Times*, for example, could throw up the information that grass-roots reaction was much less laudatory of the Report than the press celebrations of it, or that the idea of increasing black recruitment into the police was a chimera. Yet these were not the dominant themes at all, indeed were rather subversive of the general thrust of the paper's coverage. The cartoons were also out of kilter in this way.

At the same time, what above was called "the fine web of inferences to be drawn that black grievances and experiences have been blown out of proportion", was also a dynamic element within the discourse which it is almost impossible to categorise. Content analysis can identify themes, but not the intricate mechanisms by which they are traced out in practice, the chess-play of ideology.

Politically, ensuing years have demonstrated that the 1981 events enabled one policy wing of the British police to attempt a Great Leap Forward. Its public name was 'community policing', which some more traditionally minded in the police referred contemptuously as organising 'hobby bobbies'. It represented a strategy already tried and tested in the U. S. (Center for Research in Criminal Justice 1975) and in Northern Ireland (O'Dowd et al. 1980) — and no doubt elsewhere as well. On the face of it, it meant taking the police out of their cruising 'panda' cars and putting them back on their feet in the street. They were supposed to take an active interest in local goings-on, maybe even going so far as to organise clubs or discos. It looked like the return of the mythical 'neighbourhood bobby'.

The difference was that they were now equipped with radios and computers, not whistles, their equipment of twenty years before. By being closer to communities, they were in a position to hear the rumours, the word on who was who and who hated whom. They could become amateur anthropologists, in the worst tradition of that discipline. They could also learn, for instance, how people's cultures might be most effectively used to shame or control them. With huge data-banks at their disposal, they could build up an informational picture of resistant communities which could then be used for controlling their resistance.

Behind the elite press coverage of the Scarman Report, behind even its virtual obsession with the policing aspects of the 1981 events, lay a vital policy debate between the modernisers and the traditionalists among the police and public order strategists (Gilroy 1982). Even for the readership of these papers the real terms of this debate were not on public view. Community policing was seen as sensitive, not as penetrative, and had to be defended as still permitting crime to be thwarted: *'Community policing need not inhibit fight against crime'* (*The Times*, 26th November 1981, p. 5).

The only element in the power structure liable to resist such change with might and main consisted of the *The Daily Telegraph* ilk. More liberal types would be likely to take the change at face value, and approve it; those closer to police and public order circles would see it as a major opportunity for more efficient policing. In terms of financial outlay, community policing would be infinitely cheaper that doing anything substantive about racial disadvantage in jobs, housing or education. As a black US veteran pointed out in the 1969 documentary *No Vietnamese Ever Called Me Nigger*, Lyndon Johnson's Great Society reforms were all focussed on welfare, which could be given out and taken away later, not on the central, expensive questions of employment and the rest. (The same analysis turns up in Piven & Cloward 1971.) In Britain after 1981, not even welfare was expanded. Only policing was brought up to date with the latest models.

Thus elite media discourse was equally remote from two realities: from black communities in Britain and the strategic debates within the police. It focussed on the public order dimension of the 1981 events to the near-exclusion of either of these much more pressing realities. The parallel with Chaucer's Pardoner, dispensing illusory remedies to the gullible, may not be so remote after all.

*Bibliography*

Barker, Martin (1981). *The New Racism*. London, Junction Books.
Butterworth, Eric (1967) 'The smallpox outbreak and the British press', *Race* 7.4, pp. 347–64.
Center for Research on Criminal Justice (1975). *The Iron Fist and the Velvet Glove*. Center for Research on Criminal Justice, Berkeley, California.
Critcher, Charles et al. (1977). 'Race in the provincial press', *Ethnicity and the Media*. Paris, UNESCO, pp. 25–192.
Downing, John (1975). 'The (balanced) white view', in C. Husband ed. (1975), pp. 90–137.
Downing, John (1980a). *Now You Do Know*. London, War on Want Publications, for the Program to Combat Racism of the World Council of Churches.
Downing, John (1980b). *The Media Machine*. London, Pluto Press.
Elliott, Philip (1972). *The Making of a Television Series*. London, Constable.
Englehardt, Tom (1971). 'Ambush at Kamikaze Pass', *Bulletin of Concerned Asian Scholars* 3.1, pp. 1–21.
Foot, Paul (1965). *Immigration and Race in British Politics*. Harmondsworth, Penguin Books.
Gilroy, Paul (1982). 'Police and thieves', in Centre for Contemporary Cultural Studies, *The Empire Strikes Back*. London, Hutchinson, pp. 143–82.
Hall, Stuart, et al. (1978). *Policing the Crisis*. London, MacMillan.
Hartmann, Paul and Husband, Charles (1974). *Racism and the Mass Media*. London, Davis–Poynter.
Hartmann, Paul, Husband, Charles, and Clark, Jean (1974). 'Race as news', in J. D. Halloran ed., *Race as News*. Paris, UNESCO, pp. 91–173.
Holland, Patricia (1981). 'The New Cross fire and the popular press', *Multi-Racial Education* 9.3. pp. 61–80.
Husband, Charles ed (1975). *White Media, Black Britain*. London, Arrow Books, Hutchinson.
Husband, Charles (1975). 'Racism in the mass media and society: a critical interaction', in Husband, Charles ed (1975), pp. 15–38.
Husband, Charles (1977). 'News media, language and race relations', in H. Giles ed (1979), *Language, Ethnicity and Intergroup Relations*. London, Academic Press, pp. 211–40.
Husband, Charles (1979). 'Some aspects of the interaction of the British entertainment media with contemporary race relations', in H.-D. Fischer and S. R. Melnik eds (1979) *Entertainment*. New York, Hastings House. pp. 196–207.
Husband, Charles ed (1982). *'Race' in Britain: continuity and change*. London, Hutchinson.
Morrison, Lionel (1975). 'A Black Journalist's experience of British journalism', in C. Husband ed (1975), pp. 165–79.
O'Dowd, Liam et al (1980). *Northern Ireland*. London, CSE Books.
Parmar, Pratibha (1982). 'Gender, race and class: Asian women in struggle', in Centre for Contemporary Cultural Studies, *The Empire Strikes Back*. London, Hutchinson, pp. 236–75.
Piven, Frances and Cloward, Richard (1911). *Regulating the Poor*. London, Tavistock.
Reeves, Frank (1983). *British Racial Discourse*. Cambridge, Cambridge University Press.
Rose, E. J. B. et al. (1969). *Colour and Citizenship*. Oxford, Oxford University Press.
Schlesinger, Philip (1977). *Putting 'Reality' Together*. London, Constable.
Smithies, B. and Fiddick, P. (1969). *Enoch Powell on Immigration*. London, Sphere Books.

Stam, Robert and Spence, Louise (1983). 'Colonialism, Racism and Representation — an Introduction', *Screen* 24.2, pp. 2—20.
Troyna, Barry (1981). *Public Awareness and the Media*. London, Commission for Racial Equality.
Troyna, Barry (1982). 'Reporting the National Front', in C. Husband ed. (1982), pp. 259—78.
Tumber, Howard (1982). *Television and the Riots*. London, British Film Institute.
Wood, Ven. W. D. (1975). 'Black voices in the media: an interview', in C. Husband ed. (1975), pp. 41—51.

PHILIP SCHLESINGER AND BOB LUMLEY

# Two Debates on Political Violence and the Mass Media: The Organisation of Intellectual Fields in Britain and Italy

*Introduction*

This paper examines some recent debates about the role of the mass media in reporting 'terrorism'[1] in Britain and Italy. Such debates have been a matter of intense periodic political discussion in both countries and have tended to focus primarily on the extent to which media coverage promotes the propaganda aims of those using violence against the state. Consequently, much of the argument has revolved around the relative merits of the exercise of censorship *versus* the free expression of opinion within a liberal-democratic order.

In Britain, most attention has centred upon the *television* news and current affairs coverage of the Northern Ireland crisis, and especially the reporting of the Provisional IRA since it became the principal armed enemy of the British presence in the Province in 1971. In Italy, the debate has been much shorter in duration, being given an intense spur into action during the Moro affair of 1978, when questions were raised about the *press's* handling of the Red Brigades' photographs and communiques.

In this study we propose to examine, with some broad brushstrokes of comparison, the ways in which the debates on 'terrorism and the media' have been constructed. We wish to draw out the distinctive conceptions of the relationships between the state and the mass media in each society. A further central theme concerns the participants in this debate and their institutional locations.

These concerns point directly to the organisation of the 'intellectual fields' of the two societies in question. According to Pierre Bourdieu (1971: 161) an 'intellectual field' may be conceptualised as a 'system of social relations within which creation as an act of communication takes place'. Bourdieu argues for the material determination of cultural production but in a way which takes account of how 'forces of determinism' become 'a specifically

---

[1] There are problems in defining 'terrorism' in any universally acceptable way as it is a contested term of political discourse. For a recent discussion of the semantics and role of 'terrorism' in the present phase of the Cold War see Herman (1982).

intellectual determination by being reinterpreted according to the specific logic of the intellectual field, in a creative project' (Bourdieu, 1971: 185). In the terms of this position, which is non-reductionist, cultural institutions and actors do not possess complete autonomy from fundamental processes of social production, yet nevertheless operate according to practices inscribed with a distinctive cultural logic. Each intellectual field is structured in terms of 'themes and problems' which cannot be escaped. It is, in Bourdieu's conception, made up of contending intellectual alignments which are engaged in a struggle 'to impose their cultural norms on a larger or smaller area of the intellectual field' (Bourdieu, 1971: 175). At the centre of such conflicts is the effort to impose an orthodoxy of interpretation upon cultural products or attitudes.

Debates about the media coverage of political violence, terrorism especially, manifest this general conflict over the imposition of an orthodoxy of interpretation. On the one hand, there is the 'official discourse', articulated by politicians, state security personnel and some intellectuals, in which the media are viewed as instruments in a propaganda war against disorder and unreason and are expected to support the legitimate order. This position is continually outflanked by a 'reactionary populist discourse' whose proponents argue for an untramelled war against terrorism, in which all legal restraints are set to one side in order to effectively eliminate the enemy. On the other hand there are those who elaborate an 'alternative discourse' — in the main, civil libertarians, critical journalists and academics — who argue that terrorism cannot be understood without adequate context and explanation, and that an excessive reaction by the state is dangerous. Lastly, there is the 'oppositional discourse', that of the perpetrators of anti-state violence themselves. Denying this discourse any space — whether it takes the form of Red Brigade communiques or interviews with IRA spokesmen — is a central objective of those who maintain the official discourse. The proponents of the alternative variant, however, argue that oppositional views should be heard so that the public may better understand the motivations of those engaged in political violence (cf. Schlesinger *et al.* 1983; Ch. 1).

The debates are conditioned by a number of factors. Of especial importance in each society are the given media systems, media-state relations, the degree of articulation of a journalistic ideology of independence, the social role of critical intellectuals and the place of political violence in the history and culture of the society in question. We shall explore the ways in which these come into play in the case studies below.

One crucial difference which needs to be borne in mind is the distinctive nature of 'terrorism' in Britain and in Italy. In Britain, the predominant form of anti-state political violence is sectoral and nationalistic. The IRA is fighting a long-standing irredentist war, principally, but by no means exclusively, in one part of the United Kingdom. Although the Northern Ireland problem has contributed to the difficulties of the British state it has not in any clear-cut way signalled its decomposition (cf. Nairn, 1981). In Italy, the political violence of the Red Brigades and other armed groups has raised fundamental questions about the nature and persistence of the state, and has at times seemed to threaten the stability of the entire political system.

In our view, the *societal* scope of the problem in Italy and its *sectoral* nature in the United Kingdom have affected the range of debate in the two societies. In Italy, where arguments about terrorism and the state are integral to the future of the society, a wide range of participants has become involved. By contrast, in Britain, the debate is somewhat narrow and specialised. These differences are pointed up in the general remarks which preface the case studies which form the centrepiece of this paper.

Each of our case studies focuses upon a crucial moment which illuminates the mobilisation of the respective intellectual fields. In the British example we analyse the rows between the BBC and the Thatcher government over the television interview with a representative of the Irish National Liberation Army (INLA) and the filming of an IRA road-block at Carrickmore. In the Italian example we have focussed upon aspects of the D'Urso kidnapping, in particular the publication of Red Brigades material by the magazine *L'Espresso* and the debate over a news black-out.

*Some general features of the British debate*

Most debate over the media and Northern Ireland has, as noted, focussed upon television rather than the press. Nevertheless, civil libertarian and investigative journalists of both the establishment and radical presses have met with official harassment on occasion, and newspaper editors have been subject to political pressure (Curtis, 1984). Within television, it is the BBC rather than the commercial companies regulated by the Independent Broadcasting Authority (IBA) which has taken the brunt of political criticism. One reason for this is that within official circles, and more widely, the BBC is perceived as owing especial loyalty to the state. Although Independent television (ITV) has also had its problems it does not enjoy the BBC's status as an 'organisation within the constitution'. In an undeclared internal war, the BBC has been a prime target for politicians seeking a scapegoat for their lack of success.

The BBC has generally responded to criticism by accepting its obligation to support the democratic order, but also has argued that it has a duty to inform about unpalatable matters, a defence typically advanced on those relatively few occasions when programmes on police brutality or torture allegations have been screened. This typical and laudable liberal defence — that a contribution is being made to public enlightenment by presenting a range of views — has, nevertheless, not prevented the broadcasting organisations from exercising stringent internal controls. These were imposed in the early 1970s and have led to the practice of self-censorship by journalists and others. Where the limitations are transgressed, as has happened with some current affairs programmes, documentaries and dramas, the BBC and IBA have banned, censored and delayed transmissions.[2]

The public rows over broadcasting and 'terrorism' have been regular and intense, and have taken a predictable course. Typically, a given programme is denounced for aiding the terrorist propaganda war by leading governmental figures, often supported by the opposition, and parliamentary back-bench pressure mounts. The broadcasters issue periodic defensive statements, and are generally supported by the civil libertarian press and by professional organisations such as the National Union of Journalists (NUJ) and the Association of Cinematograph and Television Technicians (ACTT). The unions, while defending their members also often criticise the inadequacies of coverage. Support against both internal and external censorship has come from other organisations such as the Free Communications Group in the early 1970s, and latterly the Campaign for Free Speech on Ireland and the union-based Campaign for Press and Broadcasting Freedom. Such groupings tend to stake out a radical critique of broadcasting and the press, and accuse the broadcasters of not living up to the liberal ideals of their governing instruments. The impact of such arguments on the wider public has been rather slight, however, and the numbers committed to such campaigns are small.

In general, within Great Britain (as opposed to Northern Ireland) public involvement in the debate about 'terrorism and the media' is limited; indeed, interest in the question of political violence and its origins is only sporadically aroused when a bombing campaign or other outrage endangers the lives of the public. The defence of the 'public sphere' has been most consistently articulated by the theorists of the broadcasting organisations (notably the BBC), by liberal broadcasters such as Anthony Smith, David Elstein and Peter Taylor, radical journalists such as Jonathan Dimbleby and a few sociologists (Smith, 1972; Campaign for Free Speech on Ireland (ed.) 1979).

No major intellectual figure supporting a policy of openness has become involved in the British debates on a consistent basis. On the contrary, Dr. Conor Cruise O'Brien, who approximates closely to a European-style general intellectual, has argued strongly against the 'spiritual occupation' of the broadcasting media by terrorist sympathisers. As an ex-Minister of Posts and Telegraphs in the Irish government, a man of letters, editor-in-chief of the *Observer* and media pundit, O'Brien has carried some weight in the debates (O'Brien 1979; cf. Schlesinger *et al.*, 1983: pp. 129–132). Professor Richard

---

[2] The most thorough up-to-date account is Curtis (1984). Still of great value is the Campaign for Free Speech on Ireland (ed.), (1979). A key early article is Smith (1972). Typical BBC positions are enunciated in Francis (1979) and Hawthorne (1981). Sociological accounts include Elliott (1977) and Schlesinger (1978a).

Hoggart, in some respects a comparable figure, has made only a single foray into the field, criticising the censorship of dramas about Northern Ireland (Hoggart, 1980).

Inasmuch as intellectuals are present in the debate they tend to be ambiguously placed between the military and academia. Dr. (formerly Major-General) Richard Clutterbuck and Professor Paul Wilkinson have figured prominently in the general debate about political violence and have also made frequent observations about the role of the media, very much from within a counter-insurgency perspective (Clutterbuck 1981; Wilkinson, 1980). To the extent that there has been organised discussion, outside of television programmes and the columns of the press, this has tended to be of a restricted nature. Forums have been organised by bodies such as Royal United Services Institute for Defence Studies, the Institute for the Study of Conflict, the International Press Institute and the BBC. Such discussions in the main have involved media professionals, certain academics and members of the security forces (Schlesinger et al. 1983: 119—120).

In terms of the culture more generally, although there have been numerous novels, plays, films and television dramas dealing with terrorism both home-grown and foreign, it seems true to say that no outstanding writers have involved themselves in producing works which have become a focus of debate amongst intellectuals.

*British Case Study*

On 5 July 1979, BBC television's current affairs programme, *Tonight*, broadcast an interview with a member of the INLA. This group claimed responsibility for having killed the Northern Ireland spokesman of the Conservative Party, Mr. Airey Neave, three months earlier. During the interview, the INLA-man, who tried to offer military and political justifications for the killing, was sharply questioned by the presenter and was condemned immediately afterwards in a studio sequence by the Rev. Robert Bradford, MP, for the Loyalists, and Mr. Gerry Fitt, MP, then leader of the Social Democratic and Labour Party.

Mr. Atkins, the Northern Ireland Secretary, who had tried to dissuade the BBC from showing the interview, immediately complained to the Corporation that the broadcast had been 'ill-timed and unhelpful'. The INLA, he said, had just been declared unlawful in the UK. The BBC's immediate response was to assert its bureaucratic efficiency and its devotion to the public interest. The broadcast, it replied, had been carefully considered by the Director-General, Mr. Ian Trethowan, and by the Director, News and Current Affairs, Mr. Richard Francis, both of whom felt it added to public knowledge.[3]

---

[3] *The Guardian*, 7.7.79.

Within a few days, the row grew. The Conservative *Daily Telegraph* began a press campaign which emphasised the distress and disgust felt by Airey Neave's widow; the BBC was condemned for not ensuring that she was warned about the programme.[4] In a leading article, the *Telegraph* said that the BBC had committed 'at the very least an extreme and repulsive error of taste'. The editorial argued that there was a difference between 'thorough reporting and analysis, on the one hand, and the screening of personal interviews with men who boast of their implication in murder or their membership of terrorist groups on the other'. The paper suggested that the BBC's guidelines should be tightened up to exclude such interviews on the model of the Irish Republic's broadcasting service, RTE. The BBC, through its Director-General argued that 'we think that, very occasionally, it is right that we should remind the public of the thinking and character of those committed to terrorism and violence'.[5] The terms of the debate were now quite set: bureaucratic irresponsibility *versus* responsible judgement and negative effects *versus* serving the public interest.

On 12 July, the extent of Parliamentary fury became evident as did the possibility of legal action against the BBC. Mrs. Thatcher, the Prime Minister, announced that the Attorney-General was presently considering legal action, and said 'having seen the transcript of this programme, I am appalled that it was ever transmitted. I believe it reflects gravely on the judgement of the BBC and those who are responsible for the decision'. This condemnation was echoed by the Labour Shadow Home Secretary, Mr. Merlyn Rees, who described the programme as a grave error.

The BBC's principal spokesmen counter-attacked. The Chairman, following a discussion by the Board of Governors, defended the decision as 'falling within guidelines established some time ago' and as 'most carefully taken by senior management in the genuine belief that on balance the public interest would be served by people being reminded in this way of the murderous and intransigent nature of the problem'. He did, however, note that the Board was going to reconsider the Northern Ireland guidelines.[6] A broader defence was elaborated by the BBC's Director of News and Current Affairs, himself a party to the decision, at a meeting of the Broadcasting Press Guild on 12 July. There, Mr. Francis implied that the political storm had been manufactured, beginning as it did almost a week after the transmission. He criticised those who had reacted on the basis of reading transcripts rather than seeing the programme itself, observing that the conduct of the interview had 'made our moral stance quite plain'. Francis noted that there had been only three such interviews in the past ten years, pointing out that television could have a 'dissuasive' as well as 'persuasive' impact: 'The feeling of revulsion towards

---

[4] *The Daily Telegraph*, *The Guardian*, 11.7.79.
[5] *The Daily Telegraph*, 12.7.79.
[6] *The Daily Telegraph*, *The Guardian*, 13.7.79.

a terrorist interviewed on television, as the Rev. Robert Bradford said on the programme, is likely to strengthen the resolve of decent people to see the terrorists apprehended and their cause defeated'. He went on to comment that the BBC would be being irresponsible if it 'were to be seen interviewing the likes of Nr. Nkomo about the shooting down of airliners, talking to spokesmen for the PLO, PFLP and to Sandinista guerrillas, and yet failing to grasp the nettle in our own backyard'. In an appeal to the notion of a rational electorate, Francis asked: 'Is the public in a stable democracy such as ours to be trusted only with those threats which are distant, and those nearer to home which can be treated comfortably?'

Although the INLA was now an unlawful organisation, Francis said that contact with them had preceded the banning, that the interview had been filmed in Dublin (where the proscription did not hold), and that the INLA had been warned that information might be given to the Special Branch. He rejected the Northern Ireland Secretary's view of the programme as 'untimely' and 'unhelpful', arguing that it was appropriate to show it when the INLA was being dicussed in the Commons, and that it helped to show, as many senior army officers believed, that 'a conventional military solution was impossible'. Finally, in a positive statement of the BBC's role (recalling his response to criticisms over the exposure of police brutality in 1977), Francis stated: 'I start from the presumption that the media have a very real contribution to make, in particular, a contribution to the maintenance of the democracy which is under threat, both by providing a forum where the harshest differences of opinion can be aired, and by reporting and courageously investigating the unpalatable truths which underlie the problems of the province'.[7] The predominance of public interest arguments over bureaucratic ones is unmistakable.

Apart from the criticisms and responses, it was also reported that the Attorney-General was studying the anti-terrorism legislation, and a spokesman from his office was quoted as saying that 'The law says that people with information that may lead to the apprehension of terrorists have a duty to disclose it to the police'. This minor theme, as we shall see, was later to become of major significance.

The BBC's defence was also argued by its Director-General in a long letter to the *Daily Telegraph*, replying to its editorial. Trethowan denied any substantial difference between reporting terrorism and interviewing terrorist spokesmen. 'Newspaper reporters frequently give accounts of terrorist groups, in Northern Ireland and elsewhere, and in order to do so they must presumably hold clandestine interviews with terrorists. Reporting for television involves such interviews being presented not in print but on film.' The difference was one of impact, and for this reason the BBC had shown only four such interviews in the past decade. Trethowan acknowledged that the BBC had

---

[7] *The Listener*, 19.7.79

misjudged the emotional impact of the interview, but pointed out that there had been no undue public reaction. By inference, then, the emotional impact had been where it counted most, in the higher counsels of the Conservative Party.[8]

The NUJ, while also supporting the BBC, went further, commenting that the small number of interviews with members of proscribed organisations showed 'timidity rather than recklessness of behalf of the BBC'.[9] In an editorial, the *Guardian* echoed the BBC's arguments: 'It is not a tenable position in a democracy that whereas the political leaders know the sort of people who are responsible for the killings, and whereas the Army knows, the police knows, and the press and television people know, the public at large should be sheltered from the knowledge'.[10] The paper also rejected the Irish model as both inappropriate and inapplicable in Britain and as of dubious value in the Republic itself.

After a week the row began to peter out. The *Observer* reported that there was little likelihood of a prosecution and that the programme makers had been interviewed by the anti-terrorist squad in the presence of BBC lawyers. The paper noted that 'the prosecution of any broadcaster under the Prevention of Terrorism Act would be unprecedented'.[11] Editorially, the paper supported the BBC's stance, suggesting that Mrs. Thatcher's referral of the matter to the Attorney-General might be excessive, but that the BBC might nonetheless take another look at its guidelines.

On 17 July, the Home Secretary, Mr. William Whitelaw, condemned the BBC in the Commons, but reaffirmed the Corporation's editorial autonomy. In a typical statement of the official view, Whitelaw observed: 'Terrorists and terrorist organisations seek and depend upon publicity. A principal object of their acts of violence is to draw attention to themselves and gain notoriety ... they bomb and murder their way into the headlines. In doing so they make war on society and outlaw themselves from its privileges. The broadcasting authorities owe them no duty whatever, and owe society itself no duty whatever, gratuitously to provide them with opportunities for the publicity they want'.[12]

Thus the INLA row discloses a number of the features of the intellectual field within which the subject of media autonomy is debated. First, the limited range of actors: properly speaking no outside 'intellectuals' became involved. Rather, the argument was conducted principally between politicians, who reaffirmed a number of nostrums about negative effects, and the corporate theorists of the BBC, who juggled with the counters of bureaucratic efficiency

---

[8] *The Daily Telegraph, The Guardian*, 14.7.79.
[9] *The Guardian*, 14.7.79.
[10] *ibid.*
[11] *The Observer*, 15.7.79.
[12] *The Guardian*, 17.7.79

and the public interest. The most significant outside support came from the NUJ, since there was multipartisan condemnation of the interview in Parliament. Nothing was said during all this debate about the *content* of the interview. It was more the fact of an outsider, one beyond the pale of constitutional politics being admitted to the public media, which formed the central axis of concern.

The INLA row was rapidly followed by another, the 'Carrickmore incident'. On 9 November 1979, the London *Evening Standard* reported that a BBC *Panorama* team had filmed 140 armed IRA-men taking over a village, Carrickmore, in County Tyrone in Northern Ireland. The report said they had blocked the road for two hours and had displayed weaponry.

In an immediate response, Mrs. Thatcher said in the House of Commons that the police and Director of Public Prosecutions should be involved and that 'the Home Secretary and I think it is time the BBC put its house in order'. Mr. James Molyneaux, leader of the official Ulster Unionists, called for the TV team to be disciplined and suggested that their activity had been 'at least treasonable'. The Northern Ireland Secretary wrote to the Home Secretary deploring the incident, while the Labour leader, James Callaghan, spoke of the event as 'stage-managed'. The legal argument had now become central.

The BBC's initial response was that the standing regulations concerning the filming of terrorists had been breached. But the Corporation shortly after issued a statement denying reports that the event had been a stunt or that machine-guns and rocket-launchers had been displayed and that men had been drilling in the main square.[13] By comparison with the INLA case refuge was sought in a failure of bureaucratic controls and no appeal to the public interest was launched. Rather, the defence concentrated upon the accuracy of the allegations and the scale of the incident.

The next day the IRA denied that it had pulled a stunt. Its Tyrone unit were quoted as saying 'Operations similar to and on the scale of the Carrickmore one have been carried out in the past and will be carried out again in the future'; the BBC's presence had been coincidental. For its part, the BBC said that it had received an anonymous tip, had gone without knowing what it would find, and had neither seen nor filmed men parading or displaying arms. The source of the story, Ed Moloney, a Belfast-based reporter writing for the Dublin magazine *Hibernia*, criticised the distortions of his report in the press. He specifically denied that there had been a parade or as many weapons as alleged; there had been only one road block and 'nothing like' 140 IRA-men in the village.

The implications of bringing in the Attorney-General during the INLA incident also now became clear. At his request, Commander Peter Duffy, head of Scotland Yard's anti-terrorist squad, began investigating whether

---

[13] *The Guardian*, 9.11.79.

there had been a breach of Section 11 of the Prevention of Terrorism Act. This section concerns the withholding of information which could help arrest terrorists.[14]

In an editorial, the *Guardian* suggested that the BBC had been gullible in filming the event, but went on to say that the *Evening Standard*'s exaggerations had maximised the IRA's publicity effort. The editorial strongly defended that BBC's right to resolve the matter internally, and denied that 'contacts between the media and the Provisional IRA's were a criminal offence, cautioning the Thatcher government not to engage in a witchhunt.[15]

The *Guardian* also investigated the background to the story. Maloney had 'discovered that Carrickmore had been inundated with army patrols seeking details of an IRA exercise in the village on October 17. He also found that at least part of the exercise had been filmed by a four-man crew from *Panorama*'. Moloney's story was blown up by Fleet Street, in particular, it was not true that the BBC had been party to a stunt. Parliamentary reactions, therefore, were based on misleading evidence. The report revealed, however, that the Northern Ireland Office and the Royal Ulster Constabulary (RUC) had known about the incident within twenty-four hours of its occurrence, and that the army and RUC had withdrawn cooperation from the BBC as a result. The police had spoken with senior BBC officials, but without threat of prosecution, and it was in that context that Atkins had complained to Whitelaw. A Cabinet row had taken place only after *Hiberia* broke the story, some *three weeks* after the event, and there were suggestions that the army and the police had tried to conceal the story from Thatcher.

The *Observer* supported this account: 'Although two of her Ministers knew that the film had been shot, the news did not apparently reach the Prime Minister at Downing Street until last Thursday morning, when her attention was drawn to a story buried at the bottom of page 8 of that morning's *Financial Times*'. More light was shed on the alleged breach of the BBC's guidelines: it appeared that although senior editors in Belfast knew of the filming, the Controller, Northern Ireland, Mr. James Hawthorne, had not been informed, and was appraised of it by a Northern Ireland Office official

---

[14] *The Guardian*, 10.11.79. The relevant section of the Act reads as follows:
(1) If a person who has information which he knows or believes might be of material assistance —
(a) in preventing an act of terrorism to which this section applies, or
(b) in securing the apprehension, prosecution or conviction of any person for an offence involving the commission, preparation or instigation of an act of terrorism to which this section applies, fails without reasonable excuse to disclose that information as soon as reasonably practicable —
(i) in England and Wales to a constable, or
(ii) in Scotland, to a constable or the procurator fiscal or
(iii) in Northern Ireland, to a constable or a member of Her Majesty's forces.
He shall be guilty of an offence.
[15] *The Guardian*, ibid.

eight days after the event. 'The *Panorama* team believed that they had informed the right people in their own hierarchy and stuck to the cardinal rule that no *interviews* should be filmed with terrorists without prior permission. The rules are designed to allow a news team to film the sudden appearance of gunmen at an IRA commemoration or funeral.' The report concluded by noting — and this was the first public reference to it — that the police had submitted a report to the Attorney-General on the INLA interview.[16]

On 12 November, a *Guardian* reporter who had been travelling in the 'bandit country' of South Armagh wrote: 'I watched for more than 10 minutes on Saturday while an IRA patrol of at least seven armed and hooded men stopped cars on a border road in County Armagh. Neither I nor anyone else representing the *Guardian* had contacted the IRA beforehand. Because of the circumstances surrounding my arrival in the region, they could not have known that I would be travelling along that road at that time ... Some ten minutes before we ran into it, we had seen a helicopter flying over the area. Less than five minutes before ... we had passed an Irish police patrol car'. His investigations in the area bore out the IRA's claim to have mounted similar operations, casting doubt on the view that it was a pure propaganda exercise.

Similar points were made in the *New Statesman* by Mary Holland. 'It was predictable that in the furore over the Panorama team's filming of the Provisional IRA takeover of the village of Carrickmore, the rage of the House of Commons should be directed at the BBC. Predictable but disquieting that nobody seems to have asked the far more important question — how could it have happened that the Provos were able to seal off a village in the heart of Northern Ireland, and that the security forces should not have learnt of the incident until the next day.' Holland went on to point out the severe embarrassment for the government's security policy: 'The Northern Ireland Office, like the security forces, seems to have hoped that the incident would not surface ...' The row over *Panorama*, she concluded, was a diversion from the failure of the government's security effort, in a climate of increasing violence.[17]

The government's intimidation of broadcasters was attacked in the *Guardian*'s 'Agenda' page by a civil liberties lawyer, Geoff Robertson, who observed that 'After the INLA interview and the Carrickmore affair, every journalist preparing a programme on terrorism in Northern Ireland must reckon on at least the possibility of a Government-promoted police investigation into his conduct, his sources and his researches'. The Prevention of Terrorism Act, he thought, could well become a source of ministerial influence upon programme makers, preventing programmes on terrorism from being made at all.[18]

---

[16] *The Observer*, 11.10.79.
[17] *New Statesman*, 16.11.79.
[18] *The Guardian*, 12.11.79.

The *Guardian* also published a letter from Vincent Hanna of the NUJ's broadcasting section which pointed out 'There is not a Fleet Street newspaper that does not have its stock of "menacing IRA gunmen" shots, many of them taken at discreetly arranged photo calls'. There was no question of seeking a scoop as what the team had filmed was not out of the ordinary. Nor was *Panorama* gullible, as recording the event did not imply publication. Hanna also drew attention to the licence fee negotiations then in train between the BBC and the government, and cautioned 'It is vital that the BBC is not bullied into a denial of its hard won freedoms because of the need to get a proper licence fee'. Here, therefore, was a professional defence, a contextualisation of the BBC's action in terms of wider media practice, and an indication of the government's financial power over the Corporation.[19]

On 13 November, the police, acting under the Prevention of Terrorism Act (1976) seized a copy of the 15-minute untransmitted film shot at Carrickmore. Neither the BBC nor ITV had ever surrendered untransmitted film before.

Two weeks after the row had begun, the BBC's Board of Governors pronounced itself satisfied that there had been no collusion with the IRA. However, the Governors said that the standing rules had not been fully complied with and instituted disciplinary action against *Panorama's* editor, Roger Bolton, and John Gau; Head of TV Current Affairs. The Acting Director-General was reported as having reprimanded Mr. Gau and Mr. Bolton, and was proposing to shift the latter to another job. The offence was a failure to inform the Controller, Northern Ireland, of plans to make a programme, as directed under BBC guidelines. The threatened scapegoating of Bolton caused concern amongst BBC and ITV journalists at all levels and brought support from the NUJ.[20]

In a statement, the BBC's Board of Governors concentrated on the ways in which the incident had been exaggerated by the press and politicians. It also noted that the seized film might well not have been transmitted. The rules for referring upwards were to be reissued with 'a few changes which leave no room for doubt in any direction'. Thus, unlike the INLA interview, there were no statements of principle, nor any appeals to a rational public. The predominant concern was with the accuracy of the allegations and a legalistic concern with the adequacy of the Corporation's own procedures. By the following day, the BBC had instructed all its news and current affairs staff to inform Mr. Hawthorn personally when they were planning to film in Northern Ireland. The BBC's disciplinary hearing decided to reprimand Bolton and Gau for a technical failure to inform the Controller, Northern Ireland himself. Pressure from senior BBC journalists was said to have played

---

[19] *ibid.*
[20] *The Guardian*, 21.11.79.

a part in preventing Bolton's sacking and 'a capitulation to government pressure'.[21]

Whereas the INLA row had enabled appeals to a rational public to be a substantial element of the debate, in the Carrickmore case the predominant focus was the infraction of the law alleged by the government. The BBC's internal divisions did not help its defence, and again, most outside help (with the exceptional case of the civil liberties lawyer and letters to the press) came from other journalists, through sympathetic commentaries or NUJ statements. In the INLA case what was said about the British state was not talked about, whereas during the Carrickmore affair, the military failure was displaced from virtually all discussion.

The dispute reached a temporary conclusion in August 1980, when Sir Michael Havers, the Attorney-General, announced that he had decided not to prosecute the BBC. The threat of legal action, therefore, had lingered for a long time.

On 9 July 1980, it was reported that the Attorney-General had been told by the Director of Public Prosecutions that there was enough evidence for him to prosecute several BBC television journalists under the Prevention of Terrorism Act for their contacts with illegal paramilitary groups in Ireland. Havers, however, had decided to avoid the embarrassment of a press freedom row and instead sent a strong letter to Sir Michael Swann, who for his part defended the BBC's action.[22]

Some Conservative and Unionist MPs evidently felt that the BBC was being treated as though it were above the law, whereas, on their side, some BBC executives were hoping that a test case would resolve the question.[23]

On 1 August, a short Commons debate was held on the Attorney-General's decision. Havers promised that the government would be taking a tougher line in the future when media organisations published interviews with terrorist organisations. 'I profoundly disapprove of the conduct of the staff involved, which was in my opinion deplorable. If similar incidents take place again I would take a stricter view, and those who had participated would be warned that, subject to the evidence and circumstances of the case, they risked criminal proceedings under the Prevention of Terrorism Act'. He was satisfied that the BBC had committed a Section 11 offence under the 1976 Act. One of the factors which restrained him from prosecution was his wish not to assist the IRA's propaganda effort with an unsuccessful prosecution.[24]

To coincide with the debate, the BBC released an exchange of letters between its Chairman and the Attorney-General.[25] The substance of Havers'

---

[21] ibid.
[22] *The Guardian*, 9.7.80.
[23] *The Guardian*, *The Daily Telegraph*, 12.7.80; *The Times*, 15.7.80.
[24] *The Guardian*, 2.8.80.
[25] Havers to Swann (20.6.80) and Swann to Havers (3.7.80).

argument was that both interviews with terrorists and the negotiations leading up to them fell within the terms of Section 11 and anyone concerned was 'likely to be under a duty to disclose it as soon as reasonably practicable to the appropriate authority under the Act, unless there is a reasonable excuse for not doing so'. In the course of his letter, Havers accused the BBC of lending itself to terrorist propaganda.

Swann's reply rejected this suggestion and voiced the BBC's concern at the government's interpretation of the law. Havers' view *'could* be read as meaning that the police should be informed, at every turn, of the letters, phone calls, or meetings with go-betweens which are, I have no doubt, necessary if a journalist is ever to acquire information from known or suspected terrorists. If this is really what the law says, then all reporting of who terrorists are and what they say would, in practice, be halted abruptly'. This reply takes Havers' legal discourse and transforms it into a question of journalistic professionalism and practicality.

Havers was not slow to respond. In an adjournment debate on 4 August, he said 'I regret the manner of the reply by the BBC not accepting the law which is perfectly clear on this point'. He reiterated that BBC reporters having contacts with suspected terrorists should report them to the police.[26]

Richard Francis defended the BBC's position in the trade magazine *Broadcast*. Pointing out that the Conservative attacks had occurred when a new BBC Chairman was taking over, *Broadcast* remarked: 'Any broadcasting organisation that sees the public interest being served by pursuing inquiries involving terrorists is likely to find that it will be playing guinea-pigs before the courts. That's hardly conducive to making decisions in an atmosphere unclouded by political and legal considerations.'[27]

In the article, Francis virtually invited the government to take the BBC to the courts. 'What has yet to be tested is whether the nature of someone's business (such as reporting) legitimately makes it impossible to tell the police. If it were assumed by terrorists that everything they told you would immediately be passed on to the police, then it would be impossible to conduct business without being required as a police informer. Information would dry up, thus making business impossible. Does this constitute a "reasonable excuse"?'

The INLA and Carrickmore incidents exemplify typical dispositions of forces across the contested site of media autonomy. The general formal structure of the debate is highly predictable. The consecrated locus of Parliament is of key importance, as are the ritualised forms of denunciation, and the types of defence (whether via the projection of a rational public, a retreat into corporate procedural concerns, or an assertion of professional

---

[26] *The Guardian, The Times*, 5. 8. 80.
[27] *Broadcast*, 11. 8. 80.

freedom). The stylised rows considered above represented concentrated moments in the continual adjustments of the intellectual field.

*Some general features of the Italian debate*

Sustained debate in Italy about the relationship between terrorism and the media really began with the Moro affair of 1978, when the architect of the *modus vivendi* between the Italian Communist Party (PCI) and the Christian Democrats (DC) was kidnapped by the Red Brigades, 'tried', and eventually, found murdered.

Although prior to the kidnapping the role of the media in relation to terrorism had been discussed, the Moro case made the question one of unprecedented importance, and it received considerable publicity in the Italian press. The debate, which involved prominent commentators and intellectuals focussed upon a number of themes: whether there ought to be a 'news blackout' of Red Brigade documents and photographs, the practice of 'responsible' reporting when the state is under attack, the need for professional codes of conduct (Morcellini and Avallone, 1978; Silj, 1978: Ch. 4).

No state censorship was imposed on the reporting. However, critics of the Italian media have argued that extensive self-censorship was practised under the guise of the 'responsibility' urged upon the press by the leadership of the DC (Silj, 1978; Becchelloni, 1980: 241). It is important to note that the Italian press is much more directly linked to the interests of political parties than is the British, and that it is heavily dependent upon state subsidies. Like the press, RAI is also a 'political client' in an unambiguous way, as it is directly responsible to a parliamentary commission, and is parcelled out between the political parties (Cavazza, 1979; Iseppi, 1980). In the face of such connections it is difficult to foster the ideals of journalistic autonomy, however illusory these might be judged to be.

In the course of the debate on how to handle the Moro kidnapping, newspapers staked out a variety of positions on how to deal with the Red Brigades' propaganda gambits, and the views of prominent academics were sought, including Colletti, Bobbio, De Felice, Spriano and Romeo. Especial importance was accorded the views of the Canadian 'media guru', Marshall McLuhan, who advocated 'pulling out the plugs' on the Red Brigades. His advice to go for media silence was largely addressed to television, but in actuality, the arguments concerned the role of the press. This obviously reflects the rather unambiguous relationship between RAI and the political parties, which constrains it in rather more predictable ways than the BBC.

Since the Moro affair, the question of how journalism should deal with the problem of terrorism has periodically resurfaced, and we examine a further stage in the debate below. By contrast with Britain, the question of how to represent terrorism is locked into a much more wide-ranging discussion concerning the nature of political violence. This has involved such leading journalistic figures as Giorgio Bocca, who stands for the institutions as they ought to be (Bocca, 1978). The celebrated novelist Leonardo Sciascia has been an important interpreter of the Moro affair and of thought-provoking writings on the question of political violence (Sciascia, 1978). Film-makers such as Francesco Rosi and Gianni Amelio have explored the contradictions and tensions of contemporary attitudes to political violence, as has the didactic drama of Dario Fo. In this kind of work, reference is made to the troubling violence of the state as well as to that of its opponents. These are but a few instances of an intricately linked and much broader cultural and artistic response than is to be found in Britain, where the centrality of these questions can be avoided by bracketing them off as 'Irish'.

There has been, besides, a growing academic literature which attempts to account for contemporary forms of political violence in sociological and cultural terms. Many of the academics involved have participated in forums organised by the political parties and trade unions whereas in Britain, as noted, such discussions are more typically held in quasi-private settings.

Perhaps, at root, what is most distinctive about the Italian situation is the way in which the identity and persistence of the state have been subject to discussion, in ways that are presently unthinkable in Britain.

*Italian Case Study*

*L'Espresso*'s publication of an interview with the Red Brigades and of their interrogation of Giovanni D'Urso raised a political storm and much discussion of the rights and wrongs of investigative journalism. To put this in perspective, it is necessary to note that *L'Espresso* has a distinctive place within the Italian media.

First of all, *L'Espresso* is neither the organ of a political party nor is it part of a corporation which has publishing as just one of its activities. Secondly, it has had a record of independence in its reporting of the Valpreda case and more recently in the so called 7 April case. In an atmosphere of intolerance fostered by the political parties and sections of the press, even a simple adherent to liberal principles has to confront the charge of being a 'terrorist sympathiser'.

The *L'Espresso* case began with the delivery to the newspaper of a package containing a photograph of the kidnapped magistrate, Giovanni D'Urso, and some Red Brigades documents; the daily press responded in a variety of ways to their forthcoming publication. *La Repubblica* stressed the 'dramatic contacts' between the BR and the *L'Espresso* journalists.[28] Both *Il Corriere della Sera* and *La Stampa* cast doubts upon the integrity of *L'Espresso*'s action: 'It is

---
[28] *La Repubblica*, 31.12.80; *L'Unità*, 31.12.80.

more certain than ever that this time professional secrecy and the crime of aiding and abetting have come dangerously close together' wrote Ruggero Conteduca in *La Stampa*.[29] However, this criticism did not appear in headline or editorial form. *Il Corriere* questioned the public prosecutor's decision not to prevent publication. However, at this stage there was no press campaign for self-discipline.

The debate took off, however, when General Galvaligi was murdered after evening Mass on New Year's eve. That night, Mario Scialoja, the *L'Espresso* journalist resposible for drafting the questions put to the Red Brigades, was arrested. Two days later so was his colleague, Gianpaolo Bultrini. They were charged with 'aiding and abetting' and 'false testimony' and it was claimed that the journalists had been in regular contact with the Red Brigades since the initial contact made before Christmas, and that they were covering this up in their evidence.

Publication of *L'Espresso* went ahead as D'Amato, the public prosecutor, said that he had no powers to prevent it. However, the magazine came out in three different editions. Although sixty thousand advance copies contained all the texts, the next edition omitted them entirely, whereas the final edition cut out certain names and a section dealing with prisons in D'Urso's interrogation.[30] In this way the magazine actually censored itself.

The death of General Galvaligi brought a closing of the ranks against any form of negotiation with the Red Brigades. General Dalla Chiesa, head of anti-terrorist operations, is said to have telephoned Eugenio Scalfari, editor of *La Repubblica*, to complain about his 'scoop' headline of 31 December.[31] In the next edition Scalfari's editorial held that 'in good conscience' the *L'Espresso* journalists should have informed the police of their contacts with the Red Brigades. The arrested journalists were rapidly isolated, suspended by their union and supported only by their immediate colleagues and by those working for minority left-wing publications.

The press engaged in a bout of collective self-examination: discussion centred on the legal questions raised by the arrests, professional codes and ethics, and more generally the role of journalists in reporting terrorism.

Expert legal opinions were sought by various papers. *Il Corriere della Sera* found that the lawyers it consulted thought that it was not publishing the documents, but how they were obtained that constituted the crime.[32] While the *Corriere* tended to assume the journalists' guilt, it was on weak legal ground as citizens were under no obligation to give information to the police under the charges brought against Scialoja and Bultrini.

---

[29] *La Stampa*, 31. 12. 80.
[30] *L'Espresso*, 1. 1. 81.
[31] *Lotta Continua*, 3. 1. 81.
[32] *Il Corriere della Sera*, 2. 1. 81.

The debate on professional codes and ethics concerned the relationship of journalists both to the state and to the state's enemies. For the editors of *Il Corriere della Sera* and *La Stampa* the issue was relatively unproblematic. Leo Valliani in the *Corriere* stated that 'Not only the legitimate desire to succeed but also professional secrecy are limited by the superior duty, common to all citizens, of preventing the carrying out or continuation of serious crimes ... The Constitution affirms the safeguarding of life as a primordial need, but puts the defence of the fatherland even higher as the supreme obligation of all citizens.'[33] Vittorio Gorresio of *La Stampa* criticised those journalists who took over investigative functions properly belonging to the state, emphasising that 'the authorities need the active solidarity of citizens, and of journalists who are citizens like the rest and with the same duties.'[34] For these establishment papers, there was a strong tendency to rely on official sources in the reporting of terrorism and mistrust for investigative journalism as a potentially subversive activity. Certainly, for the *Corriere della Sera*, in a state of war there was no room for ambiguity and so it declared hostilities on 'a certain journalism, half Zoro, half Pontius Pilate, of the ambiguous persuasion which is neither with the Brigades nor with the state, which judges without being judged, is part of the salon of the politicans as well as of the slums of the rebels, and which disseminates photocopies and insinuations, demoralisation and cynicism, without worrying what grows out of it'.[35]

However, there was a shared objection to tighter state regulation of the press both on the part of the papers themselves and also on the part of the government and the police, as evidenced by the interviews with the Prime Minister and General Capuzzo in *La Stampa* on 2 January. It was suggested, rather, that 'irresponsible' behaviour would provoke a clamp-down. Thus, part of the press was assigned the task of self-policing and the bringing into line of dissidents.

*La Repubblica* adopted a more complex role, in line with its self-image of enlightened rationalism and pluralism. It permitted a debate within its column rather than presenting an unequivocal public position. Vittorio Gorresio of *La Stampa* and Livio Zanetti of *L'Espresso* were put the ring. Although Eugenio Scalfari's position was one of opposing contacts with the terrorists, he made it clear that in the D'Urso case, both the government and the political parties were attempting to satisfy the Red Brigades' demands.[36]

Arguments for unrestricted freedom to report and for the press's autonomy from state interference, direct or indirect, were most forcefully put by articles in *L'Espresso*, and by other supporters of the imprisoned journalists, who mostly wrote for papers of the extreme left. Editorials in *L'Espresso* justified

---

[33] *Il Corriere della Sera*, 2.1.81.
[34] *La Repubblica*, 4.1.81.
[35] *Il Corriere della Sera*, 4.1.81.
[36] *La Repubblica*, 4.1.81.

the publication of the Red Brigades' documents on the grounds that they provided knowledge about an 'ideology that is one of the most serious mysteries of our time', and that this was especially important since the Red Brigades were no romantics, but a cold and calculating organisation. Publication contributed to democracy as it put the reader in a position to judge for himself; it also contributed to a humane outcome as a more exact understanding of Red Brigades' stragegy allowed a more flexible response.[37]

An article by Christina Marriotti pointed out that Mario Scialoja's previous record as a journalist had included a remarkable contribution to the reportage of 'black terrorism' and analyses of the strategy of tension. Scialoja had interviewed outlawed neo-fascists and had acquired documents from undisclosed sources without earlier evoking charges of 'aiding and abetting'. His role was comparable to that of the war-correspondent: the front was terrorism.[38]

Underlying these arguments was the conviction that journalists could not abrogate their role as investigators even in the most delicate of situations, especially so as official corruption made delegating such tasks to the state unthinkable.

The general atmosphere of self-censorship ensured that a critical analysis of reporting terrorism was unlikely, in particular problems arising from the Red Brigades' control of the timing of publication and the difficulties of verifying the authenticity of the answers said to have been given by the kidnapped D'Urso. Instead, the key question had become whether or not it was 'correct' to have contact with the terrorists.

The next step came when the Red Brigades demanded publication of certain documents as a condition of D'Urso's release, once again raising the question of a 'black-out'.

On 6 January 1980, *Il Corriere della Sera* published a front-page article headlined 'To the Readers: *Il Corriere* has decided on press silence over BR demands'. The same day, *Il Tempo*, *Il Giornale Nuovo* and Channel 1 of RAI-TV (controlled by the DC) all took the same stance. Indro Montanelli evoked the image of a shopkeepers' protest: 'for the press there is no other response – pull down the shutters on all attempts at instrumentalisation. From today, *Il Giornale* will not give hospitality to the BR's messages, and will instead limit itself to recording their crimes'.

As noted earlier, the possibility of organising a black-out on what *Il Tempo* called terrorist 'proclamations, judgements and menaces' had been discussed during the Moro affair, but without any definite result. As no directives could be expected from the government, private initiatives were taken. The BR demand for the publication of specified documents contained in communique number 8 was taken as a signal for stopping the publication of anything deriving from that source.

---

[37] *L'Espresso*, 11.1.81 and 18.1.81.
[38] Cristina Marriotti, 'Chi è senza peccato scagli la prima pagina', in *L'Espresso*, 18.1.81.

In orchestrating the campaign for a black-out *Il Corriere della Sera* gave maximum coverage to its own supporters. For instance, it somewhat prematurely announced: 'The European press in agreement with *Il Corriere* — it is right not to be the loudspeakers of the terrorists'.[39] By a sleight of hand it attempted to present its own position as the only one refusing a voice to the terrorists themselves. Those disagreeing found themselves put in the camp of terrorist propagandists. A letter from an associate editor of *Il Manifesto* pointed this out: 'On page two of yesterday's edition it says that I am "against the boycott of brigade propaganda". What does this mean? That ... my paper wants to turn itself into a mouthpiece for the prisoners and the BR killers?'[40]

But a virtual news blackout did not appeal to the major dailies: *La Stampa*, *La Repubblica*, *L'Unità*, *Il Messaggero* and other papers took the view that while news should be made available to the public entire texts should not be published. The journalists of RAI's socialist controlled Channel 2 also supported this position, so that divisions cut across the state-controlled as well as the private information services.

The newspapers of the far left were out on a limb. *Il Manifesto*, *Lotta Continua* and various independent radio stations, including these controlled by the Radical Party, all insisted that full publication of documents coming from the Red Brigades was in the interest of providing maximum information to their audiences.

At one level, the debate concerned the economic determinants of journalistic practice, namely competition and ownership. The supporters of a black-out argued strongly that newspapers became the sounding-boards of terrorism because 'terrorism sold well'. So refusing to give anything other than the most minimal coverage to terrorism was an act of self-sacrifice, entailing a fall in circulation. However, *Il Corriere* was not immune from the demands of commercial logic. It has been suggested that behind the argument for a black-out was *Il Corriere*'s need to challenge the threat coming from Montanelli's *Il Giornale* over who should be the true voice of the silent majority. In addition, the *Corriere* needed to increase its readership at a time when its controlling publishing house, Rizzoli, was seeking substantial bank loans.[41]

Reference to the influence of owners in editorial policy is a regular feature of commentaries on the behaviour of the press in Italy. Not that the ownership structure is markedly more oligopolistic than in other West European countries, but rather that within the political culture and in commonsense opinion such interference is recognised as an especially salient fact.

---

[39] *Il Corriere della Sera*, 6.1.81.
[40] *Il Corriere della Sera*, 7.1.81.
[41] Giorgio Bocca interviewed in *Lotta Continua*, 8.1.81.

In interviews carried out by *La Repubblica* with the editors of several leading papers, each was asked whether the controlling interest influenced decisions about publishing terrorist documents. In each instance, the answer was 'No', leading one to conclude that only the editors believed in their own autonomy.[42] The role of ownership was highlighted by the rebellion of the staff of *Il Lavoro* (of Genoa) against Rizzoli who wanted to enforce their black-out policy across the board. A journalists' press release read 'only the conscience and professional values of journalists can limit the way they carry out their work'.[43]

The discussion of a black-out at the level of theories of communication is of interest for the picture it gives of the role of intellectuals as a source of information and interpretation and because it is a concentrated moment in which journalists are obliged to speak of their work and relationship to their audience.

The proponents of the black-out tended to rely upon McLuhan as an authority figure. McLuhan's thesis that it was necessary to 'pull out the plugs' on terrorism, because it owed its existence largely to the publicity received in the media, was taken as gospel. McLuhan's qualification that either *all* the plugs had to be pulled out, or none at all, was never mentioned. The lack of a fully elaborated case for a black-out led to an effort to impose it by *diktat*.

Those criticising a black-out, on the other hand, were inclined to be more critical of McLuhan on the basis of professional values deriving from liberal assumptions. This critique was clearly articulated by an editorial in *La Repubblica* entitled 'How dark if everyone pulls out the plugs'. The adoption of a blackout, it argued, showed authoritarian and repressive tendencies, the best example of its practical application being the USSR. In Italy, newspapers pursuing the policy 'seemed to have become official gazettes. They have front pages taken up by Forlani's speech to the *carabinieri*, or Fanfani's to the Senate, thus producing a picture of a compact, well-ordered and above all well-governed country . . . Italy seems to have become Switzerland'.[44]

The liberal critique noted that a blackout presumed that the reader or audience was rather like a minor needing protection. The alternative model proposed the reader as the best judge: the more information available, the better would the citizen be able to assess the situation. This argument for treating readers as adults was developed by Umberto Eco. Eco is an interesting figure because he is an academic, man of letters, journalist and 'opinion maker'. A regular contributor to *L'Espresso* and *La Repubblica* he could take on McLuhan as a 'guru' in his own right. Along with the novelist Leonardo Sciascia he is an intellectual with a recognised role as commentator on contemporary affairs.

---

[42] Gianpaolo Pansa interviews the editors of *Il Messaggero, Il Corriere della Sera, Il Giorno* and *Il Giornale Nuovo* in *La Repubblica*, 18. 1. 81, 20. 1. 81, 22. 1. 81 and 24. 1. 81.
[43] *Lotta Continua*, 7. 1. 81.
[44] *La Repubblica*, 8. 1. 81.

Eco's critique of McLuhan was directed, first, at his 'technological utopianism', and secondly, at his conflation of media and message. He pointed out how the very notion of the 'global village' of communication asserted by McLuhan meant it was impossible to pull all the plugs. Even in the darkness it was possible to make signals with a torch, and frequently those were the most persuasive messages. If a blackout were possible, with the state 'pretending' that it had not received certain messages, this too was flawed, as the danger was that the people would get to know more than the state and disbelieve it, as during World War Two. The dictum 'the medium is the message' did not permit McLuhan to analyse the message itself nor to ask how it could be read. The real problem, therefore, was not whether information about terrorist activities was given at all, but rather the *form* which it took.[45]

Liberal stances such as Eco's were on the defensive against the predominant view that to reproduce Red Brigades documents at all marked a victory for the enemy. Ironically, this instrumentalist view reproduced the Red Brigades' own perception of the press as something to be coerced into giving them propaganda advantages.

Following the Moro case, sections of the Italian media drew the lesson that their best contribution to combatting terrorism was not to report its activities. After the D'Urso case, it became generally apparent that the idea of a total blackout was not feasible. The editor of *Il Corriere della Sera* himself said in an interview that his paper regretted the use of the term 'press silence'.[46] The attempt had been a failure, and, when the celebrated *Corriere* made the lottery results into front page news, this brought considerable ridicule.

The publication of BR documents by the minority press, by the 'free radios' and by the use of 'TV Tribuna Flash', courtesy of the Radical Party, meant that it was impossible to maintain a blackout. Eco was, it seemed, proven right. Interestingly, though, Leonardo Sciascia, one of the chief opponents of a blackout during the kidnapping, suggested in *La Repubblica* that in certain circumstances there might be a case for a blackout. However, he argued, that had to be decided on in advance, since newspapers, as private institutions, would necessarily be subject to blackmail as it was always easier to sacrifice one's own life rather than someone else's.[47]

*Conclusions*

Leonardo Sciascia's observation that decisions about censorship are effectively the responsibility of the state rather than that of the institutions of civil

---

[45] *L'Espresso*, 18.1.81. The article is entitled 'Approfittando che McLuhan è morto'.
[46] *La Repubblica*, 20.1.81.
[47] *La Repubblica*, 17.1.81.

society has an important bearing on the development of the argument. Both in Britain and Italy it is precisely the ambiguity of the 'war against terrorism', and the lack of a clear-cut and consistent policy of intervention by the state which poses problems for the media, and which provides the impetus for the continued struggle over reporting which is manifested in the successive debates. The case studies do suggest, though, that the ambiguities may be being slowly resolved by a shift to a more stringent application of existing law. One emergent state strategy is to try and impede journalistic contact with 'terrorist sources' by the use of prosecutions (*L'Espresso*) or their threatened use (Carrickmore). In Britain, the legal interpretation of the Prevention of Terrorism Act remains undecided, whereas in Italy the obvious next step would be to move towards legislation forbidding contact and the diffusion of 'terrorist documents'. How this plays itself out is of no small consequence for the future of civil liberties and of investigative journalism.

There are points of broad similarity. Although in Britain the debate has focussed upon the public sector or publicly regulated institutions (the BBC, the IBA) and in Italy it has been predominantly private ones (newspapers), this has had less significance than might be thought. That is because British broadcasting is not, as is RAI, a largely pliant vehicle of the political class. So the terms of reference of the argument have tended to be broadly similar: the defenders of the liberal or *garantista* positions have mobilised similar rhetorics of contributing to public knowledge in a responsible fashion as part of one's democratic duty. It is interesting certainly, but not decisive for the form and content of the argument, that the main proponents should in Britain be the officials of a public corporation whereas in Italy it is journalists and other intellectuals acting within the private sector.

The critics of the liberal position base their arguments upon a composite conception of negative effects. To portray or interview terrorists is in itself damaging for it variously undermines the legitimacy of the state, offends decent-minded citizens and plays into the hands of society's enemies by promoting their propaganda aims. Built into this is, as Manconi has pointed out, a definitive perspective on the role of intellectuals when the state is facing difficult times. In essence, it is assumed that there ought to be a simple uniformity of views through which the enemy is projected as a demon and that intellectuals should reassure the public and not rock the boat (Manconi, 1980: 178—9).

However, although demonization might be the preferred option for public consumption, this is disingenuous. For the state (in Britain and in Italy, at any rate) has performed transactions with the demons, however reluctantly. *Raison d'état* may be the preferred principle, but it is not always possible to follow it. Certainly, in hostage-takings there is always an important choice to be made as Sciascia has demonstrated in his analysis of Moro's letters, one between 'the non abstract principle of saving the individual as against the most abstract principles' (Sciascia, 1978:61).

As might be expected the case studies reveal some significant differences in the construction of the debates. For one, in Britain far more importance would appear to be assigned to Parliament as the recognised locus for the production of statements about what it is proper for the media to do. The extra-institutional voices (radical critics included) are easily marginalised and terrorism in general is not debated as a political phenomenon, but rather as a manifestation of criminality. In Italy, by contrast, a variety of political definitions is available including those deriving from outside the established political arena, probably for the simple reason that they cannot, in a more fragmented political culture, be so easily excluded. The place of political violence in the routine discussion of politics is also considerably affected by the extent to which it is an integral variable of political action, which it is in Italy, but is not — outside of Northern Ireland — in the United Kingdom.

The style of the debate within the media cultures of the two societies is conditioned by the organisation of the press and of intellectual life more generally. What is especially noticeable from the Italian case study is the vigorous contention between various newspapers and the cross-referencing of the debate through commentators criticising the journalistic practice of others. The D'Urso affair was an excellent example of how the media made the running and conducted an internal argument about the proper norms of professional practice. The debate in Britain is certainly less nuanced and wide-ranging.

The unsettled nature of the professional autonomy of journalism in Italy was underscored by the was in which the Ordine dei Giornalisti suspended those accused of aiding and abetting the terrorists. The NUJ in Britain — by contrast — took a forceful line in favour of the expansion of critical journalism and in defence of the scapegoats of Carrickmore. There is a sense in which while notions of professionalism are struggling for political space in Italy, in Britain they are fighting to maintain what space already exists.

Even the most serious detractors of the BBC's performance did not argue, as did the critics of *L'Espresso*, for a 'blackout'. In Italy, however, the argument has been taken quite seriously, and was even given additional injections of cultural capital by invoking the name of Marshall McLuhan. To some extent this has permitted a more elaborated confrontation with the consequences of total censorship.

In Britain, where there has been no equivalent of the Moro and D'Urso kidnappings, the option of a blackout, at least in respect of documents emanating from an enemy of the state, has not been so clearly presented. What has been at stake, rather, has been the effort to exclude the rationale for Irish republican violence from public diffusion. This has taken the form of contesting those few interviews which have been shown as well as a broader effort at news management and largely indirect censorship.

In this paper we have used the debate over the mass media and political violence to demonstrate certain features of the organisation of intellectual fields in Britain and Italy.[48] An issue as focussed as this, viewed in comparative perspective, has enabled us to explore significant differences as well as to point out some pertinent similarities. Our intention has been to investigate the possibilities offered by such an approach. Undoubtedly, it will need some development, but it can obviously be applied to other societies and further areas of debate.

*Acknowledgements*

The authors are grateful to Thames Polytechnic and to the Nuffield Foundation for supporting the research and writing up of this study.

*Bibliography*

Becchelloni, G. (1980). The journalist as political client in Italy. In *Newspapers and Democracy*. A. Smith (ed.); Cambridge, Mass.: MIT Press.
Bocca, G. (1979). *Il terrorismo italiano, 1970—78*. Milan: Rizzoli.
Bourdieu, P. (1971). Intellectual field and creative project. In *Knowledge and Control*, M. F. D. Young (ed.). London: Collier—McMillan.
Campaign for Free Speech on Ireland (ed.), (1979). *The British Media and Ireland: Truth the First Casualty*. London: CFSI.
Cavazza, F. B. (1979). Italy: from party occupation to party partition. In *Television and Political Life*, A. Smith (ed.). London: MacMillan.
Clutterbuck, R. (1981). *The Media and Political Violence*. London: MacMillan.
Curtis, L. (1984). *Ireland: the Propaganda War*. London: Pluto.
Elliott, P. (1977). Reporting Northern Ireland. In *Ethnicity and the Media*. Paris: UNESCO.
Elliott, P. and Schlesinger, P. (1979). Some aspects of communism as a cultural category. *Media, Culture and Society* 1, 195—210.
Elliott, P. and Schlesinger, P. (1980). Eurocommunism: their word or ours'? In *The Changing Face of Western Communism*. D. Childs (ed.). London: Croom Helm.
Francis, R. (1979). Reporting under fire. *The Listener* 19 July.
Hawthorne, J. (1981). *Reporting Violence — Lessons from Northern Ireland*. London: BBC.
Herman, E. S. (1982). *The Real Terror Network*. Boston: South End.
Hoggart, R. (1980). Ulster: a 'switch-off' TV subject? *The Listener* 28 February.
Iseppe, F. (1980). The case of RAI. *Media, Culture and Society*, 2(4), 339— 350.
Lumley, B. and Schlesinger, P. (1982). The press, the state and its enemies: the Italian case. *The Sociological Review* 30(4), 603—626.
Manconi, L. (1980). *Vivere con il terrorismo*. Milan: Mondadori.
Morcellini, M. and Avallone, F. (1978). *Il ruolo dell'informazione in una situazione di emergenza*, 16 Marzo 1978. Rome: RAI-VPT.
Nairn, T. (1981). *The Break-up of Britain*. London: NLB.
O'Brien, C. C. (1979). Freedom and censorship. Lecture at the Independent Broadcasting Authority, London, 28 March.

---

[48] The present essay is part of a series of studies into intellectuals and the production of various kinds of political discourse. *Vide* Schlesinger (1978b); Schlesinger (1981); Schlesinger (1982); Elliott and Schlesinger (1979); Elliott and Schlesinger (1980). For a related article by the present authors see Lumley and Schlesinger (1982).

Schlesinger, P. (1978a). *Putting 'reality' together: BBC News*. London: Constable.
Schlesinger, P. (1978b). On the shape and scope of counter-insurgency thought. In *Power and the State*, G. Littlejohn et al. (eds.). London: Croom Helm.
Schlesinger, P. (1981). 'Terrorism', the media and the liberal-democratic state: a critique of the orthodoxy. *Social Research* 48 (1). 74—99.
Schlesinger, P. (1982). In search of the intellectuals: some comments on recent theory. *Media, Culture and Society* 4(3), 203—223.
Schlesinger, P., Murdock, G. and Elliott, P. (1983). *Televising 'Terrorism': Political Violence in Popular Culture*. London: Comedia.
Sciascia, L. (1978). *L'affaire Moro*. Palermo: Sellerio.
Silj, A. (1978). *Brigate Rosse — Stato: lo scontro — spettacolo nella regia della stampa quotidiana*. Florence: Vallecchi.
Smith, A. (1972). Television coverage of Northern Ireland. *Index on Censorship*, 2, 15—32.
Wilkinson, P. (1980). Relationship between freedom of press and information and publicity given by the mass media. Paper to the Conference on 'Defence of democracy against terrorism in Europe'. Council of Europe, Strasbourg, 12—14 November.

# Biographical Notes

*Günter Bentele* is Hochschulassistent (assistant professor) at the Free University at Berlin. Born in 1948, he has studied German Literature, Linguistics, Sociology, Politics and Communication Studies in Munich and Berlin. He received his Ph. D. from the Free University and teaches Communication Studies and Semiotics within a study program on journalism. (During the last several years he worked in a new program of further education for journalists.) Among his publications are *Semiotik — Grundlagen und Probleme* (1978) (with I. Bystrina); Zeichen und Entwicklung (1984). He edited two books entitled *Semiotik und Massenmedien* (1981) and *Wie objektiv sind unsere Medien?* (1982) and published numerous articles relating to issues of objectivity in journalism, film theory, media effects etc.

*Ian Connell* (MA., MA., PhD) is a Senior Lecturer in the Department of Art History and Communication Studies, Coventry Polytechnic. He has undertaken and been involved with various research projects on broadcasting. These include television's treatment of industrial and parliamentary affairs, the production, presentation and reception of televised ‚science', and the press and television treatment of military affairs. He is the author of several essays and reports on broadcasting, including *Television News and the Social Contract* and *Peace in our Times*.

*Howard Davis* has degrees from Cambridge and Edinburgh and is currently Lecturer in Sociology in the Faculty of Social Sciences, University of Kent. He was Research Fellow with the Glasgow University Media Group from 1974 to 1976 and has contributed to a number of their publications including *Bad News* (London, Routledge & Kegan Paul 1976) and *More Bad News* (London, Routledge & Kegan Paul 1980). Previous publications include *Beyond Class Images* (London, Croom Helm 1979). Current research interests include the impact of micro-electronic technology on mass information systems.

*Teun A. van Dijk* is professor of discourse studies at the University of Amsterdam. After earlier work on linguistic poetics, text grammar and discourse pragmatics, he has been engaged for more than a decade in research (with Walter Kintsch) about the psychology of discourse processing. The last few years, this work has been extended towards social psychology, with applications in the fields of ethnic prejudice and news in the press.

His book publications include *Some Aspects of Text Grammars* (1972), *Text and Context* (1977), *Macrostructures* (1980), *Studies in the Pragmatics of Discourse* (1981), *Prejudice in Discourse* (1984), and *News as Discourse* (1986). Besides further books in Dutch and several edited books, among which the *Handbook of Discourse Analysis*, 4 vols. (1985), he has been founder and editor of *Poetics*, and is presently editor of *Text*. With Walter Kintsch he wrote *Strategies of Discourse Comprehension* (1983), which received the AREA annual outstanding book award.

*John Downing* is, since 1981, Chair of the Communications Department, Hunter College, City University of New York. University of Massachusetts, 1980–81. Head of Sociology Division, Thames Polytechnic, London, 1972–80.

His books include: *Vicious Circle* (with W. D. Wood), London, 1968; *The Media Machine*, London, 1980; *Now You Do Know*, London 1980; *Radical Media*, Boston, USA, 1984. Presently preparing a reader on Third World Cinema, and researching the Soviet Intersputnik communication system.

*Barbara Cardillo* is currently a Ph. D. candidate at the Institute for Communication Research at Stanford University. She holds a Masters in Communication Research and a Masters in Public Relations, both from Boston University. She specializes in public communication campaigns, new communication technologies, and survey research methodology.

*Jagdish M. Chouhan* is a postgraduate research student at the University of Bradford researching in the area of new technology, communications policy and minority community rights.

*George Gerbner* is professor of Communications and dean of The Annenberg School of Communication, University of Pennsylvania. Before joining the University of Pennsylvania in 1964, he taught at the Institute of Communications Research, University of Illinois; the University of Southern California; and El Camino College and John Muir College in California. He has served on the staff of the San Francisco *Chronicle* and other newspapers, and was a member of OSS in World War II. Born in Hungary, he came to the United States in 1939, received his B.A. from the University of California at Berkeley, and his M. S. and Ph. D. from the University of Southern California. He has directed U.S. and multi-national mass communications research projects under contracts and grants from the National Science Foundation, the U.S. Office of Education, UNESCO, the International Sociological Association, the International Research and Exchanges Board (IREX), the President's Commission on the Causes and Prevention of Violence, the Surgeon General's Scientific Advisory Committee on Television and Social Behavior, and other organizations. Various projects of his ongoing research on Cultural Indicators received grant support from the National

Institute of Mental Health, the American Medical Association, the Administration on Aging, the National Science Foundation, and other sources. He is the author and editor of numerous articles, reports, and books on mass communications research, the editor of the quarterly *Journal of Communications*, and a Fellow of the International Communication Association.

*Cees J. Hamelink.* Studies in theology and psychology. Dissertation (soc.sc.): Perspectives for Public Communication (1975). Editor radio-TV stations (1975–1979). Instructor radio/TV-Communications Training Centre, Nairobi (1970). Chief Communication Research Desk, Lutheran World Federation, Geneva (1971–1976). Research Fellow Latin American Institute for Transnational Studies, Mexico City (1977–1979). Chair International Communication, Institute of Social Studies, the Hague (1980 ....). Vice-President of the International Association for Mass Communication Research.

Publications include over 50 articles, contributions to readers, several books as editor. Author of *Perspectives for Public Communications* (Baarn, 1975); *The Corporate Village* (Rome, 1977); *De mythe van de vrije informatie* (Baarn, 1978); *Derde Wereld en Culturele Emancipatie* (Baarn, 1978); *De Computer samenleving* (Baarn, 1980); *Finance and Information* (Norwood, 1982); *Transnational Data in the Information Age* (Lund, 1982); *Cultural Autonomy in Global Communications* (New York, 1982).

*Rom Harré*, Fellow of Linacre College, Oxford and University Lecturer in the Philosophy of Science; Adjunct Professor of the Philosophy of the Social and Behavioral Sciences, State University of New York at Binghamton. Originally a mathematician Rom Harré turned to philosophy of science, and came particularly under the influence of J. L. Austin, leading to a continuing interest in the relation between language and scientific method, particularly in the psychological and social sciences. His books include *Introduction to the Logic of the Sciences, The Principles of Scientific Thinking, Causal Powers* (with E. H. Madden), *The Explanation of Social Behaviour* (with P. F. Secord), *Social Being, Great Scientific Experiments,* and many others. He has been visiting professor in the Universities of Wisconsin, Nevada, Buffalo, Aarhus, Gothenberg, Padua, and others.

*John Hartley* was at the time of writing a Senior Lecturer in Mass Communication and Cultural Studies at the Polytechnic of Wales, teaching Communication Studies and leading a research project designed to develop Media Studies in secondary education. He has since taken up an appointment in the School of Human Communication, Murdoch University, Western Australia.

He is author of *Understanding News* (Methuen 1982), and co-author of *Reading Television* (Methuen 1978), *Key Concepts in Communication* (Methuen

1983), and, with Holly Goulden and Tim O'Sullivan, *Making Sense: A Course in Media Studies* (Comedia, ten booklets, 1985).

*Charles Husband* is Chair of the Postgraduate School of Social Analysis, at the University of Bradford, England. He is co-author with Paul Hartmann of *Racism and the Mass Media* (Davis-Poynter 1974) and his recent work includes *'Race' in Britain: Continuity and Change* (published by Hutchinson 1982) and *'Race' Identity and British Society* (Open University Press 1982). His current research interests are in communications policy, anti-racist strategy, and intergroup theory.

*John Hutchins* is a librarian at the University of East Anglia (Norwich, England). His research interests have concentrated mainly on the linguistic aspects of information retrieval systems, but he has also written on linguistic theory, text linguistics and machine translation. Main publications: *The generation of syntactic structures from a semantic base* (Amsterdam: North-Holland publ. Co., 1971); *Languages of indexing and classification* (Stevenage: Peter Peregrinus, 1975); 'Machine translation and machine-aided translation' *Journal of Documentation* 34 (2), June 1978, pp. 119–159.

*Theo van Leeuwen* studied film at the Netherlands Film Academy in Amsterdam and linguistics at Macquarie University in Sydney, Australia, where he is now a lecturer in Mass Communication. His main research interest is speech in the mass media, and he has published articles on interview speech and the intonation of radio announcers. He has also written and directed a number of short films and regularly performs as a jazz pianist in Sydney.

*Claire Lindegren Lerman* is a member of the research faculty of Vanderbilt University. She recently received a Ph. D. from the University of Cambridge, for an analysis of indirect discourse in the Nixon White House conversations.

*Bob Lumley* is mainly engaged in research on contemporary Italian history and politics, but also has a special interest in media studies. He has just completed a Ph. D. thesis on post-1968 social movements at the Centre for Contemporary Cultural Studies, Birmingham. His publications include articles on Gramsci, on terrorism and on Marxism and media studies.

*Adam Mills*, BA Hons (Bristol), MA(RCA). Now lectures in the History of Film and also Television Studies at the Department of Drama and Theatre Studies, Royal Holloway College, University of London. Before this he taught Film at the University of Birmingham and was also an active member of C.C.C.S. He is currently working on a critique of contemporary cultural theory and analysis in relation to theories of ideology and the social production of art.

*Martin Montgomery* studied English for a B.A. degree at the University of Birmingham and gained his M.A. (on Discourse Analysis) at the same institution. For two years he was Research Associate at the Centre for the Study of Language and Communication, University of Bristol, before taking up his present post of Senior Lecturer in Communication Studies at the Polytechnic of Wales. He co-edited with Malcolm Coulthard *Studies in Discourse Analysis* (1981) and has published papers and reviews on child language and discourse analysis (usually in collaboration with Gordon Wells and Margaret McLure). He is currently preparing a book on sociolinguistics.

*Kim B. Rotzoll* is a Professor of Advertising at the University of Illinois, Urbana. He holds a PhD in sociology from Pennsylvania State University, and is the author of a number of journal articles. His books include *Advertising in Contemporary Society* (with James Haefner and Charles Sandage), *Advertising Theory and Practice* (with Charles Sandage and Vernon Fryburger), and *Media Ethics* (with Clifford Christians and Mark Fackler).

*Philip Schlesinger* is Head of Sociology at Thames Polytechnic, London. He is the author of *Putting 'Reality' Together* (1978) and co-author of *Televising 'Terrorism'* (1983). He has written papers on journalism, Eurocommunism, the intellectuals and political violence and also writes journalistically on media matters. He is currently administrative editor of the journal *Media, Culture and Society* and has been a Social Science Research Fellow of the Nuffield Foundation.

*Douglas S. Solomon* is currently the Director of Evaluation Research for the Stanford Heart Disease Prevention Program at Stanford University in California. He holds a Ph. D. in Communication research from Stanford and a Masters in Public Health Degree from the School of Public Health and East West Center at the University of Hawaii. He specializes in formative research oriented toward the planning and evaluation of mass communications campaigns. His writing and research concerns communication campaigns, health behavior campaigns, evaluation research, market research, and the uses of marketing technologies for social purposes.

# Name Index

Abel, E., 73, 92
Abelson, R. P., 77, 93
Adam, G., 168, 184
Adorno, T. W., 145, 155
Albrecht, G., 168, 172, 182
Alexander, J., 61, 62, 67
Allen, G. D., 217, 232
Allen, S., 291
Allwardt, U., 182
Altheide, D. L., 73, 92
Althusser, L., 3, 34, 39, 41, 73
Alvarado, M., 29, 41
Amsler, R. A., 124
Anderson, D. 54, 58
Anderson, M. H., 8–9
Annenberg School, 2
Anwar, M., 277, 291
Aristotle, 127–133, 141
Armistead, N., 42
Arnheim, R., 232
Aronson, E., 67
Atkin, C. K., 61, 67
Austin, J. L., 234, 260
Avalone, F., 338, 348

Bagdikian, B. H., 73, 92
Balasz, B., 216, 232
Banton, M., 272, 291
Barker, M., 272, 291, 298, 322
Barnes, C. I., 114, 123
Barrett, M., 42, 73, 92
Barthes, R., 3, 33, 34, 41, 73, 254, 260
Bartlett, F. C., 84, 92
Bates, M. J., 110, 123
Bauer, A. 27, 41
Bauman, K. E., 68
Bauman, R., 7–8, 212
Baxendale, P. B., 117, 123
Bazalgette, C., 39, 41
Beaugrande, R. de, 1, 9, 110, 114, 123
Beccheloni, G., 338, 348
Becker, D., 123
Belkin, N. J., 111, 123
Bellour, R., 170, 182
Beltran, L. R., 148, 154
Bely, N., 116, 123

Bentele, G., 1, 6, 9, 159–184, 159, 160–162, 182–184
Berelson, B., 2, 9
Bernier, 116
Bernier, C. I., 116, 123
Bernstein, B., 44, 58, 119, 299
Bernstein, L. M., 123
Bettetini, G., 232
Birmingham Media Group, 37
Birnbaum, L., 125
Black, J. B., 85, 92
Black, J. E., 125
Blake, R. H., 196, 211
Blumler, J. G., 7, 9, 58, 92
Bobrow, D. G., 112, 123
Bocca, G., 339, 348
Bohrmann, H., 159, 183
Boorstin, 99, 105
Booth, H., 292
Borbé, T. 183
Borillo, A., 123
Bourdieu, P., 324, 325, 348
Bourne, J., 285, 291
Bouthilet, L., 68
Boyd-Barret, O., 71, 92, 148, 154
Braham, P., 272, 291
Bramer, M. A. 120, 123
Brokx, J. P. L., 232
Brough, I., 56, 59
Brown, B. W., 101, 105
Brown, R. L., 42
Brown, R. W., 185, 204, 211
Brozen, Y., 105
Burgelin, O., 34, 41
Burns, T., 52, 58
Buscombe, E., 29, 41
Butterworth, E., 274, 291, 296, 322
Bystrina, I., 159, 162, 183

Campaign for Free Speech on Ireland, 327, 348
Carby, J. V., 285, 291
Cardillo, B. A., 60–68
Carne, M., 230
Carswell, E. A., 42
Cashmore, E., 291

Cavazza, F. B.,   338, 348
Centre for Contemporary Cultural Studies,   3, 35, 44, 72, 271, 273, 291
Centre for Research in Criminal Justice,   321, 322
Ceulemans, M.,   145, 154
Chafe, W. L.,   204, 211
Chambers, I.,   37, 41
Chaney, D.,   42
Chartier, J.–P.,   216, 222, 232
Chatman, S.,   39, 41
Chibnall, S.,   29, 41, 55, 58, 275, 291
Chomsky, N.,   161
Chouhan, J. M.,   4, 270–294, 297
Cicourel, A. V.,   31, 41, 72, 93
Clark, J.,   292, 295, 322
Clarke, J.,   41, 42, 59
Clarke, P.,   68
Classe, A.,   232
Clement, W.,   145, 154
Cloward, R.,   322
Clutterbuck, R.,   328, 348
Cohen P.,   291–293
Cohen, S.,   3, 9, 26, 31, 41, 72, 92, 260, 271, 278, 291, 293
Cole, P.,   212
Compaine, B. M.,   155
Connell, I.,   3, 26–43, 39, 41
Constantini, L.,   123
Contreras, E.,   148, 154
Coward,   37
CRE,   274
Critcher, C.,   59, 274, 291, 292, 295, 322
Crystal, D.,   219, 232
Culler, J.,   241, 260
Cullingford, R.,   2,9
Curran, J.,   42, 71, 92
Curti, L.,   41
Curtis, L,   272, 326, 348
Curtis, L. P.,   291
Cutler, A.,   223, 232

Damerau, F. J.,   123
Daneš, F.,   114, 123
Darwin, C.,   131, 141
Davis, H. H.,   3, 44–59, 46, 55, 58, 73, 212
Davy, D.,   219, 232
De Bock, H.,   92
De Rooij, J. J.,   232
DeJong, G.,   118, 123
Debray, R.,   39, 41
Deer, H.,   160, 183
Deer, I.,   160, 183
Dhondy, F.,   291

Diamond, E.,   73, 92
Dijk, T. A. van, See Van Dijk
Dorfman, A.,   8–9
Doszkocs, T. E.,   110, 124
Downing, J. D. H.,   73, 92, 271, 274, 277, 291, 296, 295–323, 311, 322
Dreitzel, H.   31, 32, 41
Dressler, W. U.,   1, 9, 110, 114, 123
Dungey, J.,   277, 292


Eaton, M.,   36, 41
Eco, U.,   35, 41, 45, 58, 161, 183, 233, 260, 344, 345
Edelman, M.,   160, 183
Edholm, F.,   273, 291
Edmundson, H. P.,   117, 124
Ehlich, K.,   82
Eigen, M.,   162, 183
Eisenstein, S.,   216, 219, 232
Eiswirth, R.,   68
Elliott, P.,   29, 30, 41, 42, 59, 72, 92, 296, 297, 322, 327, 348
Ellis, J.,   36, 41, 260
Englehardt, T.,   295, 322
Enzensberger, H. M.,   146, 154
Epstein, J.   73, 92
Epstein, M. N.,   112, 124
Equity Coloured Artists Committee,   277, 291
Eschbach, A.,   160, 183
Evans, P.,   276, 274, 291
Evreinov, N.,   137, 141
Ewbank, A.,   57, 58


Fanshel, D.,   196, 200, 205, 206, 212
Farhar–Pilgrim, B.,   61, 67
Farquhar, J.,   60, 67
Fauconnier, G.,   154
Faulstich, W.,   168, 183
Fiddick, P.,   299, 322
Findahl, O.,   91–92
Findler, N. V.,   119, 124
Fischer, H. D.,   292
Fishman, M.,   6, 9, 72, 92
Fledelius, K.,   170, 183
Foot, P.,   292, 296
Foss, D. J.,   223, 232
Foucault, M.,   3, 40, 41
Fowler, R.,   4, 9, 40, 41, 73, 93, 139, 141
Fraisse, P.,   232
Francis, R.,   327, 348
Freeth, T.,   277, 278, 292
Früh, W.,   168, 183

# Name Index

Galtung, J., 180, 183
Gans, H. J., 72, 93, 145, 154
Gardin, J. C., 109, 124
Gardner, C., 271, 278, 291–293
Garrard, J. A., 292
Gartner, L. P., 292
Geipel, J., 271, 292
Geis, M. L., 193, 212
Gelder, M. G., 136, 141
Gerbner, G., 2, 3, 9, 13–25, 17, 19, 22–25, 34, 42, 148, 154, 155
Gergen, K. J., 129, 141
Gergen, M. M., 129, 141
Giles, H., 288, 292
Gilman, A., 185, 211
Gilroy, P., 277, 292, 298, 321, 322
Glasgow University Media Group, 3, 9, 29, 42–51, 55–58, 73, 93
Gledhill, C., 39, 40, 42
Goffman, E., 101, 105
Golding, P., 28, 30, 42, 55, 58, 72, 93
Goldstein, C. M., 123
Gopnik, M., 119, 124
Gordon, C., 41
Grewe-Partsch, M., 160, 184
Grice, H. P., 185, 212
Grishman, H., 120, 124
Gross, L., 23–24
Gross, L. P., 155
Guback, T. H., 148, 155
Gumperz, J., 7, 9, 193
Gurevitch, M., 71, 93

Habermas, J., 126, 141
Haddon, Jr., W., 68
Hall, S. 3, 4, 9, 30, 31, 35, 36, 38, 40–45, 59, 72, 93, 149, 155, 259, 260, 272, 275, 292, 296, 298, 322
Halliday, M. A. K., 36, 40, 42, 51, 59, 223, 232, 233, 260
Halloran, J., 4, 9, 28, 42, 55, 59
Hamelink, C. J., 143–155, 144, 145, 148, 155
Haroldson, E. O., 211
Harré, R., 7, 126–142, 142
Harris, L. R., 112, 124
Harris, P., 145, 155
Harris, Z., 120
Harter, S. P., 114, 124
Hartley, J., 4, 183, 233–269, 248, 260
Hartmann, P., 4, 9, 30, 42, 44, 55, 57, 59, 274, 275, 292, 295, 297, 322
Harwood, J., 272, 291
Hawthorne, J., 327, 348
Heath, S., 40, 42, 170, 183

Hebdige, D., 289, 292
Heck, M., 42
Hempel, C. G., 130, 141
Hendrix, G. G., 112, 124
Herman, E. S., 324, 348
Hichkethier, K., 168, 183
Hill, M. J., 275, 292
Hillman, D. J., 115, 124
Hirschman, L., 120, 124
Hobbs, J. R., 119, 124, 193, 212
Hobson, D., 155
Hodge, R., 4, 9, 41, 73, 93, 141
Hoggart, R., 328, 348
Höijer, B., 91–93
Holenstein, E., 164, 183
Holland, P., 292, 296, 322
Holmes, C., 272, 292
Holsti, O., 2, 9
Horecky, J., 124
Horkheimer, M., 145, 155
Horowitz, R., 92
Hujanen, T., 270, 292
Humphrey, D., 292
Hunt, A., 160, 183
Hurst, C., 292
Husband, C., 4, 9, 30, 42, 270–294, 272, 274, 292, 293, 295–298, 322
Hutchins, W. J., 106–125, 109, 119, 124
Hyman, R., 56, 59, 61
Hymes, D., 7, 9, 188, 212
Iseppe, F., 348

Issacharoff, R. M., 275, 292

Jacques, M., 260
Jakobson, R., 33, 35, 42, 162, 164, 183
Jameson, F., 32, 42
Jarriel, T., 208
Jefferson, T., 36, 41, 42, 59, 292
John, E., 275, 292
Johnson, M., 200, 212
Jones, L. K., 74, 93
Jones, M., 277, 292
Joshua, H., 274, 276, 292

Kant, I., 127
Kaplan, A., 42
Kaplan, R. M., 123
Katnelson, I., 292
Katz, E., 7, 9, 92
Kay, M., 123, 125
Keen, E. M., 119, 124
Kelley, A., 68
Kelly, J., 67

Khan, N., 293
Kintsch, W., 6, 7, 9, 74, 81, 84, 89–92, 193, 212
Kittredge, R., 120, 124
Klingbiel, P. H., 114, 124
Kniffka, H., 74, 93
Knilli, F., 170, 183
Knorr-Cetina, K., 72, 93, 132, 141
Koszyk, K., 183
Kozminsky, E., 84, 93
Kress, G., 4, 9, 41, 51, 59, 73, 93, 141
Krippendorff, K., 2, 9
Kriz, J., 170, 183
Kuchenbuch, T., 171, 172, 183
Kuepper, W. G., 275, 293

Labov, W., 85, 93, 196, 200, 205, 206, 212
Lacan, J., 3, 37
Lackey, E. L., 293
Laclau, E., 3, 40, 42, 233, 260
Lakoff, G., 200, 212
Lampe, G. W. H., 133, 141
Lancaster, F. W., 110, 124
Larson, S. E., 110, 124
Lawrence, E., 272, 293
Lazar, J., 68
Leach, E., 241, 260
Lebowitz, M., 125
Lehiste, I., 218, 232
Lehrberger, J., 120, 124
Lehrer, J., 196
Leitner, G., 51, 59
Lenneberg, E. H., 204, 211
Lerman, C. L., 5, 50, 59, 185–215, 185, 189, 193, 198, 200, 202, 203, 205, 210, 211
Lévi-Strauss, C., 33, 42, 241, 260
Levitt, T., 99, 105
Lindegren Lerman, See Lerman
Lindzey, G., 67
Lipset, S., 146, 155
Lisch, R., 170, 183
Local Radio Workshop, 283, 284, 289, 293
Lovelock, G., 68
Lowe, A., 155
Lüger, H.-H., 74, 93
Luhn, H. P., 117, 124
Lumley, B., 324–349, 348
Lunn, K., 272, 293

Maccoby, N., 60, 61, 62, 67
Macherey, P., 39, 42
Manconi, L., 346, 348
Mandler, J., 85, 93
Marks, I. M., 136, 141
Martin, J. G., 232

Martin, M., 216, 232
Marvanyi, G., 22, 24
Marx, K., 45
MASS, 293
Masters, R. D., 162, 183
Mathis, B. A., 117, 124
Mattelart, A., 8, 9, 144, 148, 155
Mc Alister, A., 60, 67
Mc Cann, E., 293
Mc Guire, W. J., 7, 9, 64, 67
Mc Namara, E., 67
Mc Quail, D., 1, 2, 9, 42, 164, 183
Melnik, S. R., 292
Melody, W. H., 24, 155
Meltzner, B. N., 31, 42
Mendelsohn, H., 61, 67
Merten, K., 1, 9, 168, 183
Metz, C., 170, 183, 216, 232
Middleton, S., 55, 58
Miles, R., 273, 293
Miller, G. R., 7, 9,
Mills, A., 3, 26–43
Minority Press Group, 281, 293
Minsky, M., 84, 93
Mitry, J., 216, 232
Möller, K. D., 160, 183, 184
Montgomery, C. A., 124
Montgomery, M., 4, 233–269
Morcellini, M., 338, 348
Morgan, J. L., 212
Morgan, M., 23–24
Morley, D., 42, 44, 55, 57–59
Morris, C., 162, 279, 293
Morrison, L., 274, 293
Moscovici, S., 126, 141
Mowlana, H., 147, 148, 155
Mullard, C., 285, 293
Munoz, R., 67
Murdock, G., 28, 30, 32, 42, 44, 59, 145, 155, 260

Nairn, T., 326, 348
Neale, S., 36, 39, 41, 42
Needham, R., 134, 141
Nenry, P., 42
Newman, E., 190
Nichols, B., 170, 184
Nixon, R. M., 185–215
Nooteboom, S. G., 232
Nordenstreng, K., 145, 155
Norman, D. A., 84, 93, 123
Novelli, W., 61, 67
Noyes, R. W., 68
Nunally, Jr., J. C., 19, 25

# Name Index

O'Brien, C. C., 327, 348
O'Connor, J., 111, 124
O'Dowd, L., 321, 322
O'Neill, B., 68
Oddy, R. N., 111, 123

Paech, J., 168, 183
Paisley, W., 60, 67, 68
Parker, M., 291
Parmar, P., 298, 322
Parslow, R. D., 123
Pascall, A., 293
Pateman, T., 55, 59
Paterson, R., 39, 41
Pearl, D., 68
Pêcheux, M., 33, 39, 42, 73
Peirce, C. S., 162
Peisl, A., 183
Perscke, S., 123
Peters, J. M., 216, 232
Petöfi, J., 81
Petrick, S. R., 125
Phizacklea, A., 273, 293
Piaget, J., 135
Piven, F., 322
Pool, I. de Sola, 2, 9
Popper, K. R., 106, 125, 130, 142
Postgate, R., 293
Pross, H., 160, 184
Pruyse, K. H., 183
Pudovkin, V., 232
Purer, H., 161, 184

Quasthoff, U., 82, 87, 93

Rader, W., 160, 183
Rank, H., 101, 105
Rapp, B. A., 110, 124
Ratcliffe, P., 280, 293
Ray, M., 63, 68
Reeves, F., 273, 293, 298, 299, 322
Reiss, E., 170, 183
Rex, J., 273, 299, 293
Rice, R., 67, 68
Richards, M. P. M., 141
Richstad, J., 8, 9,
Rijsbergen, See Van Rijsbergen
Roberts, B., 59, 292
Roberts, H., 291
Robertson, L. S., 68
Robertson, T. S., 61, 68
Rogers, E., 60, 64, 68
Roloff, M. E., 7, 9
Rommetveit, R., 42

Rose, E. J. B., 274, 293, 313, 322
Rosengren, K. E., 170, 184
Roshco, B., 72, 93
Rotzoll, R., 101, 94–105
Ruge, M. H., 180, 183
Rumelhardt, D., 84, 85, 93
Rush, J. E., 117, 124, 125
Russell, R., 280, 293

Saakana, A. S., 278, 293
Sacerdoti, E. D., 124
Sagalowicz, D., 124
Sager, N., 112, 120, 125
Saifullah Khan, V., 273, 286, 293
Saint–Jacques, B., 288, 292
Salt, B., 168, 184
Salton, G., 115, 125
Salvador, R., 125
Samuels, S. J., 92
Sankoff, G., 89, 93
Saracevic, T., 122, 125
Saussure, F. de, 33, 38, 164
Saville-Troike, M., 7, 9
Saxer, U., 184
Sayer, J., 291
Scarman, Lord, 300–322
Schaaf, M., 168, 184
Schank, R. C., 77, 81, 93, 118, 125
Schiller H. I., 144, 148, 155
Schlesinger, P., 4, 29, 43, 59, 72, 93, 310, 322, 324–349, 325, 327, 328, 348, 349
Schorr, D., 191, 192, 196
Schramm, W., 64, 68
Schultz, W., 160, 164, 184
Sciascia, L., 339, 346, 349
Scotton, C. M., 185, 212
Sebeok, T. A., 211
Severeid, E., 194
Shabazz, M., 277, 293
Shamsher, J. S., 280, 293
Shang, A., 277, 291
Sharf, A., 293
Sharrock, W. 54, 58
Sherif, C., 101, 105,
Sherif, M., 101, 105
Sherzer, J., 7, 8, 212
Shoemaker, F., 61, 64, 68
Shotter, J., 136, 142
Siegel, E. R., 123
Signorielli, N., 22–25
Silbermann, A., 168, 184
Silj, A., 338, 349
Singh, R., 280, 293
Siot-Decauville, N., 123

Sivanandan, A., 293
Slocum, J., 124
Smith, A., 8, 9, 327, 349
Smith, D. J., 293
Smith, H. K.,194, 209
Smith, L. C. 125
Smithies, B., 299, 322
Snowden, L., 67
Soergel, D., 114, 125
Solomon, D. S., 60—68, 61, 62, 67, 68
Sondhi, R., 291
Sparck Jones, K., 114, 115, 123, 125
Spence, L., 295, 323
Spottiswoode, R., 232
Stam, R., 295, 323
Stein, J., 60, 68
Stone, M., 293
Stone, P. J., 2, 9
Strassner, E., 73, 93, 160, 184
Sturm, H., 160, 184
Swinerton, E. N., 293

Tambs-Lyche, H., 293
Tannen, D., 92
Taplin, S., 60, 68
Taylor, R. S., 109, 125
Thomason, R. H., 193, 212
Thompson, H., 123
Thorndyke, P., 84, 91, 93
Tomlison, S., 273, 293
Torode, B., 136, 142
Tracey, M., 55, 59
Trew, T., 41, 93, 141
Troyna, B., 274—276, 291, 293, 296, 323
Tuchman, G., 6, 9, 72, 93
Tumber, H., 276, 277, 294, 296, 297, 322
Tunstall, J., 71, 93, 148, 155
Turner, J., 140, 142

Udry, J. R., 60, 68
Uhlig, P., 182
Unesco, 8, 9,

Valeriani, R., 192
Vallance, A., 293,

Van Dijk, T. A., 1—9, 1, 6—8, 69—93, 70, 74, 81, 84—86, 89—92, 116, 117, 123, 180, 183, 193, 212, 234, 260
Van Leeuwen, T., 5, 216, 222, 232
Van Rijsbergen, C. J., 110, 115
Varis, T., 145, 148, 155
Véron, E., 149, 155
Virbel, J., 123
Vološinov, V. N., 38, 43
Vygotsky, 135, 136, 142

Waletzky, J., 85, 93
Walker, D. E., 112, 119, 125
Wallace, T., 292
Walter, D. E., 123, 124
Walter, M., 275, 294
Walton, P., 46, 55, 73, 92, 212
Waltz, D. L., 111, 125
Wanjin, Z., 185, 212
Ward, M., 292
Watergate, 5, 185—215
Weil, B. H., 116, 125
Weinberg, C., 68
Weinreuter, E., 182
Weischedel, R. M., 125
Westley, B. H., 212
Wilensky, R., 85, 92—93
Wilhoit, G. C., 92
Wilkinson, P., 328, 349
Williams, A., 170, 184
Williams, M. E., 124
Williams, R., 30, 33, 38, 40, 43
Willis, P., 155
Winograd, T., 123
Wixom, C., 68
Wood, W. D., 323
Woods, W. A., 111, 125
Wortzel, L. H., 61, 68

Young, C. E., 124
Young, J., 26, 31, 41, 43, 72, 92, 260, 293

Zadeh, L. A., 193, 203, 212
Zamora, A., 125
Zampolli, A., 125
Ziman, J., 106, 125
Zimbardo, R., 64, 68

# Subject Index

Abstract, 108
Abstracting, 116–119
  automatic, 117
Accent, rhythmic, 217–218
Action discourse, 85
Action structure, 85
Adversary technique, 54
Advertisements, 94–105
  analysis of, 103–104
  and culture, 97
  and economics, 97
  and persuasion, 99
  and strategy, 100
  and technique, 100
  as symbol package, 99–103
  structures of, 101
Advertising, 94–105, 153
  forms of, 95–96
    factors explaining, 96–99
Agenda-setting, 52
Analysis, message system, 17–18
Analytical procedures, in television analysis, 247–248
Artificial intelligence, 2, 85, 111
Attention, 21–22
Attitude, 28, 82, 134–136
  change, 28
Audience, 57–58, 63
Audio-visual analysis, 159–184
Author, 47
Automatic indexing, 115

Background, in news, 87
Belief, 134
Binary opposition, US-THEM, 233
Broadcast media vs. print media, 44
Broadcasting, See Radio, and Television

Camera, and point of view, 249–251
Camerawork, 246–247
Campaign, 60–68
  definition of, 60–61
  elements of, 61–62
  evaluation of, 65–66
  implementation of, 64
  media plan in, 65
  message in, 64

  objectives of, 63
  planning of, 62–65
Class struggle, 40
Code, 45, 161
  typology, in mass media, 162–166
Cognitive factors, in news processing, 6–7
Cognitive unit, 76
Coherence, 193
Commonsense criteria, 45
Communication,
  and minorities, 270
  campaign, 60–68
  definition of, 16
  international, 8, 143–155
  mass, 16
  public, 14–15
Communicative event, 5, 7
Competence, media, 161–162
Complex proposition, 192–193
Comprehension, 90
  of news, 84
Computer analysis, 2
Computer search, 110
Consensual meaning, 32
Constituent structure grammar, 180
Content, 54–55, 69
Content analysis, 1–3, 27, 31, 46, 55, 159
  steps of, 168–170
  vs. critical discourse analysis 46
Context, 5, 70
  in news, 88
  of news, 70
  socio-cultural, 7–8
Conversation, 135
Critical analysis, 44
Cultivation, 14, 147, 150–151
Cultural
  analysis, 40
  indicators, 3, 13–25
  practice, 45
  production, 30
  studies, 35–36
  synchronization, 147
Culturalist paradigm, 45n
Culture, 14
  international communication, 145

Data-retrieval, 109
Database 119−120
Definition of the world, 26
Dialectic, 129
Direct, vs. indirect speech  47
Discourse, 1, 44
  and mass communication,  26
  impersonal,  185−215
  populist,  259−260
  racist,  295, 298−299
  scientific,  129−136
Discourse analysis,  1−11, 27, 32
  and communication studies,  159−160
  and mass communication,  1−11
  and monodrama  138
Domestic news,  248
Dominant meaning,  37

Effects, 56
  of media discourse,  7
Effects-research,  27−28
Elite, and media racism,  299−300
Emphasis,  21−22
Episode, in news,  87
Ethnic minorities,
  and radio  270−294
  and television,  274−277
  and the press,  274−277
Ethnic stereotype,  295, 298
Ethnography of communication,  7−8
Ethnomethodology,  72
Event types,  196−197
Existence,  20

Facts, of news,  195−198
Film,  216−232
Film cutting,  216−217
Formatting,  119−122
Frame,  84
Framework
  of interpretation,  55
  of understanding,  30
Functions of language  51

Global organization,  69, 75
Grammar,  73, 162
  constituent structure,  180
  media,  180
  of presentation forms,  159−184, 182
Grouping,  223, 225

Headline,  69, 86
Hierarchy of media access,  48−49
History, in news,  88

Homology, 241
Human rights,  270
Hyperbole,  99

Ideational function of language,  51
Ideological analysis,  72−73
Ideology,  3−4, 34−37, 44−45
  and international communication,  145
  and the news,  233−269
Immanent analysis,  34
Immigration,  271−274
Impersonal discourse,  185−215
  discourse, rules for,  188−189
Importance,  20−21
Indexing,  113−116
  automatic,  115
Indirect discourse,  188−190
Industrial dispute,  29, 52
  news,  56−57
Information
  computer search of,  110
  formatting,  119−122
  retrieval,  106−125
    evaluation of,  122−123
  searching,  108−113
  storage,  107
Institution,  37
Institutional
  analysis, of news,  72
  voice,  185−189
International communication,  8, 143−155
  and culture,  145
  and discourse analysis,  149−150
  and ideology,  150
  and messages,  144
  forms of,  143
  functional characteristics of,  145
  problems of,  146−149
  research in,  147−148
  structures of,  144−145
Interpersonal function of language,  51
Interruption,  207−209
Interview,  53
Interviewee,  48−49, 54
Interviewer,  54
Intonation,  222, See also Rhythm
Isochrony, perceptual,  217

Journalists, black,  297
Juncture, rhythmic,  218

Knowledge,  126
  structures,  84

Subject Index     365

Language game, 134
Law and order, 320
Lead, 86
Legitimation, 152
Lexical item, 239–240
Linguistic analysis, 73
Linguistic diversity, 286–287
Linguistics, 1
Local radio, 270–294
  and ethnic minorities, 284–290
  background of, 282–284

Macro-
  and micro-level analysis, 52
  protocol, 174
  rules, 76
  sociological analysis, 71
  strategies, 77
  structure, 69, 74, 117
  syntax 84
Main event, in news, 87
Manipulation, 126–142
Marxism, 37
Mass communication, 16
Mass production, of messages, 16
Meaning, 31, 37, 69
  consensual, 32
  production, 38
Media,
  and ethnic stereotyping, 295
  and political violence, 324–329
  and racism, 295–300
  and terrorism, 324–349
  competence, 161
  grammar, 162, 180
  influence 44
  language, 159–160
  minorities and audience, 297
  racism in, 274–279
  semiotics, 160
Mediation, 47
Message, 14, 27, 64. See also Text, Discourse
  and international communication 144
  mass production of, 16
  system, 16–17
    analysis, 13–25
Methaphor, 199–204
Micro-protocol, 173
Microsociological analysis, 71–72
Migrants, See Ethnic minorities.
Migration, to Britain, 271–274
Minority press, 279–282
Model of the situation, 81
Monodrama, 137–140

Moro affair, 338–345
Myth, 34

Narrative
  point of view, 251–252
  structure, 39
Narrator, 47
News, 69–93, 233–269
  analysis of, 173–182
  comprehension, 84, 90
  domestic, 248
  global organization of, 69
  macrosociological approaches to, 71–72
  media, and race, 295–323
  microsociological analysis of, 71–72
  police in, 300–320
  production of, 6, 72
  programs, 159–184
  routines, 72
  schema, 6, 69, 84–88
  special, format of, 187
  sociological analysis of, 70–71
  strategies of, 87–88
  strategy of production of, 81–82
  structural analysis of, 71
  study of, 70–74
  television, 159–184, 187, 245
  text, 51
    and context, 70
  thematic structure of, 74–84
  value, 72
Northern Ireland, media debate about, 326–338

Objectivity, 195–196
Official discourse, and political violence, 325
Orator, 127
Ordering, in news, 88

Parser, 115–116, 118, 120
Persuasion, 126–142
  and rules of discourse, 136
  psychology of, 134
  strategies of, 132
Picture and sound track, 253–256
Plot, 249
Point of view, 249–252
  camera, 249–251
  internal vs. external, 249–250
  narrative, 251–252
Police, in media reports, 300–320
Political
  discourse, and race, 298–299
  field, 324–325

violence,
    and media, 324–349
    and official discourse, 325
Politics, of sense-making, 259–260
Populist discourse, 259–260
Poverty, journalistic accounts of, 235
Power, and the news, 233–269
Preferred meaning, 37
Prejudice, 295, 298
Presentation forms, grammar of, 182
Presidential, speech, 185–215
Press,
    and racism, 274–277
    minority, 279–282
Primary code, 162
Private discourse, 136
Problem definition, 62–63
Problematic topic, 186–188
Production
    of news, 6, 72
    process, 29
    strategy, 90
Proposition, complex 192–193
Protocol, 170–171
Provisional Ira, 324
Psychological factors of reception, 57–58
Psychology
    as rhetoric, 140–141
    of persuasion, 134
Public, 14
    communication, 14–15
Publication, 15

Qualitative analysis, of television programs, 167–168
Quotation, 47, 204–206

Race, 295–323
Racism, 271–274
    and entertainment, 297
    and mass media, 274–279
    and mass audience, 297
    and press, 274–277
    and television, 277–279
    and the media, 295–300
Racist discourse, 295
Radio, 270–294
    and ethnic minorities, 284–290
Ranking, 222
Reading texts, 54
Reader, 90
Reality construction, 72
Realization, of thematic structure, 78, 90
Reception, 7, 57

Red Brigades (Brigate Rosse), 324, 338–345
Relational, mode of signification, 233, 236, 245–247
Relationship, 20–21
Relevance, 70, 174
    structure, 70, 79, 82
Relexicalization, 139, 141
Reported speech, 48–49
Representational, mode of signification, 233–235
Rhetoric, 128–129
    psychology as, 140–141
Rhythm,
    and timing, 226
    function of, 221–222
    initiating, 218–219, 224
    natural, 219–220
    paragraph, 225
    stylized, 219–220
    visual, 220–221
Rhythmic
    accent, 217–218, 224–225
    analysis of film, method for, 223
    editing, 219
    juncture, 218
    structure, 216–232
Routine, 29
    of news production, 72
Rules
    of impersonality, 209, 210
    system, of media, 161
    vs. strategies, 87–88

Scarman report, 300–320
Schema, 69
    news, 84–88
Scientific discourse, 129–136
    and persuasion, 129–136
    structure of, 130
Script, 77, 81, 84, 118
Secondary code, 162–163
Semantic
    categories of topics, 83
    field, 239–240
    macrostructure, 74
Semiological paradigm, 33–34
Semiology, 45 See also Semiotics
    and discourse theory, 38–41
Semiosis, 234
Semiotic
    analysis, 170–173
    paradigm, 38
Semiotics, 33–34, 159–160
Sense-making, politics of, 259–260

## Subject Index

Shot profile, 171—172
Sign, 162
Signification, 233—235
Situation model, 81
Skimming, 118
Social
   contract, 48—49, 53
   factors of reception, 57—58
   formation, 37
   practice, 38
   production of meaning, 38
Socio-cultural context, 7—8
Sociolinguistics, 45
Sociological
   analysis, 70—71
   reformation, 28—30
Sociology of knowledge, 126
Sound track, and picture, 253—256
Speaker, 47
   in news, 256—257
Specification, 83
Speech, presidential, 185—215
Stereotype, 101, 147
Story 85
   grammar, 85
   structure, 85
Strategic comprehension, 84
Strategies, vs. rules, 87—88
Strategy of news production, 81—82
Structural
   analysis, 71, 170—173
   description, of news programm, 171—178
Structuralism, 32—33, 72—73
Structuralist
   marxism, 37
   paradigm, 45n
   projection, 32
Structure, 23
Subject, 36
Summarizing, 108—109, 116
Summary, 74—75, 118
   in news, 87
Superstructure, 69, 84, 180
Supra-textual unity, 241

Symbolic functions, 18—20
Synchronization, 152—153
Television
   and racism, 277—279
   news, 159—184, 187, 245
      analysis of, 173—182
Tendency, 23
Terrorism, and media, 324—349
Tertiary code, 162—163
Text, 1—2, 30—31, 37 See also Discourse
   analysis, and information retrieval, 106—125
   and context, 5
   and mass communication, 26
   and theology, 133
   film, 216—232
   processing, 6
Textual function of language, 51
The Economist, 317—320
The Guardian, 313—317
The Times, 301—312
Thematic structure, 69, 74—77
   and semantic category, 83
   study, 55
Theme, 74—76
Theology text 133
Top-to-bottom mapping, 78
Topic shift, 206—207
Topic, 52, 69, 74—76
   as cognitive unit, 76
   semantic category of, 83
Transcendental voice, 138
   Typification, 31

Understanding, of media discourse, 7
Updating, 81

Value, 20—21
Verbal reaction, in news, 87
Viewer, role of, 245
Violence, 243—244
Vocabulary, 56, 239—240
   oppositional, 240
Voice-over, 254

# RESEARCH IN TEXT THEORY
## UNTERSUCHUNGEN ZUR TEXTTHEORIE

### Frame Conceptions and Text Understanding
Edited by Dieter Metzing

Large-octavo. XII, 167 pages. 1980. Bound DM 68,—
ISBN 3 11 008006 0 (Volume 5)

### Words, Worlds, and Contexts
New Approaches in Word Semantics
Edited by Hans-Jürgen Eikmeyer and Hannes Rieser

Large-octavo. VIII, 515 pages. 1981. Bound DM 178,—
ISBN 3 11 008504 6 (Volume 6)

### Psycholinguistic Studies in Language Processing
Edited by Gert Rickheit and Michael Bock

Large-octavo VIII, 305 pages. 1983. Bound DM 124,—
ISBN 3 11 008994 7 (Volume 7)

### Intonation, Accent and Rhythm
Studies in Discourse Phonology
Edited by Dafydd Gibbon and Helmut Richter

Large-octavo. X, 350 pages. 1984. Bound DM 148,—
ISBN 3 11 009832 6 (Volume 8)

### Linguistic Dynamics
Discourses, Procedures and Evolution
Edited by Thomas T Ballmer

Large-octavo. VIII, 366 pages. 1985. Bound DM 160,—
ISBN 3 11 010115 7 (Volume 9)

Prices are subject to change

Walter de Gruyter · Berlin · New York

P 96 .L34 D57 1985

| | DATE DUE | |
|---|---|---|
| | | |
| | | |
| | | |
| | | |
| | | |
| | | |
| | | |
| | | |
| | | |
| | | |
| | | |